PowerBuilder
Foundation Class Library
Professional Reference

Other McGraw-Hill Books of Interest

ISBN	AUTHOR	TITLE
0-07-001697-6	Anderson	*Client / Server Database Design with Sybase*
0-07-006080-0	Berson & Anderson	*Sybase and Client / Server Compluing*
0-07-913255-3	Horwood	*Optima++ Developer's Toolkit*
0-07-011662-8	Clifford	*Mastering Sybase SQL Server II*
0-07-024469-3	Green & Brown	*PowerBuilder 5*
0-07-053999-5	Roseen	*InfoMaker 5*

PowerBuilder
Foundation Class Library
Professional Reference

Howard Block

Millard Brown III

Boris Gasin

William Green

Andy Tauber

McGraw-Hill

New York San Francisco Washington, D.C. Auckland Bogotá
Caracas Lisbon London Madrid Mexico City Milan
Montreal New Delhi San Juan Singapore
Sydney Tokyo Toronto

Library of Congress Cataloging-in-Publication Data

PowerBuilder Foundation Class Library professional reference / Howard
Block...[et al.].
   p. cm.
  Includes index.
  ISBN 0-07-913267-7
  1. PowerBuilder. 2. Application software—Development.
I. Block, Howard.
QA76.76.D47P685 1997
005.2'76—dc21   97-22705
                        CIP

McGraw-Hill

A Division of The McGraw-Hill Companies

1 2 3 4 5 6 7 8 9 0 DOC/DOC 9 0 2 1 0 9 8 7

P/N 006418-0
PART OF
ISBN 0-07-913267-7

*The sponsoring editors for this book were John Wyzalek and Michael
Sprague, the editing supervisor was David E. Fogarty, and the production
supervisor was Sherri Souffrance. It was set in Century Schoolbook by
Ron Painter of McGraw-Hill's Professional Book Group composition unit.*

Printed and bound by R. R. Donnelley & Sons Company.

 This book is printed on recycled, acid-free paper containing a
minimum of 50% recycled, de-inked fiber.

McGraw-Hill books are available at special quantity discounts to use as
premiums and sales promotions, or for use in corporate training programs. For more information, please write to the Director of Special
Sales, McGraw-Hill, Inc. 11 West 19th Street, New York, NY 10011. Or
contact your local bookstore.

Contents

Foreword

Why would someone from Powersoft be recommending a book on the PowerBuilder Foundation Class Library (PFC)? Well, when you learn a new tool, you discover ways of using and extending the tool that the makers of the tool did not anticipate and therefore did not document. You also quite often learn the right way, the wrong way and the way that works (hopefully this is also the documented one). Learning from someone who has already gone through this process allows you to use the tool to its fullest capability in a much shorter time then you would on your own.

The authors of this book have a wealth of experience with PowerBuilder and the PFC. They have all designed, developed, and deployed applications that use PFC as the underlying class library. They have also switched from using other class libraries (commercial as well as their own custom written ones) and now use PFC-based libraries for their PowerBuilder development.

This book will provide you with a number of useful ways to maximize your use of PFC and make its learning curve much shorter. Make the authors insight and experience with PFC work for you. See how they can show you the right way, the wrong way, and what works for them.

The authors have provided a number of extensions to PFC with the software that comes with this book. I would suggest that you study these carefully and see how they could be used in your own applications. You can also use them as "templates" for your own extensions to PFC.

ALEX WHITNEY
Director, Companion Products
Powersoft Development Tools Division
Sybase Inc.

Preface

The book is written with a view to guiding the reader through introductory materials, learning about the objects and services provided in the PFC, and developing a base of knowledge about the product. Then the pace will pick up as we move into more advanced topics such a extending the PFC (theory and practice), building an application, and tips and techniques for building distributed and web-enabled applications.

With the expertise of the five coauthors, and additional input from known PowerBuilder experts, Steve Benfield, Kent Marsh, and William Rompala, we hope to present a complete encyclopedia of PFC knowledge. We acknowledge that the technical details presented will undoubtedly change over time (new functions added, old functions eliminated). The information provided is intended to provide a base of knowledge about the product, which the reader will be able to use to acquire the level of expertise they desire.

A CD is enclosed which includes all source code shown in the book, as well as several other demos, papers, utilities, and the sample application used as the basis for the discussion topics presented within the book. Also included are

- BSG Software's PFC Multimedia knowledge base
- Advent 2000 Source Code Commenter
- Castle Software Engineering's SBA white paper and associated software (including SBA Base Service Classes, and several utility services)
- Gateways System Inc's TimeMaster application (the sample application)

Howard Block
Millard Brown III
Boris Gasin
William Green
Andy Tauber

Acknowledgments

Howard Block: I would first like to thank Stephen Frans of BSG, Inc. for writing several topics for me. His help, as usual, was invaluable. Great appreciation goes to Rob Castle, Stephen Frans, Mark Keyser, and Paul Power of BSG, Inc. for supporting my ideas and helping me make both this book and other projects at BSG, Inc. become reality. I couldn't have done it without their support. Many thanks to Arlene Darrow, Tanzenna O'Brien, Victoria Wendt, Darryn Randle, Mary Reeping, and the BSG TPOCS Team for their invaluable code and editing contributions. Thanks to my Mom and Dad for being there when I decided to make a living in software. And finally and most importantly, thanks to my wife, Marge and my son, Scott for supporting me throughout this project. They were the ones who had to put up with my work schedule and the many countless hours of writing and editing I did at home. It meant so much to me.

Millard Brown: Thanks to Millard F. Brown, Jr. for teaching me everything I know about conquering technology and communicating with others, and to Sinclair Brown for putting up with my long hours and reminding me of my commitment to quality.

William Green: I owe an extreme debt of gratitude to my fellow authors and contributors who helped to develop and deliver this book. Their insight and expertise helped raise my own knowledge and understanding of the PFC to new heights. Special thanks to Steve Benefield, Kent Marsh, and William Rompala who contributed to this book without getting their names on the cover. To my wife Terri, and my children Lauren, Alicia, and William T. ("the deuce"), I owe so many thanks for your patience and understanding. You are my life, and my reason for doing this.

Boris Gasin: Writing a book is very difficult. Writing a technical book under a tremendous time pressure was the hardest thing I have ever done. Fortunately I was not alone. My drive came from watching the four people whose names appear next to mine making sacrifices to meet one deadline after another. I would like to thank my partners Bill Green, Millard Brown, Howard Block, and Andy Tauber for giving me the biggest incentive to keep going, the fear of letting them down. To my son Alex, who missed out on quality time with his dad and had to watch Godzilla movies by himself and to my wife Donna who took on all the additional responsibilities and made my involvement in this project possible, thank you for your patience, understanding, and support.

Andy Tauber: Thanks to Denise, the love of my life, and to Alan and Kellie. All of you provided me with the inspiration I needed.

All: Special thanks to the Director of Companion Products, Alex Whitney, and project leaders for PFC 5.0 and 6.0, Mark Overbey and Claudio Quant, for carefully sifting through the technical details, providing timely information on PFC 6.0, and keeping us honest. Last but not least, thanks to Jon Credit, Steve Katz, and Larry Cermak, who took the time out of their busy schedules to look over the material and offer suggestions.

Chapter

1

Overview

Objectives

This chapter will introduce the PowerBuilder Foundation Classes (PFC), the focus of this book. We have found that developers will begin to use a product like the PFC without really understanding why. While the remainder of the book will discuss the PFC in detail, this chapter will give you a better understanding of what the PFC is, why you should be using the PFC, what the design philosophy behind the PFC is, what service-based architecture is, and what other channels of information are available to you. Call it PFC 101.

An Introduction to the PFC

The PowerBuilder Foundation Class library (PFC), is being touted as Powersoft's major advance in the use of object orientation with the release of the 5.0 version of PowerBuilder. This library provides PowerBuilder developers with a real class library, developed by the product vendor, which utilizes the latest features and architectures available. The PFC uses a service-based architecture, which we will discuss in much more detail later in this chapter and throughout the book. The PFC offers an effective way for the developer to utilize and extend the functionality contained within the library.

The PFC actually began development in March of 1995, and was initially designed to be a PowerBuilder version 4 product. The team at Powersoft charged with this effort is led by Alex Whitney, Director of Companion Products. Whitney is an OO evangelist and the author/manager of the PowerBuilder Advanced Programming Utilities (APU) and the samples and examples included with the PowerBuilder product. His task was to replace the hopelessly outdated and outmoded Application Library, a collection of reusable objects originally designed to demonstrate reuse concepts but adopted in many organizations as a basis for a reusable class library. The cry from Powersoft customers was for a more robust offering of a reusable class library that could become the foundation for a client's development efforts. Powersoft and Alex Whitney took up the challenge.

Alex's approach was unique. He gathered as many of the existing class libraries as he could, analyzed their design philosophy (keeping in mind that in order to protect copyrights involved, Powersoft could never look at actual code, but could only review design philosophies), and put together a design for the PFC which would satisfy three main requirements. These were:

1. Provide an industrial-strength reusable class library developed and supported by the product vendor.

2. Apply the latest techniques available and utilize an architecture that would make the library usable, reusable, and extendable, while maintaining a level of ease of use.

3. Do all of this without positioning the product as a replacement for existing class libraries (mostly Powersoft CODE partners).

In our opinion, Alex succeeded admirably at everything except item 3. The resulting product (the PFC) turned out to be so good that it automatically became the standard by which class libraries were measured. This has had the side effect of having more of an impact on existing class libraries than was intended, and has sent several vendors off to either rearchitect their products to be based on the PFC or drop the product line altogether. Although this is unfortunate, because Powersoft did not intend to directly compete with its partners, we enjoy the result, which is a smaller collection of higher-quality class libraries.

Why Use the PFC?

Why use any class library? There are most certainly benefits to be had by using a class library, and, in our opinion, the winners in the visible benefits categories have been those libraries that are easiest to use, rather than those which provide the most features. It's difficult to provide a library which is comprehensive enough to be useful, while still maintaining a level of ease of use which makes the product worth using. Using any class library should provide you with most, if not all, of the following benefits.

- *Productivity.* A class library contains a set of reusable, pretested objects which developers do not have to write for themselves. Typically, class libraries provide application infrastructure objects, but some companies have begun building sets of reusable business classes on top of the class library, providing an even higher level of productivity gains, quality, and consistency.

- *Reduced overall development costs.* Using a class library will reduce development costs if the library is well designed, easy to use, and well documented. Developers have to learn how to use a class library; therefore, training and documentation become much bigger issues and do add to the project life-cycle cost. Whether that cost is offset by productivity gains depends on the quality of the training and documentation, the availability of support, and, of course, the overall ease of use of the library itself.

- *Quality.* Because a class library is utilized by many developers, objects within it are tested by many people in different ways, ensuring a higher overall quality of application. For example, for something as simple as a sort utility, which we have all written in one way or another, the object from the class library can be used within an application with the knowledge that it has been used in many other applications in many different ways. *Not* writing code is the most positive way of not introducing program bugs.

- *Consistency.* A class library ensures that application infrastructure elements are not redeveloped for each application, and are therefore consistent across applications. This leads to higher quality and lowers maintenance costs. Users benefit by not having to learn different interfaces in different applications, developers benefit by not having to concern themselves with a portion of the company's development standards as they are internally applied, and maintenance programmers working on one project developed with a class library can easily move to another project developed with the class library and have immediate knowledge of the infrastructure.

- *Robustness.* Applications typically develop only those objects which are specified for the application, and only to the level which is needed in the application. A class library provides objects which are geared toward satisfying many projects' needs, and usually includes a higher level of functionality.

- *Reduced maintenance costs.* Maintenance costs are reduced because applications do not have to maintain infrastructure code. New additions to class libraries are automatically applied to an application whenever the application is rebuilt. Furthermore, requests for infrastructure additions can be channeled through an internal library maintenance team, so that additional functionality is developed only once. As an example, at one organization, several users requested the capability of a speed search on drop-down DataWindows (DDDW). If each application team had developed this for itself, the organization would have ended up with several implementations of the speed-search DDDW, with varying levels of thoroughness and quality. Instead, the central development team developed a speed-search service class which *all* development teams picked up as soon as they implemented the latest release of the library. The cost to several application teams? Nothing.

- *Availability of experienced developers.* With commercially available class libraries, organizations can hope to go out and hire someone who already has experience with the class library they are using. For those organizations with an internally developed class library, this is of course unlikely.

Does the PFC provide these benefits?

Yes. The PFC meets the criteria shown above. Typically, a class library, even one of the successful commercial libraries, is utilized within an organization which has, at best, limited access to developers who already know the class library. Because the PFC is part of the base PowerBuilder product, more developers will be exposed to it, and those organizations which adopt the PFC as their foundation will find it easier to find developers who know the library. The PFC also meets the criteria for a good class library in that it proves a comprehensive set of reusable objects designed to make application development more productive.

The PFC provides one additional benefit which no other class library can ever offer: up-front knowledge of changes being made to the base PowerBuilder product. Because the PFC is a Powersoft product, it is part of the overall design and development plans for Powersoft and will adopt and adapt to changes within the product far more rapidly than other class libraries will. It has the additional benefit of having a direct influence on the future direction of the PowerBuilder product. For example, if the PFC highlights an area of deficiency in the base product, there is a better-than-even chance that future versions of the product will target the area of weakness, making both the PowerBuilder product and the PFC more robust and efficient.

Where does the PFC fall short?

The PFC falls short in two areas: robustness and availability of experienced developers. Both are related to the fact that this is the first release of the product. The PFC is certainly a robust product which offers many useful reusable classes. Because it is the first release, however, it has not had the chance to be utilized in real-world applications and gain the benefits of those efforts. By now, however, PFC 5.1 will be in use throughout the PowerBuilder world, and will be more robust than PFC 5.0, which is actually the first release. Also, because it is a first release, no one out there knows the product. However, since the product has been in the marketplace for almost a year now, this is changing rapidly. PFC discussions occur in all of the electronic communication forums, firmly establishing the PFC as the library of choice for many developers.

Service-Based Architecture

To gain an understanding of the PFC, we need to take a look at the underlying architecture. PowerBuilder has matured to the point where the developers of a few years ago, who eagerly dived in to produce applications as quickly as their allotted budgets would allow, are looking back and asking that age-old question, "How could I have done this better?" We are among those developers, and the answer to the question, for us, is in architecture. We tried the traditional inheritance model and achieved a great deal of reuse, often at the expense of ease of use. As the technology and our knowledge grew, we continued to add new features, extending the inheritance model to its limits. Now it's time to adapt. We need to utilize the technology for what it can provide. The current philosophy indicates that reuse is gained through infrastructure and common business functions. Where the architectures fell short was in the infrastructure area, where reuse was restricted to what developers could reuse. Service-based architecture allows for reuse within the infrastructure and extends to enhance reuse within the common business functions. To gain a better understanding of how this is achieved, we have to look at the evolution of architectures used with PowerBuilder.

First generation: The window model

In the beginning, we decided that the window was the key component of our applications. Everything was shown in a window (remember the days of no NVOs?), and we built our inheritance model around the window. We then derived new classes of windows to satisfy particular needs. Some classes would include DataWindows, others would relate multiple DataWindows, and yet others knew how to communicate to a menu. The end result was a very rigid inheritance model, with new branches extended to satisfy the multitude of business needs. Figure 1.1 shows how this model might have looked.

Second generation: The DataWindow model

We quickly discovered the limitations of the window inheritance model. Whenever you needed to have a DataWindow behave differently, either you had to do a lot of overriding or extending, or you built a new branch. We learned that the DataWindow played a more vital part in our applications and built the second generation of inheritance models with the DataWindow (inherited as a user object) as the key object, with windows acting more like a container object class. This second generation of inheritance models was still based on the traditional inheritance model, but the window hierarchy grew a little more flat. Figure 1.2 depicts what a typical DataWindow inheritance model might look like.

The drawbacks to this architecture can be summed up as follows:

- The DataWindow inheritance model placed too much emphasis on the DataWindow object, and so this portion of the inheritance model outgrew other objects, resulting in "fat client" objects.

- It was more difficult to add new functionality because the location of the function within the hierarchy was more critical.

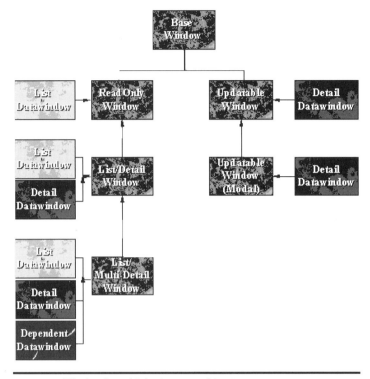

Figure 1.1   Window-based inheritance architecture.

- Changing the level of functionality we wanted required significant effort, even if we could actually determine which level of the inheritance tree we wanted to use in the first place.
- Partitioning of code and data was next to impossible.

Third generation: Introducing service-based architecture

We needed solutions to the drawbacks of the DataWindow inheritance model. We wanted more encapsulation, improved ease of use, better performance, less maintenance, greater flexibility. Enter service-based architecture (SBA).

SBA is based on the premise of placing reusable client object behavior in a delegation class or service class. Figure 1.3 shows the SBA architectural premise.

What are the benefits of utilizing the service-based approach?

Service-based architecture provides a number of benefits.

Added power. SBA adds power to the already powerful language by providing the developer with the means to achieve a result similar to multiple inheritance, an object-oriented (OO) feature not available in PowerBuilder. SBA is

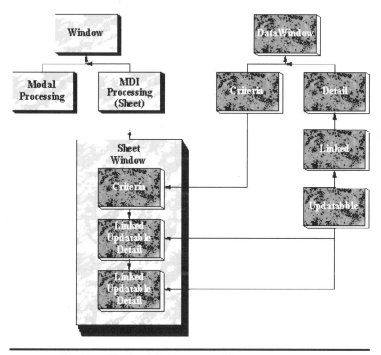

Figure 1.2   The DataWindow inheritance model.

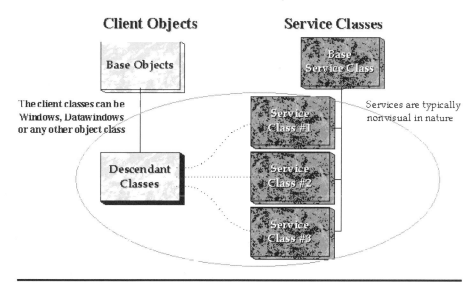

Figure 1.3   Service-based architecture delegates behavior to an external service class.

not a form of inheritance; rather, it is the implementation of delegated behavior in a developer-definable fashion. New services can easily be added to an existing client, allowing you to make new, tested service classes available to your developers without affecting their existing code base. For example, we recently added generic stored-procedure services to our DataWindow client class, allowing developers to change from their SPUD-generated stored-procedure code to a single service class declaration, with the service taking care of the remainder of the requirements.

Further promotion of encapsulation.   This is the premise of the service objects in the first place: Encapsulate processing into small, manageable chunks which are completely independent of one another, other than by ancestry. For example, row processing can be encapsulated into a single service. Row selection services may be one service that can be implemented as part of row processing, allowing even further encapsulation. For example, you might create a family of row selection services, say single-row selection or multirow selection, and give the developer the choice of implementing one of these as part of row processing. Now the developer can choose to alternate the service by DataWindow, or even within the DataWindow. When a change to multirow selection is required, the service class developer knows it is contained within the multirow selection service class.

Easier maintenance.   If services are well encapsulated, easier maintenance is almost a given. It's one of the OO fundamentals that reuse will reduce maintenance. What's less well known is that good encapsulation promotes easier maintenance. Good encapsulation also means that when a change is made to a service class, the developers that use the services in that class are less likely to be affected, because smaller chunks of code are easier to write, test, and document, almost assuring you of higher quality. We said "almost." Bad code in an object of any size causes severe problems in a reusable class environment—it is simply easier to trace the problem to a specific service, correct it, retest that service, and redistribute the corrected object. Service classes still follow a traditional inheritance model, however, promoting reuse at the service class level. One thing this means is that your classes will be easier to use.

Ease of use.   Have you used a hierarchy which seemed simple enough at first, only to realize just how complicated simple hierarchies can become? For example, we had a class library which featured three main types of DataWindow objects, Search-Criteria, Search-Results, and Parent-Child. This sounds simple enough, but it causes masses of confusion and enhancement nightmares. Let us elaborate. Suppose we are working on a project and we are preparing a particular window which contains three DataWindow objects: a criteria object, a list of data driven by the criteria, and a maintenance object linked to the list of data. This seems simple. We mapped the criteria object to our Search-Criteria, the list to Search-Results, and the maintenance object to Parent-Child. But what if we were told that the list of data might need update capabilities, and might be driven by a different lookup on occasion? Well, Search-Results is not updatable, and Parent-Child is the master of linking DataWindows together, so perhaps we want to go Search-Criteria, Parent-Child, Parent-Child. Okay. So we're carrying more than half of the Parent-Child functionality as overhead, never to be used. So what? It's OO, right? We can override whatever is not needed!

So now the system is developed and the user comes back and says, "That list object will not be updatable after all. Make sure it's nonupdatable." Do we go back and change the inheritance? We could, but with only two days to user acceptance testing (UAT), do we take a chance on the export–change inheritance–reimport capabilities? Multiply this a few times and add in a few more complex scenarios, and you can see that this process can quickly escalate to Nightmare on Inheritance Street.

With SBA, you no longer have to choose the level of functionality beforehand. In our new client hierarchy of base→client→application customization layer, you always use the application client object. No more choosing. Inside the application client object, you can choose to activate the services necessary to implement the behavior required by the client object; for example, Build SQL, Manage Transactions, and Manage Relationships. When the user says, "No, that list must be updatable," you open the object, activate the Update services, and *voila!* Updatable list object. If you change your mind, you can deactivate the service. Now your application can adapt to user requirements much more quickly and safely.

Flexibility.   Two things spring to mind when thinking about flexibility: We must be able to specify what each individual object is capable of doing, and we must be able to specify what an object is capable of doing at runtime. SBA allows the developer to choose what services to make available to the client object. This does not mean that these services are all activated immediately, although you could code them that way if you chose to. Allowing each client object to determine its capabilities *without* overriding a lot of code is a powerful technique. When you figure that client capabilities could also be controlled at runtime by the user, it becomes even more powerful.

Market growth.   With services being available in small, manageable components, we see an opening for a new market for PowerBuilder components, be they PowerScript, DLL, OCX, or other forms. In addition, with Powersoft's own PFC library being SBA-based, developers who learn the PFC library will become more marketable to organizations that use any library based on the PFC. This is an area of increasing importance. Have you worked with a class library and been in the position of having to try to hire someone for your organization? We have. A premium is being placed on people who have experience with your specific class library; those with experience with any class library are rising to second on the list, and those without any reusable class library experience are often being overlooked. With SBA, we might begin to see a standard being developed for service object components which will promote even further reuse, and drag PowerBuilder into the commercial marketplace. OCXs are enjoying huge popularity at the moment because they offer a standard for design and implementation so that developers and tool makers alike can utilize them. The newer ActiveX architecture builds upon the foundation prepared by OCXs. PB offers the capability to build inbound OLE automation servers, a fancy way of saying a class built on a specification for linking, which opens up a door of huge opportunity. Can you imagine your small utility object, which can change the colors of a PB object, suddenly becoming a commercially available object? Imagine!

What are the drawbacks of utilizing SBA?

SBA is not without drawbacks. No architecture is. The biggest drawback to SBA is that it introduces yet another paradigm to the clutter of client-server paradigms. Developers will have to learn a new method of developing. However, we believe that the end justifies the means. The second drawback is that for already established code bases, the costs of moving to SBA might be prohibitive. Here are the major drawbacks to SBA:

- Implementation style must be chosen carefully. While SBA is not extremely difficult to change, changes can cause confusion.

- SBA requires a new way of thinking—it adds one more learning curve for developers to overcome.

- Existing libraries using first- or second-generation architecture will not be easy to convert—this will not be cost-effective over the short term.

- Thousands of applications based on pre-SBA libraries become "legacy" systems.

- Evolution of the architecture leaves us wondering how long it will be before the next generation arrives to make this one obsolete.

The PFC Design Philosophy

The PFC design philosophy is to follow service-based architecture and maintain a level of reuse and ease of use that will make using the library a worthwhile investment. To do this, the PFC varies from the standard theme proposed by SBA (i.e., that objects should be loosely coupled to promote maximum reuse) in order to enhance ease of use. There are some elements which will make the classes and methods of the PFC easier to recognize. They are defined as follows.

Classes

The PFC contains four basic categories of classes: service classes, abstract client classes, concrete client classes, and extension classes.

Service classes.   Classes in this category contain the delegated behavioral content of the library. Services are divided into further categories which are explained in detail in this book. Service classes are referenced directly at the extension layer, resulting in the tight coupling mentioned earlier. This means that to extend a service class, the recommended method would be to insert a new inheritance layer between the base service class and the extension layer. Service classes *can* be extended through inheritance, but the implications of this need to be understood. Chapter 3 discusses extending the PFC and the extension classes in detail.

Abstract client classes.   Abstract client classes are those client classes which are used through inheritance. Examples of these classes are the userobject DataWindow class (pfc_u_dw) and the various generalized window classes, such as pfc_w_master and pfc_w_sheet. The intent is that these classes are inherited from by the developer and then specialized depending on the need. For example, when you place a u_dw object on a window, you are in fact inheriting from the u_dw object. If you create a sheet window for your application, you would inherit it (physically) from w_sheet. Extending these classes follows the same philosophy as extending the service classes.

Classes such as pfc_w_master are not only abstract, but pseudo-virtual as well. They are intended to classify descendant classes, rather than be used on their own. For example, pfc_w_sheet is inherited from w_master, which is inherited from pfc_w_master. We would not actually descend a class directly from the w_master class; rather, we would choose the client class which was still abstract, but more specific to our task, such as w_sheet.

Concrete client classes.   Concrete client classes are those which you do not inherit; rather, they are used as is. Examples of this type of class are the About dialog window, the Splash window, the Login window, etc. Basically, these classes include any class that is specialized to the point where it would no longer be specialized functionally. These are classes which could be omitted from the extension layer completely, but are not, for two reasons. The first is that the library needs to be consistent. The second is that concrete classes are often the classes that would be modified by developers to reflect appearance standards. Extending these classes can be done by inheritance, by insertion, *or* by peer object generation.

Extension classes.   The extension classes provided in the PFC are the developers' gateway to affecting the appearance and behavior of defined classes. The extension layer is an empty layer of objects descended from the base objects. Basically, this means that the PFC has done some of the work you would ordinarily do yourself if you were using a regular class library. The service-based approach allows the use of the extension layer quite nicely, although typically, only the service classes truly require an extension layer. Client classes can be extended through inheritance anyway. The extension layer is discussed in detail in Chap. 3.

Methods

The methods used in the PFC fall into one of the following categories.

Events

- *Standard.* These are the events that are standard to the control in which they are found. Events such as clicked fall into this category.

- *Delegated.* These are events which are included to delegate the behavioral responsibility of the action to a different user-defined event. For example, the clicked event "delegates" its actions to the pfc_clicked event.

- *Precoded.* These are events which contain code prior to your using them. Most events fall into this category, even if they are delegating their behavior.

- *Placeholder.* These are events created for developers to extend where the class library cannot make the decision of processing. For example, a post_insert event would be part of the insert cycle, but would not be coded within the class library.

Functions

- *Standard.* These are standard PowerBuilder functions.

- *PFC internal.* These are used within PFC objects, defined as private.

- *Attribute.* This is a wrapper function allowing read or write access to an attribute, typically a Get or Set function. It is usually defined as public or protected.

- *Action.* This is a function that performs a specific action. It is typically the object's application programming interface (API).

- *Service management.* These are functions used to enable and disable services. In the PFC, these are typically of_Setxxxx(TRUE/FALSE), where xxxx is the name of the service and the true/false switch determines whether to enable or disable the service.

Summary/Conclusions

This concludes the introduction to the PFC. This chapter has introduced you to the concepts and philosophy behind the PFC, and how and why this architecture is better than prior generations. The remainder of the book will go into much more detail about all of the classes and objects defined to the PFC.

2

Supporting the PFC

Introduction

This chapter introduces concepts necessary for the successful support of the PFC. We will examine the issues involved in successfully supporting the PFC in a multideveloper environment, as well as the infrastructure of the organization needed to provide this support. In addition, we will look at the issues involved in the make-versus-buy decision with respect to adding functionality to the PFC, and gain an understanding of this decision-making process. We will also look at the issues involved in deciding whether or not to rearchitect your existing class library. Finally, we will discuss some available third-party software that already supports the PFC.

One point we strongly emphasize is that using the PFC correctly will take a larger up-front investment than you are probably used to. This includes time to develop a support structure that will serve its purpose without bringing development to a standstill and time at the beginning of each project to properly architect functionality for reuse in future applications.

Team Buy-in—Critical for Success

Over time, we have been involved with many projects, some for very large companies. Many were successful; some were doomed to fail from the start. In fact, there are more of the latter than one would believe. Why? Most companies that make an investment in new technology like client/server want to see quick, visible results to validate their decision. This leads to the "There is never enough time or money to do it right, but there is always enough time and money to do it over" syndrome. Companies that make a commitment to the process enjoy a much higher degree of success.

To be successful in the use of the PFC, there has to be commitment to that success. *Commitment* is a funny word, with many interpretations. Let us define commitment as we view it.

When looking at a ham-and-eggs breakfast:

The chicken was involved in the success.

The pig was committed to the success.

This commitment must come from all levels of the organization. Management must buy into the fact that results will not be instantaneous. Using the PFC correctly is a longer-term investment than just turning out code; however, this investment will have a large return. In fact, the more you invest along the way, the larger the return.

In this sense, management is not limited to the management of the information services organization. This commitment must come from the top. If it does, it can be enforced even if the pressure from the user community for the delivery of new systems is increased. We have seen many situations where IS management is committed, but does not have the support of the corporate management team. In these cases, any methodology will fail as it is forced to yield to time pressures.

The payback comes in the form of increased productivity, greater ease of maintenance, and more robust systems down the line. It takes time to develop the reusable objects that will be required to support an organization's business rules and interface requirements.

Perhaps the hardest of these benefits to sell is the gain in productivity, since initially it appears to take longer to deliver anything, and performing an accurate measurement of productivity gains may seem more witchcraft than science. Think of this as being like building a computer. Without prebuilt components, you must solder chips to a board, build disk drives, and bend metal to make a chassis. After you have been in business for a while, these parts are sitting finished on a shelf, and producing a finished computer from the component parts will take less time.

Productivity gains are easiest to measure on small, simple systems. If the first system developed using the PFC needs a minimal architecture and can use the PFC as is, gains in productivity will be easily identified. These gains may be measured by observing how quickly generic tasks, such as inserting a new row into a DataWindow with a pop-up menu, can be accomplished. Upon saving a row, the PFC will perform normal and required field processing without the developer's having to write a line of code.

In the case of large-scale systems or organizations, the measurement of productivity becomes more complex. Many of the gains beyond the ones already discussed will not be visible until new objects are architected and developed. Once a solid base of reusable objects containing processes and business rules has been developed, then gains may be measured in the reduced development, debugging, and maintenance times on new systems.

Ease of maintenance is achieved through common objects. Common objects can be developed as loosely coupled (no dependency on other objects) or tightly coupled (interobject dependencies are built in). The PFC is actually a combination, containing service classes which are loosely coupled, but implementing an extension layer which is tightly coupled. The ultimate goal for an OO developer is to have loose coupling, while trying to avoid the natural complexity implicit within this type of programming. These objects are highly encapsulated and loosely coupled. By this I mean that each object contains the code that affects it and is not dependent on other objects. This means that code that needs to be maintained is easily located and needs to be changed in only one place. Also, with a product such as the PFC, someone else is maintaining and enhancing the product, removing this cost from your organization.*

Robustness is ensured by the fact that these reusable objects are in continual use and therefore have been tested in various real-world applications. Furthermore, these objects tend to be more robust because they were developed to satisfy many requirements, whereas individual project teams tend to develop only the functionality needed for the current iteration of their project's development life cycle. For example, a project team would most likely write a query object used to search for records to support only the needs of that project as opposed to building it for reuse across multiple applications.

What does all of this have to do with the PFC? Once you start using it and see the benefits, you will rush to add your own objects and extensions.

Next, the development team needs to commit to the process, whatever the process may be. Using the PFC to its best advantage is a more painful process than working in a vacuum. First of all, it means doing things in a predetermined way, thereby removing some of the creativity of programming. Second, it increases the effort in the design phase of a project by requiring developers to look for existing objects for reuse and to design new objects with reuse in mind. Third, once the use of a class library is widespread, there is a risk that changes may have a negative impact on existing systems. This requires that some restrictions be placed on the modification of objects used by multiple applications.

We can't emphasize enough the requirement for buy-in from the team. Having standards is not a solution, as can be seen in all the places that have fat standards manuals stuck up on a shelf covered by two inches of dust. Standards and policies themselves are not enough. They *must* be enforced. In order for the enforcement to work in a way that is not detrimental to the well-being of the organization, everyone must be committed to the process. Using a class library such as the PFC implies enforcement of some standards because of the nature of using inheritance. Once a company's standards are built on top of the PFC objects supplied (for example, size and font used on something as

---

*Current proposed enhancements to the PFC will be discussed in later chapters.

simple as a command button), you are assured that avoiding these standards would require manual intervention from the developer.

Organizational Roles

There are several roles needed to properly support development with the PFC in a multideveloper environment. Several of these roles may be performed by a single individual, but they are all needed. Successful organizations will have clearly defined roles with little or no functional crossover between them.

Roles include those of the system/object architect, object designer, librarian, developer, and quality assurance team. This is by no means an exhaustive list, and any structure that an organization chooses must fit within the reality of the world the organization works in. By this we mean that it is all well and good to have volumes of standards, practices, and methodologies; however, if they are too cumbersome to use in the day-to-day work of the organization, they will sit on a shelf and gather dust.

Project Manager

Project management in the object-oriented arena is a different animal from the project management we have done over the last 20 years. Traditionally we have used the waterfall approach to system design. This approach is a serial process that normally had the users involved in the beginning during analysis, and then again at the end for system testing. In the mainframe world, the time between these points could be two years. Often, after this two years of effort, we heard from the users, "That's not what I asked for." Or we found that the users or business requirements had changed. Figure 2.1 shows the waterfall approach to traditional project management.

In the object-oriented metaphor, we tend to use a prototyping approach to development. This allows the users to see the software at various stages of

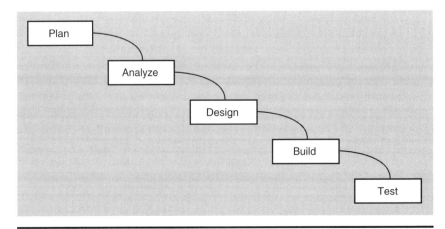

Figure 2.1 Waterfall project management.

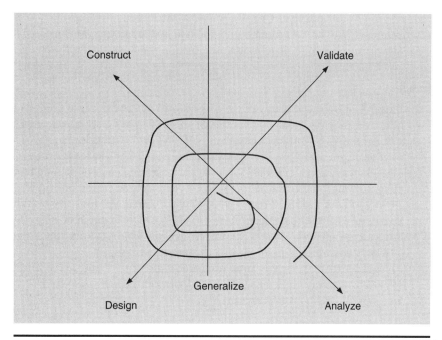

Figure 2.2 The spiral model.

development and permits more flexibility in the process. As an outgrowth of this approach, we are beginning to see a new model for project management: the spiral model. The spiral model is essentially a never-ending spiral moving out from the center. Figure 2.2 shows the spiral model.

As can be seen, the spiral continually moves through five steps:

1. Analyze
2. Generalize
3. Design
4. Construct
5. Validate/test

Since in the prototyping model we are always analyzing, we are assured of always having the most current requirements. Generalization refers to making every object as generic as possible to maximize its potential for reuse. The remaining steps are self-explanatory and will not be discussed here.

As can be seen, the object-oriented project life cycle is an ever-evolving target. This makes the management of an OO project more challenging. As a rule of thumb, we break up all projects into three-month pieces to reduce the scope and make for more manageable implementations. This reduction in scope helps to make the project more manageable.

We should point out that the spiral model is our current choice for development. However, OO methodologies are still evolving, and we are seeing a move toward object modeling as the technique for developing systems.

System Architect

The role of the system architect is to design the system from the object level. This entails defining each object, including its attributes and services, and defining any interobject communications and dependencies.

It is important that any system under development go through such a design step. It will help to identify objects that already exist and may be reused. While it is not the purpose of this book to teach object orientation, Fig. 2.3 shows a simple object model. This figure shows a DataWindow class with some attributes and functions defined and a DataWindow insertrow class with its attributes and methods. Such models serve as a way to validate our design and identify the objects needed and their relationships.

There are many tools and methodologies available to accomplish this task (Fig. 2.3 was created using VISIO Technical), and your organization is free to use whichever best suits your needs.

Object designer

The object designer translates the object model into a specification that can be coded. He or she needs to define the public interface for the object and how it will communicate with other objects. The public interface of an object is how the programmers will communicate with it. For example, the Powerbuilder DataWindow object has a private-instance variable that stores what the current row is. Programmers can find this value by calling the GetRow() function; this is part of the public interface. Figure 2.4 shows an object's public interface.

Object administration

The object administrator is responsible for the coordination of maintenance of the PFC and other reusable objects. It must be stressed that changes to

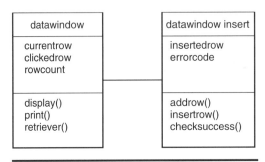

Figure 2.3 A simple object model.

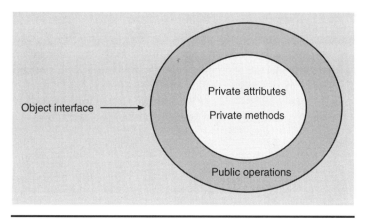

Figure 2.4 The public interface.

reusable objects can have a enormous impact on existing systems that are using them. It is highly recommended that changes to these objects be thoroughly tested before they are incorporated into the PFC. In one shop we are aware of, the PFC is located on a network drive that only two people have write access to. These people are responsible for all changes made to the PFC.

Design review team

It is the responsibility of this group to ensure that all systems are as well designed as possible. Design review can be a touchy subject and must be handled properly to prevent those whose work is being reviewed from taking it personally. In our organization, we view design review as a learning process. The designer presents his or her design and is prepared to support it as the group tries to find any holes. Remember, the goal of design review is to produce the best possible systems.

We do at least two design reviews in our shop. The first is at the system level, and the second is at the object design level. In this way, we ensure that both designs take advantage of existing objects.

Code reviewer

A code reviewer's popularity is somewhere up there with that of the tax collector and poison ivy. No programmer we have ever met likes having someone look over his or her shoulder and tell him or her how to write code. After all, we're artists.

However, one achievable goal when using a class library such as the PFC is to not be able to tell who wrote a script by the style of the coding. This is where standards such as naming conventions come into play. Attaining this goal is worth the investment, because when the code needs to be maintained or resources on a project need to shift, or when someone leaves the development team, the learning curve for the replacement is minimized.

Tester

While not the most glamorous of jobs, testing is absolutely critical to the successful implementation of any system. On the bright side, once an organization has built up a library of reusable objects, testing will become less time-consuming. The theory behind this is that if an object is being used successfully in several places, it probably works. There are now several products on the market, such as SQA Test Suite, that will automate the testing process.

The organization

Figure 2.5 shows what the optimum organization would be in a perfect world. There are many benefits derived from this type of organization.

- *Maximized ability to manage the project.* This type of organization clearly defines the responsibilities of all those involved. The project manager can devote his or her time to managing the project and need not be immersed in the technical details.

- *Sound design.* Effectively managing the design process and performing design reviews will ensure a more solid system design.

- *More rapid development.* The speed of systems development will increase as more reusable objects are developed.

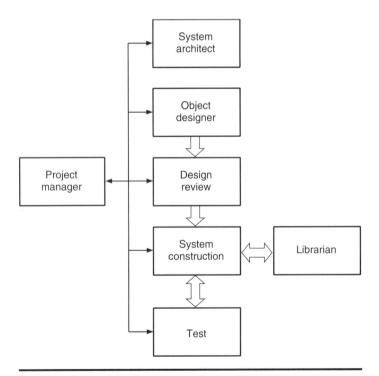

Figure 2.5 The organization.

■ *Robust systems.* The use of existing objects that have been thoroughly exorcised in multiple systems, will lead to the development of more robust systems, with the added benefit of reducing the time required for testing.

While the above structure has many benefits, there are some downsides to it also. As in all things, placing controls on anything will eventually lead to bottlenecks. Having a limited number of people who can update the PFC and corporate objects will at times slow things down a little. However, it is our belief that this is worth any minor problems it might cause. We strongly suggest that at least two people have this capability so that they can back each other up.

In many organizations, it is common for one person to wear several of the above hats. This can work as long as that person has a backup so that if he or she is unavailable for any reason, the process can continue.

Start Fresh or Rearchitect? The Big Question

Starting from scratch

There are many factors involved in the make-versus-buy decision. Each needs to be evaluated in deciding whether to rearchitect an existing class library, start with the PFC as delivered and develop from there, or purchase an add-on to the PFC to provide functionality that is not included with the shipped product.

The first criterion is the technical expertise of the developers in your organization. To use the PFC and create reusable objects correctly requires a strong knowledge of object orientation. This is not to be confused with Powerbuilder development. I have met many excellent Powerbuilder programmers who do not possess an in-depth knowledge of OO principles or know how to apply them in Powerbuilder. I call this "Powerbuilder using the COBOL approach." These people know the Powerscript language and can do anything they want with the product, but with a process- rather than an object-oriented approach.

Using the PFC will force your organization to become more object-oriented; however, the maximum gains with the PFC will be realized only if you have an understanding of OO principles before you start.

Therefore, the first question to ask and answer is, "Does my organization have the knowledge to start from scratch?" Even if the answer to this is yes, you might still want to look at available add-ons as a way to reduce start-up time.

Next, ask yourself, "How much time do I have to get started?" If a fast start-up is a necessity, then purchasing an add-on can give an organization a head start in providing functionality.

Next ask, "Do I want to reinvent the wheel?" If the functionality you want exists in a third-party product, why develop it yourself? Many organizations will balk at add-ons, seeing them as an additional cost. It must be remembered that it costs to develop this functionality in-house.

Buying an extended library

When deciding whether to purchase an extension to the PFC, there are several points to be considered. Following is a list of questions we would ask when evaluating any library extensions for the PFC.

Is it architected for the PFC? By this we mean, is the extension designed to fit seamlessly with the PFC? If any of the extension's code must reside in the top level of the PFC (PBLs that begin with PFC), we would be concerned. This is the layer that Powersoft will maintain and ship new versions of. If any extension puts code here, it will need to be reinstalled each time a new version of the PFC is shipped from Powersoft.

Does it follow PFC standards? Did the architects of the extension follow the naming conventions used within the PFC? If not, this will make the extension harder to integrate. Is it service-based, or do its objects carry all the code and overhead? As an example, the PFC separates DataWindow update services from querymode services. Service-based architecture allows you to use only those services you want, without carrying the overhead of unused services.

How do I customize the extension? Does the extension have its own extension layer? This is important, as any organization will most likely want to customize purchased objects to work in its environment.

What does it cost? Is the cost based on the number of developers? Is there a runtime licensing fee? We would be more concerned about a licensing fee than about the cost per developer. A good extension can pay for itself quickly in productivity gains.

How is it supported? What is the cost of maintenance? How often will updates be issued? These are the questions that must be asked on any software purchase. The support policies need to be understood. Remember that any time a class library is updated, all applications using it or their associated PBDs will need to be recompiled before they will be affected by the changes.

Rearchitecting your library

Whether to rearchitect your existing library or not is often an emotional issue. We had a class library we had developed over the years that had a lot of ourselves invested in it. It was a hard decision, but we threw it out in favor of the PFC. Why? Mainly because our attachment to our library was mostly emotional, and as consultants we need to be doing what the mainstream is doing, which in our opinion will be the PFC.

Having said that, we did not discard it in its entirety but incorporated several sets of functionality that are not native in the PFC into the PFC.

With the introduction of PowerBuilder 5.0, there is much to learn. There are several new controls, as well as the ability to do distributed processing and the PFC. We started using the PFC as it shipped, then incorporated those functions that we use and that were not included in the PFC. In some cases we did not agree with the way that the PFC accomplished a task and chose to override its functionality with our own.

Once again, the technical expertise of the developers is an issue. The PFC is highly object-oriented and uses many nonvisual objects to incorporate functionality. A thorough understanding of these principles will be required in order to rearchitect an existing library. The ease of the rearchitecture will depend on how highly encapsulated and how object-oriented your library is.

If you decide to incorporate functionality from an existing library into the PFC, the organization will need to have a thorough working knowledge of PFC internals. This is a highly complex library with a lot of interobject communication which must be understood before radical changes can be made.

Another issue is the time that will be required to rearchitect and develop from an existing class library versus the learning time for the PFC. The time it will take to become proficient with the PFC is not trivial; however, it is less than that needed to develop a library with similar functionality.

One final point to always keep in mind is that there is a cost associated with rearchitecting your library. There is also another cost, and that is that either the applications you already have developed without the PFC will have to be converted to the new library, or a copy of the old library will have to be maintained and supported in parallel with the new library.

Application Design/Development Tools

There are several tools available today to help in the design and development of objects for the PFC. Following is a discussion of some of these tools. These are not product reviews, but rather an overview of some of the capabilities of these tools.

Riverton HOW for PowerBuilder*

Riverton's HOW product is an interactive design tool designed specifically for object-oriented analysis and design. It is designed to be a foundation class–based design and component assembly environment built specifically for PowerBuilder and N-tier development.

HOW provides for object domains, visual storyboards, workflows, and a repository to help in the development of reusable business objects and technology components. Using a drag-and-drop interface, the product provides use-case analysis for the gathering of system requirements using a graphical approach.

In the context of HOW, an object domain is a collection of class objects and their interrelationships. Business objects are derived from an organization's business rules. Technology components are the building blocks for an application's interface and services.

---

*Riverton Software, One Kendall Square, Building 200, Cambridge, MA 02139, (617) 588-0500, http://www.riverton.com.

Use-case analysis is an industry-standard approach for systems analysis, detailing specific functions and their interactions or the roles that interact with them.

HOW allows for the management of multiple projects. The repository stores information about objects, and an explorer is provided for sorting and retrieving information about objects and projects. A task builder allows for the assembling of objects into applications by storyboarding application flow and behavior.

There are also generation and synchronization features for creating databases and applications, and for specifying the type of application to be developed: two-tier or multitier.

The steps for developing applications using HOW are as follows:

1. *Define use cases and business rules.* In this step, use cases for each segment of functionality within the scope of the application are created. You can also create use case views that illustrate a group of use cases and roles (see Fig. 2.6). This allows you to define information about who is doing what work. Each use case can be expanded to include an overview, specific steps, preconditions, etc. Roles that interact with the system are fully defined.

2. *Derive objects.* Nouns defined within use cases are primary candidates to become business objects. Application behavior may also be derived in this way. For example, a single use case, such as process an order, might become a specific service within an application. This service can be defined as a task for later storyboarding.

3. *Complete the object model.* Business objects are defined in the domain builder, which provides a flexible environment. Each domain will reference a subset of the objects contained in the Open Tool repository. For each object, you can define attributes, methods, and relationships, including inheri-

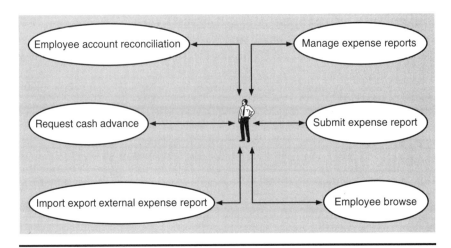

Figure 2.6 Use-case analysis.

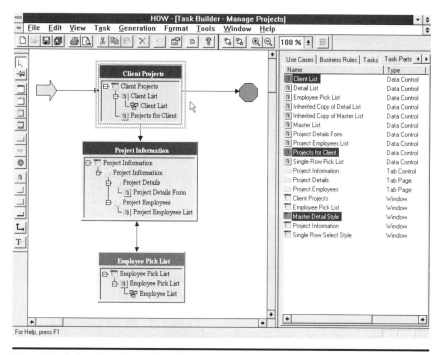

Figure 2.7 A simple task storyboard.

tance. These definitions serve as the foundation for your database, and will become properties and functions of PowerBuilder custom class objects.

4. *Storyboard tasks.* The task builder is designed to assemble the parts of the application by creating storyboards of the application's flow and interface (see Fig. 2.7). Within the task builder, you may use existing objects or create descendants of a more specialized nature. From the storyboard, Open Tool generates PowerBuilder windows, DataWindows, tab controls, and queries.

5. *Define work flows.* This component helps you to design comprehensive business workflows (see Fig. 2.8). These workflows may be used as documentation of the work in your business and as specifications for workflow applications.

6. *Generate the database.* Databases may be generated from one or more of the class object domains. A data model for either Logic Works' Erwin or Powersoft's S-Designor will be created. The database design is then completed in the data-modeling tool of your choice.

7. *Import a data model.* The data model for an existing application may be imported into Open Tool and the class objects for it will be created.

8. *Generate the application.* The application is generated in two stages, resulting in an application with an object-oriented architecture.

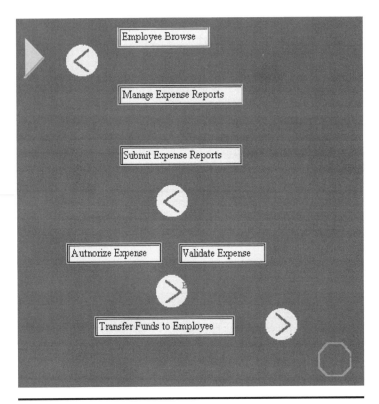

Figure 2.8   A simple workflow.

Open Tool will support any commercially available class library, including the PFC. This product is currently offered for Windows 95.

S-Designor by Powersoft*

S-Designor provides modules for process, data, and application modeling, as well as the capability to develop templates for use with various class libraries to generate objects for a PowerBuilder application. In this chapter we discuss the AppModeler and Template pieces of the product.

The AppModeler will generate application objects, leveraging off the data models created in the DataArchitect module. These objects are based upon a physical data model and a set of standard or customized templates.

The data modeling workspace in AppModeler is an easy-to-use interface where various details necessary to define a database are specified. You can create tables and columns. Depending on the DBMS you are using, check constraints, alternative keys, indexes, referential integrity, triggers, and stored procedures may be created.

*Powersoft, (800) 395-3525, http://www.powersoft.com.

At the time of this writing, AppModeler supports the generation of objects for 16- and 32-bit PowerBuilder, versions 4.0 and 5.0.

AppModeler uses templates to generate application objects. The product provides predefined, customizable templates, each corresponding to a specific type of object in the physical data model and creating a specific application object. As an example, the template for a reference between two tables will create a master-detail presentation. Table 2.1 depicts the relationship between the model objects and their corresponding application objects.

Templates define and encapsulate appearance (for visual objects) and behaviors. Therefore, generated applications have a common look and feel. This allows users to learn new systems more quickly and reduces training time.

Any template may be customized to meet the standards of your organization. The associations between model-level templates and object-level templates can be overridden. For example, the default presentation style for a table or view is freeform; you may, however, assign one or more individual tables to a template that uses a different presentation style.

The objects generated for a PowerBuilder application are inherited from a class library. At this writing, AppModeler provides templates for the Application Library for PowerBuilder 4.0 and the PFC. Templates for other class libraries may be developed.

The PowerBuilder templates are divided into three categories:

- *Model.* These include the application object, main (MDI) window, main menu, and sheet window.

- *Table or view.* This is a window object containing a single DataWindow.

- *Reference.* This is a window with two DataWindow controls in a master-detail relationship.

Template objects may also be PowerBuilder user objects. All of these templates are stored in a PowerBuilder library (PBL). This library can contain multiple template objects of each type. This means that, for example, there can be more than one window object template, each with a different appearance and behaviors.

TABLE 2.1   Model-to-Object Relationship

Model object	PowerBuilder object
Physical data model	Application object MDI frame window Main menu
Table or view	Window Freeform DataWindow
Reference	Window Master (freeform) DataWindow Detail DataWindow (grid)

These template objects are assigned to the tables in a model via extended attributes. Certain template objects are assigned as defaults and may be overridden in the AppModeler physical data model workspace.

ObjectComposer by BusinessSoft*

ObjectComposer is a graphical code generator for PowerBuilder 5.0. The product uses a Windows 95 Wizard to step the user through building objects based on the PFC.

ObjectComposer consists of three composers, two utilities, and two PowerBuilder links. The composers provide a graphical interface for defining and generating PowerBuilder objects, including application objects, windows, and nonvisual user objects.

- *Window Composer.* The Window Composer is used to build selection dialogs and maintenance objects. You can also define DataWindows and their relationships and associate menus. The developer may choose from many models, such as master-detail, form, list, treeview, listview, and tabs.

- *Preload Composer.* This composer allows the developer to specify data that will be preloaded and cached.

- *Navigation Composer.* Use this composer to create an interface for navigating between windows in your application. Options include menus, listview, treeview, and tab interfaces.

ObjectComposer contains two utilities to simplify application development and object management.

- *Application Wizard.* The Application Wizard walks you through a step-by-step dialog to specify the decisions necessary to generate an application.

- *Object Manager.* This tool helps you to organize and develop objects and to manage the scope of the definitions. It also allows for the sharing of objects among developers.

ObjectComposer's links to PowerBuilder allow you to work in the DataWindow and menu painter from within the product. You can use these links to develop your own custom menus, or ObjectComposer can use the menu from the PFC.

ObjectComposer stores the object definitions in a database. Each developer logs on with a unique user id. Therefore, each object definition in the database has a specific owner. The owner defines the scope of the object definition. The scope determines who has what kind of access to an object definition. Private restricts the object definition to the owner. Public read-only and public all-access scopes may also be set.

---

*BusinessSoft, 2500 City West Blvd., Suite 800, Houston, TX 77042, (800) 888-BUSSOFT, http://www.bsisoft.com.

ObjectComposer supports multiple databases for storing object definitions. Placing the database on a server allows team development access across multiple systems. The currently supported databases are Sybase SQL Anywhere, Microsoft SQL Server, Sybase, and Oracle.

PFC Add-Ons

CornerStone 5.0*

CornerStone 5.0 is an object-oriented service-based class library that augments the PFC by providing developers with prebuilt application objects that can quickly be incorporated in PowerBuilder 5.0 applications.

The product is designed to help organizations take advantage of new features in PowerBuilder 5.0 and maximize its object-oriented capabilities. CornerStone 5.0 is built on the PFC, thereby ensuring compatibility with Powersoft's class library strategy. CornerStone 5.0 includes a comprehensive set of customizable business-oriented objects, services, and templates that can be readily assembled into robust business applications. CornerStone 5.0 greatly reduces the PFC learning curve and addresses the needs of a wide range of development organizations.

The PFC is a foundation for experienced developers to build upon. CornerStone 5.0 builds upon this foundation by significantly extending and enhancing the PFC's core functionality, and adding the kinds of business-oriented services, visual metaphors, and reusable templates that PFC does not provide. CornerStone is an excellent learning tool that helps organizations manage the transition to the new service-oriented paradigm. New developers can draw from the library's extensive set of prebuilt window templates and get started building applications quickly; experienced developers and architects can learn how to properly extend functionality and add corporate-specific services by following CornerStone's example.

CornerStone was designed specifically for the PFC and therefore does not need to maintain backward compatibility as other pre–PowerBuilder 5.0 libraries do.

The product includes well-documented source code, and the help file is built mainly on Lotus ScreenCams to help you get started using the product quickly.

The CornerStone architecture provides all of the features and benefits of the PFC plus:

- Extensions of the PFC services to provide more robustness and flexibility. CornerStone 5.0 extends and augments many of the PFC services to include additional real-world, business-oriented events, functionality, and features.

---

*Financial Dynamics Inc., 7900 Westpark Drive, Suite A515, McLean, VA 22102, (800) 4FI-NDYN, http://www.findyn.com.

- Extensions to existing PFC services, as well as several services of its own, all developed in full compliance with PFC's architecture and naming conventions. Some of these services are listed below.

  New: Ad hoc Query/Report Builder
  New: Business Rule Service—to facilitate application partitioning
  New: Bubble Help
  Enhanced: Data-Driven Tree View
  Enhanced: Data-Driven List View
  New: DataWindow Output Medium Manager
  Enhanced: DataWindow Cache Manager
  New: DataWindow Column Manager
  New: Environment Manager
  Enhanced: Error logging
  New: Explorer interface objects
  New: Inter/Intra Object Message Manager
  Enhanced: Linkage Manager
  New: Properties Manager (colors, sort and filter styles, error logging, etc.)
  New: Security Manager
  New: Spell Checking
  New: Split Screen Manager
  New: Surrogate Key Manager
  New: Tag Value Manager
  New: Validation Manager

- Visual metaphors that provide options for your application's look and feel, such as

  "Workbook" metaphor for MDI frames
  "Sticky" or Post-it Notes
  Graphical timeline
  Wizard (business rule–driven)

CornerStone also provides a Component Library of commonly used encapsulated visual controls (pop-up/drop-down calendars, progress meters, etc.).

This is a very powerful and full-featured product that would be a great help in starting you on your way with the PFC.

Summary

As can be seen, successful implementation of the PFC requires some knowledge of object-oriented concepts, the definition of new roles within the organization, and above all a commitment to the process from the top down. We take this opportunity to once again emphasize the importance of this commitment, for without it the success of the organization will be impaired.

In addition, as you make your way down the path, there are tools and add-ons available to help guide you along the way. These tools will help you to manage your projects, design objects, and maintain your databases, and will provide objects for your use. Some of them will even generate the code, windows, menus, etc., required for your application.

As you take the first steps down the road to developing with the PFC, remember that it may sometimes appear difficult, but if you have half as much fun learning and using it as we have, then you'd best be prepared to give up your other hobbies.

3

Extensibility

Introduction

Class libraries allow us to capitalize on many benefits of object-oriented technology.

Applications can be built faster by reusing the objects in the library. The class library is a programmer's toolbox. After the initial learning curve, solving a problem becomes simply a matter of recognizing a specific pattern, then applying a proven solution.

Stable and tested objects yield fewer bugs. This is not to say that the initial class library release is always bug-free, but as the object's usage increases, so does its reliability. This is especially true for such a widely used class library as PFC.

Insulated from the tedious low-level implementation details, we can concentrate on solving the real business and design issues. This allows us to construct ever more complex applications. We are able to build upon a enormous amount of knowledge invested in a class library by its developers.

None of the above can be beneficial unless we can adjust the class library to fit the needs of a specific project. There can be no argument—the success of a class library lies in its flexibility. The true test of any class library is how easily it can be extended.

Chapter Objectives

Class libraries provide instant gratification. It is possible to achieve very impressive results with little effort. The payoff is great, and it is very tempting to jump right in and start developing. You should, since there is no better learning tool than hands-on experience. But it is also very important not to lose sight of the bigger picture. An interesting observation is that children learn by asking why. It is very easy to follow instructions to accomplish a certain task, but it may be more beneficial to determine why this specific solution is the best. Taking the time up front to understand the reasoning behind the choices made by class library developers will make it a lot easier to extend their vision and resolve the issues of a specific project.

Extensibility is crucial to successful use of any class library. This chapter will present the concept of the extension layer adopted by PFC. It will take you through the history of different techniques and provide the ways to extend and customize that are best fitted for each. It will also cover some techniques specific to service-based architecture.

Extensibility in Inheritance-Based Architecture

The goal of a typical class library is to provide as much functionality as possible while staying flexible. While the class library developers concentrate on constantly improving the techniques required to reach their objectives, the task of determining the best way to extend and customize the library has historically been the responsibility of the end user.

Extensibility requirements

After the initial awe at all the benefits received from the class library, many questions arise. How do we change the default behavior to satisfy the needs of this specific project? Can additional functionality be added without interfering with any of the objects in the class library?

The extensibility requirements can be summarized as follows:

- Ability to add new functionality to the library
- Ability to modify the existing behavior
- Ability to integrate any modifications with future class library releases

Object-oriented technology has reached adulthood. There are many different approaches to adding functionality through inheritance. Determining the best approach to extension requires an understanding of the internal structure of the class library itself. There are two common techniques in an inheritance-based architecture.

- General-purpose classes
- Nested generalization classes

These techniques differ in philosophy, performance, and results. We will discuss these techniques in more detail in the following sections.

General-purpose classes

One of the first approaches to class library/framework design is a general-purpose class method. This method is based on placing all the functionality in the ancestor object. The required functionality is then enabled for a specific object instance by using a "set" function or an instance variable.

Note: The general-purpose ancestor is considered to be an abstract class.

Definitions:

abstract class A class that is never instantiated itself, but is used only to provide common functionality for its descendants.

concrete class A class that can be either inherited or instantiated.

A good example of this method is a DataWindow ancestor control. Figure 3.1 shows a typical general-purpose DataWindow ancestor.

In the example shown in Fig. 3.1, the ancestor datawindow provides the row selection and enhanced sort capabilities. All the datawindows will be inherited from this ancestor. When row selection is required for a specific instance, it can be enabled by calling the of_SetRowSelect(TRUE) function. This function will set an instance variable ib_RowSelect = true. In the appropriate events, the ancestor datawindow can check this variable and decide whether or not to execute the code related to row selection.

If additional functionality is required in the future, it will be added to the same ancestor object.

It's time to put the general-purpose method through the extensibility test and ask the questions:

- How do I extend?
- How do I customize?

The first instinct is to add the code to the objects in the class library itself. The problem is that although you may have paid for the software, the ownership remains with the vendor. The vendor has the right to modify the objects to add new features or fix existing bugs. As long as the interface remains stable, the vendor can change the internal operation of its objects in any way it wishes. When a new release is shipped, any changes you have made to the class library directly will be overwritten. Therefore, these changes will have to be reapplied.

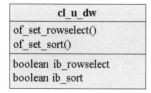

Figure 3.1 General-purpose DataWindow ancestor.

In some cases, the internal code may have changed so much that your changes cannot be easily applied. Adding the code directly to the class library objects violates the requirement of not being affected by future releases.

It is obvious that there is a need for a technique that allows you to extend and enhance the class library's functionality without being subject to these effects. The insulation-layer technique allows you to modify a class library's features and behavior, yet remain consistent with the published interface and safe from the effects of future releases.

Insulation layer

Inheritance, an old standby, can be used to solve this problem. Adding another layer between the class library objects and the concrete application classes provides an adequate solution. Figure 3.2 illustrates the addition of an insulation layer.

For every object in a class library, there is a descendant in the insulation layer. Any new functionality is added to the objects in the insulation layer, not to the class library itself. The classes in the class library become abstract, and the classes in the insulation layer become concrete.

Figure 3.3 shows an example of multitable update added to the insulation-layer DataWindow ancestor. The row-selection functionality is customized by changing the of_SetRowSelect function and other related code. Because the ancestor was never changed, it can be easily replaced by a new version when one becomes available.

Unfortunately, technology moves at the speed of light, leaving many with whiplash and a set of yesterday's techniques. Soon after we start to use the general-purpose framework, its disadvantages become apparent. The ancestor object size grows with every new added feature. Each descendant inherits every single method, including the ones it has no intention of using. There is no way to exclude any logic—it all comes in one package. As a direct result of the object's size, it takes longer to read it into memory. This produces long instantiation times and very sluggish applications. The next approach, nested generalization, solves this problem, while providing some new challenges for extensibility.

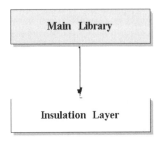

Figure 3.2 Adding an insulation layer protects your modifications.

Class Library

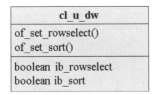

Insulation Layer

Figure 3.3 Insulation-layer example.

Nested generalization (specialized inheritance approach)

Nested generalization again uses inheritance, but this time very little function-ality resides in the top ancestor itself. Instead of a single ancestor, a hierarchy of inheritance is used. Only very generic methods are placed in the top ancestor. At every descendant level, more specific functionality is added. When using such a library, you select functionality by choosing a specific ancestor. A typical MDI application window hierarchy, shown in Fig. 3.4, illustrates this method.

At the top of the hierarchy is w_cl_master. It contains only very generic logic common to all the windows. At the next level, windows are more specialized; w_cl_sheet, w_cl_frame, and w_cl_response are each intended to perform spe-cific tasks. Finally, at the bottom level is w_cl_logon, a very specialized window that can be used only for a single purpose.

The first approach to extending a framework based on nested generalization would be to try the proven method of an insulation layer. By applying the insu-lation-layer techniques, you add another inheritance level with a descendant for every object in the class library (see Fig. 3.5).

After a close examination of this approach, some limitations become obvious.

Insulation-layer limitations

Figure 3.6 shows how eventual extensibility is limited by the nested generaliza-tion insulation-layer approach. In the original inheritance hierarchy, w_cl_logon is a descendant of w_cl_response. Any logic added to w_cl_response trickles down to w_cl_logon. That is not true for the objects in the insulation layer. W_logon is not a descendant of w_response. Any logic added to w_response does not make it to w_logon. The same holds true for all the other objects. The insulation layer can be used to extend only the objects themselves, not their descendants. This

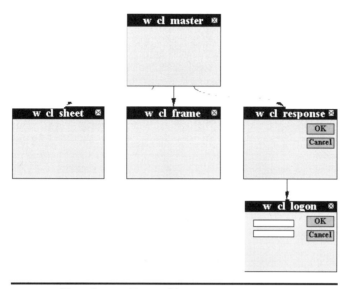

Figure 3.4 Nested generalization library structure.

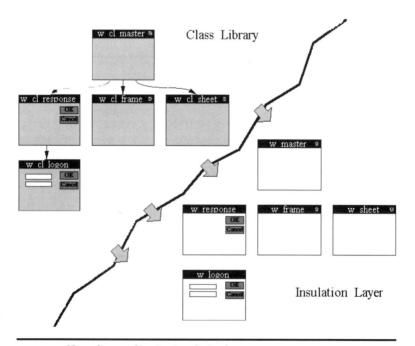

Figure 3.5 Nested generalization insulation layer.

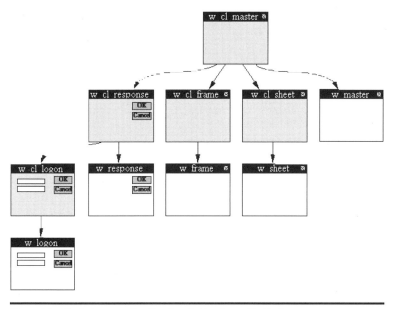

Figure 3.6   Nested generalization insulation-layer limitations.

inhibits extensibility. The relationships between ancestors and descendants are not the ones the designers intended.

Extension Layer

Clearly a different approach is needed to provide extension capabilities for all the objects in the library. In order to accomplish this, an extension layer must be implemented in the class library itself.

Extension library structure

At first glance, Fig. 3.7 looks very similar to the insulation-layer technique. In fact, the extension layer shares some of the principles of its predecessor. Both begin by creating a descendant for every object in the main library. This is where the similarities end. With the extension-layer approach, the descendant objects in the class library are not inherited from the other objects in the main library; instead, they are inherited from the corresponding objects in the extension layer. The extension layer becomes an integral part of the class library itself.

Extension-layer example

Let's take a look at how the extension layer is implemented, using the previous nested generalization example. Figure 3.8 shows how an extension layer is incorporated into the design of the library.

The integration of the extension layer and the benefits it brings now become

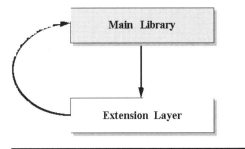

Figure 3.7   Extension library structure.

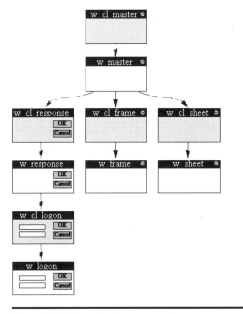

Figure 3.8   Extension-layer example.

clear. It is now possible to extend any object and all of its descendants. Since this time w_logon is a descendant of w_response, any logic added to w_response in the extension layer does make it to w_logon.

Extension-layer drawbacks

Each extension layer adds extra inheritance levels. Adding an extension layer to a three-level class hierarchy brings the number of levels up to six. Fortunately, in Powerbuilder, starting from version 4, the number of inheritance levels has a minimal impact on performance. This has been further improved in version 5, bringing the performance penalty due to the inheritance down to insignificant levels.

Any changes in the extension layer make their way back into the original class library. This is a double-edged sword. It provides the capability to extend all the descendants in the hierarchy, but it also makes it easier to inadvertently change the class library behavior. Changes to the extension layer must be made with care.

Tip: To minimize the possibility of inadvertently changing the behavior of other objects, add any additional logic at the lowest possible descendant.

Service-Based Architecture

Looking back at the nested generalization approach, there are some major limitations. The appropriate functionality is "turned on" by selecting the appropriate ancestor. By design, the ancestor and descendant objects are very tightly coupled. This creates very rigid objects. When a change in functionality is required, the only possible solution is to change the inheritance.

Because many languages, including Powerbuilder, do not support multiple inheritance, it is impossible to select functionality from two different ancestors. To achieve the desired result, duplication of code may be necessary.

The inheritance is determined at compile time. Once defined, it cannot be changed at runtime.

Fortunately, the technology keeps changing, and once again a new, exciting technique has emerged to help resolve some limitations of the inheritance-based methods.

Service-based architecture presents an alternative to inheritance. Most of the functionality is moved from the base objects into service objects. Each service object is responsible for a single, distinct function. When this function is needed on the base object, the required service is instantiated and all the work is delegated to the service object. The service provider objects are very loosely coupled to one another.

Because the functionality is determined by selecting the appropriate services, any change is as easy as selecting a different set of services. The results of multiple inheritance can be simulated by using multiple services. Finally, in contrast to the situation with inheritance, the object behavior is determined at runtime. It can be changed dynamically by associating the object with a different service provider.

Extension layer and the service-based architecture

The extension layer is intended to extend the functionality in an inheritance-based framework. How does the extension-layer approach fit with the service-based architecture?

A framework based on service delegation consists of service requesters and providers. Even though the framework as a whole is based on service delegation, its components, the service providers and requesters, are constructed using either general class or nested generalization methods. The extension-layer approach works equally well with either one.

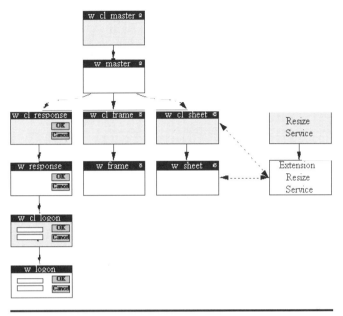

Figure 3.9   Extension layer in a service-based framework.

Let's take a look at the familiar example of the typical window hierarchy. This time, the resize functionality will be provided by a resize service object.

In Fig. 3.9, the service requester is a window (w_sheet), and the service provider is a nonvisual user object which contains the logic needed to resize all the controls when the window is resized.

Note: Any direct references are always made to the service object in the extension layer and not to its ancestor.

Any direct references to the resize service in w_cl_sheet and w_sheet are made to the resize service object in the extension layer. Whenever an instance of w_sheet is created, it will see any new functionality added to the resize service in any layer.

Extending the service-based architecture

As mentioned earlier in this chapter, when extending a class library it is very important that you understand the methodology used by the original developers. Understanding the underlying reasons behind the choices they have made makes it easier to expand and build upon their original ideas. If you take the time to familiarize yourself with the specific methodology and the techniques involved, you will find yourself naturally going with the flow instead of feverishly paddling against the current.

Applying the theory of service-based architecture opens new opportunities for class library expansion. Instead of adding new logic through inheritance, it is possible to add new services. Let's examine the different approaches to extending the service-based framework. There are three possible approaches:

- Adding logic through inheritance to the base objects
- Adding new service objects
- Adding logic through inheritance to the service objects

Many different factors should be considered when selecting the best approach. This topic alone contains enough material for a separate book, and this chapter will not attempt to cover every detail, but outlining the major advantages and shortcomings of each approach should make some design decisions more obvious.

Adding logic through inheritance to the base objects.   The first approach is the easiest to implement, but it may result in somewhat rigid objects. All the limitations of the nested generalization inheritance model when extending a class library still apply. The descendant objects by design are tightly coupled to their ancestors. In some cases, the ancestor's properties and methods are exposed to its descendants. It is very tempting to reference these directly and break the object's encapsulation. Although it is possible to hide the effects of this method by defining a set of interface methods in the ancestor and making the other methods private, it is still very easy to inadvertently alter the descendant's behavior while making changes to the ancestor. In cases where the base object is responsible for many different functions, the number of interface methods may also grow to be unmanageable.

Adding new service objects.   The service objects are designed to function as stand-alone entities. The user interface is typically very well defined. Because the object is responsible for a single function, its interface is not overly complicated. A well-defined interface brings all the benefits of encapsulation.

Encapsulation and dynamic creation open up many new opportunities. It is possible for an object to exhibit different behavior based on dynamic conditions. The conventional way to accomplish this was to create different functions or to overload an existing function in the inheritance tree of the same object. At run-time, based on some input, an appropriate function would be called.

An alternative solution is to define two different service objects that share the same interface. At runtime, the appropriate service is selected. The advantage of this method is that only one function has to exist in memory. It also makes it easier to add new objects in the future. This technique is called *operational polymorphism.*

Service objects also make ideal business logic containers. If necessary, these objects can be easily converted to distributed objects and deployed as application servers.

Adding the new functionality as a stand-alone service object does not increase the size of the base class. The functionality can be requested dynamically only when it is required.

There are many more advantages to partitioning the functionality into distinct services, but there are also some disadvantages. It is possible to overpartition, which results in many more objects. Dynamic service creation, while offering flexibility, may result in some performance overhead.

Adding logic through inheritance to the service objects. Extending the existing service objects is another natural choice. Many benefits of the service-based architecture come from cohesion within service provider objects. Each individual object carries its own distinct purpose. It is perfectly acceptable to add new functionality to an existing service as long as this new functionality is directly related to the object's original function.

Summary

No class library can meet everyone's needs out of the box. Utilizing appropriate techniques to extend the default functionality is crucial to the project's success. The act of constructing an application is nothing more than extending the class library to meet a set of specific requirements.

The extension layer is an exciting concept that provides the ability to extend any object in a class library. It facilitates the propagation of applied changes to all of its descendants, including the objects in the class library itself. The extension-layer approach works equally well with inheritance-based and service-based architectures.

Service-based architecture opens new opportunities for extensibility. In addition to using standard inheritance techniques, it is also possible to extend by adding new service objects. Creating new service objects requires more effort up front, but it does encourage object reuse, both for single and for multiple applications. In addition, it also encourages application partitioning and produces more flexible designs.

By following the techniques outlined in this chapter, you can further extend and customize the PFC, or any other class library, to meet the requirements of your future projects.

4

What's in the PFC

Introduction

The PFC is delivered as a set of PowerBuilder libraries (PBLs). These libraries contain the ancestor and descendant objects needed to write an application with the PFC. In order to understand and use the PFC effectively, it is important to know what these different PBLs are and how they are designed. It is also necessary to understand how the different objects in the PFC libraries are subclassed and named.

Chapter Objectives

This chapter will

- Explain the two components of the PFC and explain extension layers.
- Discuss the PFC library structure.
- Explain the PFC naming conventions.
- Provide an objects overview.
- Describe the client objects in the PFC.
- Describe the server objects in the PFC.
- Describe the transport objects in the PFC.
- Describe the global functions in the PFC.
- Discuss the dynamic link libraries (DLLs) in the PFC.
- Discuss the help files in the PFC.
- Discuss what's not in the PFC.

Two Major Components of the PFC

The PFC is a set of PBLs. The objects in these PBLs must be made available to PFC-based applications by adding them to the application's library list. The PFC is distributed with PBLs containing ancestor objects and PBLs containing extension-layer objects. The PBLs containing ancestor objects are referenced as PowerBuilder Foundation Class (PFC)–layer PBLs. These PBLs contain instance variables, coded events, and coded functions. The PBLs that contain extension-layer objects are referenced as PowerBuilder Foundation Extension (PFE)–layer PBLs. These PBLs contain unmodified descendants of corresponding objects in the PFC library. Figure 4.1 shows the relationship between the PFC PBLs and PFE PBLs.

The objects in the PFE-layer PBLs (extension-layer objects) are used for customizing the PFC to meet the needs of your application. These objects allow a developer to modify or extend the behavior of any object in the PFC-layer PBLs by extending or overriding code. The objects in the PFC-layer PBLs should never be modified because Powersoft will change these objects in future upgrades. The PFE-layer PBLs are always delivered as unmodified descendants of corresponding objects in the PFC library, and Powersoft will never place code in these objects. This guarantees that custom coding for objects in the PFE-layer PBLs is not overwritten.

Note: Never place code in objects that are part of the PFC-layer PBLs. Code that is placed in these objects will be overwritten by Powersoft's upgrades to the PFC.

The PFC Library Structure

The PFC libraries are located under the Advanced Developer Toolkit (ADK) directory within the Powersoft directory. Figure 4.2 shows the library structure for the PFC (for Windows 95, using the short filenames installation option).

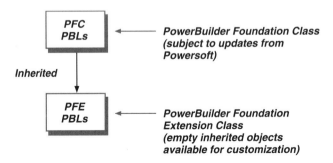

Figure 4.1 Two components in the PFC.

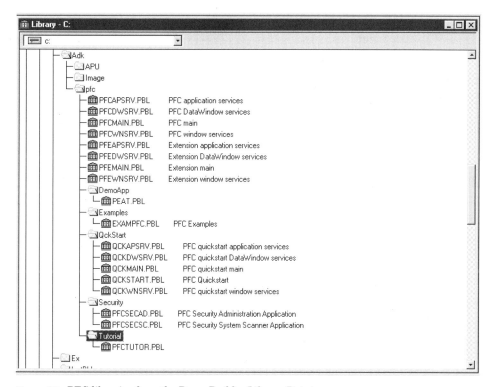

Figure 4.2 PFC libraries from the PowerBuilder Library Painter.

The ADK directory contains the PFC and PFE PBLs, as well as sample applications that were built using the PFC. These components of the ADK directory are explained in this section.

The PFC PBLs

The PFC is delivered with eight PBLs. Four of these PBLs define the PFC-layer PBLs, and the other four define the PFE-layer PBLs. Table 4.1 describes the eight PBLs in the PFC.

The PEAT Demo application

The PEAT Demo application is included in the demoapp directory within the PFC directory. It was built using the PFC and provides examples of how the PFC can be used in an application. The PBL for this application is PEAT.PBL. One nice feature included in the PEAT application is the addition of two new services, the vertical splitter bar and the explorer interface service. This gives you an idea of how to add new services to the PFC.

TABLE 4.1   The PFC PBLs

PFC PBL name	Description
PFCAPSRV	Basic application services and global services, such as a debugger object, a caching object, a file services object, a message object, etc.
PFCDWSRV	Basic DataWindow services, such as a find object, a drop-down DataWindow search object, a report object, etc.
PFCMAIN	Visual and standard class user objects, such as a command button object, a transaction object, a DataWindow control object, etc.
PFCWNSRV	Basic window services, such as a resizing object, a sheet manager object, etc.
PFEAPSRV	Unmodified descendants of corresponding objects in the PFCAPSRV PBLs
PFEDWSRV	Unmodified descendants of corresponding objects in the PFCDWSRV PBLs
PFEMAIN	Unmodified descendants of corresponding objects in the PFCMAIN PBLs
PFEWNSRV	Unmodified descendants of corresponding objects in the PFCWNSRV PBLs

The PFC Examples application

The PFC Examples application is included in the examples directory within the PFC directory. It was built using the PFC and has examples of some of the different services provided with the PFC. The PBL for this application is EXAMPFC.PBL.

Tip: The PFC Examples application is a great way to learn how you can use many of the PFC services.

The PFC Quick-Start PBLs

The PFC Quick-Start PBLs are included in the qckstart directory within the PFC directory. They were built using the PFC and are used to get an application up and running quickly. These PBLs contain a selected subset of precoded extension-layer objects. The functionality provided by these PBLs is the rough equivalent of the PowerBuilder GenApp application, but with the addition of all the built-in PFC functionality. When a new project is created in PowerBuilder, you are given the choice of having PowerBuilder create some basic objects and code for you. This code is referred to as the PowerBuilder GenApp. Table 4.2 shows the PFC Quick-Start PBLs.

TABLE 4.2   PFC Quick-Start PBLs

Quick-Start PBL name	Description
QCKAPSRV.PBL	PFC Quick-Start application services
QCKDWSRV.PBL	PFC Quick-Start DataWindow services
QCKMAIN.PBL	PFC Quick-Start main
QCKSTART.PBL	PFC Quick-Start
QCKWNSRV.PBL	PFC Quick-Start window services

TABLE 4.3   The PFC Security Administration Utility

Security PBL/database name	Description
PFCSECAD.PBL	Security administration utility. This utility allows you to define users, groups, items to be secured, and user access.
PFCSECSC.PBL	Security scanner. The utility scans user-specified windows to gather information on all items that can be secured.
PFC.DB	Security database and a message table used for the error service. The security database contains information on users, groups, items to be secured, and user access to those secured items. It is delivered as a local database. The security tables included in the PFC database must be replicated in the database that will be used for your application. The message table contains message definitions used by the PFC.

The PFC security administration utility

The PFC security administration utility is a PowerBuilder application that can be used in conjunction with the PFC security services to provide security for an application built using the PFC. The security administration utility can be used to

- Define users and groups.
- Run the security scanner.
- Define security for windows and controls.
- Associate users and groups with windows and controls.

Table 4.3 describes the components of the PFC security administration utility.

Note: Make sure that the security tables in the PFC database (PFC.DB) are present in your application's database if PFC security is being used.

The PowerBuilder Foundation Class tutorial

The *PowerBuilder Online Books,* a CD that is part of the Advanced Developers Kit (ADK), contains a simple tutorial to get you started with the PowerBuilder Foundation Class library. The PBL that accompanies the tutorial is PFCTUTOR.PBL. It includes a skeleton application object and several DataWindows to save you time. The application object includes precoded calls to the application manager.

PFC Naming Conventions

The PFC is composed of many objects, events, and functions. This section provides a detailed explanation of the naming conventions used.

Object naming

All objects in the PFC are named to reflect the layer, object type, and object name. The PFC uses the following prefix standard for object names:

pfcobject_type_objectname

pfcobject indicates whether the object is part of the PFC layer or the extension layer. All objects in the PFC layer are prefixed with pfc_. If an object is in the PFE layer, pfcobject will not be present.

type indicates the object type, such as w_, n_cst, n_cst_dwsrv, etc. The name prefixes for type are shown in Table 4.4.

objectname describes the object, such as sort, search, linkage, etc.

Table 4.4 shows the types used in the PFC, and Table 4.5 shows some examples of objects in the PFC using the naming conventions described.

Note: When placing code in an object, make sure the object is not prefixed with pfc_. If the object is prefixed with pfc_, it is in the PFC layer and should not be modified. Always use the PFE layer when customizing.

TABLE 4.4   Type

Type	Description
m_	Menu
n_	Standard class user object
n_cst	Custom class user object
n_cst_dwsrv	Custom class user object that provides DataWindow services
n_cst_wnsrv	Custom class user object that provides window services
s_	Global structure
u_	Visual user object
w_	Window

TABLE 4.5   PFC Object-Naming Convention Examples

Description	PFC object	PFE object
Transaction standard class user object	pfc_n_tr	n_tr
Error custom class user object	pfc_n_cst_error	n_cst_error
DataWindow visual user object	pfc_u_dw	u_dw
DataWindow sort custom class user object	pfc_n_cst_dwsrv_sort	n_cst_dwsrv_sort
Window preference custom class user object	pfc_n_cst_wnsrv_preference	n_cst_wnsrv_preference
Response window	pfc_w_response	w_response
Master menu	pfc_m_master	m_master

Event naming

All events in the PFC have a *pfc_* prefix.

Examples: Some PFC events in pfc_u_dw, the PFC's base DataWindow control, are

pfc_addrow

pfc_clear

pfc_copy

pfc_insertrow

pfc_retrieve

pfc_validation

When you trigger a PFC event from code, use the format

*object.*Event pfc_*eventname* ()

or

*object.*Triggerevent ("pfc_*eventname*")

Function naming

All functions in the PFC have an *of_* prefix.

Examples: Some PFC functions in pfc_u_dw are

of_SetBase

of_SetFilter

of_SetFind

of_SetLinkage

When you call a PFC function from code, use the format

*object.*of_*Functionname* ()

Objects Overview

The PFC consists of three types of objects—client, service, and transport—and several global functions. The PFC uses windows, standard class user objects, and custom class user objects to isolate related types of processing. These related types of processing are grouped together in objects called "services." Services are then requested by the client objects in your application. Examples of the type of services a client object in your application would request are DataWindow caching, sorting, and window resizing. Transport objects are used to pass data from object to object. All of these objects will be discussed in greater detail throughout the remainder of the book.

Client objects

Client objects in the PFC request services when they are needed. They have reference variables declared for the different services available to them as well as functions that automatically create and destroy service objects for the services that the client object requests. Reference variables are instance variables for each type of service that an object has available to it. For example, the DataWindow object pfc_u_dw has an instance variable of the following declared:

n_cst_dwsrv_sort   inv_Sort

Inv_Sort is a reference variable defined in pfc_u_dw.

To create a service for a client object, a function in the format *client.of_SetService(TRUE)* would be called to instantiate the service instance. Some examples of the reference variables and the of_SetService functions for the client object pfc_u_dw are shown in Table 4.6.

These functions of the client object create or destroy the service object based on a boolean (TRUE/FALSE) value that is passed. A value passed of TRUE will create the service object, and a value passed of FALSE will destroy the service object.

Selectively instantiating service objects from within the client object provides complete flexibility in the PFC functionality used by the application. Client objects call functions and redirect events in the service object to extend functionality. An example of how the PFC redirects an event in the client object to the service object is shown for the clicked event code fragment of pfc_u_dw below.

pfc_u_dw—clicked event

```
// Sort services.
IF IsValid (inv_Sort) THEN
        // Notify the sort service, since it may have a request
        // to sort on column header.
        inv_Sort.Event pfc_clicked ( xpos, ypos, row, dwo )
END IF
```

TABLE 4.6   **Examples of Client Object Functions That Instantiate Services**

This function	Instantiates this service object	And is referenced in code by this instance variable
of_SetRowManager(TRUE)	n_cst_dwsrv_rowmanager	inv_RowManager
of_SetLinkage(TRUE)	n_cst_dwsrv_linkage	inv_Linkage
of_SetRowSelect(TRUE)	n_cst_dwsrv_rowselection	inv_RowSelect
of_SetSort(TRUE)	n_cst_dwsrv_sort	inv_Sort

If the sorting service in the above code were instantiated, the IsValid would pass, and the pfc_clicked event in inv_Sort of type n_cst_dwsrv_sort would be triggered. The advantage of this approach is that if the service was not requested in your code, its code is not loaded into memory. This allows for leaner client objects.

All client objects in the PFC destroy the services that were requested by calling the client object function *of_Set*Service (FALSE) to cause the service object to be destroyed. This makes the cleanup of services automatic. An example of this is shown in the code fragment from the destructor event of pfc_u_dw.

pfc_u_dw—destructor event

```
of_SetBase (FALSE)
of_SetRowManager (FALSE)
of_SetQuerymode (FALSE)
of_SetLinkage (FALSE)
of_SetReport (FALSE)
```

Service Objects

The PFC uses windows, standard class user objects, and custom class user objects to isolate related types of processing. These related types of processing are grouped together in objects called services. Services are then requested by the client objects in your application. Service objects in the PFC are implemented in two different ways: an *aggregate relationship* and an *associative relationship*.

- The aggregate relationship occurs when the service object cannot function apart from the owning client object. This relationship is sometimes called a *whole-part relationship*. For example, the u_dw DataWindow visual user object uses the n_cst_dwsrv_sort user object to provide sorting services. You cannot use the sorting service alone. It must be used in conjunction with the u_dw DataWindow object.

- The associative relationship occurs when a service object can function alone. For example, string services provided by the n_cst_string user object are available to objects throughout the application and can be used in non-PFC applications.

Service objects in the PFC are instantiated (created) when they are needed. Any service object in the PFC that is instantiated will be destroyed automatically.

Global functions

The PFC has very few global functions. The ones that are in the PFC are needed for operating system–specific uses. Most functions are grouped as services in custom class user objects that are instantiated as needed.

Client Objects

The following will describe the different types of client objects in the PFC. These objects include standard visual user objects, standard window objects, and standard menu objects.

Standard visual user objects

All standard PowerBuilder controls have been subclassed in the PFC as standard visual user objects. Instances of standard visual user objects are placed on the surface of a window or custom user object instead of standard controls. Each PFC standard visual user object class has predefined code in it that extends the corresponding control with additional code. You can add code as needed to customize the PFE layer to suit the needs of your application. Table 4.7 shows the standard visual user objects in the PFC.

Use the standard visual user objects in place of standard PowerBuilder controls. In this way, if new services are added to these user objects by Powersoft or to the PFE standard visual user objects by your application architects, the new services are immediately available to the object desired (by the use of the appropriate of_SetService function).

To use these controls on a window or a standard visual user object:

TABLE 4.7   Standard Visual User Objects in the PFC

Control	Description
pfc_u_cb	PFC Commandbutton class
pfc_u_cbx	PFC CheckBox class
pfc_u_ddlb	PFC DropDownListBox class
pfc_u_ddplb	PFC DropDownPictureListBox class
pfc_u_dw	PFC DataWindow class
pfc_u_em	PFC Editmask class
pfc_u_gb	PFC GroupBox class
pfc_u_gr	PFC Graph class
pfc_u_hsb	PFC HorizontalScrollBar class
pfc_u_lb	PFC ListBox class
pfc_u_lv	PFC ListView class
pfc_u_mle	PFC MultLineEdit class
pfc_u_oc	PFC OleControl class
pfc_u_p	PFC Picture class
pfc_u_pb	PFC Picturebutton class
pfc_u_plb	PFC PictureListBox class
pfc_u_rb	PFC Radiobutton class
pfc_u_rte	PFC RichTextEdit class
pfc_u_sle	PFC SingleLineEdit class
pfc_u_st	PFC StaticText class
pfc_u_tab	PFC Tab class
pfc_u_tabpg	PFC TabPage class
pfc_u_tv	PFC TreeView class
pfc_u_vsb	PFC VerticalScrollBar class

1. Select the user object control from the control drop-down button on the toolbar or select Controls→UserObject from the menu.

2. Find the correct standard visual user object in the PFEMAIN PBL (remember to always use the PFE-layer PBL) and select it.

3. Place the object on the window or on a custom visual user object.

Standard visual user object hierarchy.   Figure 4.3 shows the object hierarchy for standard visual user objects using the Commandbutton control as an example.

Examples of services requested by standard visual user objects.   The following is a code fragment from the rowfocuschanged event of pfc_u_dw. It requests linkage services if the service has been instantiated.

To instantiate this service, you would call the function of_SetLinkage(TRUE) in your code. The function could be placed in any event that occurs as the object is created, such as the constructor event of the DataWindow object. Requesting the service causes the instance variable inv_Linkage to point to the instantiated service object of type n_cst_dwsrv_linkage. When the rowfocuschanged event executes, the pfc_rowfocuschanged event in inv_Linkage is triggered if the service is instantiated. If the service is not instantiated, the pfc_rowfocuschanged event will not be triggered because it will not pass the IsValid test.

pfc_u_dw—rowfocuschanged event

```
/* Linkage Service */
IF IsValid ( inv_Linkage ) THEN
        inv_Linkage.Event pfc_rowfocuschanged (currentrow)
END IF
```

The following is a code fragment from the resize event of pfc_u_tab. It requests resize services if the service has been instantiated.

To instantiate this service, you would call the function of_SetResize(TRUE) in your code. The function could be placed in any event that occurs as the object is created, such as the constructor event of the tab object. Calling this function causes the instance variable inv_Resize to point to the instantiated service object of type n_cst_resize. When the resize event executes, the pfc_resize event in the inv_Resize object is triggered if the service is instantiated. If the service is not instantiated, the pfc_resize event will not be triggered because it will not pass the IsValid test.

Figure 4.3 Commandbutton hierarchy.

pfc_u_tab—resize event

```
// Notify the resize service that the object size has changed.
IF IsValid (inv_Resize) THEN
        inv_Resize.Event pfc_resize (sizetype, This.Width, This.Height)
END IF
```

Standard window objects—w_master and its descendants

The ancestor for all PFC windows is pfc_w_master. It includes instance variables, events, and functions that are accessed by many PFC objects. All windows that want to take advantage of the PFC must descend from w_master. Descendants of w_master that are included with the PFC are w_child, w_frame, w_main, w_popup, w_response, and w_sheet. These correspond to the six window classes available to you through PowerBuilder. Table 4.8 describes these window classes.

Note: Code that needs to affect all windows should be placed in w_master. Code that is specialized for a particular window is placed in that specific window ancestor.

Standard window object hierarchy. Figure 4.4 shows the object hierarchy for all standard window objects.

Note: When creating windows for your application, always inherit from window classes in PFEMAIN.PBL.

Examples of services requested by standard window objects. The following is a code example from the resize event of pfc_w_master. It requests resize and preference services if these services have been instantiated.

To instantiate these services, you would call the functions of_SetResize(TRUE) and of_SetPreference(TRUE) in your code. These functions can be placed in any event that occurs as the object is created, such as the pfc_preopen event of the window. Requesting these services causes the instance variables inv_Resize and inv_Preference to be instantiated as objects of type n_cst_winsrv_preference and

TABLE 4.8   Standard Window Objects in the PFC

Window	Description
pfc_w_master	Ancestor for all PFC windows
pfc_w_main	Ancestor main window for all SDI applications
pfc_w_child	Ancestor for all PowerBuilder Class Library child windows
pfc_w_frame	Ancestor frame window for all MDI applications
pfc_w_response	Ancestor for all PFC response windows
pfc_w_sheet	Ancestor for all PowerBuilder Class Library sheet windows
pfc_w_popup	Ancestor for all PowerBuilder Class Library pop-up windows

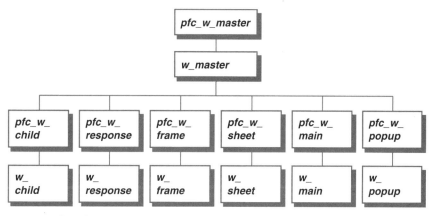

Figure 4.4 Standard window object hierarchy.

n_cst_resize. When the resize event executes, the pfc_resize event for inv_resize is triggered and the function of_SetPosSize() is executed for inv_Preference if these services are instantiated. If these services are not instantiated, the pfc_resize event and the of_SetPosSize() function would not execute because they would not pass the IsValid test.

pfc_w_master—resize event

// Notify the resize service that the window size has changed.
IF IsValid (inv_Resize) THEN
        inv_resize.Event pfc_resize (sizetype, This.WorkSpaceWidth(),
            This.WorkSpaceHeight()
END IF

The following is a code example from the pfc_postopen event of pfc_w_frame. This event is called in the open event of the ancestor window pfc_w_master. It requests statusbar services if this service has been instantiated.

To instantiate this service, you would call the function of_SetStatusbar(TRUE) in your code. This function can be placed in any event that occurs as the object is created, such as the pfc_preopen event of the window. Requesting the service causes the instance variable inv_Statusbar to point to the instantiated service object of type n_cst_winsrv_statusbar. When the pfc_postopen event is executed, the of_Open function in inv_Statusbar will be called because the service was instantiated.

When the pfc_postopen event executes, the of_Open function in inv_Statusbar is called if the service is instantiated. If the service is not instantiated, the function the of_Open will not execute because it will not pass the IsValid test in the PFC code.

pfc_w_frame—pfc_postopen event

```
// Opens statusbar if applicable.
IF IsValid (inv_Statusbar) THEN
        inv_statusbar.of_Open(TRUE)
END IF
```

Standard menu objects

In PFC applications, all menus typically inherit from pfc_m_master (or a pfc_m_master descendant) and add, modify, or hide items as needed. The m_master menu provides items for use with all PFC windows, DataWindows, and visual controls.

The m_frame menu is a descendant of m_master with most items disabled and hidden. This menu is to be used as the frame menu for an application. You can modify and add menu items, as necessary.

Tip: It is not necessary to use pfc_m_master if you prefer another menu. If you create your own menu, be sure to add the PFC function of_SendMessage to the menu so that the message-routing service (discussed in later chapters) can be used. In PowerBuilder, maintaining many menu items can be expensive, making the opening of windows slower. If an application does not need all the menu items provided with pfc_m_master, it might be wise to create a new menu and add the message routing service, or to copy pfc_m_master and delete the items you don't need.

Standard menu object hierarchy. Figure 4.5 shows the object hierarchy for the standard menu objects.

Examples of services requested by standard menu objects. The following is a code example from the m_new menu item of pfc_m_master. It uses the message routing service to send a message to the currently active window sheet associated with the menu to perform the pfc_new event.

pfc_m_master—m_new menu item

```
SetPointer (hourglass!)
of_SendMessage ("pfc_new")
```

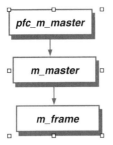

Figure 4.5 Standard menu object hierarchy.

Service Objects

The following sections describe the different types of service objects in the PFC. These objects include standard class user objects and custom class user objects.

Standard class user objects

All PowerBuilder built-in system objects have been subclassed in the PFC as standard class user objects. They extend any system object with additional code. Table 4.9 shows the standard class user objects in the PFC.

Standard class user object hierarchy. Figure 4.6 shows the object hierarchy for standard class user objects, using the transaction object as an example.

Custom class user objects

Custom class user objects encapsulate attributes and functions that are not visible to the user. They are defined to create units of processing that have no visual component, such as database services. Objects of this type are often called nonvisual user objects. The PFC uses custom class user objects for specialized services.

Table 4.10 shows the custom class user objects in the PFC. Most of the utility services have an associative relationship and can function alone. These objects can be used anywhere in the application. They have many functions grouped by service type, such as string services. Many of the utility custom class user objects have the autoinstantiate property. This property allows the object to be instanti-

TABLE 4.9   Standard Window Objects in the PFC

Standard class user object	PowerBuilder system object
pfc_n_cn	Connection
pfc_n_msg	Message
pfc_n_ds	Datastore
pfc_n_pl	Pipeline
pfc_n_err	Error
pfc_n_tr	Transaction
pfc_n_ms	Mail session
pfc_n_trp	Transport

Figure 4.6 Transaction object hierarchy.

TABLE 4.10   Custom Class User Objects in the PFC

Type of service	Custom class user object	Description
Application services	pfc_n_cst_appmanager	PFC application manager service
	pfc_n_cst_dwcache	PFC caching service
	pfc_n_cst_debug	PFC debugging service
	pfc_n_cst_sqlspy	PFC SQL spy service
	pfc_n_cst_security	PFC security service
	pfc_n_cst_error	PFC error service
Menu services	pfc_n_cst_menu	PFC menu service
Window services	pfc_n_cst_winsrv	PFC basic window service
	pfc_n_cst_wnsrv_preference	PFC preference service
	pfc_n_cst_wnsrv_sheetmanager	PFC window sheet manager service
	pfc_n_cst_wnsrv_statusbar	PFC window statusbar service
	pfc_n_cst_resize	PFC window resize services
DataWindow services	pfc_n_cst_dwsrv	PFC basic DataWindow service
	pfc_n_cst_dwsrv_rowmanager	PFC DataWindow rowmanager service
	pfc_n_cst_dwsrv_querymode	PFC DataWindow querymode service
	pfc_n_cst_dwsrv_linkage	PFC DataWindow linkages service
	pfc_n_cst_dwsrv_report	PFC DataWindow reporting service
	pfc_n_cst_dwsrv_multitable	PFC DataWindow multitable service
	pfc_n_cst_dwsrv_rowselection	PFC DataWindow row selection service
	pfc_n_cst_dwsrv_filter	PFC DataWindow filter service
	pfc_n_cst_dwsrv_reqcolumn	PFC DataWindow required column service
	pfc_n_cst_dwsrv_dropdownsearch	PFC DataWindow drop-down search service
	pfc_n_cst_dwsrv_find	PFC DataWindow find service
	pfc_n_cst_dwsrv_printpreview	PFC DataWindow print preview service
	pfc_n_cst_dwsrv_sort	PFC DataWindow sorting service
	pfc_n_cst_dssrv	PFC datastore service
Utility services	pfc_n_cst_conversion	PFC conversion service
	pfc_n_cst_datetime	PFC date and/or date-time service
	pfc_n_cst_filesrvwin16	PFC Win16 file-handler service
	pfc_n_cst_filesrvwin32	PFC Win32 file-handler service
	pfc_n_cst_filesrvmac	PFC Macintosh file-handler service
	pfc_n_cst_filesrvso12	PFC Unix (Solaris) file-handler service
	pfc_n_cst_inifile	PFC INI file service
	pfc_n_cst_numerical	PFC numerical service
	pfc_n_cst_platformwin16	PFC Win16 cross-platform service
	pfc_n_cst_platformwin32	PFC Win32 cross-platform service
	pfc_n_cst_platformmac	PFC Macintosh cross-platform service
	pfc_n_cst_platformso12	PFC Unix (Solaris) cross-platform service
	pfc_n_cst_rtefind	PFC RTE find/replace service
	pfc_n_cst_selection	PFC selection service
	pfc_n_cst_string	PFC string service
	pfc_n_cst_sql	PFC base SQL service
	pfc_n_cst_trregistration	PFC transaction registration service

ated at reference time without the need to use the Powerscript Create(object-name) function. Autoinstantiated objects are destroyed when the code in which they are referenced goes out of scope. There is no need to code a Destroy(object-name) statement.

Tip: Always check to see if the utility custom class user object you are using has the autoinstantiate property. If the object has this property, it doesn't need to be created with the Powerscript Create(objectname) function. It will be created automatically when the object is referenced and will be destroyed automatically when the code that uses the object is out of scope. You will also get a compiler error if you attempt to create an autoinstantiated object.

Custom class user object hierarchy.   The object hierarchies for some of the more frequently used custom class user objects are shown in this section. The other custom class user objects follow a similar hierarchy. The custom class user object hierarchy for all application and utility services is shown in Fig. 4.7. In this figure, XXX is the object service name (e.g., debug, error, string).

The custom class user object hierarchy for all window services is shown in Fig. 4.8. All window services are descendants of the custom class user object pfc_n_cst_wnsrv, which provides basic window services.

The custom class user object hierarchy for all DataWindow services is shown in Fig. 4.9. All DataWindow services are descendants of the custom class user object pfc_n_cst_dwsrv, which provides basic DataWindow services.

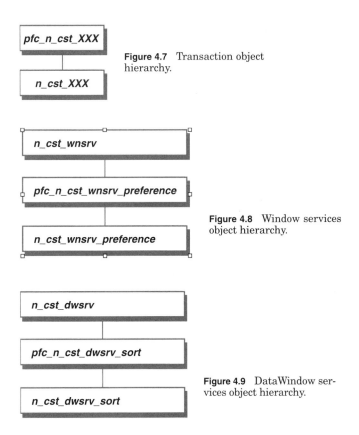

Figure 4.7 Transaction object hierarchy.

Figure 4.8 Window services object hierarchy.

Figure 4.9 DataWindow services object hierarchy.

Transport Objects

The following sections describe the different types of transport objects in the PFC. These objects include structure replacement objects and global structures.

Structure replacement objects

Structure replacement objects are autoinstantiated custom class user objects that consist solely of instance variables. These objects provide all the functionality of global structures.

Structure replacement objects are used in the PFC because structures cannot be inherited. Structure replacement objects can be inherited, making it easy to extend these objects by adding instance variables in the PFE layer. The PFC contains many structure replacement objects to communicate between two objects. Table 4.11 shows all the structure replacement objects that are part of the PFC.

Structure replacement object hierarchy.   Figure 4.10 shows the structure replacement object hierarchy, where XXX is the object replacement service name (findattrib, linkageattrib, etc.).

Global structures

Table 4.12 shows all the global structures that are part of the PFC.

TABLE 4.11   Structure Replacement Objects in the PFC

Object	Description
pfc_n_cst_aboutattrib	Contains information displayed in w_about
pfc_n_cst_dirattrib	Contains information used in n_cst_filesrv and its descendant
pfc_n_cst_dwobjectattrib	Contains information used in n_cst_dwcache, n_cst_dssrv, n_cst_dwsrv, and their descendants
pfc_n_cst_errorattrib	Contains information used in n_cst_error and w_message
pfc_n_cst_filterattrib	Contains information used in n_cst_dwsrv_filter and the Filter dialog boxes
pfc_n_cst_findattrib	Contains information used in n_cst_dwsrv_find, u_rte, w_find, and w_replace
pfc_n_cst_itemattrib	Contains information used in u_lb, u_plb, and u_tv
pfc_n_cst_linkageattrib	Contains information used in n_cst_dwsrv_linkage
pfc_n_cst_logonattrib	Contains information used in n_cst_appmanager
pfc_n_cst_returnattrib	Contains return code and associated text
pfc_n_cst_selectionattrib	Contains information used in n_cst_selection and w_selection
pfc_n_cst_sortattrib	Contains information used in n_cst_dwsrv_sort and the Sort dialog box
pfc_n_cst_splashattrib	Contains information used in n_cst_appmanager and w_splash
pfc_n_cst_sqlattrib	Contains information used in n_cst_sql
pfc_n_cst_textstyleattrib	Used by u_rte-based RichTextEdit controls to access text style
pfc_n_cst_toolbarattrib	Contains information used in w_frame and w_toolbars
pfc_n_cst_zoomattrib	Contains information used in n_cst_dwsrv_printpreview and w_zoom

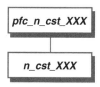

Figure 4.10 Structure replacement object hierarchy.

TABLE 4.12   Global Structures

Structure	Description
s_pagesetupattrib	Contains information used in n_cst_platform and w_pagesetup
s_paperattrib	Contains information used in s_pagesetupattrib
s_svalue	Contains information used in n_cst_dwsrv_querymode
s_printdlgattrib	Contains information used by n_cst_platform for printing
s_dwdebugger	Contains information used in w_dwdebugger
pfc_n_cst_findattrib	Contains information used in n_cst_dwsrv_find, u_rte, w_find, and w_replace
pfc_n_cst_itemattrib	Contains information used in u_lb, u_plb, and u_tv
pfc_n_cst_linkageattrib	Contains information used in n_cst_dwsrv_linkage
pfc_n_cst_logonattrib	Contains information used in n_cst_appmanager
pfc_n_cst_returnattrib	Contains return code and associated text

TABLE 4.13   Global Functions

Structure	Description
f_SetFileServ	This function creates an operating system–specific descendant of n_cst_filesrvwin. For example, for Windows 3.1, it creates n_cst_filesrvwin16; for Windows 95 and Windows NT, it creates n_cst_filesrvwin32; for Macintosh, it creates n_cst_filesrvmac; for Unix (Solaris), it creates n_cst_filesrvso12
f_SetPlatform	This function creates an operating system–specific descendant of n_cst_platform. For example, for Windows 3.1, it creates n_cst_platformwin16; for Windows 95 and Windows NT, it creates n_cst_platformwin32; for Macintosh, it creates n_cst_platformmac; for Unix (Solaris), it creates n_cst_platformso12.

Global Functions

Table 4.13 shows all the global functions that are part of the PFC. Notice that there are few global functions in the PFC. This is because the PFC takes advantage of custom class user objects that contain many functions grouped by service type, such as string services.

PFC Dynamic Link Libraries (DLLs)

Some objects in the PFC call platform-specific external functions. The PFC contains three DLLs to help support some of the platform-specific calls made in some of the PFC objects. Table 4.14 lists and describes these DLLs.

These DLL files must reside on the client machine in a directory that is

TABLE 4.14   PFC DLLs

PFC DLL name	Object DLL referenced in	Description
PFCFLSRV.DLL	pfc_n_cst_filesrvwin16	Platform-specific file-management functions for applications running under Windows 3.1
PFCCOMM.DLL	pfc_n_cst_platformwin16	Platform-specific functions for applications running under Windows 3.1
PFCCOM32.DLL	pfc_n_cst_platformwin32	Platform-specific functions for applications running under Windows 95

accessible to your application if you make use of platform-specific application or file-management services.

PFC Help Files

The PFC has an extensive on-line help system that supplements the information in the PFC documentation. This on-line help system provides step-by-step directions for using the PFC and all of its objects. The PFC help also supports context-sensitive help. Whenever you want to access context-sensitive help for a PFC function, select the function and press Shift+F1.

Additional information can be found in the *Powersoft Online Books,* which is delivered on a CD. In the *Online Books,* under the "Advanced Developer Toolkit," there are two chapters documenting the PFC: "The PFC User's Guide" and "The PFC Object Reference Guide."

What's Not in the PFC

Windows and widgets

The PFC is a great starting point for a framework for any application. However, because the PFC is service-based, it lacks many of the visual objects needed for any application. Many of the frameworks that were built prior to the PFC had visual objects for use by the developer.

For example, many frameworks had a master/detail window. You as the developer would inherit from this window and save it. You would then assign DataWindow objects for the master DataWindow and the detail DataWindow. All the code for handling the master/detail relationship was already coded in the ancestor window. This worked well for many cases, but there were problems. If the requirements changed and the master/detail paradigm was not desired, you were forced to copy code to another window because the master/detail window was inherited from a window that had code for handling only the master/detail paradigm.

Also, these framework objects were not very flexible and could be used only in specific ways. It was very hard to change their behavior without doing some coding changes.

By using a service-based framework like the PFC, you can create a window with a master/detail paradigm by setting the linkage services of the PFC with a small amount of code. If you decide to change your mind and not use the master/detail paradigm, all you need to do is eliminate the code that sets the PFC linkage services. It is up to you to design the type of visual objects/widgets that your application will have and to use the services provided by the PFC to obtain the desired effects. It is very important to understand this concept. A service-based framework like the PFC contains many services that can be used to design the visual objects needed in your application.

Services

The PFC is built with a very flexible architecture. Because no framework can meet the needs of all developers, the PFC allows you to extend the Framework and build additional services. You as the developer are responsible for deciding what additional services you will need. New services can be added to the PFC very easily by adding new custom class user objects that contain the services and instance variables in the appropriate client objects. The PFC is delivered with a PFE layer that is to be used by you to extend and modify any of the services that you need.

For example, one company wanted all microhelp messages to be standard. To do this, it modified code by overriding and overloading some of the functions in n_cst_error object in the PFE layer. This allowed all microhelp messages to be displayed from the error message database.

Summary

This chapter discusses the PFC library structure so that you can become familiar with everything that is part of the PFC. It also provides an overview of all the different types of objects that are in the PFC. It is important for you to understand the different types of objects that are part of the PFC if you are to understand how the PFC is built. You as a developer will begin to understand the real benefits of the PFC and how to extend and modify the PFC only after you know how the PFC has been designed and built. The following chapters in this book will discuss these how these objects are built and how to use these objects to make your application development effort successful. And remember one important thing when building your applications—it isn't rocket science.

5

PFC Menus and Windows

Introduction

PowerBuilder developers have a love/hate relationship with menus. Yes, they are powerful and flexible. However, menu objects grow large quickly, are sometimes problematic to inherit, and suffer from poor performance when inheritance is used.

The Powersoft Foundation Classes provide PowerBuilder developers with significant menu functionality while avoiding some of the difficulties. This chapter will show you how the PFC menus work, and how to make use of them.

The PFC windows work hand in hand with the PFC menus, using precoded events to implement the functionality inherent in the menus. There is a PFC window class for each PowerBuilder window type, and each window class implements behavior appropriate to its intended use.

Chapter Objectives

This chapter will teach the reader to

- Understand the basics of standard PowerBuilder menu functionality.
- Understand the PFC menu strategy.
- Know and use the functionality of the PFC menus.
- Understand the PFC message router.
- Use and extend the PFC menus as provided by Powersoft.
- Develop and use alternative solutions to the PFC menu strategy and structure.

- Use the right mouse menus.

- Create customized right mouse menus.

- Manage the toolbars.

- Understand and use the windows provided in the PFC.

- Extend the PFC windows.

PFC Menus

Standard PowerBuilder menu functionality

PowerBuilder provides a very flexible menuing facility. You can code as much or as little Powerscript as you desire in each menu item's clicked event. You can also inherit from any menu to create a new menu, and extend or override the ancestor's functionality as needed.

In order to gain this flexibility, you pay a price in terms of size, speed, and stability. PowerBuilder's menus are implemented as a set of discrete objects, one for each menu item. Thus, any time you instantiate a menu, a CREATE occurs for each menu item and all of its associated script. The code associated with the creation and destruction of the various menu items, as well as the script, can combine to make a PowerBuilder menu object very large. Even worse, the impact is exaggerated whenever you use inheritance to try to construct your menus in an object-oriented way.

Over time, PowerBuilder developers have learned to follow two strategies when developing menus:

- Minimize inheritance.

- Minimize script within menu items' clicked events.

The inheritance penalty is greatly relieved in PowerBuilder 5.0 and beyond. However, the need to keep menu script to a minimum is still very much with us. Even though the PFC provides a great deal of functionality in precoded menus, the script within the menu items is kept to a minimum. The PFC menus reduce the code necessary to respond to a menu selection to single generic function calls.

The PFC menu strategy

The PFC menu strategy is one of controlled overkill. What I mean by this is that the menus included with PFC have an overabundance of items, meant to handle almost any need. You'll still need to add items to cover custom aspects of your application's functionality, but the core of the PFC provides menu selections for a huge number of standard events.

Table 5.1 shows the menu selections and their associated events for the File item on the m_master menu. You can find more information on the other items

TABLE 5.1   m_master File Menu Items and Events

Menu item	Action	Object containing user event
New	Calls pfc_new	w_master
Open	Calls pfc_open	u_rte, w_master
Close	Calls pfc_close	w_master
Save	Calls pfc_save	u_rte, w_master
Save As	Calls pfc_saveas	u_rte, w_master
Print	Calls pfc_print	u_dw, u_rte, w_master
Print Preview	Calls pfc_printpreview	u_dw, u_rte
Page Setup	Calls pfc_pagesetup	u_dw, w_master
Print Immediate	Calls pfc_printimmediate	u_dw, u_rte, w_master
Delete	Empty menu item. Add your own events or functions.	
Properties	Empty menu item. Add your own events or functions.	
Exit	Calls pfc_exit	N_cst_appmanager

in the m_master menu, as well as the items on the predefined right mouse button menus, in the *PowerBuilder Online Books*.

A standard method used by many PowerBuilder developers has been to place minimum functionality in ancestor menus and gradually build up more functionality through the descendants. You need to turn this strategy around to use the PFC menus effectively. The way you use these menus is to selectively disable or hide menu items that are not appropriate to your application. For instance, the tutorial included with PFC uses the sheet menu as the ancestor for the frame menu. The frame menu typically sports far less functionality than a sheet menu. The frame's only job is to bring sheets into existence and manage their affairs. To accommodate the leaner functionality of the frame menu, you simply turn off the menu items that don't apply. This method actually will improve performance. The sheet menus are used more often than the frame menu. Since the sheet menus are higher in the ancestry hierarchy, they will instantiate faster than if they were inherited and extended from a menu with less functionality.

Tip: Be sure to uncheck the visible attribute in both the style and toolbar tabs for each menu item that you are hiding. This prevents phantom toolbar icons from appearing and providing inappropriate functionality.

The PFC menu functionality

Figure 5.1 shows the standard PFC menu hierarchy. The primary value added in the PFC menus is the of_SendMessage() function. This function allows menu events to send a predefined message, the name of a user event, to the active object in such a way that the menu item need not know what window is active, or what the active object is within that window. All PFC menu selections are implemented as a simple call to the of_SendMessage() function.

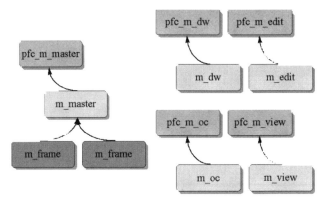

Figure 5.1 The PFC menu hierarchy.

Since each menu selection contains only one line of code, the size of each menu is kept to the absolute minimum. This helps performance and reduces the complexity of future maintenance.

The real magic of the PFC menus lies in the message router. The message router is implemented as a function call to of_SendMessage() in the menus and another function, pfc_MessageRouter(), in the PFC window objects.

Understanding the PFC message router

The PFC menus use the of_SendMessage function to trigger the appropriate event in the active window or control. The of_SendMessage function is passed a string argument that you use to specify the user event that will be fired when the message is received. Figure 5.2 shows the flow of a message from the of_SendMessage function to the intended recipient.

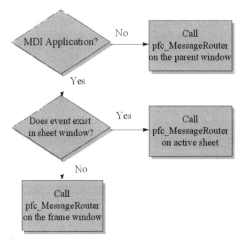

Figure 5.2 PFC's of_SendMessage function initiates delivery of menu messages.

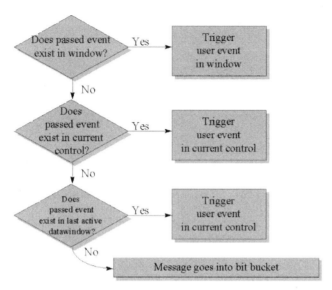

Figure 5.3 The pfc_MessageRouter function uses a predetermined decision path to find the optimal recipient for a message.

In the case of an MDI application, the message is routed to the active window first. If the event exists on the active sheet, the sheet window's pfc_MessageRouter() function is called. However, if no event is found that satisfies the message, the pfc_MessageRouter() function is called on the MDI frame instead. The method differs slightly if the application is an SDI application. In that case, the pfc_MessageRouter function is called on the parent window of the menu.

Once the pfc_MessageRouter function receives the message, the function attempts to deliver the message to the correct object. Figure 5.3 illustrates the way pfc_MessageRouter determines the best recipient.

First, pfc_MessageRouter() attempts to trigger the passed message as a window user event. If the event doesn't exist, it is sent to the active control. If that also fails, then the event is triggered on the last active DataWindow. Finally, if that fails, the message falls into the bit bucket and is not delivered to any other object on the window.

Using the PFC menus

Powersoft demonstrates a typical use of the PFC menus in the PFC tutorial application. You inherit from m_master to create your sheet menu. Then you add any new menu items that you need. The existing menu items in the PFC menus utilize the Slide Over/Down attribute to direct the positioning of any new items that you add. As you add menu items, they will be inserted into the menus as shown in Table 5.2

TABLE 5.2   Positions for New Items Added to
the PFC m_master Menu

Where you add new items	Position for new items
Menu bar	Between Tools and Window
File menu	Above Delete
Edit menu	Above Update Links
View menu	Above Ruler
Tools menu	Above Customize Toolbars
Window menu	Below Undo
Help menu	Above About

Adding items to the frame and window menus

Each item that you add needs to have a supporting script for its clicked event. Most often, you will simply add a call to of_SendMessage() with a string specifying the name of the user event to invoke. If you need to add more information to your call, pattern your code after the model used in m_master's File | Open menu selection. Pass any additional information in the message object before calling of_SendMessage() as shown here:

```
message.stringparm = "w_qcksheet"
of_SendMessage ("pfc_open")
```

Finally, create the custom user event on the appropriate object. Use the message router diagram shown in 5.3 to help you decide where to place the functionality. You don't always need to place events or code in the window to ensure delivery to the active object. The message router will take care of that for you. However, you might need to always direct an action to a given object, whether or not it is active. Under these circumstances, it is best to place the custom user event and its script in the window.

Remember, many of the precoded events in the PFC menus will initiate the correct processing in their associated PFC objects. In these cases, using the menus is a simple matter of enabling the menu items and extending the associated events as necessary.

Developing and using alternative strategies

You may find that the menus provided with the PFC do not meet your needs perfectly. They may be too large or too heavily inherited. You may need more functionality than they provide, yet not need any of the functionality that is already included. Or, you may be using an object such as the u_tv treeview user object that doesn't directly support a right mouse button menu. Here are some alternative strategies you can use:

- Instead of inheriting from m_master to create your sheet menu, alter m_master directly and use that as your sheet menu.

- Instead of using PFC menus at all, create your own menus.

■ Implement your own right mouse menu for objects that don't already have one.

The first strategy, alter m_master directly, is easy to implement and saves space and one layer of inheritance. This means improved performance. You will find m_master in PFEWNSRV.PBL. Add items as necessary and select the pre-coded events that you need to make visible.

The second strategy, creating your own menus, takes a bit more work, but can greatly improve performance by eliminating the extensive inheritance hierarchy of the PFC menus. You must first create the of_SendMessage() function on your custom menu. The of_SendMessage function takes a string as an argument and returns an integer. The simplest method you can use to create the body of the function is to copy the function in its entirety from m_master.

Note: You will need to make sure that your of_sendMessage() function is updated whenever the PFC is updated so that it matches the current implementation within PFC.

Tip: To reduce maintenance requirements, you might want to create a service object that you implement on each menu that contains an of_sendMessage() function. That way, you'll need to update the code in only one place. As of the time of this writing, the upcoming release of PowerBuilder is expected to implement an of_SendMessage() service.

We'll discuss the last alternative strategy, implementing your own right mouse button menus, in the following sections.

Using the right mouse button menus

The PFC right mouse button (RMB) menus are a bit different from the standard menus. The RMB menus don't have an of_Sendmessage() function. These menus are meant to invoke functionality directly on the active, focused object. PFC uses the function of_SetParent() to establish a pointer to the object that is using the RMB menu. This is the body of the of_SetParent() function as implemented in pfc_m_edit:

```
integer  li_rc = 1
IF IsValid (adrg_parent) THEN
        idrg_parent = adrg_parent
ELSE
        li_rc = −1
END IF
return li_rc
```

Each PFC user object that supports a RMB menu establishes its own addressability within the RMB menu by calling the of_SetParent() function. Here is a section of the rbuttonup script that the pfc_u_mle object uses to create its RMB menu:

```
// Create popup menu
lm_edit = create m_edit
lm_edit.of_SetParent (this)
// Enable menu items if appropriate
lm_edit.m_edititem.m_copy.enabled = false
lm_edit.m_edititem.m_cut.enabled = false
IF Len (this.SelectedText()) >0 THEN
        lm_edit.m_edititem.m_copy.enabled = true
        IF NOT this.displayonly THEN
                lm_edit.m_edititem.m_cut.enabled = true
        END IF
END IF
```

The pfc_u_mle object creates the RMB menu, then calls the of_SetParent() function to establish a pointer to itself. Finally, menu items are selectively enabled according to the conditions that exist when the menu is called.

The clicked script for each menu item contains code to directly invoke functionality on the parent object:

```
idrg_parent.dynamic event pfc_copy()
```

Note the use of the *dynamic* keyword to allow the menu to address an event that may or may not exist on the parent object. The menu instance variable idrg_parent is of type dragobject to allow the parent to be any type of control that is descended from dragobject.

Creating your own right mouse button menu

The process of creating your own RMB menu can be illustrated with an example from the sample application GSI TimeMaster, included on the CD. The GSI TimeMaster application needs a right mouse button menu to implement functionality on the treeview of clients, projects, and tasks. The PFC treeview user object, u_tv, does not support a right mouse button menu. Here are the steps taken to implement an RMB menu on a treeview object.

To add an RMB menu to an object, you will need to

- Create an RMB menu object. The easiest way to accomplish this is to inherit from the pfc_m_object that best matches your requirements. This also gives you access to the of_SetParent() function on the ancestor.

- Code the script to create, setparent, and invoke the menu in the rbuttonup or rightclicked event in the object.

- Code the script in the RMB menu to call the appropriate event on the parent object.

- Add custom user events and scripts as necessary on the parent object to implement the desired behavior.

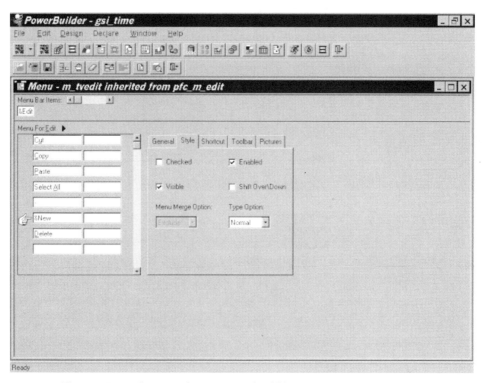

Figure 5.4 The treeview right mouse button menu for GSI TimeMaster.

Note: For a complete description of the GSI TimeMaster sample application, see Chap. 18.

Create an RMB menu object. We inherited from m_edit to create the treeview RMB menu. Figure 5.4 shows the menu items as implemented on the descendant menu.

We didn't need any of the standard m_edit functionality, so the next step is to disable the visible attributes of the Cut, Copy, Paste, and Select All menu items. Then we added the New and Delete items.

Create the right mouse button script. Next, we created a custom event, gsi_rmbmenu, on the treeview object. Then we added code to the rightclicked event to post the gsi_rmbmenu event:

```
this.event Post gsi_rmbmenu()
```

Note: The events are preceded with an identifier, gsi_, to signify events specifically created for the GSI TimeMaster example program.

We copied the code in the gsi_rmbmenu event from the pfc_u_dw user object. We deleted the code specific to DataWindow operations, and added code to enable the treeview menu items and dynamically alter the text of the New menu item:

```
//////////////////////////////////////////////////////////////
//
//         Event: gsi_rmbmenu
//
//         Description: Popup menu
//
//////////////////////////////////////////////////////////////
//
//         Revision History
//
//         Version
//         5.0 Initial version
//
//////////////////////////////////////////////////////////////
//
//         Copyright © 1996 Gateway Systems, Inc. All Rights Reserved.
//
//////////////////////////////////////////////////////////////
boolean lb_frame
m_tvedit                    lm_tv
window                            lw_parent
window                            lw_frame
Long    ll_current, ll_return, ll_row
n_ds    lds_datastore
string ls_dataobject
string ls_newtext

// Determine if RMB popup menu should occur
IF Not ib_rmbmenu
        return 1
END IF

// Determine parent window for PointerX, PointerY offset
this.of_GetParentWindow (lw_parent)
IF IsValid (lw_parent) then
        // Get the MDI frame window if available
        lw_frame = lw_parent
        do while IsValid (lw_frame)
                IF lw_frame.windowtype = mdi! or lw_frame.windowtype = mdihelp!
THEN
                        lb_frame = true
                        exit
                ELSE
                        lw_frame = lw_frame.ParentWindow()
                END IF
```

```
                loop
                IF lb_frame THEN
                        lw_parent = lw_frame
                END IF
        ELSE
        //      return 1
        END IF

        // Create popup menu
        lm_tv = create m_tvedit
        lm_tv.of_SetParent (this)
        // Set the New item text according to the level selected
        ll_current = this.FindItem(CurrentTreeItem!, 0)
        ll_return = this.of_GetDataRow(ll_current, &
                lds_datastore, ll_row)
        IF ll_return = -1 THEN
                /* New Client */
                ls_newtext = is_newclient
        ELSE
                ls_dataobject = lds_datastore.dataobject
                ls_newtext = ""
                choose case ls_dataobject
                        CASE "d_tlg_client"
                                /* New Project */
                                ls_newtext = is_newproject
                        CASE "d_tlg_project"
                                /* New Task */
                                ls_newtext = is_newtask
                        CASE "d_tlg_task"
                                /* New Time Entry */
                                ls_newtext = is_newtimeentry
                        CASE ELSE
                END CHOOSE
        END IF
        is_newtext = ls_newtext

        // Allow for any other changes to the popup menu before it opens
        this.event pfc_prermbmenu (lm_dw)

        lm_tv.m_edititem.m_new.enabled = TRUE
        lm_tv.m_edititem.m_new.text = is_newtext

        // Popup menu
        lm_tv.m_edititem.PopMenu (lw_parent.PointerX() + 5, lw_parent.PointerY() + 10)
        destroy lm_tv
        //return 1
```

The strings used for the New menu item text are declared and initialized as instance variables. This centralizes their definition and eases maintenance.

Create RMB menu script to call events on the parent object.   Each new menu item must have code to call the corresponding event on the parent treeview object. This is the script for the clicked event of the Delete menu item:

idrg_parent.dynamic event gsi_delete()

This code is replicated, except for the name of the event, for the New item.

Create scripts on the parent object to implement the desired behavior.   This is the script for the treeview's gsi_new event:

```
// execute appropriate event depending on is_newtext
CHOOSE CASE is_newtext
        CASE is_newclient
                w_timelogframe.event gsi_ClientMaint()
        CASE is_newProject
                w_timelogframe.event gsi_projectMaint()
        CASE is_newTask
                w_timelogframe.event gsi_TaskMaint()
        CASE is_newTimeEntry
                /* New Time Entry */
                dw_1.event gsi_start()
END CHOOSE
```

That's all there is to it. The treeview object now has context-aware right mouse button support, courtesy of the PFC.

Managing the toolbars

The predefined PFC menu items usually have a toolbar picture associated with them. The picture appears as a button on the toolbar if the menu item is visible and the toolbar picture is visible. These properties are controlled by the property tabs in the menu painter. Each menu item's visible property appears on the Style tab. The visible property for the toolbar picture appears on the Toolbar tab, and the picture can be chosen using the Picture tab. Figure 5.5 shows the menu painter and properties tabs.

The PFC menu items trigger events on the associated windows and objects according to the algorithm of the message router. Next, we will discuss the various PFC windows and the functionality they implement.

PFC Windows

PFC window functionality

The PFC provides seven window classes, one for each type of PowerBuilder window:

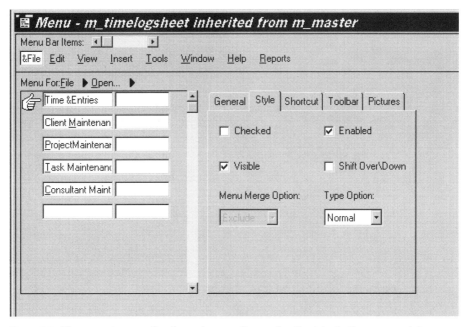

Figure 5.5 You can set properties for each menu item using the tabs in the menu painter.

1. w_master—descended from pfc_w_master

2. w_child—descended from pfc_w_child

3. w_main—descended from pfc_w_main

4. w_popup—descended from pfc_w_popup

5. w_response—descended from pfc_w_response

6. w_frame—descended from pfc_w_frame

7. w_sheet—descended from pfc_w_sheet

The ancestor of all other PFC window classes, pfc_w_master, implements a number of instance variables and functions, as well as precoded events and empty events to be extended by the developer. Each of the other window classes is descended from its own pfc_ ancestor, which in turn is descended from w_master. That is, for each window class, the hierarchy looks like Fig. 5.6.

Instance variables defined in pfc_w_master. The instance variables defined in pfc_w_master are:

■ ia_helptypeid (protected)—controls the way PFC calls the ShowHelp function.

■ ib_closeStatus (protected)—indicates whether the window is closing.

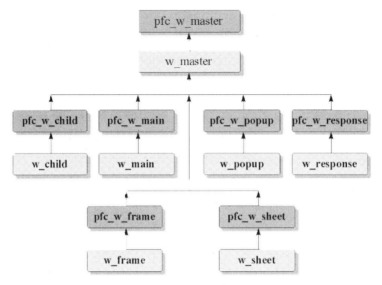

Figure 5.6 The PFC window common hierarchy.

- ib_disableCloseQuery (protected)—indicates whether CloseQuery processing is enabled.
- idw_active (protected)—indicates the current DataWindow or the last active focus DataWindow.
- inv_base (public)—provides a pointer to the basic window services.
- inv_preference (public)—provides pointer to the window preferences service.
- inv_resize (public)—provides a pointer to the resize service.

Functions defined in pfc_w_master.   pfc_w_master implements three functions to establish services: of_SetBase(), of_SetPreference(), and of_SetResize(). These functions are called to instantiate and initialize the pointers to their associated services.

Note: The window services are discussed in detail in Chap. 8.

- of_SetBase()—This function instantiates or destroys the basic window service (n_cst_winsrv). The basic window service provides the capability to center the window. It also provides the basic functionality to associate a window with any service object through the of_SetRequestor() function. Usually, you will not call of_SetBase. Since all window services are descended from n_cst_winsrv, the basic window service functions are available whenever you instantiate any window service.
- of_SetPreference(). This function instantiates or destroys the preference service (n_cst_winsrv_preference). The preference service will be instantiated as an instance variable named inv_Preference. The window prefer-

ences service provides functions to save the values of window properties, and to control which properties are saved.

- of_SetResize()—This function instantiates or destroys the resize service (n_cst_resize). The resize service provides functions to control the resizing of objects on a window (or tab control) as the window or tab control is resized.

Pfc_w_master also implements a function to access a protected variable: of_GetCloseStatus(). Finally, of_UpdateChecks() is used to determine if any updates are pending and to process data validation.

Events defined in pfc_w_master. pfc_w_master defines both precoded events and empty events. The precoded events are:

- *Close.* Stores preference information and destroys any existing window service objects.
- *CloseQuery.* Accesses all DataWindows, checks for validation errors, and, if changes are pending, prompts the user to save the changes.
- *Move.* Stores the window position and size if the preferences service is on.
- *Open.* Triggers the pfc_preopen event and posts the pfc_postopen event. If the window preference service is enabled, this event also restores window settings.
- *pfc_accepttext.* Issues a DataWindow AcceptText function to all DataWindows on the current window. The DataWindows to be included are passed in as an array, and may or may not be the same as the DataWindows in the window's control array. This event features recursive processing for tab controls and user objects.
- *pfc_close.* Closes the window.
- *pfc_controlgotfocus.* If MicroHelp is on, this event is triggered when a PFC visual control gets focus. This event keeps track of the current control.
- *pfc_descendant.* Called by PFC events and functions to determine if the window is inherited from w_master. This event always returns TRUE for a PFC object, and is meant for internal use only.
- *pfc_help.* Calls the ShowHelp function by index, topic, or keyword, based on the ia_helptypeid instance variable.
- *pfc_messagerouter.* Invokes PFC MessageRouter processing. This event combines with the menu's of_SendMessage() function to provide the PFC's message router capability. The first part of this chapter discusses the message router in detail.
- *pfc_postupdate.* Resets the DataWindow update flags after a successful database update.
- *pfc_save.* Calls w_master user events and functions to save changes for all DataWindows in the window. This user event calls pfc_updatespending, pfc_preupdate, pfc_endtran, and pfc_postupdate.

- *pfc_update.* Calls the DataWindow Update function for all modified, updatable DataWindows in the array of powerobjects passed to the function.

- *pfc_updatespending.* Searches for unsaved DataWindows and saves references to unsaved DataWindows. When CloseQuery calls this user event, validation messages are suppressed.

- *pfc_validation.* Searches for errors in DataWindows with pending updates.

- *Resize.* Triggers automatic resize processing, if enabled in n_cst_resize.

The precoded events can be extended to perform additional processing, but they provide valuable functionality to pfc_w_master and its descendants without any additional coding by the developer. The empty events in pfc_w_master are intended to be extended by the developer to provide custom processing. The pfc_w_master empty events are:

- *pfc_begintran.* Place any start-of-transaction processing in this event. By convention, return 1 if the processing succeeds and -1 if an error occurs.

- *pfc_endtran.* Place end-of-update processing, such as COMMIT and ROLLBACK, in this event. You can access the return code from the pfc_update event using the ai_update_results argument.

- *pfc_microhelp.* Descendants such as pfc_w_frame and pfc_w_sheet add code to this event to control the display of Micro Help in the MDI frame status bar.

- *pfc_new.* Place code that performs processing to add a new entity to the current window, window control, or DataWindow in this event.

- *pfc_open.* Place code that performs processing to open an existing entity (such as a file) in the current window, window control, or DataWindow in this event.

- *pfc_pagesetup.* Place code in this event to display a Page Setup dialog box.

- *pfc_postopen.* Place code in this event to perform processing that is to occur after the window is opened, but before any other processing has occurred.

- *pfc_preclose.* Place any code that you want to be executed just before CloseQuery processing into this event.

- *pfc_preopen.* Place any code that you want to occur just before the window opens into this event.

- *pfc_preupdate.* Use this event to perform any application-specific presave processing. Return 1 if the processing succeeds and -1 if it fails. A return of -1 will abort the save process.

- *pfc_print.* Place code into this event to initiate print processing. The difference between this event and the similar pfc_printimmediate is that you would typically display a Print Setup dialog box before printing from this event.

- *pfc_printimmediate.* Place code into this event to initiate print processing. Normally you would not display a Print Setup dialog box before printing from this event.

- *pfc_saveas.* Add code to this event to save all or part of the window or its controls, typically providing a dialog box that allows the user to select file type and content.

pfc_w_child.   The pfc_w_child window is a descendant of w_master. It is a window of type *child.* No additional instance variables, events, or functions are defined within pfc_w_child.

pfc_w_frame.   The pfc_w_frame window adds MDI-frame specific functionality to w_master.

Instance variables defined in pfc_w_frame

- *inv_SheetManager.* Pointer to the MDI sheet manager service.
- *inv_StatusBar.* Pointer to the status bar service.

Functions defined in pfc_w_frame.   pfc_w_frame defines two additional functions, of_SetSheetManager() and of_SetStatusBar(), which are used to instantiate and initialize the sheet manager and status bar services, respectively.

Note: The window services are discussed in detail in Chap. 8.

- *of_SetSheetManager().* Instantiates or destroys the sheet manager service (n_cst_winsrv_sheetmanager). The sheet manager service provides functions to allow the developer to manage and manipulate MDI sheets.
- *of_SetStatusBar().* Instantiates or destroys the status bar service (n_cst_winsrv_statusbar). The status bar service provides functions that allow you to control the status bar display.

Events defined in pfc_w_frame.   pfc_w_frame adds code to the following events:

- *Activate.* Calls the n_cst_appmanager of_SetFrame function to establish this window as the active frame.
- *pfc_cascade.* Calls the n_cst_winsrv_sheetmanager pfc_cascade event.
- *pfc_layer.* Calls the n_cst_winsrv_sheetmanager pfc_layer event.
- *pfc_minimizeall.* Minimizes all open sheets. Calls the pfc_minimizeall event on the sheet manager if the sheet manager is available.
- *pfc_pretoolbar.* Populates the attributes of the toolbar before passing an object to the toolbar window.
- *pfc_tilehorizontal.* Tiles sheets horizontally. This event calls the pfc_tilehorizontal event on the sheet manager if the sheet manager is available.
- *pfc_tilevertical.* Tiles sheets vertically. This event calls the pfc_tilevertical event on the sheet manager if the sheet manager is available.
- *pfc_toolbars.* Displays the w_toolbars dialog box.
- *pfc_undoarrange.* Calls the pfc_undoarrange event on the sheet manager.

In addition, pfc_w_frame extends the following events:

- *Move.* Adjusts the position of the status bar when the user moves the window.

- *pfc_microhelp.* If MicroHelp is enabled in the application manager, displays the argument as_microhelp in the frame window's status bar.

- *pfc_postopen.* Opens the status bar if it is available.

- *Resize.* Calls the pfc_Resize function on the status bar if it is available.

pfc_w_main. The pfc_w_main window is a descendant of w_master. It is a window of type *main.* No additional instance variables, events, or functions are defined within pfc_w_main.

pfc_w_popup. The pfc_w_popup window is a descendant of w_master. It is a window of type *popup.* No additional instance variables, events, or functions are defined within pfc_w_popup.

pfc_w_response. The pfc_w_response window is a descendant of w_master. It is a window of type *response.* No additional instance variables or functions are defined within pfc_w_response. Pfc_w_response defines the following user events:

- *pfc_apply.* Empty user event to which you add code that applies dialog box specifications to the associated sheet or window.

- *pfc_cancel.* Empty user event to which you add code that closes the window without accepting changes.

- *pfc_defaults.* Add code to this event to apply changes and close a response window. It is meant to be triggered by the default command button (typically cb_ok); however, it could be triggered by Cancel, Close, or some other command button.

Pfc_save event sequence

W_master contains the functionality to automatically update every DataWindow on the window. The save process consist of several steps. These include:

- Validation

- Preupdate processing

- Update (within a single logical unit of work)

- Postupdate processing

- Error handling

The update process is triggered by calling the pfc_save event. In turn, the pfc_save event calls the events shown in Table 5.3. The first three events are a

TABLE 5.3   pfc_save Events and Error Codes

	Event	pfc_save error code
Validation	pfc_accepttext	-1
	pfc_updatespending	0 (no changes)
		-2 (error)
	pfc_validation	-3
Preupdate	pfc_preupdate	-4
Logical unit of work	pfc_begintran	-5
	pfc_update	-6
	pfc_endtran	-7
Postupdate	pfc_postsave	-8
Error handling	pfc_dberror	N/A

part of the validation process. When an update is a result of a closequery event, the first three events are bypassed to prevent the display of validation error messages during the automatic closing of a window.

The next event, pfc_preupdate, is a placeholder for any preupdate processing. This event should be used with caution when preupdate processing includes any additional database updates. The reasons have to do with transaction management and are discussed in the next event group.

The next three events are a part of a logical unit of work. The pfc_save transaction management behavior depends on the setting of the autocommit transaction attribute. The first case is when autocommit is set to true and the transaction is started manually. In this case, pfc_begintran will contain code to start the LUW:

```
long ll_sqlcode
ll_sqlcode = SQLCA.of_execute("Begin Transaction")
IF ll_sqlcode <> 0 THEN return −1
return 1
```

If the transaction is started in pfc_begintran, then the pfc_preupdate event falls outside of the LUW. Any database I/O will be committed and rolled back separately from the other updates on the window.

The second case is when autocommit is set to false (default). In this case, no code needs to be added to pfc_begintran, but the LUW will be started when the last transaction has ended. Furthermore, pfc_preupdate will be a part of the same LUW as all the other DataWindows, but another issue comes up. With any update, insert, or delete statement, locks will be acquired. This may happen in pfc_preupdate or even before the pfc_save event. The locks will remain until the transaction is committed or rolled back in pfc_endtran. A cardinal rule of transaction management is not to release the control to the user while the transaction is open. It is very important not to display any modal windows from the time the tables were locked to the time the transaction is committed or rolled back.

A pfc_update event triggers a pfc_update event on every DataWindow. If an update fails, the error message is not displayed in the DataWindow's dberror event. Instead, the error message is saved in an instance variable and the pfc_save event sequence is allowed to complete.

Note: The DataWindows are updated in the order of the control array. If the update sequence is important, the control array may be rearranged or the linkage service may be used to specify the update sequence.

The next event, pfc_postsave, is a placeholder for postupdate logic. Whether autocommit is set to true or false, pfc_postsave is always outside of the logical unit of work. This is not the right event to use if you are adding embedded SQL to perform additional updates. If you need to add preupdate or postupdate logic that must remain within the same transaction, the pfc_update event must be extended as shown in the example below:

```
int li_rc
this.of_PreUpdate()
li_rc = Super::Event pfc_update()
this.of_PostUpdate()
return li_rc
```

Finally the last event, pfc_dberror, is responsible for the error message display. This event is called to display an error message in case any of the DataWindows fail. The event is called after the error message is saved and the transaction is rolled back in pfc_endtrans.

Using and extending the PFC windows

You can create windows for your application by inheriting from the PFC window of the appropriate class. As with all PFC objects, you should inherit from the w_ objects, not from the pfc_w_ objects.

You can extend the functionality of the windows provided with the PFC by adding your application-specific code to the w_ objects in the extension layer.

Summary

In this chapter you learned the specifics of the PFC menu and window functionality. You learned how the PFC menus implement a great deal of functionality while remaining small and performing well. You learned how the message router operates. We showed you how to implement and extend the PFC menus and how to develop and use alternative strategies within the PFC menu framework. Finally, you learned about the PFC window hierarchy and the events, variables, and functions that give each window class its personality and power. Chapter 8 delves into more detail about the various window services mentioned here.

6

Standard Visual Controls

Introduction/Objectives

This chapter will describe the visual user objects which are included in the PFC package. Much of this information can be obtained from the user manuals, but we will try to present the information in a way which will give you some insights into what can be done with the controls and possible extensions.

Visual controls are typically client objects which implement services. Although the DataWindow object (u_dw) is considered a visual control, it will not be discussed in this chapter; rather, it will be included in Chap. 9, "PFC DataWindow Services," as the information in that chapter is more pertinent to the DataWindow class.

The purpose of having user object versions of the visual controls is twofold: First, they allow you to implement your organization's standards for visual presentation, and second, they allow you to implement behavior that you want present in the class being used. They also provide you with a stepping-stone to develop specialized *families* of object classes that implement very specific behavior.

In general, all of the visual controls can simply be dropped onto a window (or custom user object) and used in place of their standard PowerBuilder counterparts. Keep in mind that you should always use the PFE extension objects rather than the PFC base objects, even if you choose to implement an inserted corporate layer, as all of the controls follow a typical base/extension hierarchy as shown in Fig. 6.1.

When using the controls is a little more complex than just dropping them on the window, we have shown an example of how the object could be used. In cases where an extension to an object is mentioned, a sample of the extension is included in Chap. 13, "PFC Extensions."

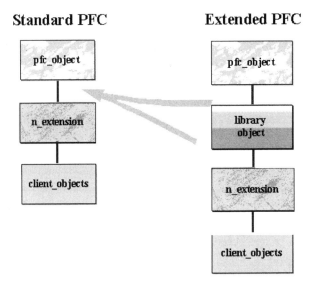

Figure 6.1 Standard PFC hierarchy and extended PFC hierarchy.

General Description

The way we will present the information about these controls is to utilize a table display for the control information. There are tables describing the control, followed by an example* of the control being described. The format of these tables is shown in Tables 6.1, 6.2, 6.3, and 6.4. The content of each column in each table is described in these examples.

Table 6.3 describes an example of why the object might be extended to add standard behavior. Standard behavior is that which all descendant objects of the class might want to have access to. Standardized extensions may be applied

---

* All sample extensions are included with Chap. 13, "PFC Extensions."

TABLE 6.1 Description Table

Object name	The name of the object; for example, pfc_u_cb	Object type	The type of object, based on the classifications described in Chap. 1
Ancestry	What standard control is the base for this object	Extension	The name of the standard extension-layer object
Description	A description of the object		
Usage	What the control would typically be used for		
Purpose	The purpose of the PFC enhanced control		

TABLE 6.2   Methods and Attributes Table

Method/attribute	Type	Access	Description
Attribute	Data type	Access level	Description of attribute
Event	Event type	Public	Description of event
Function	Function type	Access level	Description of function

TABLE 6.3   Extending the Object (Standardization Layer)

Sample extension	N/A
Description	

TABLE 6.4   Extending the Object (Specialization Layer)

Sample extension	N/A
Description	

using a corporate layer or directly to the PFE layer, depending on your approach to extensions (see Chap. 3).

Table 6.4 describes an example of why the object might be extended and specialized. Specialization creates object classes which serve a specific purpose, and seldom deviate from that purpose. This form of extension is always by inheritance, and such extensions should not be added to the PFE (or standardization-layer) libraries, but should be provided in a separate library. Specializing object classes can change the object type from abstract to concrete.

The Custom Visual Objects

The controls that will be described in this chapter are as follows:

pfc_u_cb	Command button
pfc_u_cbx	Checkbox
pfc_u_ddlb	Drop-down listbox
pfc_u_ddplb	Drop-down picture listbox
pfc_u_em	Editmask
pfc_u_gb	Groupbox
pfc_u_gr	Graph
pfc_u_hsb	Horizontal scroll bar
pfc_u_lb	Listbox
pfc_u_lv	Listview control
pfc_u_mle	Multiline edit

pfc_u_oc	OLE control
pfc_u_p	Picture control
pfc_u_pb	Picture button
pfc_u_plb	Picture listbox
pfc_u_rb	Radio button
pfc_u_rte	Rich text edit
pfc_u_sle	Single-line edit
pfc_u_st	Static text
pfc_u_tab	Tab control
pfc_u_tabpg	Tab page
pfc_u_tv	Treeview
pfc_u_vsb	Vertical scroll bar

pfc_u_cb (command button)

Description

Object name	pfc_u_cb	Object type	Abstract visual client
Ancestry	CommandButton	Extension	u_cb

Description	Standard user object command button.
Usage	Used instead of normal command button class.
Purpose	Allows standardization of size/font used on command buttons within an application.

Methods/attributes

Method/attribute	Type	Access	Description
None			
GetFocus	Standard event		Calls the pfc_controlgotfocus event on the parent window to establish that this control now has the focus. This means that the control can be a recipient of a menu action if the parent window is of type pfc_w_master* or a descendant.
of_GetParentWindow	PFC function		Establishes who the parent window is, regardless of the object's location.

*pfc_w_master and other window classes are described in Chap. 5.

Extending the object (standardization layer)

Sample extension	Auto_Click
Description	Automatically fires a user event based on one of three settings: the button text, the class name, or the tag value. This sample is based on the text value of the button. This allows the user to simply drop a button on an object (typically a window), and then enter the text description of the button. The code will pick up the text, remove any special characters (except for underscores), and trigger that user event on the parent. For example, putting a u_cb on a window with text of OK will translate to a user event of ue_ok (or whatever prefix you establish if you prefer not to use "ue").
	Another method of extending the command button is to have the command button "detect" the user event as above, but then use the PFC's message router to trigger the event based on the message router's rules.

Extending the object (specialization layer)

Sample extension	Update/Insert/Delete buttons (et al.)
Description	Inherited from the u_cb class, these buttons can incorporate the code necessary to fire the update/insert/delete events on the active DataWindow, allowing them to be "dropped" onto response windows which contain updatable DataWindows and eliminating the need for writing the code each time. *Note:* Use this only if you use these command buttons often.

pfc_u_cbx (checkbox)

Description

Object name	pfc_u_cbx	Object type	Abstract visual client
Ancestry	CheckBox	Extension	u_cb
Description	Checkbox user object		
Usage	Used in place of the standard control		
Purpose	Allows standardization and extension of the normal checkbox control		

Methods/attributes

Method/attribute	Type	Access	Description
None			
GetFocus	Standard event		Calls the pfc_controlgotfocus event on the parent window to establish that this control now has the focus. This means that the control can be a recipient of a menu action if the parent window is of type pfc_w_master or a descendant. Getfocus is also used to initiate the display of MicroHelp (display the tag value of the control to the frame window MicroHelp bar).
of_GetParentWindow	PFC function	Public	Establishes who the parent window is, regardless of the object's location.

pfc_u_ddlb (drop-down listbox)

Description

Object name	pfc_u_ddlb	Object type	Abstract visual client
Ancestry	DropDownListbox	Extension	u_ddlb

Description	Replacement drop-down listbox which supports speed searching (like the search capabilities within the windows help environment, where each character entered narrows or expands the search-results possibilities).
Usage	Used in place of the standard drop-down listbox control.
Purpose	The control is already extended to support copy, cut, and paste as well as right mouse menu support and speed searching.

Methods/attributes

Method/attribute	Type	Access	Description
ib_autoselect	Boolean	Public	Determines whether the first row is automatically selected when the control receives focus.
ib_rmbmenu	Boolean		Determines whether or not the control will support a right mouse popup menu.
ib_search	Boolean	Public	Determines whether or not the control should support speed searching.
cbneditchange	User event		This event allows speed searching on the drop-down list box much like the drop-down DataWindow (DDDW) speed-search capabilities. To activate the search capabilities, set the ib_search attribute to TRUE. To deactivate, set ib_search to FALSE.
GetFocus	Standard event		Calls the pfc_controlgotfocus event on the parent window to establish that this control now has the focus. This means that the control can be a recipient of a menu action if the parent window is of type pfc_w_master or a descendant.
pfc_cut	PFC event		Triggered from menu actions.
pfc_copy	PFC event		Triggered from menu actions.
pfc_paste	PFC event		Triggered from menu actions.

Method/attribute	Type	Access	Description
pfc_clear	PFC event		Triggered from menu actions.
pfc_selectall	PFC event		Triggered from menu actions.
rbuttonup	User event		This event will display a popup menu if the ib_rmbmenu attribute is set to true.
Prermbmenu	User event		This event is fired to allow you to set the attributes of the pop-up menu to match the object contents.
of_GetParentWindow	PFC function	Public	Obtains a handle back to the parent window.

Extending the object (standardization layer)

Sample extension	Automatically populate from a datastore.
Description	Add the ability to populate the drop-down list from a datastore. Add this capability as a service so that it can be reused by other list-style controls.

Extending the object (specialization layer)

Sample extension	Create a drop-down listbox which contains a list of states.
Description	Create a descendant of the u_ddlb class which contains a list of states and codes which can then be used on any window which requires such a lookup. (*Note:* An alternative to this would be to create a drop-down DataWindow which could then be used inside of DataWindows.) The state list should be prepopulated from a data source to enhance reusability and maintainability.

pfc_u_ddplb (drop-down picture listbox)

Description

Object name	pfc_u_ddplb	Object type	Abstract visual client
Ancestry	DropDownPictureListbox	Extension	u_ddplb
Description	Replacement drop-down picture listbox which supports speed searching. Drop-down picture listboxes can be used instead of normal drop-down listboxes so that a picture can be displayed representing the item in the list, much like the File Open dialog in the Windows 95 interface ("Look-In" is a drop-down listbox which displays a picture next to each item in the list).		
Usage	Use in place of the standard drop-down listbox control.		
Purpose	The control is already extended to support copy, cut, and paste as well as right mouse menu support and speed searching.		

Methods/attributes

Method/attribute	Type	Access	Description
ib_autoselect	Boolean	Public	Determines whether the first row is automatically selected when the control receives focus.
ib_rmbmenu	Boolean	Public	Determines whether or not the control will support a right mouse pop-up menu.
ib_search	Boolean	Public	Determines whether or not the control should support speed searching.
cbneditchange	User event		This event allows speed searching on the drop-down list box much like the drop-down DataWindow speed-search capabilities. To activate the search capabilities, set the ib_search attribute to TRUE. To deactivate, set ib_search to FALSE.
GetFocus	Standard event		Calls the pfc_controlgotfocus event on the parent window to establish that this control now has the focus. This means that the control can be a recipient of a menu action if the parent window is of type pfc_w_master or a descendant.
pfc_cut	PFC event		Triggered from menu actions.
pfc_copy	PFC event		Triggered from menu actions.
pfc_paste	PFC event		Triggered from menu actions.
pfc_clear	PFC event		Triggered from menu actions.
pfc_selectall	PFC event		Triggered from menu actions.

Method/attribute	Type	Access	Description
rbuttonup	User event		This event will display a pop-up menu if the ib_rmbmenu attribute is set to true.
prermbmenu	User event		This event is fired to allow you to set the attributes of the pop-up menu to match the object contents.
of_GetParentWindow	PFC function	Public	Obtains a handle back to the parent window.

Extending the object (standardization layer)

Sample extension	Add capability to load data from a datastore.
Description	Add the ability to populate the drop-down picture list from a datastore. Add this capability as a service so that it can be reused by other list-style controls (see example on CD).

Extending the object (specialization layer)

Sample extension	Create a drop-down listbox which displays drives, directories, and/or files.
Description	Create a descendant of the u_ddlb class which contains code to populate the drop-down listbox with drives, directories, or files.

pfc_u_em (edit mask)

Description

Object name	pfc_u_em	Object type	Abstract visual client
Ancestry	EditMask	Extension	u_em

Description	Edit mask control user object.
Usage	Use in place of the standard edit mask control.
Purpose	PFC version supports the clipboard functions cut, copy, and paste. It also supports clear and undo as well as selectall and a pop-up menu with default attributes set based on the edit mask content.

Methods/attributes

Method/attribute	Type	Access	Description
ib_autoselect	Boolean	Public	Determines whether the first row is automatically selected when the control receives focus.
ib_rmbmenu	Boolean	Public	Determines whether or not the control will support a right mouse pop-up menu.
ib_search	Boolean	Public	Determines whether or not the control should support speed searching
GetFocus	Standard event		Calls the pfc_controlgotfocus event on the parent window to establish that this control now has the focus. This means that the command button can be a recipient of a menu action.
pfc_cut	PFC event		Triggered from menu actions—will cut selected text.
pfc_copy	PFC event		Triggered from menu action—will copy selected text.
pfc_paste	PFC event		Triggered from menu actions—will paste contents of clipboard at the specified insertion point.
pfc_clear	PFC event		Triggered from menu actions—will clear the contents of the control.
pfc_selectall	PFC event		Triggered from menu actions—will select the entire contents of the control.
pfc_undo	PFC event		Triggered from menu actions—will undo previous keystrokes.
rbuttonup	User event		This event will display a pop-up menu if the ib_rmbmenu attribute is set to true.

Method/attribute	Type	Access	Description
of_GetParentWindow	PFC function	Public	Establishes who the parent window is, regardless of the object's location.

Extending the object (standardization layer)

Sample extension	Preset default values.
Description	Allows the control to use specified defaults when the control is initialized; for example, a date field can be initialized to today's date + or − an offset number of days.

Extending the object (specialization layer)

Sample extension	Data entry assistant family—amounts, dates, etc.
Description	Creates descendants of the u_em class that are specialized for entry of specific formats. Allows the user to enter abbreviations for certain elements and translate the abbreviations to valid entries; for example, 1B = 1,000,000,000 on the financial class.

pfc_u_gb (group box)

Description

Object name	pfc_u_gb	Object type	Abstract visual client
Ancestry	GroupBox	Extension	u_gb
Description	User object version of the groupbox control.		
Usage	Use in place of the standard groupbox control.		
Purpose	This control apparently has no reason to be in a class library. Groupboxes do not support events, although you could add functions and attributes to the object. There really is no reason why the control is part of the library other than to aid in standardization of font and colors. We must, however, keep in mind that while groupboxes behave this way today, there is no reason why we should assume that this will always be the case.		

pfc_u_gr (graph)

Description

Object name	pfc_u_gr	Object type	Abstract visual client
Ancestry	Graph	Extension	u_gr
Description	User object version of the graph control.		
Usage	Use in place of the standard graph control.		
Purpose	Allows standardization of size/font used on command buttons within an application.		

Methods/attributes

Method/attribute	Type	Access	Description
None			
GetFocus	Standard event		Calls the pfc_controlgotfocus event on the parent window to establish that this control now has the focus. This means that the command button can be a recipient of a menu action.
of_GetParentWindow	PFC function		Establishes who the parent window is, regardless of the object's location.

Extending the object (standardization layer)

Sample extension	Select graph style.
Description	Extension allowing the selection of graph style, colors, etc.

pfc_u_hsb (horizontal scroll bar)

Description

Object name	pfc_u_hsb	Object type	Abstract visual client
Ancestry	Horizontal Scroll Bar	Extension	u_hsb
Description	Horizontal scroll bar user object.		
Usage	Use instead of standard horizontal scroll bar.		
Purpose	Allows adition of predefined actions for scroll bars.		

Methods/attributes

Method/attribute	Type	Access	Description
None			
GetFocus	Standard event		Calls the pfc_controlgotfocus event on the parent window to establish that this control now has the focus. This means that the command button can be a recipient of a menu action.
of_GetParentWindow	PFC function		Establishes who the parent window is, regardless of the object's location.

Extending the object (standardization layer)

Sample extension	N/A
Description	

Extending the object (specialization layer)

Sample extension	N/A
Description	

pfc_u_lb (listbox)

Description

Object name	pfc_u_lb	Object type	Abstract visual client
Ancestry	Listbox	Extension	u_lb
Description	Standard user object version of the listbox control.		
Usage	Use instead of standard control.		
Purpose	Allows standardization of control attributes and behavior. Also allows specialization of behavior.		

Methods/attributes

Method/attribute	Type	Access	Description
None			
GetFocus	Standard event		Calls the pfc_controlgotfocus event on the parent window to establish that this control now has the focus. This means that the command button can be a recipient of a menu action.
pfc_invertselection	PFC event		Inverts the current selection, i.e., selected rows become unselected, while unselected rows become selected.
pfc_selectall	PFC event		Selects all available items.
of_GetParentWindow	PFC function		Establishes who the parent window is, regardless of the object's location.
of_GetSelected	PFC function		Gets data from the selected item and populates an array of data structures of type n_cst_itemattrib.

Extending the object (standardization layer)

Sample extension	Add capability to load data directly from a datastore.
Description	Add the ability to populate the drop-down list from a datastore. Add this capability as a service so that it can be reused by other list-style controls.

Extending the object (specialization layer)

Sample extension	Extend to hold predefined lists of data.
Description	Build specialized list objects that are precoded to display lists of data.

pfc_u_lv (listview control)

Description

Object name	pfc_u_lv	Object type	Abstract visual client
Ancestry	ListView	Extension	u_lv
Description	User object version of the listview control.		
Usage	Use instead of standard control.		
Purpose	Allows standardization of control attributes and behavior. Also allows specialization of behavior.		

Methods/attributes

Method/attribute	Type	Access	Description
ib_rmbmenu	Boolean		Use this instance variable to enable or disable right mouse button support. By default, this is set to TRUE. To disable right mouse button support, set this variable to FALSE in the listview's constructor event.
ids_source	n_ds*		DataStore containing the DataWindow object used to populate u_lv items.
igrs_currentsort	GrSortType[†]		Tracks sort status.
ii_currentsortcol	Integer		Contains the column used for the current sort.
il_lasthandle	Long		Tracks the last listview item.
il_rightclicked	Long		Contains the handle of the right-clicked listview item.
im_view	m_view[‡]		Reference variable for the m_view pop-up menu.
is_colformat[]	String		String array containing DataWindow format information for all displayed columns.
is_coltype[]	String		String array containing data type information for all displayed columns.
is_columns[]	String		String array listing displayed columns.
is_labelcolumn	String		Tracks the column in the DataWindow object that u_lv uses as the item label.
is_overlaycolumn	String		Tracks the column in the DataWindow object that u_lv uses for overlay picture information.
is_picturecolumn	String		Tracks the column in the DataWindow object that u_lv uses for picture information.
is_statecolumn	String		Tracks the column in the DataWindow object that u_lv uses for state information.

Method/attribute	Type	Access	Description
is_xposcolumn	String		Tracks the column in the DataWindow object that u_lv uses for x-position information.
is_yposcolumn	String		Tracks the column in the DataWindow object that u_lv uses for y-position information.
ColumnClick	Standard		Sorts the listview contents, using the column whose heading was clicked. If the column is already sorted, this event reverses the sort order.
Destructor	Standard		Destroys the m_view pop-up menu instance, if one exists.
EndLabelEdit	Standard		Updates the DataStore with user edits to the item label. This function updates the DataStore only. You must update the database explicitly, using the of_Update function.
GetFocus	Standard		Calls the pfc_controlgotfocus event on the parent window to establish that this control now has the focus. This means that the command button can be a recipient of a menu action.
pfc_preRMBmenu	PFC delegated		User event allowing you to modify m_view contents prior to display.
RButtonUp	PFC precoded		Displays the m_view pop-up menu.
RightClicked	PFC precoded		Event that executes when the user presses the right mouse button.
of_AddColumn	PFC function	Public	Adds a column to the listview control.
of_AddItem	PFC function	Public	Adds a column to the listview control for each visible DataWindow column. PowerBuilder displays columns in report view only.
of_CreateKey	PFC function	Public	Creates a single-column unique key for each row and adds the keys to ids_source.
of_DeleteItem	PFC function	Public	Creates a single-column unique key for each row and adds the keys to ids_source.
of_FormatData	PFC function	Public	Converts DataWindow data from its native format to the String data type.
of_GetCurrentSort	PFC function	Public	Returns information on listview sorting.
of_GetDataRow	PFC function	Public	Returns the source DataWindow and row that corresponds to a specified item in the listview control.
of_GetDataSource	PFC function	Public	Returns the DataStore used as the source of listview items.

Method/attribute	Type	Access	Description
of_GetItemForRow	PFC function	Public	Returns the handle of the listview item that points to a specified row in the ids_source DataStore.
of_GetParentWindow	PFC function	Public	Establishes who the parent window is, regardless of the object's location.
of_Populate	PFC function	Public	Populates the listview with information from the ids_source DataStore.
of_Refresh	PFC function	Public	Refreshes the listview with updated items from the ids_source DataStore.
of_RefreshItem	PFC function	Public	Refreshes a single listview item, updating it with data from the associated row in the ids_source DataStore.
of_ResetUpdate	PFC function	Public	Resets the update flags for the ids_source DataStore.
of_SetAttributes	PFC function	Public	Sets the attributes of a listview item using data from the ids_source DataStore.
of_SetDataSource	PFC function	Public	Registers a data source for the listview control. The data source is a DataWindow object, which u_lv maintains in the ids_source DataStore.
of_Update	PFC function	Public	Saves all rows in the DataStore associated with the listview.

*The datastore object is described in Chap. 9.
†GrSortType is an enumerated data type with the values Ascending!, Decending!, Unsorted!, and UserDefinedSort!
‡The menu m_view is described in Chap. 5.

Extending the object (standardization layer)

Sample extension	N/A
Description	The PFC object is already significantly enhanced to allow data access from a DataStore.

Extending the object (specialization layer)

Sample extension	N/A
Description	

pfc_u_mle (multiline edit)

Description

Object name	pfc_u_mle	Object type	Abstract visual client
Ancestry	MultiLineEdit	Extension	u_mle

Description	Standard user object version of the control.
Usage	Use instead of standard control.
Purpose	Allows standardization of the object's appearance and behavior. The control also implements the PFC clipboard services (cut, copy, and paste), right mouse menus, and a SelectAll behavior.

Methods/attributes

Method/attribute	Type	Access	Description
ib_autoselect	Boolean	Protected	Activates or deactivates the AutoSelect behavior of the control. This behavior implies that when the control initially gets focus, the entire contents of the control are automatically selected.
ib_rmbmenu	Boolean	Protected	Activates or deactivates the right mouse menu services.
GetFocus	Standard event		Calls the pfc_controlgotfocus event on the parent window to establish that this control now has the focus. This means that the control can be a recipient of a menu action if the parent window is of type pfc_w_master or a descendant. If the AutoSelect attribute is set to true, the control will automatically select the contents of the control when focus is received.
RButtonUp	Standard event		Displays the right mouse menu if the ib_rmbmenu attribute is set to TRUE.
pfc_preRMBmenu	PFC delegated		Event is fired immediately after the pop-up menu is displayed to allow manipulation of the menu's attributes.
pfc_cut	PFC event		Triggered from menu actions—will cut selected text.
pfc_copy	PFC event		Triggered from menu actions—will copy selected text.
pfc_paste	PFC event		Triggered from menu actions—will paste contents of clipboard at the specified insertion point.

Method/attribute	Type	Access	Description
pfc_clear	PFC event		Triggered from menu actions—will clear the contents of the control.
pfc_clear	PFC event		Triggered from menu actions—will clear the contents of the control.
pfc_selectall	PFC event		Triggered from menu actions-will select the entire contents of the control.
pfc_undo	PFC event		Triggered from menu actions—will undo previous keystrokes.
of_GetParentWindow	PFC function	Public	Establishes who the parent window is, regardless of the object's location.

Extending the object (standardization layer)

Sample extension	N/A
Description	

Extending the object (specialization layer)

Sample extension	N/A
Description	

pfc_u_oc (OLE control)

Description

Object Name	pfc_u_oc	Object type	Abstract visual client
Ancestry	OLEControl	Extension	u_oc

Description	Standard user object version of the control.
Usage	Use instead of standard control.
Purpose	Allows standardization of the object's appearance and behavior. The control also implements the PFC right mouse menu services and some specific behavior for OLE controls, such as Cut, Copy, Paste and Paste Special, EditObject, InsertObject, and UpdateLinks.

Methods/attributes

Method/attribute	Type	Access	Description
ib_rmbmenu	Boolean	Protected	Activates or deactivates the right mouse menu services.
GetFocus	Standard event		Calls the pfc_controlgotfocus event on the parent window to establish that this control now has the focus. This means that the control can be a recipient of a menu action if the parent window is of type pfc_w_master or a descendant.
RButtonUp	Standard event		Displays the right mouse menu if the ib_rmbmenu attribute is set to TRUE.
pfc_preRMBmenu	PFC delegated		Event is fired immediately after the pop-up menu is displayed to allow manipulation of the menu's attributes.
pfc_clear	PFC event		Triggered from menu actions— will delete the selected object from the OLE control.
pfc_cut	PFC event		Triggered from menu actions— will delete the selected object or text from the OLE control.
pfc_copy	PFC event		Triggered from menu actions— will copy the selected object to the clipboard.
pfc_editobject	PFC event		Triggered from menu actions— activates the in-place OLE object.
pfc_insertobject	PFC event		Triggered from menu actions— activates the OLE 2.0 Insert Object dialog, allowing you to select an object to insert into the OLE control.

Method/attribute	Type	Access	Description
pfc_openobject	PFC event		Triggered from menu actions—activates the object off-site.
pfc_paste	PFC event		Triggered from menu actions—will paste contents of the clipboard into the control.
pfc_pastespecial	PFC event		Triggered from menu actions—invokes the OLE 2.0 Paste Special dialog to allow selection of an OLE control.
pfc_updatelinks	PFC event		Triggered from menu actions—invokes the OLE 2.0 Update Links dialog to allow the user to update the established links in an OLE object.
of_GetParentWindow	PFC function	Public	Establishes who the parent window is, regardless of the object's location.

Extending the object (standardization layer)

Sample extension	Save data to database as a blob.
Description	Add services to the control to allow the OLE object to be saved to a database as a blob.

Extending the object (specialization layer)

Sample extension	OLE controls family.
Description	One of the most obvious specializations of this control is, of course, various flavors of existing OLE controls accessible to us. The most common of these is the MS Office suite of products, including Word and Excel. By creating descendants of the u_oc control, you can create u_oc_word or u_oc_excel controls, which can then have further behavioral implementations specific to those types of objects. These can then be further specialized into specific Word documents, such as a mailing list merge or a budget spreadsheet. There are literally hundreds of OLE controls available. Included with PowerBuilder Enterprise is a Component Gallery which includes several OCX controls from Gamesman Inc. and Visual Tools, giving you even more options.

pfc_u_p (picture control)

Description

Object name	pfc_u_p	Object type	Abstract visual client
Ancestry	Picture	Extension	u_p
Description	Standard user object version of the control.		
Usage	Use instead of standard control.		
Purpose	Allows standardization of the object's appearance and behavior.		

Methods/attributes

Method/attribute	Type	Access	Description
None			
GetFocus	Standard event		Calls the pfc_controlgotfocus event on the parent window to establish that this control now has the focus. This means that the control can be a recipient of a menu action if the parent window is of type pfc_w_master or a descendant.
of_GetParentWindow	PFC function	Public	Establishes who the parent window is, regardless of the object's location.

Extending the object (standardization layer)

Sample extension	Animation service.
Description	Add a service to the object which allows you to specify several "frames" which the control cycles through based on a set timer.

Extending the object (specialization layer)

Sample extension	N/A
Description	

pfc_u_pb (picture button)

Description

Object name	pfc_u_pb	Object type	Abstract visual client
Ancestry	PictureButton	Extension	u_pb
Description	Standard user object version of the control.		
Usage	Use instead of standard control.		
Purpose	Allows standardization of the object's appearance and behavior.		

Methods/attributes

Method/attribute	Type	Access	Description
None			
GetFocus	Standard event		Calls the pfc_controlgotfocus event on the parent window to establish that this control now has the focus. This means that the control can be a recipient of a menu action if the parent window is of type pfc_w_master or a descendant.
of_GetParentWindow	PFC function	Public	Establishes who the parent window is, regardless of the object's location.

Extending the object (standardization layer)

Sample extension	Depress service.
Description	Add a service to allow the button to be used as a "sticky" button with a normal and a depressed mode of display.

Extending the object (specialization layer)

Sample extension	N/A
Description	

pfc_u_plb (picture listbox)

Description

Object name	pfc_u_plb	Object type	Abstract visual client
Ancestry	PictureListbox	Extension	u_plb

Description	Standard user object version of the listbox control.
Usage	Use instead of standard control.
Purpose	Allows standardization of control attributes and behavior. Also allows specialization of behavior.

Methods/attributes

Method/attribute	Type	Access	Description
None			
GetFocus	Standard event		Calls the pfc_controlgotfocus event on the parent window to establish that this control now has the focus. This means that the command button can be a recipient of a menu action.
pfc_invertselection	PFC event		Inverts the current selection, i.e., selected rows become unselected, while unselected rows become selected.
pfc_selectall	PFC event		Selects all available items.
of_GetParentWindow	PFC function	Public	Establishes who the parent window is, regardless of the object's location.
of_GetSelected	PFC function	Public	Gets data from the selected item and populates an array of data structures of type n_cst_itemattrib.

Extending the object (standardization layer)

Sample extension	Add capability to load data directly from a DataStore.
Description	Add the ability to populate the drop-down list from a DataStore. Add this capability as a service so that it can be reused by other list-style controls.

Extending the object (specialization layer)

Sample extension	Extend to hold predefined lists of data.
Description	Build specialized list objects that are precoded to display lists of data.

pfc_u_rb (radio button)

Description

Object name	pfc_u_rb	Object type	Abstract visual client
Ancestry	RadioButton	Extension	u_rb

Description	Standard user object version of the control.
Usage	Use instead of standard control.
Purpose	Allows standardization of the object's appearance and behavior.

Methods/attributes

Method/attribute	Type	Access	Description
ib_example	Boolean	Protected	Sample attribute.
GetFocus	Standard event		Calls the pfc_controlgotfocus event on the parent window to establish that this control now has the focus. This means that the control can be a recipient of a menu action if the parent window is of type pfc_w_master or a descendant.
of_GetParentWindow	PFC function	Public	Establishes who the parent window is, regardless of the object's location.

Extending the object (standardization layer)

Sample extension	N/A
Description	

Extending the object (specialization layer)

Sample extension	N/A
Description	

pfc_u_rte (rich text edit)

Description

Object name	pfc_u_rte	Object type	Abstract visual client
Ancestry	RichTextEdit	Extension	u_rte

Description	Standard user object version of the control.
Usage	Use instead of standard control.
Purpose	Allows standardization of the object's appearance and behavior. The control also implements the PFC clipboard services (cut, copy, and paste), right mouse menus, and a SelectAll behavior. Additionally, consistent behavior for rich text edit (RTE) controls is implemented.

Methods/attributes

Method/attribute	Type	Access	Description
ib_continuouspages	Boolean	Protected	Indicates whether continuous page numbering is enabled when printing.
ib_ignorefileexists	Boolean	Protected	Indicates whether u_rte asks the user to confirm when saving a file that already exists.
ib_ongoingfind	Boolean	Protected	Indicates whether a find operation is in progress.
ib_rmbmenu	Boolean	Protected	Indicates whether right mouse button support is enabled.
il_currentinstance	Boolean	Protected	Tracks continuous printing.
il_currentprintpage	Boolean	Protected	Tracks current page number.
il_startpagenumber	Boolean	Protected	Specifies the first page that receives a page number.
inv_filesrv	Boolean	Protected	Reference variable for the file service.
inv_find	Boolean	Protected	Structure containing information used in find and replace processing.
is_filename	Boolean	Protected	Name of the current file.
is_pageinputfield	Boolean	Protected	Specifies the name of the field that PFC uses to place the page number.
Destructor	Standard event		Destroys the created instance of the file services object (inv_filesrv).
FileExists	Standard event		Informs the user that the selected filename already exists. This is not done if the ib_ignorefileexists instance variable is set to TRUE.
GetFocus	Standard event		Calls the pfc_controlgotfocus event on the parent window to establish that this control now has the focus. This means that the control can be a recipient of a menu action if the parent window is of type pfc_w_master or a descendant.

Method/attribute	Type	Access	Description
RButtonUp	Standard event		Displays the right mouse menu if the ib_rmbmenu attribute is set to TRUE.
pfc_preRMBmenu	PFC delegated		Event is fired immediately before the pop-up menu is displayed to allow manipulation of the menu's attributes.
pfc_firstpage	PFC event		Scrolls to the first page.
pfc_insertfile	PFC event		Displays a dialog allowing the user to select the name of the file that must be inserted at the current insertion point.
pfc_insertpicture	PFC event		Displays a dialog allowing the user to choose a bitmap image that should be copied at the current insertion point.
pfc_lastpage	PFC event		Scrolls to the last page.
pfc_nextpage	PFC event		Scrolls to the next page.
pfc_open	PFC event		Prompts the user to select a file to insert into the control. If there is already a document in the control, the user is prompted to save it first.
pfc_preprintdlg	PFC delegated		Empty event allowing the developer to modify the properties passed on to the print dialog function.
pfc_previouspage	PFC event		Scrolls to the prior page.
pfc_print	PFC event		Calls the pfc_PrintDlg function to print the contents of the control.
pfc_printdlg	PFC event		Initializes the s_printdlgattrib structure with the RichTextEdit control's current settings, displays the Print dialog box by calling the n_cst_platform of_PrintDlg function, and resets the settings, as specified by the user.
pfc_printimmediate	PFC event		Prints the control without displaying the print dialog.
pfc_printpreview	PFC event		Toggles print preview mode and edit mode.
pfc_ruler	PFC event		Toggles the display of the ruler and tab bar.
pfc_save	PFC event		Initiates the save of the control's contents. If the control is associated with a file, then the save is direct. If not, the user will be prompted for the name of a file to save to.
Pfc_saveas	PFC event		Allows the user to save the data to another file.
pfc_selectall	PFC event		Triggered from menu actions—will select the entire contents of the control.
pfc_undo	PFC event		Triggered from menu actions—will undo previous keystrokes.
of_GetContinuousPages	PFC function		Indicates whether PFC uses continuous page numbering when the RichTextEdit control is shared to a DataWindow.

(Continued)

Method/attribute	Type	Access	Description
of_GetFileName	PFC function		Returns the name of the file associated with the RichTextEdit control.
of_GetIgnoreFileExists	PFC function		Indicates whether PFC displays a message before overwriting an existing file.
of_GetPageInputField	PFC function		Returns the name of the field PFC uses to place the page number.
of_GetParentWindow	PFC function		Establishes who the parent window is, regardless of the object's location.
of_GetStartPageNumber	PFC function		Retrieves the number of the page on which page numbers are initially displayed. For example, if this value is 3, the first two pages do not display page numbers and the third page displays a 3.
of_GetTextStyle	PFC function		Calculates all text style settings for the currently selected text.
of_InsertDocument	PFC function		Displays the Insert File dialog box, prompting the user for the name of the file to copy into the current document, placing it at the current insertion point.
of_InsertPicture	PFC function		Displays the Insert Picture dialog box, prompting the user for the name of the bitmap to copy into the current document, placing it at the current insertion point.
of_OpenDocument	PFC function		Displays the Open dialog box, prompting the user for the name of the file to place into the RichTextEdit control. This function prompts you before discarding the control's current contents.
of_SetContinuousPages	PFC function		Specifies whether PFC uses continuous page numbering when the RichTextEdit control is shared to a DataWindow.
of_SetFileName	PFC function		Specifies the name of the file associated with the RichTextEdit control.
of_SetFind	PFC function		Enables or disables n_cst_rtefind, which provides find and replace services.
of_SetIgnoreFileExists	PFC function		Specifies whether PFC displays a message before overwriting an existing file.
of_SetPageInputField	PFC function		Specifies the name of the field PFC uses to place the page number.
of_SetStartPageNumber	PFC function		Specifies the number of the page upon which page numbers are initially displayed. For example, if this value is 3, the first two pages do not display page numbers and the third page displays a 3.
of_SetTextStyleBold	PFC function		Sets the currently selected text to bold, leaving all other text attributes as they were.
of_SetTextStyleItalic	PFC function		Sets the currently selected text to italic, leaving all other text attributes as they were.

Method/attribute	Type	Access	Description
of_SetTextStyleStrikeout	PFC function		Sets the currently selected text to strikeout, leaving all other text attributes as they were.
of_SetTextStyleSubscript	PFC function		Sets the currently selected text to subscript, leaving all other text attributes as they were.
of_SetTextStyleSuperscript	PFC function		Sets the currently selected text to super-script, leaving all other text attributes as they were.
of_SetTextStyleUnderline	PFC function		Sets the currently selected text to underline, leaving all other text attributes as they were.

Extending the object (standardization layer)

Sample extension	N/A
Description	

Extending the object (specialization layer)

Sample extension	Mail merge.
Description	Create a standard form letter with replaceable parameters that can then be used with any data brought in via a DataStore.

Note: Don't use the RTE control or its PFC replacement if you're planning to deploy on the NT platform. Powersoft blames a repaint problem on a "Microsoft anomaly." Microsoft has no announced plans to fix this "anomaly."

pfc_u_sle (single-line edit)

Description

Object name	pfc_u_sle	Object type	Abstract visual client
Ancestry	SingleLineEdit	Extension	u_sle

Description	Standard user object version of the control.
Usage	Use instead of standard control.
Purpose	Allows standardization of the object's appearance and behavior. The control also implements the PFC clipboard services (cut, copy, and paste), right mouse menus, and a SelectAll behavior.

Methods/attributes

Method/attribute	Type	Access	Description
ib_autoselect	Boolean	Protected	Activates or deactivates the SelectAll behavior of the control. This behavior implies that when the control initially gets focus, the entire contents of the control are automatically selected.
ib_rmbmenu	Boolean	Protected	Activates or deactivates the right mouse menu services.
GetFocus	Standard event		Calls the pfc_controlgotfocus event on the parent window to establish that this control now has the focus. This means that the control can be a recipient of a menu action if the parent window is of type pfc_w_master or a descendant.
RButtonUp	Standard event		Displays the right mouse menu if the ib_rmbmenu attribute is set to TRUE.
pfc_cut	PFC event		Triggered from menu actions—will cut selected text.
pfc_copy	PFC event		Triggered from menu actions—will copy selected text.
pfc_paste	PFC event		Triggered from menu actions—will paste contents of clipboard at the specified insertion point.
pfc_clear	PFC event		Triggered from menu actions—will clear the contents of the control.
pfc_preRMBmenu	PFC delegated		Event is fired immediately after the pop-up menu is displayed to allow manipulation of the menu's attributes.

Method/attribute	Type	Access	Description
pfc_selectall	PFC event		Triggered from menu actions—will select the entire contents of the control.
pfc_undo	PFC event		Triggered from menu actions—will undo previous keystrokes.
of_GetParentWindow	PFC function	Public	Establishes who the parent window is, regardless of the object's location.

Extending the object (standardization layer)

Sample extension	N/A
Description	

Extending the object (specialization layer)

Sample extension	N/A
Description	

pfc_u_st (static text)

Description

Object name	pfc_u_st	Object type	Abstract visual client
Ancestry	StaticText	Extension	u_st
Description	Standard user object version of the control.		
Usage	Use instead of standard control.		
Purpose	Allows standardization of the object's appearance and behavior.		

Methods/attributes

Method/attribute	Type	Access	Description
None			
GetFocus	Standard event		Calls the pfc_controlgotfocus event on the parent window to establish that this control now has the focus. This means that the control can be a recipient of a menu action if the parent window is of type pfc_w_master or a descendant.
of_GetParentWindow	PFC function	Public	Establishes who the parent window is, regardless of the object's location.

Extending the object (standardization layer)

Sample extension Description	N/A

Extending the object (specialization layer)

Sample extension	Specialized AutoSize.
Description	We are in charge of a class library team at a client. One of our daily tasks is to teach our developers how to use the class library. One of the ways we do that is by examples. We needed a way to put some text on the example that would describe what the example is doing, how the developer should be looking at it, etc. After doing this individually a few times, we decided to code a specialized version of the static text control which automatically resizes itself to fit on either the top or the bottom of the window and automatically resizes itself when the window is moved or resized—sort of a sheet status bar service. Now you simply drop the new object on a window, type in the text, and leave it wherever you dropped it. It automatically moves itself to where it should go, and resizes itself to use up the minimum amount of space.

pfc_u_tab (tab control)

Description

Object name	pfc_u_tab	Object type	Abstract visual client
Ancestry	TabPage	Extension	u_tab

Description	Standard user object version of the control.
Usage	Use instead of standard control.
Purpose	Allows standardization of the object's appearance and behavior.

Methods/attributes

Method/attribute	Type	Access	Description
None			
GetFocus	Standard event		Calls the pfc_controlgotfocus event on the parent window to establish that this control now has the focus. This means that the control can be a recipient of a menu action if the parent window is of type pfc_w_master or a descendant.
of_GetParentWindow	PFC function	Public	Establishes who the parent window is, regardless of the object's location.

Extending the object (standardization layer)

Sample extension	N/A
Description	

Extending the object (specialization layer)

Sample extension	N/A
Description	

pfc_u_tabpg (tab page)

Description

Object name	pfc_u_tabpg	Object type	Abstract visual client
Ancestry	TabPage	Extension	u_tabpg

Description	Standard user object version of the control.
Usage	Use instead of standard control.
Purpose	Allows standardization of the object's appearance and behavior. The control also implements the PFC clipboard services (cut, copy, and paste), right mouse menus, and a SelectAll behavior.

Methods/attributes

Method/attribute	Type	Access	Description
None			
GetFocus	Standard event		Calls the pfc_controlgotfocus event on the parent window to establish that this control now has the focus. This means that the control can be a recipient of a menu action if the parent window is of type pfc_w_master or a descendant.
Resize	Standard event		Allows the resize service to resize the controls within a tab (new in 5.0.02).
of_SetResize	PFC function	Public	Enables/disables the resize service (new in 5.0.02).
of_GetParentWindow	PFC function	Public	Establishes who the parent window is, regardless of the object's location.

Extending the object (standardization layer)

Sample extension Description	N/A

Extending the object (specialization layer)

Sample extension Description	N/A

Tip: Tab-page usage is a source of many headaches for first-time PFC users. It's not immediately obvious how to add a tab page to a PFC tab control. If a control inherited from u_tab is placed on a window, the "insert tabpage" and "insert user object" options are disabled.

The problem with the tab page is not unique to PFC. It is related to the nature of a native tab and tab-page controls. Once inherited, the Powerbuilder tab control behaves a lot like a visual user object. When a user object is placed on a window, it cannot be modified in a window painter. Instead, any changes to the user object must be done in a user object painter. When an inherited tab control is placed on a window the Insert Tabpage and Insert User Object options are disabled, because just like a user object, any changes to the control must be done in a user object painter. Follow these simple steps to use the PFC's tab objects:

1. For each tab page, create a new user object, inherited from u_tabpg. Add all the necessary DataWindows and other controls as well as the code directly related to the controls on the user object. An example would be in u_dw's pfc_retrieve event: Return This.Retrieve().

2. Create a new user object for the tab, inherited from u_tab. In the user object painter, select Insert User Object from the RMB popup menu. Select the previously created tab-page user object and populate the appropriate properties. Repeat for every tab page.

3. Place the tab object created in step 2 on the target window. From this point on, the tab and tab-page objects can be treated just like any other custom visual user object.

pfc_u_tv (treeview)

Description

Object name	pfc_u_tv	Object type	Abstract visual client
Ancestry	TreeView	Extension	u_tv

Description	Standard user object version of one of the most popular visual presentation aids around. A treeview control (previously known as the outline control), has been developed or presented in many different ways, usually with the same goal in mind.
Usage	Use instead of standard control.
Purpose	Allows standardization of the object's appearance and behavior. The control also implements the PFC clipboard services (cut, copy, and paste) and SelectAll behavior.

Methods/attributes

Method/attribute	Type	Access	Description
ids_buffer	n_ds	Protected	DataStore containing the DataWindow object used to populate u_tv items.
il_dragtarget	Long	Public	Handle of the target for the drop operation.
il_dragsource	Long	Public	Handle of the dragged item.
istr_ds[]	os_datastore	Protected	Structure array containing information displayed in a treeview level.
itr_obj	n_tr	Protected	Transaction object used for the ids_buffer DataStore.
il_dragsource	Long	Public	Handle of the dragged item.
BeginDrag	Standard		Saves the handle of a dragged item in the il_DragSource public instance variable.
Constructor	Standard		Creates the ids_buffer DataStore.
Destructor	Standard		Destroys the ids_buffer DataStore.
DragDrop	Standard		Saves the handle of the dropped item in the il_DragTarget instance variable.
EndLabelEdit	Standard		Updates the DataStore with user edits to the item label. This function updates the DataStore only. You must update the database explicitly, using the of_Update function.
ItemExpanding	Standard		Populates an item with its children.

Method/attribute	Type	Access	Description
GetFocus	Standard		Calls the pfc_controlgotfocus event on the parent window to establish that this control now has the focus. This means that the control can be a recipient of a menu action if the parent window is of type pfc_w_master or a descendant.
pfc_searchcompare	PFC precoded		Compares treeview data or item text with a target string.
of_BuildTree	PFC function	Public	Builds the data used for printing a treeview.
of_CreateKey	PFC function	Protected	Creates a computed column containing a single-column unique key for each row and adds the keys to the passed DataStore.
of_DeleteItem	PFC function	Protected	Deletes an item from the treeview along with its associated row in the DataStore. The function also removes any of the row's children from their DataStores.
of_DiscardChildren	PFC function	Public	Removes all treeview items below a specified item. The function also removes the item's rows from the DataStores.
of_FindFirstItemLevel	PFC function	Public	Returns the handle of the first item on a specified level.
of_FindItem	PFC function	Public	Searches by label or data for a specified treeview item.
of_GetArgs	PFC function	Public	Returns the retrieval arguments for a specified treeview level.
of_GetDataRow	PFC function	Protected	Returns the DataStore and row associated with a specified treeview item.
of_GetDataStore	PFC function	Public	Returns a reference to the DataStore associated with a specified treeview level.
of_GetItemForData	PFC function	Protected	Returns a handle to the treeview item associated with a specified DataStore row.
of_GetParentWindow	PFC function	Public	Establishes who the parent window is, regardless of the object's location.
of_InitialRetrieve	PFC function	Public	Retrieves data to populate the first level of the treeview.
of_InsertItem	PFC function	Public	Adds a new line to the treeview using data from the DataStore.

(Continued)

Method/attribute	Type	Access	Description
of_ParseArgs	PFC function	Protected	Creates an array of retrieval arguments from a passed string.
of_PopulateLevel	PFC function	Public	Populates a treeview item with its child items.
of_RefreshItem	PFC function	Public	Refreshes a treeview item. This includes removing all children and resetting label and data attributes from the DataStore.
of_RefreshLevel	PFC function	Public	Refreshes all items at a specified treeview level. This includes removing all children and resetting label and data attributes from the DataStore.
of_ResetUpdate	PFC function	Public	Resets the update flags for the DataStore associated with the specified treeview level.
of_SearchChild	PFC function	Protected	Searches for a string in either the label or the data treeview item attribute.
of_SetDataSource	PFC function	Public	Associates a data source with a treeview level. A data source is a DataWindow object that u_tv associates with a DataStore and uses to populate the treeview items for a specified level.
of_SetItemAttributes	PFC function	Protected	Sets a treeview item's attributes using data from the associated DataStore.
of_SetPictureColumn	PFC function	Public	Associates a DataWindow column with one of the picture indexes. This column contains a number that contains the appropriate picture index for its row.
of_Update	PFC function	Public	Updates one or all DataStores associated with the treeview.

Extending the object (standardization layer)

Sample extension	N/A
Description	

Extending the object (specialization layer)

Sample extension	N/A
Description	

Note: There is an example with extensive use of the treeview including extension to support a RMB menu in the GSI TimeMaster sample application.

pfc_u_vsb (vertical scroll bar)

Description

Object name	pfc_u_vsb	Object type	Abstract visual client
Ancestry	Vertical Scroll Bar	Extension	u_vsb

Description	Vertical scroll bar user object.
Usage	Use instead of standard vertical scroll bar.
Purpose	Allows addition of predefined actions for scroll bars.

Methods/attributes

Method/attribute	Type	Access	Description
None			
GetFocus	Standard event		Calls the pfc_controlgotfocus event on the parent window to establish that this control now has the focus. This means that the command button can be a recipient of a menu action.
of_GetParentWindow	PFC function		Establishes who the parent window is, regardless of the object's location.

Extending the object (standardization layer)

Sample extension	N/A
Description	

Extending the object (specialization layer)

Sample extension	N/A
Description	

Summary and Conclusions

This chapter took a look at the visual controls included in the PFC. Maintenance releases can affect the contents shown here, so please refer to the on-line help and release notes to ensure that there are no differences. We also tried to show you how you could extend client objects for standardization (adding standard behavior suitable for all usages of the control type) as well as specialization [deriving from the lowest inheritable layer (usually the PFE) and creating specialized classes with specific behavioral intentions]. As you can see, the standardization layer is useful for applying your corporate standards and/or corporate behavior and seems limited (how much generic functionality could you add?). The specialization layer can very easily outgrow the original library, so you should take care to collect the specialized classes into easily distinguishable libraries of easily reused classes.

7

Application Services

Introduction/Objectives

This chapter will introduce and describe the PFC application services, including

- Application manager
- DataWindow caching
- Debugging
- Error
- Transaction registration
- Security

Each service section contains a general service overview which outlines the features of the service and its purpose. The overview is followed by the description of each function and event. To ease navigation through numerous PFC events and functions, they are broken down into the categories shown in Tables 7.1 and 7.2.

Each section concludes with the description of the service usage. Step-by-step instructions and examples are provided for each principal service feature.

TABLE 7.1 Event Types

Standard	Standard event defined by Powerbuilder
Delegated	Service provider events, redirected from the service requester object
Precoded	Events defined by PFC, containing code
Placeholder	Empty events defined and triggered by PFC, intended to perform specific action

TABLE 7.2   Function Types

Standard	Standard function defined by Powerbuilder
Get	A wrapper function allowing read access to private or protected variables
Set	A wrapper function allowing write access to private or protected variables
Information	A function that returns information about objects' behavior or environment
Action	A function that initiates a specific action
Service Switch	A function used to enable and disable services
Service Control	A function used to configure the specific service behavior
Internal	Used internally by PFC; declared as protected.

Application Manager Service

Overview

The application manager is declared as a global variable that must be typed gnv_app.* Because of its scope, it also serves as a container for the many functions and properties requiring global access. These properties include application and user INI file locations, reference to the frame window, help file location, registry key path, application version, title, and bitmap. All of these attribute variables are declared as protected. To allow external access, a "get" function is declared for each variable. To get access to these properties from anywhere within the application, the wrapper functions are called using the dot notation. For example, gnv_app.of_GetFrame() will return the reference to the application's mdi frame window. Each individual function is described later in this chapter.

The other role of the application manager is the replacement of the application object. Because the application object cannot be inherited, PFC has chosen to use a nonvisual object to replace it. This was accomplished by redirecting all the application object events to the application manager object. Figure 7.1 shows how the application events are redirected to the application manager.

The application manager is also unique in the way it serves as both a service provider and a requester. The application manager acts as an anchor for the

*Other PFC objects contain direct references to the gnv_app global variable.

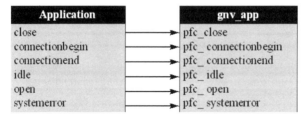

Figure 7.1   Application manager service redirected events.

services that are persistent throughout the life of the application and have to be referenced by other objects and services, including

- Transaction registration
- DataWindow caching
- Debugging
- Error

All of the above are considered to be application services but are actually services of the application manager object. Because the application manager is declared as a global variable, all of these services are accessible at any time. Just like the object manager functions, these services are accessed by using the dot notation. For example, to display a message in the debug window, the debug service is accessed as:

```
gnv_app.inv_Debug.of_Message("Hello world")
```

Events/functions

Table 7.3 lists all the events and functions of the application manager.

Usage

In order to use the application manager, a global reference variable must be declared:

```
n_cst_appmanager        gnv_app
```

In case the n_cst_appmanager was extended by inheritance, gnv_app should be declared as a variable of a descendant type:

```
n_cst_myappmanager      gnv_app
```

Actually, there are a few more global variables, masked as standard class types. These include transaction, dynamicdescriptionarea, dynamicstagingarea, error, and message. PFC provides extensions to transaction, error, and message, but currently only the transaction object contains any logic. The PFC extended transaction, n_tr, contains functions to load its attributes from the INI file, perform a rollback on disconnect, commit, and roll back, along with many others. Other PFC objects may assume that any transaction is of n_tr type and refer to these functions. Although currently this is not mandatory, the application's SQLCA type should be changed from transaction to n_tr. Furthermore, if any other transactions are declared in an application, they should be of n_tr type and not transaction type. If error or message is further extended, the type should be changed from error or message to n_err or n_msg, as shown in Figure 7.2. This will ensure that any future additions to these

TABLE 7.3   pfc_n_cst_appmanager Events and Functions

Object name	pfc_n_cst_appmanager	Object type	Abstract service
Ancestry	nonvisualobject	Extension	n_cst_appmanager

Description	Application manager service user object.
Usage	Created as a global variable.
Reason for use	Application object replacement. Global properties and methods and service container.
Layered extensions	Extend by inheritance and/or insertion.

Event (standard)	Constructor	Can be used to initialize the application properties and to create the appropriate services.
Event (standard)	Destructor	Contains the code to destroy any created services.
Event (delegated)	pfc_close	This event is triggered from the application close event.
Event (delegated)	pfc_connectionbegin	Triggered from the application connectionbegin event.
Event (delegated)	pfc_connectionend	Triggered from the application connectionend event.
Event (delegated)	pfc_exit	Triggered to close the application.
Event	pfc_logon	Triggered from the w_logon window. Intended as a placeholder for the code necessary to connect to the database.
Event (delegated)	pfc_open	Triggered from the application open event. It is typically used to open the main window and initialize the transaction object.
Event (placeholder)	pfc_preabout	Triggered prior to opening the about window. Intended as a placeholder event to allow for runtime modifications of the about window properties.
Event (placeholder)	pfc_prelogondlg	Triggered prior to opening the logon window. Intended as a placeholder event to allow for runtime modifications of the logon window properties.
Event (placeholder)	pfc_presplash	Triggered prior to opening the splash window. Intended as a placeholder event to allow for runtime modifications of the splash window properties.
Event (delegated)	pfc_systemerror	Triggered from the application systemerror event.

Function (action)	of_About	Opens the w_about window.
Function (get)	of_GetAppINIFile	Returns the current application INI file location (path+filename).
Function (get)	of_GetAppKey	Returns the registry key for the application information.
Function (get)	of_GetCopyright	Returns the copyright notice string.
Function (get)	of_GetFrame	Returns the reference to the frame window.
Function (get)	of_GetHelpFile	Returns the current help file location (path+filename).
Function (get)	of_GetLogo	Returns the name of the logo bitmap.

TABLE 7.3   pfc_n_cst_appmanager Events and Functions (*Continued*)

Function (get)	of_GetMicroHelp	Returns the state of MicroHelp (enabled/disabled).
Function (get)	of_GetUserId	Returns the current user ID.
Function (get)	of_GetUserINIFile	Returns the current user INI file location (path+filename).
Function (get)	of_GetUserKey	Returns the registry key for the user information.
Function (get)	of_GetVersion	Returns the current application version.
Function (information)	of_IsRegistryAvailable	Determines if the registry is available on the current platform.
Function (action)	of_LogonDlg	Opens the logon window. The Pfc_logon event is triggered when the window is closed.
Function (set)	of_SetAppINIFile	Sets the location of the application INI file.
Function (set)	of_SetAppKey	Sets the location of the registry key for the application information.
Function (set)	of_SetCopyright	Sets the copyright notice.
Function (service switch)	of_SetDebug	Turns the debug service on or off.
Function (service switch)	of_SetDWCache	Turns the DataWindow cache service on or off.
Function (service switch)	of_SetError	Turns the transaction registration service on or off.
Function (set)	of_SetFrame	Assigns a reference to the current MDI frame.
Function (set)	of_SetHelpFile	Sets the location of the help file.
Function (set)	of_SetLogo	Sets the application logo bitmap.
Function (set)	of_SetMicroHelp	Enables or disables the MicroHelp behavior.
Function (service switch)	of_SetTrRegistration	Turns the error service on or off.
Function (set)	of_SetUserId	Sets the current user ID.
Function (set)	of_SetUserINIFile	Sets the location of the user INI file.
Function (set)	of_SetUserKey	Sets the location of the registry key for the user information.
Function (set)	of_SetVersion	Sets the version displayed on the splash screen and the about window.
Function (action)	of_Splash	Opens a splash window for the specified duration.

objects will be automatically integrated into your application. Next, all the application events are redirected:

```
// application open event
gnv_app = create n_cst_appmanager
gnv_app.Event pfc_open (commandline)
```

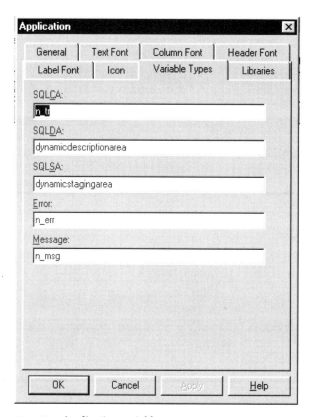

Figure 7.2 Application variable types.

```
// application close event
gnv_app.Event pfc_close()
destroy gnv_app

// application connectionbegin event
gnv_app = create n_cst_appmanager
return gnv_app.Event pfc_connectionbegin (userid, password, connectstring)

// application connectionend event
gnv_app.Event pfc_connectionend ()
destroy gnv_app

// application idle event
gnv_app.Event pfc_idle()

// application systemerror event
gnv_app.Event pfc_systemerror()
```

We are now ready to use the application manager. In the constructor event of the application manager, PFC saves references to the current application object and environment. The constructor event also serves as a placeholder for all the appropriate properties to be initialized and services to be "turned on." Template code for populating these properties is provided by PFC and commented out. The example below shows the code from this book's sample application.

```
// n_cst_appmanager constructor event
// Name of the application
iapp_object.DisplayName = "GSI TimeMaster"

// Enable the MicroHelp functionality
of_SetMicroHelp (TRUE)

// The filename of the application INI file
of_SetAppINIFile ("app.ini")

// The filename of the user INI file
of_SetUserINIFile ("TimeMstr.ini")

// Application registry key
of_SetAppKey
("HKEY_LOCAL_MACHINE\Software\GatewaySystems\TimeMaster")

// User registry key
of_SetUserKey
("HKEY_CURRENT_USER\Software\GatewaySystems\TimeMaster")

// The filename of the application's on-line help file
of_SetHelpFile ("gsi_time.hlp")

// The application version
of_SctVcrsion ("Vcrsion 1.0")

// The application logo (bitmap filename)
of_SetLogo ("timproc2.bmp")

// Application copyright message
of_SetCopyright ("Copyright @ 1997 Gateway Systems, Inc")
```

Our next task is to establish a database connection. This is typically done from the pfc_open event. After the transaction is initialized, the frame window is opened.

```
// n_cst_appmanager pfc_open event
IF sqlca.of_Init (is_userinifile, "Gateway Systems Time Master") = -1 THEN
        MessageBox (is_title, "Initialization failed from file" + is_userinifile)
        halt
```

END IF
Open (w_timelogframe)

The of_LogonDlg() function is then used to open the logon window. In this example, the logon window is opened from the open event of the MDI frame window. The order in which logon, splash, and frame windows are opened is a matter of personal preference.

Tip: If the splash window is opened before the logon window from the same event, this may cause the logon window to automatically close with the splash window. To avoid this problem, add a Yield() between two calls or open these windows from different posted events.

The logon window will trigger the pfc_logon placeholder event on the application manager. The code needed to connect to the database is placed in this event.

```
// n_cst_appmanager pfc_logon event
// Perform logon
sqlca.of_SetUser (as_userid, as_password)

IF sqlca.of_Connect()> = 0 THEN
        return 1
ELSE
        MessageBox (is_title, "Connect failed")
        return −1
END IF
```

DataWindow Caching Service

Overview

The DataWindow caching service allows frequently used data to be cached in memory. When this data is required, it can be accessed from the caching service, thus saving costly database hits. There are three different cache sources. Data can be retrieved from the database, passed in a structure, or saved in the DataWindow object. Each cached source can be refreshed individually or in a group. The DataWindow caching service provides access to the handle of the DataStore but currently does not provide any method of automatically sharing the data with the cache target DataWindows.

Events/functions

Table 7.4 shows the functions and events for the DataWindow caching service.

Usage

The first step in using the DataWindow cache service is to register the source of the data to be cached. The service offers three possible sources:

TABLE 7.4   pfc_n_cst_dwcache Events and Functions

Object name	pfc_n_cst_dwcache	Object type	Abstract service
Ancestry	nonvisualobject	Extension	n_cst_dwcache
Description	DataWindow cache service user object.		
Usage	Used to reduce the database access for static data.		
Reason for use	Cache the data used by multiple DataWindows throughout the application. Typically used for drop-down DataWindows.		
Layered extensions	Extend by insertion.		
Event (standard)	Constructor	Not used.	
Event (standard)	Destructor	Used by PFC to destroy all the registered objects.	
Function (get)	of_GetCount	Returns the total number of registered objects.	
Function (get)	of_GetRegistered	Returns information about the registered cache objects. Function is overloaded to return a list of all registered DataStores, a single DataStore with a specified ID, or a list of all IDs.	
Function (information)	of_IsRegistered	Determines if the DataStore with a specified ID has been registered.	
Function (service control)	of_Refresh	Refreshes the data in the DataStores which originated from the database. Function is overloaded to refresh all or a single DataStore.	
Function (service control)	of_Register	Register a new cache source. Overloaded to allow for sources from the database or the structure or embedded in the DataWindow object.	

1. Database
2. Array of structures or user objects
3. DataWindow object

The appropriate method is selected by calling the corresponding version of the of_Register() function. The first one is probably the most commonly used. The data is retrieved from the database table once when the object is registered. In this case, the arguments must include a valid and connected transaction object of n_tr type, a DataWindow object, and retrieval arguments, if any. The example below provides a syntax for adding a list of states to the cache service.

```
// Enable the cache service
gnv_app.of_SetDWCache(TRUE)

// Register the data source
gnv_app.inv_dwcache.of_Register( "states", "d_states", SQLCA)
```

If the DataWindow has arguments these should be passed as well.

Note: The retrieval arguments are passed as a bounded array of 20 elements of type any. Even if only a single argument is used, it should be passed in an array of 20.

```
// Register the data source with a retrieval argument.
String ls_country[20] = {"USA"}
gnv_app.inv_dwcache.of_Register( "states", "d_states", SQLCA, ls_country)
```

The second function version accepts the data in an array of powerobjects. This should be an array of either structures or user objects. It still requires a DataWindow object that matches the data definition of the user object or a structure. This method may become useful when more control of retrieve timing is required.

```
// Structure declaration
global type s_states from structure
          string          s_id
          string          s_state
          string          s_capital
end type
```

```
// Register the data source with an array of structures.
s_states lstr_states[]
lstr_states = dw_states.Object.Data
gnv_app.inv_dwcache.of_Register( "states", "d_states", lstr_states)
```

The final method assumes that the data was saved in the data object. This time only the cache id and the data object name are required:

```
// Register the data source with an array of structures.
gnv_app.inv_dwcache.of_Register( "states", "d_states")
```

Once the DataWindow is registered with the cache service, the data is accessed by getting a handle to the registered object.

```
Datawindowchild ldwc_states
```

```
// Get the drop-down DataWindow handle
dw_parent.GetChild("state", ldwc_states)
```

```
// Get the cache DataStore handle
n_ds lds_cache
gnv_app.inv_dwcache.of_GetRegistered( "states", lds_cache)
```

The data can be retrieved by sharing or copying.

```
// Populate the drop-down by sharing the data
lds_cache.ShareData(ldwc_states)
```

```
// Or populate the drop-down by copying the data
ldwc_states.Object.Data = lds_cache.Object.Data
```

Another important feature of the cache service is its capability to refresh the data in one or all of the cache objects.

Note: The ability to refresh the cache data is limited to the objects registered with a database source. Of_Refresh has no effect on the cache objects whose data originated from an array of powerobjects or the DataWindow object.

of_Refresh called without any arguments will refresh all the cache DataStores with a database data source. When of_Refresh is used with a cache ID as an argument, only the specified cache will be refreshed.

```
// Refresh all the registered cache objects
gnv_app.inv_dwcache.of_Refresh()
```

```
// Refresh only the state's cache object
gnv_app.inv_dwcache.of_Refresh( "states" )
```

Error/Message

Overview

The user interface is one of the most volatile areas of any design. A typical application contains many messages, such as information, error, warning, or user input. These messages are usually the first casualties of dynamic user requirements. The message content is guaranteed to go through many iterations before and after the production release. Most of the class libraries offer some kind of a method for isolating the messages from the rest of the application. The primary role of the error service is as a message repository, but it offers much more. The error service features include the following:

- A file or database error messages repository.
- Error messages allow for argument substitution.
- The error may be displayed using a MessageBox or a custom PFC response window.
- PFC response window allows capability to print the error message.
- PFC response window allows capability to add user input.
- PFC response window allows an optional "beep on error" feature.
- PFC response window may be closed automatically after a defined time period.
- Messages can be optionally logged to a file.
- Automatic e-mail notification (MAPI).
- E-mail and log severity level.

Events/functions

Table 7.5 shows the events and functions of the PFC error service.

Usage

Message source. The first step is to select the source of the message repository. The initial message table is included in the PFC SQL Anywhere database, pfc.db, located in the default PFC directory. The table can be copied to the application database by using a pipeline or by exporting the table definition and data. The contents of the message table are described in Table 7.6.

For the file message source, the file format is tab-separated text. The field format is the same as in the message table.

Tip: Create a DataWindow against the message table to help with the message maintenance. D_definedmessages may be used as a starting point. For the file message source, use Rows/Import and File/SaveAs DataWindow painter commands.

To set the message source to the database, a valid and connected transaction should be passed as an argument to of_SetPredefinedSource.

```
int li_rtc
// Set the file predefined source
li_rtc = inv_error.of_SetPredefinedSource(SQLCA)
```

When of_SetPredefinedSource is called, the service will attempt to retrieve the predefined messages into the ids_messages DataStore. In the example above, of_SetPredefinedSource will return an error code if the transaction is not connected.

```
int li_rtc
// Set the file predefined source
li_rtc = inv_error.of_SetPredefinedSource("d:\data\quickmgs.txt")
```

The last option allows the developer not to use any predefined message sources. Each message can be specified dynamically by using the appropriate syntax of the of_Message() call. The of_Message function is described in the section on message display. In early revisions PFC did assume the predefined message mode for some internal messages. Even if the predefined message repository is not used, specifying the file message source with the standard PFC messages may be recommended.

Message display. The messages are displayed using the of_Message function. The function is overloaded to provide many different versions, but these versions fall into two major groups. The first one allows the display of the predefined message. It accepts up to three arguments: a string specifying the message ID and

TABLE 7.5   pfc_n_cst_error Events and Functions

Object name	pfc_n_cst_error	Object type	Abstract service
Ancestry	nonvisualobject	Extension	n_cst_error

Description	Error message service.	
Usage	Used to display or log messages.	
Reason for use	Cache the data used by multiple DataWindows throughout the application. Typically used for drop-down DataWindows.	
Layered extensions	Extend by insertion.	

Event (standard)	Constructor	Not used.
Event (standard)	Destructor	Used by PFC to destroy all the created objects.

Function (internal)	of_CreateLogText	Constructs the text string for the log. Used internally, but can be extended or overridden to add custom information to the log file.
Function (internal)	of_CreateNotifyText	Constructs the text string for the e-mail notification. Used internally, but can be extended or overridden to add custom information to the message.
Function (get)	of_GetBeep	Provides access to the current setting of the "beep on error" attribute.
Function (get)	of_GetLogFile	Provides access to the current name and location of the log file.
Function (get)	of_GetLogSeverity	Provides access to the current severity setting at which the log should be generated.
Function (get)	of_GetNotifyConnection	Provides access to the current mail session configured for auto-notify.
Function (get)	of_GetNotifySeverity	Provides access to the current severity setting at which e-mail notification should be sent.
Function (get)	of_GetNotifyWho	Provides access to the list of users on the auto-notify list.
Function (get)	of_GetPredefinedSource	Overloaded to provide a transaction of the database source or a predefined message file location.
Function (get)	of_GetPredefinedSourceType	Returns the type of the predefined message source: "File" or "Database."
Function (get)	of_GetStyle	Returns the current message style: 0, MessageBox; 1, PFC message window.
Function (get)	of_GetTimeOut	Provides access to the current timeout setting after which PFC message style window is automatically closed.
Function (get)	of_GetUnattended	Provides access to the current setting of unattended (log only) mode.
Function (action)	of_LoadPredefinedMsg	Retrieves the predefined messages from the specified datasource. Automatically called by PFC when the source is defined.
Function (action)	of_Message	Displays the message. If appropriate, the message is also logged and e-mailed. Overloaded to display the message from the predefined source or provided directly.

TABLE 7.5   pfc_n_cst_error Events and Functions (*Continued*)

Function (internal)	of_ProcessLog	Logs message to file. Used internally, but may be overridden or extended to log the message to a different target.
Function (internal)	of_ProcessMessage	Processes the message initiated with of_Message.
Function (internal)	of_ProcessMessageSubstitution	Replaces the substitution parameters.
Function (internal)	of_ProcessNotify	Sends the e-mail notification to the specified recipients.
Function (set)	of_SetBeep	Specifies the setting of the "beep on error" attribute for the PFC message style window.
Function (set)	of_SetLogFile	Specifies the name and location of the log file.
Function (set)	of_SetLogSeverity	Specifies the severity level at which the log entry should be generated.
Function (set)	of_SetNotifyConnection	Specifies the mail session to be used for auto-notify.
Function (set)	of_SetNotifySeverity	Specifies the severity level at which the e-mail notification should be sent.
Function (set)	of_SetNotifyWho	Specifies a list of users to be notified.
Function (set)	of_SetPredefinedSource	Overloaded to specify a transaction for the database source or a predefined message filename and location.
Function (set)	of_SetStyle	Specifies the message style: 0, MessageBox; 1, PFC message window.
Function (set)	of_SetTimeOut	Species the timeout value after which the PFC message style window is closed automatically.
Function (set)	of_SetUnattended	Turns the unattended mode (not displayed) on or off.

TABLE 7.6   Message Table Contents

Column name	Type	Description	Valid values
msgid	char(40)	The message ID, used in of_Message()	Any string
msgtitle	char(255)	The message title	Any string
msgtext	char(255)	The message text	Any string
msgicon	char(12)	The message icon displayed on the left side of the window"	Information", "StopSign", "Exclamation", "Question", "None"
msgbutton	char(17)	Command button combinations	"OK", "OKCancel", "YesNo", "YesNoCancel", "RetryCancel", "AbortRetryIgnore"
msgdefaultbutton	integer	The default button	1, 2, 3
msgseverity	integer	The message severity level	0–32,000
msgprint	char(1)	The message print indicator	"Y", "N"
msguserinput	char(1),	The message user input indicator	"Y", "N"

an optional array of strings containing the substitution parameters and override message title. The error service is accessed through the application manager. The example below will prompt the user to save changes.

```
// Prompt to save changes
gnv_app.inv_error.of_Message("pfc_closequery_savechanges")
```

The ability to use substitution parameters is a powerful feature of the message service. It allows the definition of fewer, more generic messages, with "%s" specifying a place where the specific parameter should be substituted. One example of a message with substitution parameters is "pfc_requiredmissing", intended to be used when a required field was left empty. In this case, the error text is defined as "Required value missing for %s on row %s. Please enter a value." At runtime the "%s" are replaced with parameters passed in a string array argument.

```
// Required entry missing on row 1 (predefined source)
gnv_app.inv_error.of_Message("pfc_requiredmissing",&
{"Customer maintenance", "1"} )
```

The second version of the of_Message function allows the display of a message specified in a string.

```
// Required entry missing on row 1 (w/o predefined source)
gnv_app.inv_error.of_Message("Application",&
"Required value missing for Customer maintenance"+&
"on row 1 Please enter a value.",&
Information!, Ok!, 1, 5, False, False )
```

All the arguments except the first two are optional and will assume the default values if omitted. For example, if the severity value of 0 was acceptable for the previous message, it could be called as

```
// Required entry missing on row 1 (w/o predefined source)
gnv_app.inv_error.of_Message("Application",&
"Required value missing for Customer maintenance"+ &
"on row 1 Please enter a value.")
```

Message log. Any message can also be logged to a specified file. The log process is automatic for every message with severity greater than or equal to the specified severity log threshold. of_SetLogFile can be used to specify the log file location and of_SetLogSeverity to set the minimum severity level for the messages to be added to the log.

```
// Set the log file location
li_rtc = inv_error.of_SetLogFile("d:\data\quicklog.txt")
// Set the log severity level
li_rtc = inv_error.of_SetLogSeverity(5)
```

E-mail notification.   E-mail notification is very similar to the log feature. The e-mail connection is specified by providing a valid MAPI mail session object and a list of users to be notified. The example below shows the required steps to enable the e-mail notification.

```
mailSession                               mSes
mailReturnCode              mRet

// Create the mail session and login
mSes = create mailSession
mRet = mSes.mailLogon ( ls_userid, ls_userpassword, mailNewSession! )
IF mRet <> mailReturnSuccess! THEN
        // signal error
        return -1
END IF

// Register the mail session with the error service
string ls_notifywho[] = {"administrator", "developer"}
int li_rtc // error checking removed for clarity
li_rtc = gnv_app.inv_errror.of_SetNotifyConnection(mSes)
li_rtc = gnv_app.inv_errror.of_SetNotifyWho(ls_notifywho)
li_rtc = gnv_app.inv_errror.of_SetNotifySeverity(5)
```

Unattended mode.   Often there is a need to log or e-mail a message without displaying the message window. PFC addresses this requirement by providing the unattended mode. When the unattended mode is turned on, the message display is bypassed.

```
gnv_app.inv_error.of_SetUnattended( TRUE )
gnv_app.inv_error.of_Message("log_messageid")
gnv_app.inv_error.of_Message("email_messageid")
gnv_app.inv_error.of_SetUnattended( FALSE )
```

In the above case, the message will not be displayed, but if the log or the e-mail severity meets the threshold, the message will be logged or mailed to the selected users.

Security

Overview

PFC security provides a client-side security solution. It allows access restriction to the different components of a PFC-based application. The objects that can be secured are menu items, graphic objects, and DataWindow columns. Each object may be enabled/disabled or made invisible.

The security service allows us to grant the rights to window objects to pre-designated users. Users may be combined into groups. The access to each control may be granted on a user or a group level. The setting for each control may be assigned to an individual user or to a group.

All the security information is saved in the database. The security definition changes are completely transparent to the application. The same database may be used for multiple applications.

The security service consists of two administration utilities and the runtime security service object. The security administration utilities include

- Security administration utility
- Security scanner utility

The two applications are used to populate and maintain the security database. They are described in detail in Chap. 10. Because this chapter deals with application services, it will concentrate on the runtime security module and its use within the application. It is important to know that before the security service can be used, the security database should be established and the appropriate rights should be granted. If you are ready to implement the security in your application, you may want to skip to Chap. 10 and follow the steps needed to establish the security database, scan the application, and grant the appropriate rights.

Events/functions

Table 7.7 lists the events and functions in the PFC security service module.

Usage

At first glance, the list of security functions in Table 7.7 may be intimidating. After a closer look, it becomes obvious that most of the functions are used internally by the scan and secure procedures. Only a few functions are used to enable and initialize the security service and then secure each window.

Enabling the security service. The application manager contains the by now familiar of_SetSecurity function used to create the security service. After the security service is enabled, it needs to know how to connect to the security database, what is the current user id, and what is the current application. This information is provided by the of_InitSecurity function. The security can be enabled in the pfc_open event of the application manager.

```
// Enable the security service
of_SetSecurity(TRUE)

// Initialize the security service
inv_security.of_InitSecurity(SQLCA, ClassName(iapp_object),&
of_GetUserID(), "Default")
```

The last argument is a default group, which will be used if the user was not assigned to any other group.

TABLE 7.7   **pfc_n_cst_security Events and Functions**

Object name	pfc_n_cst_security	Object type	Abstract service
Ancestry	nonvisualobject	Extension	n_cst_security
Description	Security service user object.		
Usage	Used to secure the window controls according to the predefined settings in the security database.		
Reason for use	It's free.		
Layered extensions	Extend by insertion		
Event (standard)	Constructor	Not used.	
Event (standard)	Destructor	Used by PFC to destroy all the created objects.	
Function (internal)	of_AddObject	Adds an object to the security template. Used internally by the scan process.	
Function (internal)	of_FindEntry	Determines if a specific control exists in the security template. Used internally by the scan process.	
Function (internal)	of_GetTag	Gets the control description from its tag "MicroHelp" value. Used internally by the scan process.	
Function (internal)	of_GetType	Converts the enumerated object type to a string. Used internally by the scan process.	
Function (internal)	of_InitScanProcess	Initializes the database connection and library search path. Used internally by the scan process.	
Function (service control)	of_InitSecurity	Initializes the transaction, application, user ID, and default group to be used by the security service.	
Function (internal)	of_LoadSecurity	Retrieves the security information about the window and appends it to the DataStore. Used internally by the secure process.	
Function (internal)	of_ScanControlArray	Scans the control array and secures the controls as specified in the security database. Used internally by the secure process.	
Function (internal)	of_ScanDataWindow	Scans the DataWindow and saves the information about each control. Used internally by the scan process.	
Function (internal)	of_ScanWindow	Scans and captures the information about the controls and DataWindow columns on the window. Used by the security scanner application.	
Function (internal)	of_SetControlArray	Scans the control array and sets the security on the controls. Used internally by the secure process.	
Function (internal)	of_SetControlStatus	Sets the control properties as specified in the database security tables. Used internally by the secure process.	
Function (internal)	of_SetMenuStatus	Sets the menu properties as specified in the database security tables. Used internally by the secure process.	

TABLE 7.7   pfc_n_cst_security Events and Functions (*Continued*)

Function (service control)	of_SetSecurity	Secures the window as specified in the database security tables.
Function (internal)	of_SetState	Sets the control's enabled and visible properties. Used internally by the secure process.

If a separate security database is used, a different transaction object should be substituted for SQLCA. The transaction must be successfully connected prior to the of_InitSecurity call.

Securing a window.   The function to secure any window was intentionally made very simple to use. All it needs is a reference to the window. It returns a boolean success/failure indicator. It is typically called from the window open event.

```
IF Not gnv_app.inv_security.of_SetSecurity(this) THEN
        gnv_app.inv_error.of_Message("security_fail")
        Post Event pfc_close()
END IF
```

Note: of_SetSecurity may fail if none of the controls on the window is secured. To prevent that, set at least one control to be enabled.

Transaction Registration

Overview

In a typical PowerBuilder application, a system global variable SQLCA is used as an application transaction. When more than one database connection is required, another global variable is declared, and it gets the job done. The transaction registration service provides an alternative to global variables. The main purpose of the service is to manage multiple transaction objects in an application. It provides the following features for the transactions of an n_tr or its descendant type:

- Ability to register the transaction object with the service
- Ability to access a registered transaction object by a logical name
- Ability to determine the total number of registered transactions
- Ability to obtain a list of all registered transaction objects
- Ability to determine if a specific transaction object has been registered

Instead of declaring a global variable, it is possible to register the transaction with the service and give it a logical name. This name can be used later to gain access to the registered transaction. The first benefit of a transaction name is that it is self-documenting. The name, such as "accounting" or "inventory," can describe the purpose of the transaction. The second and more important benefit is that a transaction name, in conjunction with the registration service, provides a layer of abstraction. The fact that a transaction is always referenced by its alias makes it easier to implement operational polymorphism. This technique allows the runtime substitution of objects with the same interface but different functionality. Substitution of any transaction with the same name is completely transparent to the rest of the system.

Events/functions

Table 7.8 shows the events and functions in the PFC transaction registration service.

Usage

The transaction registration is one of the easier services to use. The transaction is registered and then assigned a name. The order is not important.

gnv_app.of_SetTrregistration(TRUE)

TABLE 7.8   pfc_n_cst_trregistration Events and Functions

Object name	pfc_n_cst_trregistration	Object type	Abstract service
Ancestry	nonvisualobject	Extension	n_cst_trregistration
Description	Transaction registration service user object.		
Usage	Used to create a pool of registered transaction objects.		
Reason for use	Reduce the number of global variables. Assign a logical transaction name.		
Layered extensions	Extend by insertion.		
Event (standard)	Constructor	Not used.	
Event (standard)	Destructor	Used by PFC to destroy all the created objects.	
Function (get)	of_GetByName	Gets a reference to the registered transaction with the specified name.	
Function (get)	of_GetCount	Returns the total number of registered transaction objects.	
Function (get)	of_GetRegistered	Returns all the registered transaction objects.	
Function (information)	of_IsRegistered	Determines if a transaction is registered.	
Function (service control)	of_Register	Registers the specified transaction object with the service.	
Function (service control)	of_Unregister	Unregisters the specified transaction object with the service.	

```
gnv_app.inv_trregistration.of_Register(ltr_oracle)
ltr_oracle.of_SetName("accounting")
ltr_sybase.of_SetName("inventory")
gnv_app.inv_trregistration.of_Register(ltr_sybase)
```

A reference to the specific transaction is provided by the of_GetByName function.

```
n_tr ltr_parts
IF gnv_app.inv_trregistration.of_IsRegistered("inventory") THEN
        gnv_app.inv_trregistration.of_GetByName("inventory", ltr_parts)
        dw_parts.of_SetTransObject(ltr_parts)
END IF
```

Having all the transactions in one place makes it possible to perform group operations. For example, one function could roll back every registered transaction.

```
n_tr ltr_obj[]
int i, li_TotalRegistered
li_TotalRegistered = gnv_app.inv_trregistration.of_GetRegistered(ltr_obj)
FOR i = 1 to li_TotalRegistered
        ltr_obj[i].of_rollback()
NEXT
```

Debugging

Overview

The PFC provides a lot of functionality, giving us a head start on the application design. Unfortunately, it shares one common trait with all the class libraries: It may be difficult to debug. The asynchronous nature of events does not work well with the debugger. Debugging any focus-related events has always been an unpleasant task. The debugger grabs the focus away from the application and may interfere with the event flow. Many functions and events are deeply nested or called recursively. Stepping through lines of code becomes much like surfing the Web: What you see is very interesting, but not at all what you were originally looking for.

The debug service addresses all of these issues. The debug service does not provide any features that extend the application functionality. Its sole purpose is to make the developer's life easier.

The debug service consists of two components, a nonvisual log, implemented with a DataStore, and a visual component to display the debug log. Messages can be added to the log and displayed independently. This feature can be used to debug the focus-sensitive events by adding the messages to the log and displaying them at a later time.

The debug service also contains properties that contain information about the current revision of the PFC library and the application build date and time.

Events/functions

Table 7.9 lists the events and functions in the PFC debug service.

Usage

The debug service is created as a service of the application manager. A separate function is provided to open the debug window. Destroying the debug service will automatically close the debug window.

```
// Enable the debug service
gnv_app.of_SetDebug(TRUE)
```

To add a debug message to the log, check to see if the debug service was enabled.

TABLE 7.9   pfc_n_cst_debug Events and Functions

Object name	pfc_n_cst_debug	Object type	Abstract service
Ancestry	nonvisualobject	Extension	n_cst_debug
Description	Debug service user object.		
Usage	Used to allow display and logging of the debug messages.		
Reason for Use	Use where the debugger is too intrusive or cumbersome.		
Layered extensions	Extend by insertion.		
Event (standard)	Constructor	Not used.	
Event (standard)	Destructor	Used by PFC to destroy all the created objects.	
Function (service control)	of_ClearLog	Clears all the messages from the log buffer.	
Function (service control)	of_GetAlwaysOnTop	Gets the current setting of the debug window position.	
Function (action)	of_Message	Adds a message to the log buffer.	
Function (action)	of_OpenLog	Opens or closes the debug window, which is used to display the log buffer.	
Function (action)	of_PrintLog	Prints the messages in the log buffer.	
Function (service control)	of_SetAlwaysOnTop	Specifies the debug window position.	
Function (service switch)	of_SetSqlSpy	Enables or disables the SQL Spy service.	

```
IF IsValid(gnv_app.inv_debug) THEN
        gnv_app.inv_debug.of_Message("Something really important")
END IF
```

To open the debug window:

```
IF IsValid(gnv_app.inv_debug) THEN
        gnv_app.inv_debug.of_OpenLog(True)
END IF
```

Logical Extensions

Application Manager. The application manager is a good place for functions requiring access from anywhere within the application. However, it may not be a good idea to have application manager become a placeholder for any global function. As a general rule, the extensions to the application manager should contain functionality related to the application. One example is the capability to determine if another instance of the same application is already running.*

Datawindow caching. A natural extension to the DataWindow cache service would be to allow the data to be shared automatically.

Debugging. Debug service is a good placeholder for the information about the current application revision. Additional instance variables may be added to contain the revision information.

PFC documentation recommends using the debug service only during development. There are a couple of different ways to eliminate the debug service calls from the production version of the application. The first one is to physically remove every call to the debug service; the second is to never instantiate the debug service in production code. An *IsValid()* function call should be added before each call to the debug service.

```
IF IsValid(gnv_app.inv_debug) THEN
        gnv_app.inv_debug.of_Message("Debugging PFC is a piece of cake")
END IF
```

Another method takes advantage of the "conditional compile" behavior of the IF statement:

```
IF FALSE THEN
        //...The code here will be optimized out by the compiler
END IF
```

---

*This example is outlined in Chap. 13.

This behavior remains the same when the "false" literal is replaced by a constant variable.

```
IF CON.IB_DEVELOPMENT THEN
        IF IsValid(gnv_app.inv_debug) THEN
                gnv_app.inv_debug.of_Message("Debugging PFC takes a lot of
                    typing")
        END IF
END IF
```

To make the debug calls easier, all of this code could be encapsulated in an n_cst_appmanager function:

```
public function integer of_DebugMsg (string as_debugmsg);

IF CON.IB_DEVELOPMENT THEN
        IF IsValid(inv_debug) THEN
                return inv_debug.of_Message(as_debugmsg)
        ELSE
                return -1
        END IF
END IF
return 1
```

To add a debug message to the log from anywhere in the application, use

```
gnv_app.of_DebugMsg("Now that's much better!")
```

Error. One idea for the error service extension comes from a typo in the PFC documentation, that is, the ability to log the errors to a database. That would be a welcome feature, and it is not that difficult to implement by extending the of_ProcessLog function.

A second extension is to allow two error messages, one intended for the user and a second, more technical, message intended for the developer. The service can be toggled between the user and the developer message mode. A variation of the same theme is to provide a short and a long message. The user would see a short description of the error and then would press the More button to see a detailed error message.

There is often a need to display multiple messages in a single window. Consider an example of the save cycle validation process. There could be a number of different validation rules on a single window. Seeing multiple validation error messages one after another can wear a little thin. One solution is to display only one failure message for each save attempt. When the error is resolved and the save is initiated again, the next error is displayed. Another solution is to extend the error service and provide a function to add messages to a queue and another function to display all the messages in a queue.

Transaction registration. Any function that allows common processing for all the registered transactions is a good extension candidate. Setting the "rollback on disconnect" property for all the transactions is one such example.

Security. The security definitions provided by the security service are static. The windows are secured on a class level. All the instances of the window share the same security definition. Often there is a need to enable or disable controls based on dynamic conditions. One such example is a requirement to disable the Save menu item when there is nothing to save and to enable it when the data on the window was changed. This requirement is easy to implement, but it necessitates manipulation of the menu item properties. If the window is secured when it's first opened, any manipulation of the secured properties may inadvertently override the security setting for the control. In the above example, a user may not have been granted the rights to save, and so the Save menu item was disabled by the security service. Enabling the Save menu item in this case would override the database security setting and defeat the purpose of the security service.

One solution to the problem above would be to extend the security service to allow a check to verify that a change in the visible/enabled properties is allowed by the security. Before any manipulation of these properties, this function would be called to "ask permission" for the change in the control status. Another way to solve this problem is to avoid the manipulation of enabled and visible properties. Instead, enable, disable, show, and hide functions may be added to the security service. When there is a need to dynamically change the control status, the appropriate function on the security service would be called, accepting the control as an argument. The function would check whether any security was assigned to the control, resolve any potential conflicts, decide whether the request should be allowed, and enable or disable the control itself.

Summary/Conclusions

All of the application services play an integral part in any PFC-based design, but some are more important than others. One advantage of the service-based architecture is that you do not have to know every detail of each service to become productive and begin integrating PFC in your next application. On the other hand, few of the services are crucial to the success of any PFC-based project. Application manager and error services fall into the "more important" category. Application manager is at the center of any application. The error service encourages good programming practices and should be a part of the application standards. It is also very difficult to implement afterwards. If you are new to PFC, become proficient with these services first. DataWindow cache, transaction registration, security, and debugging services each offer very valuable features, but do not require in-depth knowledge up front.

8

Window Services

Introduction

The PFC provides many services which may be used in your application. This chapter will discuss the window services of the PFC. Window services provide functionality for managing window objects within the application. These services include centering, preferences processing, sheet management, and status bar processing, among many others. Window services are implemented within the PFC window hierarchy from which most of your applications windows will be inherited.

Chapter Objectives

In this chapter you will gain an understanding of the structure of the window services objects and the functionality they will provide.
Objectives for this chapter include the following:

- Explain the structure of window services.
- Discuss the functions provided by the window services.
- Learn how to use window services in your application.

Window Services

The window services included in PFC are:

- Menu service
- Resize service
- Base window service

TABLE 8.1   Base Class for Window Services

Object name	pfc_n_cst_winsrv	Object type	Abstract service
Ancestry	nonvisualobject	Extension	n_cst_winsrv
Description	Window base service user object.		
Usage	Created as an instance service for a window.		
Reason for use	Provides basic window services.		
Layered extensions	Extend by inheritance and/or insertion.		
Function (action)	of_Center	Centers the window relative to the dimensions of the current display resolution.	
Function (set)	of_SetRequestor	Associates a window with this service.	

- Preference service
- Status bar service

Base window services

The base window services are implemented in the object pfc_n_cst_winsrv and via window functions (Table 8.1).

PFC window services include automatic closequery processing for all DataWindows in a window. This processing saves all pending changes if the user clicks Yes in the Save Changes dialog box. If you want to implement application-specific save processing, override the closequery event in your application's windows. (To do this globally, override closequery in w_master or disable closequery processing by setting the w_master ib_disableclosequery instance variable to TRUE.)

The closequery process uses the same functions and events as save processing. In these processes, the control array of the window is searched, looking for DataWindows or any control that can contain a DataWindow, such as a tab control. All DataWindows on the window will be processed unless the DataWindow is disabled via the of_SetupDataBale(FALSE) function.

Basic PFC window functionality includes:

- Message router and menu integration
- Empty user events, which are triggered by PFC menu items
- Toolbar control (w_frame only)
- Automatic database save
- Centering a window on the screen

Message router

The message router is designed so that it can be called from menus or scripts. To invoke the message router, use the of_SendMessage("event_name") function from a menu or call the active window's pfc_messagerouter user event, passing the user event to be called: this.Event pfc_messagerouter("event_name")

The message router will sent the message to the active window. If the event is not found, the message will be sent to the control that has focus, and if that control does not contain the event, the message will be sent to the last active DataWindow control.

Window-centering service

One of the services provided by the base window service is the ability to center a window on the screen.

To center a window on the screen,

- Enable the base window service:

  this.of_SetBase(TRUE)

- Call the n_cst_winsrv of_Center function:

  this.inv_base.of_Center( )

You might use the window-centering service to center dialog windows regardless of screen resolution.

Preference service

The preference service is implemented via the n_cst_winsrv_preference user object (Table 8.2).

The PFC preference service provides functions that save and restore a user's window settings using either the registry or an INI file. The preference service can be configured to save

- ToolBarVisible
- ToolBarAlignment
- ToolBarItemOrder
- Toolbar size (ToolbarHeight and ToolbarWidth)
- Toolbar position (ToolbarX and ToolbarY)
- Window size (height and width)
- Window state
- Window position (X and Y)
- Menu item attributes

The service provides functions allowing you to control which parameters are saved.

TABLE 8.2   The Window Preferences Service Class

Object name	pfc_n_cst_winsrv_preference	Object type	Abstract service
Ancestry	nonvisualobject	Extension	n_cst_winsrv_preference

Description	Window preference service user object.
Usage	Created as an instance service for a window.
Reason for use	To save and restore window settings from an INI file or the registry.
Layered extensions	Extend by inheritance and/or insertion.

Function (get)	of_GetMenuItems	Reports if the service is to restore the attributes on the menu items.
Function (get)	of_GetToolbarItemOrder	Reports if the service is to restore the order attributes on the toolbar item order.
Function (get)	of_GetToolbarItemSpace	Reports if the service is to restore the Space attribute on the menu items.
Function (get)	of_GetToolbarItemVisible	Reports if the service is to restore the ToolbarItemVisible attribute on the menu items.
Function (get)	of_GetToolbars	Reports if the service is to restore the toolbar attributes.
Function (get)	of_GetToolbarTitles	Reports if the service is to restore the toolbar titles.
Function (get)	of_GetWindow	Reports if the service is to restore the window attributes.
Function (internal)	of_Restore	Restores the preference information either from the Registry or from an .INI file.
Function (internal)	of_RestoreMenu	Recursively restores all menu items from either the registry or an INI file. If a desired value is not found, then the current value found on the menu is left as it is.
Function (internal)	of_RestorePositiveNumber	Performs a get to the registry or to an .INI file. It then checks and reports if it got a valid positive number.
Function (internal)	of_Save	Saves the preference information either to the registry or to an .INI file.
Function (internal)	of_SaveMenu	Recursively saves all menu items that have pictures into the registry. Function will continue to save even if an error is found.
Function (set)	of_SetMenuItems	Tells the service to restore or not to restore the attributes on the menu items.
Function (set)	of_SetPosSize	Store in the service the current position and size of requestor. This is needed so that the service knows the normal size of the requestor even when the requestor is closed as maximized/minimized. *Note:* This function should be called from the resize and move events. It should be called only when the WindowState is of type Normal!.

TABLE 8.2   The Window Preferences Service Class (*Continued*)

Function (set)	of_SetToolbarItemOrder	Tells the service to restore or not to restore the ToolbarItemOrder attribute on the menu items.
Function (set)	of_SetToolbarItemSpace	Tells the service to restore or not to restore the ToolbarItemSpace attribute on the menu items.
Function (set)	of_SetToolbarItemVisible	Tells the service to restore or not to restore the ToolbarItemVisible attribute on the menu items.
Function (set)	of_SetToolbars	Tells the service to restore or not to restore the attributes from the toolbars.
Function (set)	of_SetToolbarTitles	Tells the service to restore or not to restore the toolbar titles.
Function (set)	of_SetWindow	Tells the service to restore or not to restore the window attributes.

Using this service allows an application to store a window's size and position along with its menu and toolbar attributes so that they may be restored to the saved positions when the application is run again.

Tip: Windows descended from w_master save and restore settings automatically *if* the service is enabled.

To enable the window preference service, call the w_master of_SetPreference function. This function is available in all windows developed with PFC (w_master is the ancestor of all PFC windows):

```
this.of_SetPreference(TRUE)
```

The PFC destroys the service automatically when the window closes. The preference service should be enabled in the pfc_preopen event before the window's open event. The open event contains code to restore the window settings if the preference service is enabled.

To configure the preference service for what attributes are saved, call the appropriate of_Setxxx function. Table 8.3 lists these functions.

To save current window settings, call the of_Save function.

```
Integer li_return
li_return = this.inv_preference.of_Save (gnv_app.of_GetUserINIFile( ),
"WindowSettings")
IF li_return = –1 THEN
        MessageBox("Settings", "Unable to save window settings")
END IF
```

TABLE 8.3   **Preference Service Functions**

of_SaveMenu	Saves menu items.
of_SetMenuItems	Specifies if the service restores menu items.
of_SetPosSize	Saves the current window position and size.
of_SetToolbarItemOrder	Specifies if the service restores toolbar item order.
of_SetToolbarItemSpace	Specifies whether the service restores the ToolbarItemSpace property.
of_SetToolbarItemVisible	Specifies whether the service restores the ToolbarItemVisible property.
of_SetToolbars	Specifies whether the service restores toolbars.
of_SetToolbarTitles	Specifies whether the service restores toolbar titles.
of_SetWindow	Specifies whether the service restores window properties.

This code would be placed in the windows close event.

To restore current window settings from an INI file, call the of_Restore function. This example restores the window settings that were saved:

```
Integer li_return
li_return = this.inv_preference.of_Restore
(gnv_app.of_GetUserINIFile(),"WindowSettings")
IF li_return = –1 THEN
      MessageBox("Settings", "Unable to restore window settings")
END IF
```

The above code already exists in the window open event and should be used only when there is need to restore the window settings after the open event.

Sheet management service

The PFC sheet management service provides functions that help you manage multiple sheets in an MDI application. PFC enables the sheet management service through the n_cst_winsrv_sheetmanager user object (Table 8.4).

To enable the window sheet management service, call the w_frame of_SetSheetManager function. This function is available in all windows that descend from w_frame.

```
this.of_SetSheetManager(TRUE)
```

The PFC destroys the service automatically when the frame window closes. The example below closes all the sheets of a w_employee_maint class.

```
w_sheet lw_employee[]
w_frame lw_frame
int li_idx, li_TotalSheets
```

TABLE 8.4   Window Sheet Manager Service Class

Object name	pfc_n_cst_winsrv_sheetmanager	Object type	Abstract service
Ancestry	nonvisualobject	Extension	n_cst_winsrv_sheetmanager

Description	Window sheet manager service user object.	
Usage	Created as an instance service for a window.	
Reason for use	To manage multiple sheets in an MDI application.	
Layered extensions	Extend by inheritance and/or insertion.	

Function (get)	of_GetCurrentState	Gets the current arrange state of open windows.
Function (get)	of_GetSheetCount	Returns sheet count for frame requestor.
Function (get)	of_GetSheets	Gets reference to all open sheets.
Function (get)	of_GetSheetsByClass	Gets reference to all open sheets with class name specified.
Function (get)	of_GetSheetsByTitle	Gets reference to all open sheets with title specified.
Function (set)	of_SetCurrentState	Sets the current arrange type of the sheets to allow for undo.
Function (set)	of_SetRequestor	Associates a frame window with this service.
Event (precoded)	Constructor	Sets arrange state to null.
Event (precoded)	pfc_cascade	Cascades sheets.
Event (precoded)	pfc_layer	Layers sheets.
Event (precoded)	pfc_minimizeall	Minimizes all open sheets.
Event (precoded)	pfc_tilehorizontal	Tiles horizontally.
Event (precoded)	pfc_tilevertical	Tiles vertically.
Event (precoded)	pfc_undoarrange	Undoes last arrange.

```
lw_frame = gnv_app.of_GetFrame()
li_TotalSheets = lw_frame.inv_sheetmanager.of_GetSheetsByClass(lw_employee)
FOR li_idx = 1 TO li_TotalSheets
        lw_employee[li_idx].Post Event pfc_close()
NEXT
```

Status bar service

The PFC status bar service displays date, time, memory information, and other user-specified text in the lower right corner of an MDI frame window.

PFC enables the status bar service through the n_cst_winsrv_statusbar user object. Status bar information displays in the w_statusbar pop-up window (Table 8.5).

You call n_cst_winsrv_statusbar functions to control the items displayed.

To enable the window status bar service, call the w_frame of_SetStatusBar function.

TABLE 8.5   Windows Status Bar Service Class

Object name	pfc_n_cst_winsrv_statusbar	Object type	Abstract service
Ancestry	nonvisualobject	Extension	n_cst_winsrv_statusbar

Description	Window status bar service user object.
Usage	Created as an instance service for a frame window.
Reason for use	To manage the status bar.
Layered extensions	Extend by inheritance and/or insertion.

Function (internal)	of_CalculateMicroHelpHeight	Calculates MicroHelp height.
Function (set)	of_CreatedWObject	Builds and validates the string used to create the actual visual status bar.
Function (get)	of_GetBorderType	Gets the default border type for any object created.
Function (get)	of_GetGapWidth	Gets the default gap width for any object created. The gap width is the spacing between the previous object created and the next object created.
Function (get)	of_GetGDI	Reports TRUE if GDI memory is being reported; otherwise FALSE.
Function (get)	of_GetGDIThreshold	Gets the current GDI memory threshold value.
Function (get)	of_GetMem	Reports TRUE if computer memory is being reported; otherwise FALSE.
Function (get)	of_GetMemThreshold	Gets the current computer memory threshold value.
Function (get)	of_GetRefreshRate	Gets the current refresh rate.
Function (get)	of_GetTimer	Reports TRUE if a timer is being reported; otherwise FALSE.
Function (get)	of_GetUser	Reports TRUE if user memory is being reported; otherwise FALSE.
Function (get)	of_GetUserThreshold	Gets the current user memory threshold value.
Function (internal)	of_IsPredefined	Determines if the passed ID is a predefined ID.
Function (set)	of_Modify	Modifies the value of the user-defined object. The object can be either a text value or a bitmap name.
Function (action)	of_Open	Opens an instance of w_statusbar window. Sets the desired refresh rate. Makes sure focus stays on the frame window.
Function (set)	of_Register	Registers a new object to be displayed on the GUI status bar.
Function (internal)	of_RegisterPredefined	Registers a predefined object to be displayed on the GUI status bar.
Function (set)	of_SetBorderType	Sets the default border type for any *future* object.
Function (set)	of_SetGapWidth	Set the default gap width for any *future* object.
Function (set)	of_SetMem	Sets the flag to indicate if computer memory is to be reported on the status bar.
Function (set)	of_SetMemThreshold	Sets a new computer memory threshold value.

TABLE 8.5   Windows Status Bar Service Class (*Continued*)

Function (set)	of_SetMemWidth	Sets a new computer memory width value.
Function (set)	of_SetRefreshRate	Sets a new refresh rate for the GUI status bar.
Function (set)	of_SetTimer	Sets the flag to indicate if a timer is to be displayed on the status bar.
Function (set)	of_SetTimerFormat	Sets the new format to be used on a timer object.
Function (set)	of_SetTimerInterval	Sets the new timer interval to be used in updating the timer object (if any has been requested or is later requested).
Function (set)	of_SetTimerWidth	Sets a new timer width value.
Function (set)	of_SetUser	Sets flag to display user memory.
Function (set)	of_SetUserThreshold	Sets a new user memory threshold value.
Function (set)	of_SetUserWidth	Sets a new user memory width value.
Function (set)	of_Unregister	Unregisters the desired user-defined object.
Function (set)	of_UnregisterPredefined	Unregisters the desired predefined object.
Event (precoded)	Constructor	Gets system environment.
Event (precoded)	pfc_move	Notifies status bar window that the frame has moved. *Note:* This causes the w_statusbar window to be resized/moved to its parent's new size/position.
Event (precoded)	pfc_resize	Notify status bar window that the frame has resized. *Note:* This causes the w_statusbar window to be resized/moved to its parent's new size/position.
Event (precoded)	pfc_statusbarclick	A click has occurred on the status bar. *Note:* This event can be used to take some action when the user performs the action on the status bar.
Event (precoded)	pfc_statusbardoubleclick	A doubleclick has occurred on the status bar. *Note:* This event can be used to take some action when the user performs the action on the status bar.
Event (precoded)	pfc_statusbarrbuttonup	A right button up has occurred on the status bar. *Note:* This event can be used to take some action when the user performs the action on the status bar.

```
this.of_SetStatusBar(TRUE)
```

This function is available in all windows that descend from w_frame. PFC destroys the service automatically when the frame window closes. The status bar service is enabled by default. It is set to display the time. The code below will configure the service to display free memory instead:

```
inv_statusbar.of_SetTimer(FALSE)
inv_statusbar.of_SetMem(TRUE)
```

In addition to displaying time and free memory, the status bar service can be used to display a custom status object, containing text or a bitmap. The status bar service also contains several events which are fired when a user interacts with the displayed objects. This feature can be used to display status or to set applicationwide options. Some of the possible uses of this feature are

- Save progress indicator
- Database connection indicator
- User ID
- User security access indicator
- Debug service control
- SQL debug control

The example below illustrates the use of the status bar service to toggle the debug service and to open the debug log window. First, in the w_frame open event, two bitmaps are registered with the service:

```
string ls_picture
IF IsValid(inv_statusbar) THEN
        IF IsValid(gnv_app.inv_debug) THEN
                ls_picture = "bug_no.bmp"
        ELSE
                ls_picture = "bug_yes.bmp"
        END IF
        inv_statusbar.of_Register("debug", "bitmap", ls_picture, 75)

        IF IsValid(w_debuglog) THEN
                ls_picture = "foldopen.bmp"
        ELSE
                ls_picture = "folder.bmp"
        END IF
        inv_statusbar.of_Register("debuglog", "bitmap", ls_picture, 75)
END IF
```

To modify the status bar pictures, open and close events of w_debuglog and of_setdebug in n_cst_appmanager are extended.

w_debuglog close event

```
w_frame lw_frame
lw_frame = gnv_app.of_GetFrame()
IF IsValid(lw_frame.inv_statusbar) THEN
        lw_frame.inv_statusbar.of_Modify("debuglog", "folder.bmp")
END IF
```

w_debuglog open event

```
w_frame lw_frame
lw_frame = gnv_app.of_GetFrame()
IF IsValid(lw_frame.inv_statusbar) THEN
        lw_frame.inv_statusbar.of_Modify("debuglog", "foldopen.bmp")
END IF
```

n_cst_appmanager of_SetDebug

```
int li_rtc
w_frame lw_frame

li_rtc = Super::of_SetDebug(ab_switch)

IF li_rtc <> 1 THEN return li_rtc

lw_frame = of_GetFrame()
IF IsValid(lw_frame) THEN
        IF IsValid(lw_frame.inv_statusbar) THEN
                string ls_picture
                IF IsValid(gnv_app.inv_debug) THEN
                        ls_picture = "bug_no.bmp"
                ELSE
                ls_picture = "bug_yes.bmp"
                END IF
                lw_frame.inv_statusbar.of_Modify("debug", ls_picture)
        END IF
END IF
return li_rtc
```

Resize service

The PFC resize service provides functions that automatically move and resize controls when the user resizes a window or tab. This service allows you to control how and whether controls resize when the window or tab resizes.

PFC enables the resize service through the n_cst_resize user object (Table 8.6). Use this service to control window resizing.

To enable the resize service, call the w_master or u_tab of_SetResize function:

```
this.of_SetResize(TRUE)
```

PFC destroys the service automatically when the window or tab closes. To register resizable controls, call

```
this.inv_resize.of_Register(control, <resize method>)
```

The values of the resize method and their effect are described in Table 8.7.

TABLE 8.6   **Window Resize Service Class**

Object name	pfc_n_cst_resize	Object type	Abstract service
Ancestry	nonvisualobject	Extension	n_cst_resize

Description	Window resize service user object.
Usage	Created as an instance service for a window.
Reason for use	To manage the controls on a window.
Layered extensions	Extend by inheritance and/or insertion.

Function (get)	of_GetMinMaxPoints	Determines the four extreme points of the controls within a control array by looking at the X, Y, Width, Height, BeginX, BeginY, EndX, and EndY attributes.
Function (set)	of_Register	Registers a control which needs to be either moved or resized when the parent object is resized. The action taken on this control depends on the four attributes ab_movex, ab_movey, ab_scalewidth, and b_scaleheight. *Note:* The service object needs to be initialized (of_SetOrigSize()) prior to any registering (this function) of objects.
Function (internal)	of_Resize	Moves or resizes objects that were registered with the service. Performs the actions that were requested via the of_SetOrigSize() and of_Register() functions.
Function (set)	of_SetMinSize	Sets the current object minimum size attributes. *Note:* If the window was resized prior to the service's being enabled, the service object needs to be initialized (of_SetOrigSize()) before setting the minimum size of the object.
Function (get)	of_SetOrigSize	Initializes the resize object by setting the current object size. *Note:* If the window was resized prior to the service's being enabled, the service object needs to be initialized (this function) before the registering (of_register()) of objects.
Function (internal)	of_TypeOf	Determines the type of an object for the purpose of getting to its attributes.
Function (set)	of_Unregister	Unregisters a control that was previously registered.
Event (precoded)	pfc_resize	Executes the of_Resize() function.

The resize service also allows you to set the minimum size for each control, beyond which the control is no longer resized.

When the resize service is enabled, it takes a snapshot of the current window size and the current size and position of each control. When each control is reg-

TABLE 8.7   Options Used in the Resize Service

FixedToRight	Control is moved, keeping the original distance to the right edge.
FixedToBottom	Control is moved, keeping the original distance to the bottom edge.
FixedToRight&Bottom	Control is moved, keeping the original distance to the right and bottom edges.
Scale	Control is resized in proportion to the window.
ScaleToRight	Control is resized, keeping the original distance to the right edge.
ScaleToBottom	Control is resized, keeping the original distance to the bottom edge.
ScaleToRight&Bottom	Control is resized, keeping the original distance to the right and bottom edges.
FixedToRight&ScaleToBottom	Control is moved, keeping the original distance to the right edge. Control is resized, keeping the original distance to the bottom edge.
FixedToBottom&ScaleToRight	Control is moved, keeping the original distance to the bottom edge. Control is resized, keeping the original distance to the right edge.

istered with the of_Register function, the resize service takes a snapshot of the size and position of that control. It later uses these original values to properly resize/move the controls when the window is resized. The resize service will not work properly if the window is resized before the resize service is enabled. In this case, the resize service will store an erroneous original window size. This may occur when the window is opened in a mode other than original! or if the preference service restores the window size before the resize service is enabled. To resolve this problem, one of two solutions should be used.

1. When both resize and preference services are used, the resize service needs to be enabled and configured before the preference service resizes the window.

2. If the window was resized before the resize service is enabled, of_SetOrigSize must be used to set the original window size before the controls are registered. Often it is difficult to dynamically derive the window's original size. If a window was opened in layered! mode, it is resized before any window event fires.

Summary

As can be seen, window services provide a variety of capabilities for the management of windows. Windows may be centered in the workspace, selected controls automatically resized, and MDI sheets managed. Using the PFC window services will greatly reduce the amount of tedious code we often write to manage our applications' windows.

PFC DataWindow Services

Introduction

The DataWindow is the most important object in PowerBuilder and is the object that most developers will use to interface with the database in most applications. Because of this importance, it is easy to see why a major portion of the PFC concentrates on the DataWindow and its services. Much of the DataWindow behavior provided by the PFC was implemented in previous PowerBuilder frameworks in many ways, without much consistency. The major difference now is that the PFC has implemented additional DataWindow behavior as services that are requested by the client DataWindow control. The intent of this chapter is to describe how the DataWindow object is set up, what services are available to it, how and when to instantiate the services, how the developer should utilize the DataWindow object, and how and when the DataWindow object and service objects should be extended. Finally, after all the services have been explained, we will show you how implement some of the services by referencing the GSI TimeMaster application, included on the CD.

Chapter Objectives

This chapter will teach the reader to

- Understand how to use the DataWindow standard visual user object provided in the PFC.

- Understand the different DataWindow services provided in the PFC.

- Understand how to use the different DataWindow services in the PFC.

- Extend the DataWindow standard visual user object in the PFC.

- Extend the different DataWindow services in the PFC.

- Understand how some of the services are used in an application like the GSI TimeMaster application.

Ancestry

pfc_u_dw is the ancestor visual user object for all DataWindow controls in applications written using the PFC. This DataWindow user object includes

- Functions to enable and disable DataWindow services
- Events that automatically make use of enabled DataWindow services
- Precoded user events that provide basic editing functionality
- Template user events to which you can add application-specific functionality

The DataWindow control has been subclassed in the PFC as a standard visual user object, pfc_u_dw. The object is further subclassed to u_dw, which is in the PFC extension layer. Figure 9.1 shows the DataWindow control hierarchy.

Usage

Instances of the DataWindow user object can be placed on the surface of a window or custom user object instead of the standard DataWindow control. To do this, the following is done:

1. Place a u_dw user object on your window. This is done as follows:
    - Select the user object control from the control drop-down button on the toolbar or select Controls =>UserObject from the menu.
    - Find u_dw in the PFEMAIN PBL (remember to always use the PFE-layer PBL).
    - Click the OK button.
2. In the DataWindow constructor event (or some other appropriate place), enable DataWindow services, as needed by your application.
3. Add application-specific functionality, as needed.

Instance Variables

Table 9.1 lists and describes in general the different instance variables that are defined in pfc_u_dw. Some of the instance variables are used as pointers for ser-

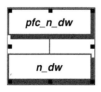

Figure 9.1 The DataWindow control hierarchy.

TABLE 9.1   pfc_u_dw Instance Variables

Instance variable	Type	Scope	Description (from the *PowerBuilder Online Books*)
ib_isupdateable	Boolean	Protected	Indicates whether the DataWindow can be updated.
ib_rmbmenu	Boolean	Protected	Controls whether the m_dw menu displays when the user presses the right mouse button over the DataWindow control.
ib_rmbfocuschange	Boolean	Protected	Used to track focus change while the right mouse button is down.
inv_base	n_cst_dwsrv	Public	Reference variable for basic DataWindow services.
inv_dropdownsearch	n_cst_dwsrv_dropdownsearch	Public	Reference variable for the drop-down DataWindow search service.
inv_filter	n_cst_dwsrv_filter	Public	Reference variable for the DataWindow filter service.
inv_find	n_cst_dwsrv_find	Public	Reference variable for the DataWindow find service.
inv_linkage	n_cst_dwsrv_linkage	Public	Reference variable for the DataWindow linkage service.
inv_multitable	n_cst_dwsrv_multitable	Public	Reference variable for the DataWindow multitable update service.
inv_printpreview	n_cst_dwsrv_printpreview	Public	Reference variable for the DataWindow print preview service.
inv_querymode	n_cst_dwsrv_querymode	Public	Reference variable for the query-mode service.
inv_report	n_cst_dwsrv_report	Public	Reference variable for the reporting service.
inv_reqcolumn	n_cst_dwsrv_reqcolumn	Public	Reference variable for the required service.
inv_rowmanager	n_cst_dwsrv_rowmanager	Public	Reference variable for the row manager service.
inv_rowselect	n_cst_dwsrv_rowselection	Public	Reference variable for the rowselection service.
inv_sort	n_cst_dwsrv_sort	Public	Reference variable for the sort service.
itr_object	n_tr	Public	Reference variable for the transaction object.

vices that can be instantiated. An example of this is the PFC sorting service, n_cst_dwsrv_sort. The instance variable inv_Sort is used as a pointer to the instantiated sorting service of type n_cst_dwsrv_sort. You can find more information on the different pfc_u_dw instance variables in the *PowerBuilder Online Books* and in the PFC on-line help.

Events

There are many precoded and template events in the user object pfc_u_dw, both in the standard DataWindow control events and in those events that have been added by the PFC in the pfc_u_dw object. Precoded events in pfc_u_dw have extensive precoded functionality. This means that when a specific PFC DataWindow service is enabled, pfc_u_dw detects the enabled service and performs the processing defined in the precoded events. An example of a precoded event is the rowfocuschanged event, which calls certain DataWindow service functions if they are enabled. Template user events are provided to you so that you can add application-specific functionality. An example of this type of event is the pfc_retrieve event. It is used as the event in which to place all retrieval code for the DataWindow.

Examples of how to use some of these events will be shown as appropriate when showing how to implement the different DataWindow services. Table 9.2 lists and describes the different precoded events that are defined in pfc_u_dw. You can find more information on the different pfc_u_dw precoded events in the *PowerBuilder Online Books* and in the PFC on-line help.

Table 9.3 lists and describes the different template events that are defined in pfc_u_dw. You can find more information on the different pfc_u_dw template events in the *PowerBuilder Online Books* and in the PFC on-line help.

Functions

There are many precoded object functions to control DataWindow services. Table 9.4 lists and describes the different precoded functions that are defined in pfc_u_dw. You can find more information on the different pfc_u_dw functions in the *PowerBuilder Online Books* and in the PFC on-line help.

Where to Place the Code

Where to place PFC code is an interesting question, and one that is especially interesting when dealing with DataWindows. In fact, we can cut the question several different ways: in which *event,* in which *object,* and in which *layer* do we place our code? And our choices in cases in which the PFC object spans a number of objects (e.g., multiple DataWindows participating in the DataWindow linkage service) are some of the most complex. While there are no hard and fast rules, there are some guidelines we can share.

Which event?

The constructor event is our favorite for the instantiation of all the simple DataWindow services—that is, those services that do not involve any other objects (e.g., row manager and sort). There are a number of advantages to this strategy. The first is that DataWindow controls may be added and removed without fear of redoing scripts in other events (for example, upon removing a DataWindow that had a number of services instantiated in the *open* event of the

TABLE 9.2   pfc_u_dw Precoded Events

Precoded event	Description (from the *PowerBuilder Online Books*)
clicked	Calls DataWindow selection service and sort service functions, if enabled.
dberror	Displays a message box informing the user that a database error occurred.
destructor	Destroys all existing DataWindow service objects.
getfocus	Notifies the parent window so that it can track the current control.
itemerror	Calls the required column service; if enabled, it returns a 3, causing the DataWindow to accept the value.
itemfocuschanged	If MicroHelp is enabled for the application, this event calls the pfc_microhelp event on the parent.
buttondown	Calls the row selection service's pfc_lbuttondown event.
buttonup	Calls the row selection service's pfc_lbuttonup event.
pfc_addrow	Calls the row manager service to add a row at the end of the DataWindow.
pfc_clear	Deletes selected text.
pfc_copy	Copies selected text to the clipboard.
pfc_cut	Deletes selected text and stores it on the clipboard.
pfc_deleterow	Deletes either the current row or, if the row manager service is enabled, all selected rows. If the linkage service is enabled, this event calls that service's pfc_deleterow event.
pfc_descendant	PFC events and functions trigger this event to determine if the DataWindow control is inherited from u_dw.
pfc_filterdlg	Displays a Filter dialog box by calling the n_cst_dwsrv_filter service's pfc_filterdlg event.
pfc_finddlg	Displays a Find dialog box by calling the n_cst_dwsrv_find service's pfc_finddlg event.
pfc_firstpage	Scrolls to the first page of the DataWindow.
pfc_insertrow	Inserts a row just prior to the current row.
pfc_lastpage	Scrolls to the last page of the DataWindow.
pfc_nextpage	Scrolls to the next page of the DataWindow.
pfc_operators	Calls the n_cst_dwsrv_querymode pfc_operators event, which displays a w_selection dialog box containing operators.
pfc_pagesetup	Calls the pfc_pagesetupdlg event to display the Page Setup dialog box.
pfc_pagesetupdlg	Displays the Page Setup dialog box by calling the n_cst_platform of_PageSetupDlg function, passing the DataWindow's page display properties.
pfc_paste	Inserts (pastes) the contents of the clipboard at the insertion point.
pfc_previouspage	Scrolls to the previous page of the DataWindow.
pfc_print	Calls the pfc_PrintDlg function and prints the DataWindow, as specified in the Print dialog box.
pfc_printdlg	Initializes the s_printdlgattrib structure with the DataWindow's current settings, displays the Print dialog box by calling the n_cst_platform of_PrintDlg function, and resets the DataWindow's settings, as specified by the user.
pfc_printimmediate	Prints the current DataWindow without displaying the Print dialog box.

TABLE 9.2   pfc_u_dw Precoded Events (*Continued*)

Precoded event	Description (from the *PowerBuilder Online Books*)
pfc_printpreview	Toggles the DataWindow between preview and edit modes.
pfc_replacedlg	Displays a Replace dialog box by calling the n_cst_dwsrv_find service's pfc_replacedlg event.
pfc_restorerow	Calls the row manager pfc_restorerow event, which displays the w_undelete dialog box.
pfc_rowchanged	Calls the linkage service's pfc_RowFocusChanged function.
pfc_ruler	Toggles the DataWindow between displaying and hiding rulers in print preview mode.
pfc_selectall	Selects all text in the current DataWindow cell.
pfc_sortdlg	Displays a Sort dialog box by calling the n_cst_dwsrv_sort service's pfc_sortdlg event.
pfc_undo	Cancels the last edit to the DataWindow.
pfc_update	Updates the DataWindow. If the multitable update service is enabled, this event updates all specified tables.
pfc_updatespending	Determine if any updates are pending on this DataWindow.
pfc_validation	Calls of_CheckRequired to make sure all required fields have been entered if required services are turned on.
pfc_values	Calls the cst_dwsrv_querymode pfc_values event, which displays a w_selection dialog box containing a list of values.
pfc_zoom	Displays the w_zoom dialog box, allowing the user to control DataWindow display while in print preview mode.
rbuttondown	Calls the row selection service's pfc_rbuttondown event.
rbuttonup	Calls the row selection service's pfc_rbuttonup event.
rowfocuschanged	Used by the linkage service, if enabled, to coordinate scrolling among the linkage chain.
Sqlpreview	Calls SQL Spy functions, if enabled for the application.

TABLE 9.3   pfc_u_dw Template Events

Template event	Description (from the *PowerBuilder Online Books*)
pfc_debug	Empty user event allowing you to add code that displays the DataWindow debugger (w_dwdebugger).
pfc_prepagesetupdlg	Empty user event allowing you to modify the properties passed to the n_cst_platform of_PageSetupDlg function.
pfc_preprintdlg	Empty user event allowing you to modify the properties passed to the n_cst_platform of_PrintDlg function.
pfc_prermbmenu	Empty user event allowing you to modify m_dw contents prior to display.
pfc_retrieve	Empty user event to be called for all database retrieves.
pfc_retrievedddw	Empty user event to be called for all drop-down DataWindow retrieves.

TABLE 9.4   pfc_u_dw Functions

Function	Description (from the *PowerBuilder Online Books*)
of_CheckRequired	Determines if any required columns contain NULL values.
of_GetParentWindow	Returns a reference to the parent window.
of_GetUpdateable	Indicates whether the DataWindow is updatable and should be included in a window's default save processing.
of_SetBase	Enables or disables n_cst_dwsrv, which provides basic DataWindow services.
of_SetDropDownSearch	Enables or disables n_cst_dwsrv_dropdownsearch, which provides drop-down DataWindow search services.
of_SetFilter	Controls or destroys an instance of n_cst_dwsrv_filter, which provides filtering services.
of_SetFind	Enables or disables n_cst_dwsrv_find, which provides the DataWindow find service.
of_SetLinkage	Controls or destroys an instance of n_cst_dwsrv_linkage, which provides master/detail services.
of_SetMultitable	Controls or destroys an instance of n_cst_dwsrv_multitable, which provides multitable update services.
of_SetPrintPreview	Controls or destroys an instance of n_cst_dwsrv_printpreview, which provides the print preview service.
of_SetQueryMode	Controls or destroys an instance of n_cst_dwsrv_querymode, which provides querymode services.
of_SetReport	Controls or destroys an instance of n_cst_dwsrv_report, which provides reporting services.
of_SetReqColumn	Controls or destroys an instance of n_cst_dwsrv_reqcolumn, which provides DataWindow required-field services.
of_SetRowManager	Controls or destroys an instance of n_cst_dwsrv_rowmanager, which provides row management services.
of_SetRowSelect	Controls or destroys an instance of n_cst_dwsrv_rowselection, which provides row selection services.
of_SetSort	Controls or destroys an instance of n_cst_dwsrv_sort, which provides sorting services.
of_SetTransObject	Sets the transaction object for the DataWindow and initializes instance variables for use by DataWindow services.
of_SetUpdateable	Specifies whether the DataWindow is updatable and should be included in a window's default save processing.

window, the *open* script of the window would have to be modified). Second, one can exercise object-oriented practices (e.g., using the pronoun *this* to refer to the DataWindow control), emphasizing encapsulation—always an important factor when dealing with the PFC effectively. What about services, such as the linkage service, that affect multiple objects? This can be a bit more problematic when using the constructor event, as the order in which the constructor events are fired for multiple controls on a window depends on the order in which they have been dropped on the window. This is not a robust method when the existence of specific objects in a script is required (e.g., the detail DataWindow referencing the master DataWindow for a LinkTo relationship). To resolve this problem, one needs to be very careful when using the constructor event for multiple object services, or start looking at other objects (see the next section, "Which object?")

Which object?

Encapsulation is probably the most important tenet of object-oriented programming, at least where the PFC is concerned. So wherever and whenever possible, place the code in the object that is to exhibit the behavior. For DataWindow services, that almost always means placing the code in the DataWindow control u_dw. However, as pointed out above, things can get complicated when dealing with something like the linkage service. If you cannot stand having to be careful to drop your DataWindow controls in order (master first, detail second, etc.), you can place the multiple-object PFC code in the parent object of the objects that are related. In the case of the linkage service, that would probably be the window object or the tab page object. And in that parent object, you should place the code in the constructor event (e.g., open event or equivalent).

Which layer?

Most of the time you will place your code in the DataWindow control that you inherit from the empty u_dw object. However, placing code directly in the u_dw object of the PFE layer can help to maintain standards across a large number of developers or teams. For example, if DataWindows are always to have the row manager service functionality, then doing away with the burden (and ambiguity) of each developer's placing the code in his or her objects, by placing the *this.of_SetRowManager(TRUE)* call in the PFE layer is a sound move. Even if it is only 90 percent true, it is easier to destroy the service in 10 percent of the cases than to instantiate it in 90 percent.

Services

n_cst_dwsrv (base DataWindow service)

All DataWindow services are descendants of the custom class user object pfc_n_cst_dwsrv which provides basic DataWindow services. Figure 9.2 shows the DataWindow services hierarchy.

The functions in this user object are called to obtain basic information about a DataWindow object and its contents. This object should be used when you require basic DataWindow services only. If you are using any DataWindow services, you will have any n_cst_dwsrv functions available to use. pfc_u_dw instantiates this object as an instance variable, inv_Base.

If the service is instantiated as a descendant DataWindow service of

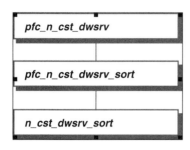

Figure 9.2 The DataWindow services hierarchy.

n_cst_dwsrv_base, the functions are accessed through the instantiated descendant service (e.g., n_cst_dwsrv_sort).

Enabling the service

Syntax

instancename.of_SetBase (boolean)

Argument	Description
instancename	Instance name of u_dw.
boolean	Boolean specifying whether to enable (TRUE) or disable (FALSE) basic DataWindow services.

The return value is an integer. The return is 1 if the function succeeds and -1 if an error occurs.

Example: In order to instantiate the service n_cst_dwsrv, the following function is called:

this.of_SetBase(TRUE)

Call base DataWindow service functions, as needed. Once the service has been instantiated, base DataWindow service functions can be called as needed. Table 9.5 lists and describes the functions available through this service.

As you can see, most of the above functions were written to eliminate the need to call more complicated PowerScript functions that require additional code to get the specific information needed. You can find more information on the different base DataWindow service functions in the *PowerBuilder Online Books* and in the PFC on-line help.

Two of my favorite base functions are the of_GetItem and of_GetObjects functions. To get a value from a DataWindow column, you must use DataWindow Powerscript functions such as GetItemString and GetItemNumber. You are responsible for calling the correct version of the DataWindow GetItem function. The of_GetItem function eliminates the need to figure out what DataWindow GetItem function to call. It will decide the data type of the column and call the correct Powerscript DataWindow GetItem function.

TABLE 9.5   **pfc_n_cst_dwsrv Functions**

Function	Description (from the *PowerBuilder Online Books*)
of_Describe	Describes DataWindow attributes. There are two ways: 1. Describe multiple columns or bands. 2. Describe a single column.
of_DWArguments	Determines DataWindow and drop-down DataWindow arguments. There are two ways: 1. Determine drop-down DataWindow arguments. 2. Determine DataWindow arguments.
of_GetColumnNameSource	Returns the column name source. n_cst_dwsrv maintains this as the ii_Source instance variable.
of_GetDefaultHeaderSuffix	Returns the default header suffix. n_cst_dwsrv maintains this as the ii_DefaultHeaderSuffix instance variable.
of_GetHeaderName	Returns a header name for the passed DataWindow column name.
of_GetHeight	Returns the height of the DataWindow object in the associated DataWindow control.
of_GetItem	Returns the formatted text of any DataWindow column, regardless of the column's data type. The returned text includes formats, edit masks, and display values, if any.
of_GetItemAny	Returns a column's value, cast to the Any data type.
of_GetObjects	Parses the list of objects contained in the associated DataWindow, placing their names into a string array passed by reference and returning the number of names in the array.
of_GetWidth	Retrieves the width (in the units specified for the DataWindow object) of the associated DataWindow.
of_Modify	Modifies DataWindow attributes. There are two ways: 1. Modify multiple columns or bands. 2. Modify a single column.
of_RefreshDDDWs	Determines if a DataWindow has any drop-down DataWindows and, if so, reretrieves drop-down DataWindow rows.
of_SetColumnNameSource	Specifies how Sort, Filter, and Querymode dialog boxes will display DataWindow column names.
of_SetDefaultHeaderSuffix	Specifies the default suffix that your application uses in DataWindow objects to designate headers. n_cst_dwsrv maintains this as the ii_DefaultHeaderSuffix instance variable.
of_SetItem	Returns the formatted text of any DataWindow column, regardless of the column's data type. The returned text includes formats, edit masks, and display values, if any.
of_SetRequestor	Associates a DataWindow service with a DataWindow control.

The of_GetObjects function parses the list of objects contained in the associated DataWindow, placing their names into a string array passed by reference and returning the number of names in the array. This is a nice way to get all the columns on a DataWindow so that you can loop through the array and modify the column attributes, such as the font, for example.

n_cst_dwsrv_dropdownsearch (drop-down search service)

The PFC drop-down DataWindow search service can add a very polished look to your application by providing a smart search capability for your drop-down DataWindows. This capability, like that of Windows 3.x Help and Quicken's check register, completes the field as the user types by searching the rows of the drop-down DataWindow for matches. As each match is found, the non-matching text is displayed and highlighted for the user and the drop-down DataWindow scrolls to that row (even if the drop-down DataWindow is not currently dropped). Figures 9.3 and 9.4 show the drop-down search service in action. In Fig. 9.3, the letter N was typed and New Jersey was found. In Fig. 9.4, typing is continued with the letter O and North Carolina was found.

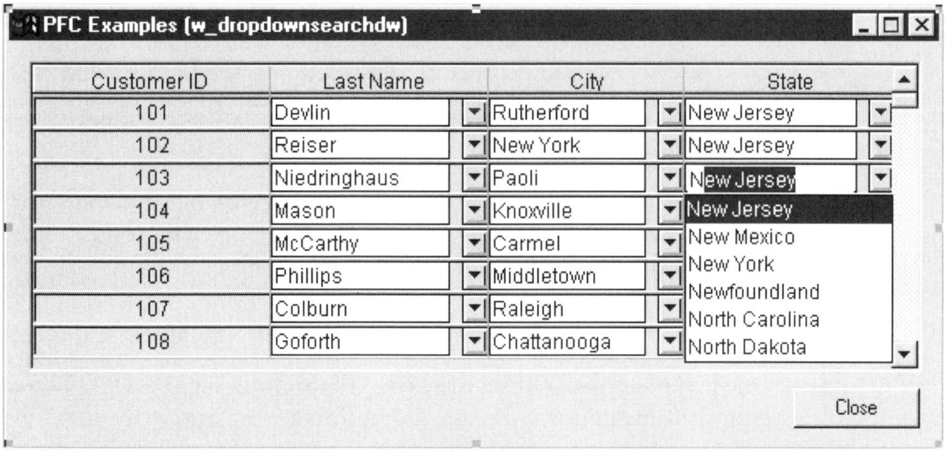

Figure 9.3 The drop-down search service—the letter N typed.

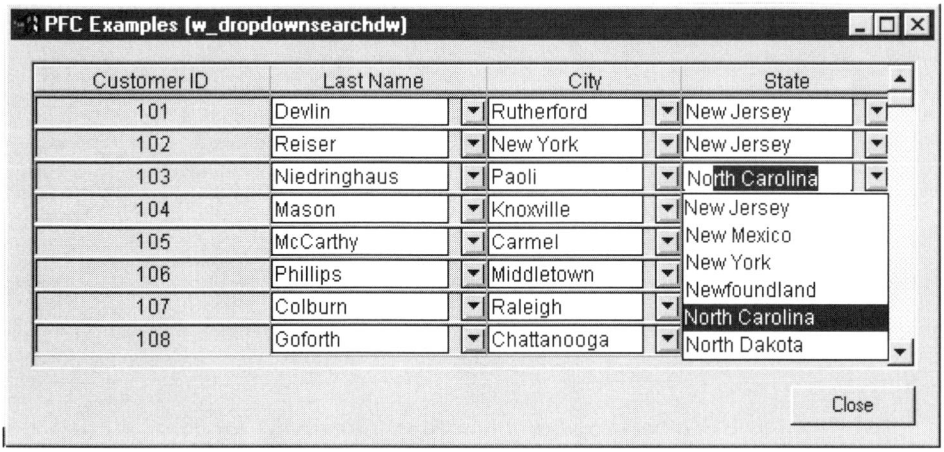

Figure 9.4 The drop-down search service—the letter N typed, then the letter O typed.

Enabling the service. Like many of the PFC DataWindow services, this service is a *set it and forget it* service, requiring only a couple of function calls to kick it off. However, unlike many of the other PFC services, this one requires you to add code in two of the u_dw events to redirect the event to this service. Why is this not already coded in the pfc_udw of the PFC? Probably because of the expense of these events (*editchanged* fires on every keystroke, and *itemfocuschanged* fires on changing item focus).

Syntax

dwcontrol.of_SetDropDownSearch (boolean)

Argument	Description
dwcontrol	Instance name of the u_dw DataWindow control.
boolean	Boolean specifying whether to enable (TRUE) or disable (FALSE) drop-down DataWindow search services. This service is automatically destroyed upon the destruction of the DataWindow control.

The return value is an integer. The return is 1 if the function succeeds and -1 if an error occurs.

Example: In order to instantiate the service n_cst_dwsrv_dropdownsearch, the following function is called, typically in the constructor event of the DataWindow control:

this.of_SetDropDownSearch(TRUE)

Once the service is instantiated, *all* columns on the DataWindow that are of edit style drop-down DataWindow have the search functionality enabled. In addition, code must be added to two events of the DataWindow control u_dw.

Add code to the editchanged event. In the u_dw *editchanged* event, redirect the event to the n_cst_dropdownsearch pfc_editchanged event:

IF IsValid(inv_dropdownsearch)THEN

this.inv_dropdownsearch.Event pfc_editchanged(row, dwo, data)

Add code to the itemfocuschanged event. In the u_dw *itemfocuschanged* event, redirect the event to the n_cst_dropdownsearch pfc_itemfocuschanged event:

IF IsValid(inv_dropdownsearch)THEN

this.inv_dropdownsearch.Event pfc_ItemFocusChanged(row, dwo)

Invoke other drop-down functions through the service. While the default behavior for this service is to add *all* available drop-down DataWindow columns that have the editable attribute on a DataWindow, the developer can control which columns are to use the search functionality by using the object functions of_AddColumn(column) and of_RemoveColumn(column).

The overloaded function of_AddColumn adds one or more columns to the list of columns that will use the service, while the of_RemoveColumn function removes a column from the list of columns that will use the service.

Syntax

dwcontrol.instancename.of_AddColumn([column])

Argument	Description
dwcontrol	Instance name of the u_dw DataWindow control.
instancename	Instance name of the n_cst_dwsrv_dropdownsearch object, inv_dropdownsearch.
[column]	With no arguments passed in, this function turns on this service for all columns of the edit style drop-down DataWindow. This is the same behavior as would occur if the service were instantiated and no of_AddColumn call was made. If a column name is passed in, the service will be activated only for those columns included in the of_AddColumn call(s).

Return value is an integer. The return is the number of drop-down DataWindow columns found if the function succeeds, 0 if the column cannot be found, and −1 if an error occurs.

Example: In order to make only the city and state columns drop-down searchable, the following code is added to the constructor event of the DataWindow control:

```
this.of_SetDropDownSearch(TRUE)
this.inv_dropdownsearch.of_AddColumn("city")
this.inv_dropdownsearch.of_AddColumn("state")
```

Syntax

dwcontrol.instancename.of_RemoveColumn (column)

Argument	Description
dwcontrol	Instance name of the u_dw DataWindow control.
instancename	Instance name of the n_cst_dwsrv_dropdownsearch object, inv_dropdownsearch.
column	The drop-down DataWindow search service will be deactivated for the column specified.

The return value is an integer. The return is the number of drop-down DataWindow columns remaining for the search service if the function succeeds, 0 if the column cannot be found, and −1 if an error occurs.

Example: In order to deactivate the city and state columns' drop-down searchable functionality, the following code is added to the event in which these drop-downs need to be drop-down search deactivated:

```
dw_1.inv_dropdownsearch.of_RemoveColumn("city")
dw_1.inv_dropdownsearch.of_RemoveColumn("state")
```

Tip: Use the drop-down DataWindow service sparingly on columns that have drop-down DataWindows that retrieve many rows, as this may produce significant performance problems as text is typed into the column. This service will perform a search of the drop-down DataWindow on each and every keystroke (as a result of the editchanged event).

Tip: If you are using retrieval arguments on a field defined as a drop-down DataWindow and the values are not retrieved until after an action has been taken (such as entering a value on another drop-down DataWindow that will be used as the retrieval argument), you will have to use the of_RemoveColumn function and then the of_AddColumn function for that DataWindow field if you want the drop-down search service to work properly.

n_cst_dwsrv_filter (filter service)

The PFC filter service adds some very nice extensions to the filter functionality already available to DataWindow controls. The non-PFC filter functionality allows the developer to programmatically filter data retrieved in DataWindows, as well as allowing the user to enter filters of his or her own through the Specify Filter dialog box (using the SetFilter() and Filter() functions). However, there are a number of shortcomings in using the non-PFC functionality that are handily addressed using the PFC service n_cst_dwsrv_filter—especially those regarding users entering filters of their own. Some of these include not being able to restrict filtering on specific columns and not being able to control how the columns are named in the dialog box.

In addition to providing a rich set of functions that control which columns will be presented as filterable to the user, the n_cst_dwsrv_filter service adds a number of dialog box styles to the Specify Filter dialog box. By using this service, the developer is able to provide a powerful interface to the user for filtering data, while still retaining control over the presentation and choices given to the user.

Enabling the service. To activate the PFC filter functionality for the user, the developer needs minimally to instantiate the service using the *dwcontrol.of_SetFilter* function (notice that this is a function of the u_dw object, and is not to be confused with the *dwcontrol.instancename.of_SetFilter* function of the nonvisual object n_cst_dwsrv_filter, which sets the filter string).

Syntax

dwcontrol.of_SetFilter (boolean)

Argument	*Description*
dwcontrol	Instance name of the u_dw DataWindow control
boolean	Boolean specifying whether to enable (TRUE) or disable (FALSE) the filter service. This service is automatically destroyed upon the destruction of the DataWindow control.

The return value is an integer. The return is 1 if the function succeeds and -1 if an error occurs.

Example: In order to instantiate the service n_cst_dwsrv_filter, the following function is called, typically in the constructor event of the DataWindow control:

    this.of_SetFilter(TRUE)

The Filter dialog box is then typically invoked by the user selecting View =>Filter on the menu. This menu item triggers the pfc_filterdlg event of the active DataWindow using the message router (which ultimately gets passed to n_cst_dwsrv_filter). The pfc_filterdlg event can also be triggered from another object; for example, in the clicked event of a button:

    dw_1.inv_filter.Event pfc_filterdlg( )

Notice also that both the of_SetFilter *and* the of_Filter function calls are made in the n_cst_dwsrv_filter pfc_filterdlg event; therefore, it is not necessary to do either the of_SetFilter or the of_Filter call manually.

Extract of the n_cst_dwsrv_filter pfc_filterdlg event:

    ...
    li_rc = of_SetFilter(ls_nullformat)
    IF li_rc <= 0 THEN Return li_rc
    Return of_Filter()

Specify filter style dialog box. The simple instantiation of the service using of_SetFilter provides the default PFC filter service behavior; however, one can optionally set the style of the dialog box, restrict the columns displayed to the user, and specify how the columns are named in the Filter dialog box using the functions described below.

To set the style of the filter dialog box, use the of_SetStyle function:

Syntax

dwcontrol.instancename.of_SetStyle (style)

Argument	*Description*
dwcontrol	Instance name of the u_dw DataWindow control.
instancename	Instance name of the n_cst_dwsrv_filter object, inv_filter.
style	Integer specifying the filter style:
	0, PowerBuilder Filter dialog box (default)
	1, w_filterextended dialog box
	2, w_filtersimple dialog box

The return value is an integer. The return is 1 if the function succeeds and -1 if an error occurs.

Example: In order to set the style of the Filter dialog box, this function is called after instantiating the filter service, typically in the constructor event of the DataWindow control:

```
this.of_SetFilter(TRUE)
this.inv_filter.of_SetStyle(2)
```

The three available dialog box styles are shown in Figs. 9.5, 9.6, and 9.7.

Select the columns to exclude from the filter dialog box. To restrict the columns available to the user for filtering, the developer can select from the following functions.

of_SetExclude allows the developer to specify which columns are to be excluded from the filter dialog box.

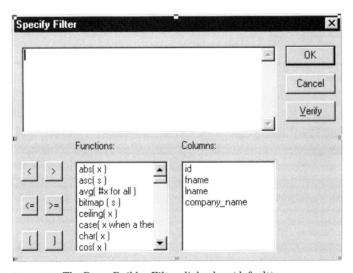

Figure 9.5 The PowerBuilder Filter dialog box (default).

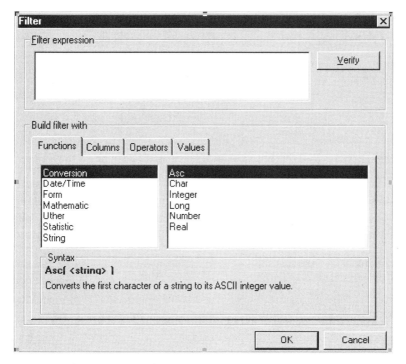

Figure 9.6   The w_filterextended dialog box.

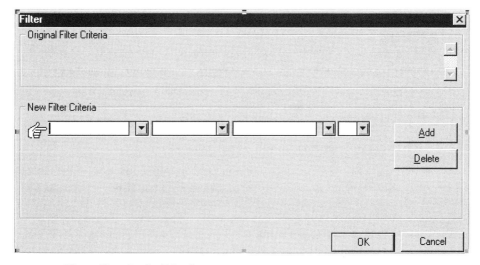

Figure 9.7   The w_filtersimple dialog box.

dwcontrol.instancename.of_SetExclude (excludecols[])

Argument	Description
dwcontrol	Instance name of the u_dw DataWindow control.
instancename	Instance name of the n_cst_dwsrv_filter object, inv_filter
excludecols[]	String array specifying the columns to exclude from the Filter dialog box.

The return value is an integer. The return is 1 if the function succeeds and −1 if an error occurs.

Example: In order to remove the emp_id and dept_id columns from the Filter dialog box, this function is called after instantiating the filter service, typically in the constructor event of the DataWindow control:

```
string ls_excludecols[]
this.of_SetFilter(TRUE)
ls_excludecols[1] = "emp_id"
ls_excludecols[2] = "dept_id"
this.inv_filter.of_SetExclude(ls_excludecols)
```

Restrict display to only visible columns in the filter dialog box. The of_SetVisibleOnly function allows the developer to more generally restrict display to only visible columns in the Filter dialog box.

dwcontrol.instancename.of_ SetVisibleOnly (boolean)

Argument	Description
dwcontrol	Instance name of the u_dw DataWindow control.
instancename	Instance name of the n_cst_dwsrv_filter object, inv_filter.
boolean	Boolean that switches the display of visible columns only on (TRUE) and off (OFF).

The return value is an integer. The return is 1 if the function succeeds and −1 if an error occurs.

Example: In order to remove all invisible columns from the Filter dialog box, this function is called after instantiating the filter service, typically in the constructor event of the DataWindow control:

```
this.of_SetFilter(TRUE)
this.inv_filter.of_SetVisibleOnly(TRUE)
```

Control the text displayed in the filter dialog box. Finally, the developer can control the text displayed in the Filter dialog box so that the user sees either the

DataWindow column names, the database column names, or the DataWindow column label/header names (i.e., those labels that match the column names with a _t suffix) by using the of_SetColumnNameSource function:

Syntax

dwcontrol.instancename.of_SetColumnNameSource (source)

Argument	*Description*
dwcontrol	Instance name of the u_dw DataWindow control.
instancename	Instance name of the n_cst_dwsrv_filter object, inv_filter.
source	Integer indicating which source to use as the filter dialog column labels:
	0, DataWindow column names (default)
	1, database column names
	2, DataWindow label/header text

The return value is an integer. The return is 1 if the function succeeds and -1 if an error occurs.

Example: To use the typically more friendly DataWindow label text (which is what the user sees on the DataWindow anyway), this function is called after instantiating the filter service, typically in the constructor event of the DataWindow control:

```
this.of_SetFilter(TRUE)
this.inv_filter.of_SetColumnNameSource(2)
```

Tip: The of_SetColumnNameSource function is an ancestor function of n_cst_dwsrv_filter, belonging to the n_cst_dwsrv base DataWindow service object. So look for it in n_cst_dwsrv. This fact may come in handy while debugging, and also when trying to locate specifics about this function in the help documentation.

n_cst_dwsrv_find (find service)

The PFC find and replace functionality, as embodied by the n_cst_dwsrv_find service, provides a common user interface behavior that more and more users are coming to expect from professionally written software. The Find and Replace dialog boxes invoked through this service allow the user to search through a DataWindow, finding and/or replacing text in specific columns. This powerful functionality is provided by the PFC at the cost of basically one line of code.

The Find and Replace dialog boxes that may be invoked by the user are shown in Figs. 9.8 and 9.9.

Enabling the service. To activate the PFC find and replace functionality for the user, the developer merely needs to instantiate the service using the *dwcontrol.of_SetFind* function.

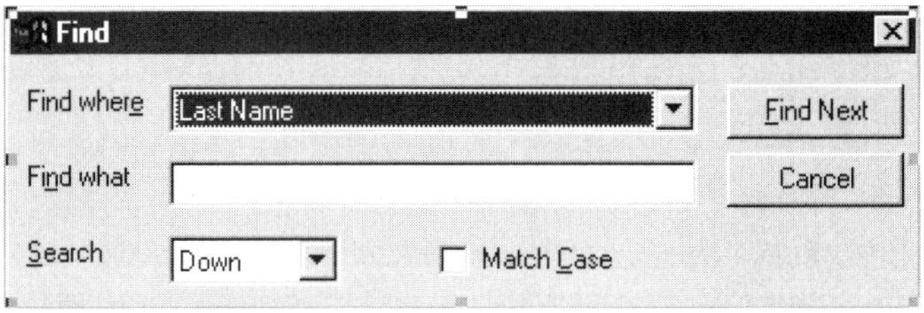

Figure 9.8 The Find dialog box.

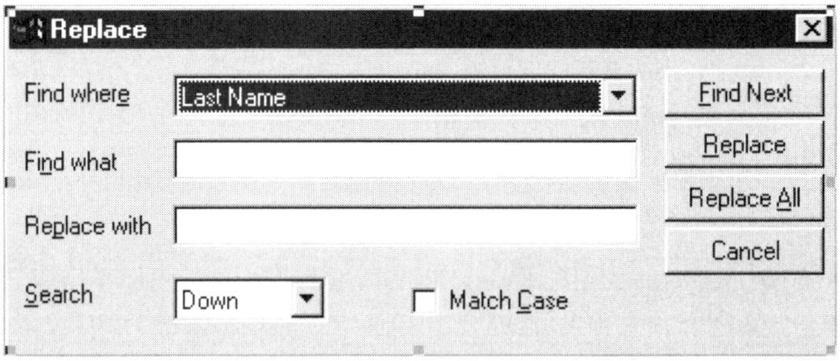

Figure 9.9 The Replace dialog box.

Syntax

dwcontrol.of_SetFind (boolean)

Argument	Description
dwcontrol	Instance name of the u_dw DataWindow control.
boolean	Boolean specifying whether to enable (TRUE) or disable (FALSE) the find service. This service is automatically destroyed upon the destruction of the DataWindow control.

The return value is an integer. The retun is 1 if the function succeeds and -1 if an error occurs.

Example: In order to instantiate the service n_cst_dwsrv_find, the following function is called, typically in the constructor event of the DataWindow control:

this.of_SetFind(TRUE)

The Find and Replace dialog boxes are then typically invoked by the user's selecting Edit =>Find and Edit =>Replace, respectively, on the menu. These menu items trigger the pfc_finddlg and pfc_replacedlg events, respectively, of the active DataWindow using the message router (which ultimately gets passed to n_cst_dwsrv_find). The pfc_finddlg and pfc_replacedlg events can also be triggered from another object, for example, in the clicked event of a button, one can trigger the find event:

dw_1.inv_filter.Event pfc_FindDlg( )

n_cst_dwsrv_linkage (linkage service)

Most frameworks developed before the PFC implemented some kind of master/detail processing. The PFC also provides a service for linking DataWindows, and it is fairly easy to use. This service is typically used for master/detail processing, but it can be used for other purposes. This object also includes several functions that will help you coordinate typical DataWindow functions among groups of related DataWindows.

There are many functions included in n_cst_dwsrv_linkage. Table 9.6 lists and describes the linkage functions that control the relationships among DataWindows. You can find more information on the different linkage functions that control the relationships among DataWindows in the *PowerBuilder Online Books* and in the PFC on-line help.

Table 9.7 lists and describes the linkage functions that control the relationships among DataWindows. You can find more information on the different linkage functions that control the relationships among DataWindows in the *PowerBuilder Online Books* and in the PFC on-line help.

Table 9.8 lists and describes the linkage functions that allow you to perform basic processes through the linkage chain among DataWindows. You can find more information on the different linkage functions that allow you to perform basic processes through the linkage chain among DataWindows in the *PowerBuilder Online Books* and in the PFC on-line help.

Table 9.9 lists and describes the linkage functions that update linked DataWindows from either the bottom up or the top down. You can find more infor-

TABLE 9.6   Linkage Functions That Control the Relationships among DataWindows

Function	Description (from the *PowerBuilder Online Books*)
of_LinkTo	Links this DataWindow to the specified master DataWindow. This function sets the idw_master instance variable and calls the master DataWindow's of_LinkDetail function.
of_CreateUpdateSequence	Returns an array containing the default update sequence. An ordered list of the DataWindows to be updated.
of_LinkDetail	Adds the specified DataWindow to a master DataWindow's idw_details array.
of_SetUseColLinks	Establishes the method by which the linkage service relates DataWindows.
of_Unlink	Removes a detail DataWindow from the linkage chain.
of_UnlinkDetail	Removes the specified DataWindow from a master DataWindow's idw_details array.

TABLE 9.7   Linkage Functions That Coordinate Processing among DataWindows

Function	Description (from the *PowerBuilder Online Books*)
of_RetrieveDetails	Retrieves rows for detail DataWindows based on the current row values in the detail's master.
of_ScrollDetails	Scrolls the DataWindows in the linked chain, starting with this DataWindow, down through the linkage chain.
of_FilterDetails	Filters detail DataWindows based on current row values in the detail's master.
of_TriggerEvent	Triggers the specified user event in the DataWindows in the linked chain, starting with this DataWindow, down through the linkage chain.

TABLE 9.8   Linkage Functions That Allow You to Perform Basic Processes through the Linkage Chain among DataWindows

Function	Description (from the *PowerBuilder Online Books*)
of_Reset	Clears data from the DataWindows in the linked chain, starting with the current DataWindow, down through the linkage chain.
of_ResetUpdate	Clears the update flags for the DataWindows in the linked chain, starting with this DataWindow, down through its linkage chain.
of_SetTransObject	Sets the transaction object for all DataWindows in the linked chain, from this DataWindow on down through the linkage chain.

TABLE 9.9   Linkage Functions That Allow You to Update Linked DataWindows

Function	Description (from the *PowerBuilder Online Books*)
of_Update	Updates the linked DataWindows in the direction specified in the of_SetUpdateBottomUp function. Depending on the arguments specified, this function calls the PowerScript AcceptText function before calling the Update function. You can also specify whether to clear each DataWindow's update flags.
of_UpdateBottomUp	Updates the DataWindows in the linked chain, starting with the current DataWindow and going up the chain. This logic does not follow the same chain as of_UpdateTopDown.
of_UpdateTopDown	Updates the DataWindows in the linked chain, starting with the current DataWindow and going down the chain. This logic does not follow the same chain as of_UpdateBottomUp.

mation on the different linkage functions that allow you to that update linked DataWindows in the *PowerBuilder Online Books* and in the PFC on-line help.

The following steps will describe in detail what is needed to use the linkage service to set up a master/detail relationship. The steps for retrieving data for the master/detail relationship will then be discussed. Additional information on some of the more important linkage functions will be described so that you will have a better understanding of all the functionality available to you using the

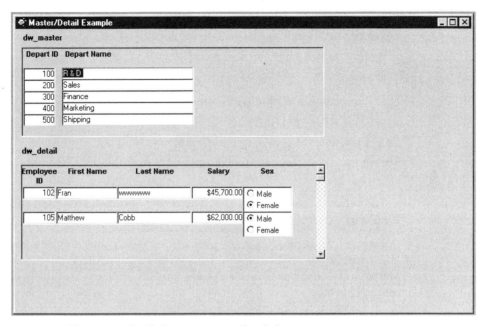

Figure 9.10 The w_mastdetail_sheet—a master/detail sheet.

linkage service. You will see that this service is very powerful and rich in functionality. Figure 9.10 shows a master/detail sheet. This figure will be used to illustrate exactly how to use the linkage service to implement a master/detail sheet and use additional linkage functions.

As stated earlier in the chapter, the placement of code is very important when using the linkage services. Problems can occur when the constructor event is used, as the order in which the constructor events are fired for multiple controls on a window depends on the order in which they have been placed on the window. This is not a robust method when the existence of specific objects in a script is required (e.g., the detail DataWindow referencing the master DataWindow for a LinkTo relationship). To resolve this problem, one needs to be very careful when using the constructor event for multiple object services, or start looking at other objects. One way to resolve this is to place code in an event that is guaranteed to be triggered after all objects on the window have been instantiated.

Tip: Place code in an event that is guaranteed to be triggered after all objects on the window have been instantiated when using linkage services, for example, in the window open event or a postconstructor event.

Although the following examples place the code in the constructor event, it could have been placed in other events on the window to guarantee that all objects have been instantiated.

Enabling the service. To activate the PFC linkage functionality for the user, the developer needs to first instantiate the service using the *dwcontrol.of_SetLinkage* function for each DataWindow that will need to be linked.

Syntax

instancename.of_SetLinkage (boolean)

Argument	*Description*
instancename	Instance name of u_dw.
boolean	Boolean specifying whether to enable (TRUE) or disable (FALSE) the linkage service.

The return value is an integer. The return is 1 if the function succeeds and −1 if an error occurs.

Example: In order to set the linkage services, this function can be called in the constructor event of the DataWindow control. Figure 9.10 shows two DataWindows that will need to have linkage services instantiated, dw_master and dw_detail.

The constructor event for dw_master is

this.of_SetLinkage(TRUE)

The constructor event for dw_detail is

this.of_SetLinkage(TRUE)

Link the detail DataWindow to the master. After linkage services for each DataWindow have been instantiated, the detail DataWindow must be linked to the master DataWindow to establish the master/detail relationship by calling the linkage service function *of_LinkTo*.

Syntax

dwcontrol.instancename.of_LinkTo (master)

Argument	*Description*
dwcontrol	Instance name of the u_dw-based DataWindow control.
instancename	Instance name of n_cst_dwsrv_linkage. The u_dw default for this value is inv_linkage.
master	DataWindow variable pointing to the master DataWindow.

The return value is boolean. The return is TRUE if the function succeeds and FALSE if the master does not exist.

Example: To link the detail DataWindow dw_detail to the master DataWindow dw_master in Fig. 9.10, the following code can be written in the constructor event of the dw_detail control:

this.inv_linkage.of_LinkTo(dw_master)

Specify which columns are to be linked.   Now that you have specified what the DataWindow relationships are, a relationship must be made between a column in the master DataWindow and a column in the detail DataWindow. This is done so that when a row in the master is changed, a retrieval of details can be made using the columns specified in the relationship. The linkage service function *of_SetArguments* can be called multiple times for multiple column arguments.

Tip: If the DataWindow you are using is linked by more than one column, make sure that this function is called for each column.

Syntax

dwcontrol.instancename.of_SetArguments (mastercol, detailcol)

Argument	Description
dwcontrol	Instance name of the u_dw-based DataWindow control.
instancename	Instance name of n_cst_dwsrv_linkage. The u_dw default for this value is inv_linkage.
mastercol	String specifying the column in the master DataWindow that is a linkage argument.
detailcol	String specifying the column in the detail DataWindow that relates to mastercol.

The return value is an integer. The return is 1 if the function succeeds and -1 if an error occurs.

Example: To link a column on the detail DataWindow dw_detail to the master DataWindow dw_master in Fig. 9.10, the following code can be written in the constructor event of the dw_detail control. In this example, dw_master and dw_detail have a column that can be used so that for every record on dw_master there are related records by column dept_id on dw_detail.

```
this.inv_linkage.of_SetArguments("depart_id","depart_id")
Establish the method by which the linkage service relates
```

Call the linkage service function *of_SetUseColLinks* in each detail DataWindow to specify the method, or linktype, by which the linkage service relates to the master DataWindow. Depending on the linktype specified, the way the data is displayed in the details will change. If the linktype is a 1, then the PFC uses columns in the master DataWindow as filter criteria for the detail DataWindow. If the linktype is a 2, then the PFC uses columns in the master DataWindow as retrieval arguments for the detail DataWindow. Finally, if the linktype is a 3, then the PFC uses columns in the master DataWindow to control scrolling in the detail DataWindow. Most typical master/detail relationships will require a linktype of 2 for retrieval.

Syntax

dwcontrol.instancename.of_SetUseColLinks (linktype)

Argument	Description
dwcontrol	Instance name of the u_dw-based DataWindow control.
instancename	Instance name of n_cst_dwsrv_linkage. The u_dw default for this value is inv_linkage.
linktype	Integer specifying the linkage type:

1. PFC uses columns in the master DataWindow as filter criteria for the detail DataWindows.

2. PFC uses columns in the master DataWindow as retrieval arguments for the detail DataWindow.

3. PFC uses columns in the master DataWindow to control scrolling in the detail DataWindow.

The linktype values (1, 2, and 3) mentioned might be good candidates for constants so that you, the developer, will know what these values represent.

The return value is an integer. The return is 1 if the function succeeds and -1 if an error occurs.

Example: To specify the method by which the dw_detail linkage service relates to dw_master in Fig. 9.10, the following code can be written in the constructor event of the dw_detail control. In this example, dw_detail uses columns in dw_master as retrieval arguments for the detail.

```
dw_detail.inv_linkage.of_SetUseColLinks(2)
```

Retrieve data through the linkage services

Setting the DataWindow's transaction object. Before a retrieve of the DataWindow can be done, the transaction object must be set. Do not use the SetTransObject PowerScript function or the base DataWindow service of_SetTransObject function; instead, use the linkage service function of_SetTransObject. This will in turn call the of_SetTransObject function in u_dw for all DataWindows in the linkage chain. This will establish the variables for use by other DataWindow services.

Syntax

dwcontrol.instancename.of_SetTransObject (transaction)

Argument	Description
dwcontrol	Instance name of the u_dw-based DataWindow control.
instancename	Instance name of n_cst_dwsrv_linkage. The u_dw default for this value is inv_linkage.
transaction	n_tr variable specifying the transaction object to use for the DataWindow

The return value is an integer. The function sets the s_linkage_errors error_rc variable to 1 if the function succeeds and to −1 if an error occurs.

Example: To set the transaction object for dw_master and dw_detail in Fig. 9.10, the following code can be written in the pfc_postopen event of w_mastdetail_sheet, which was inherited from w_sheet:

dw_master.inv_linkage.of_SetTransObject(transaction)

Retrieving data. Call the linkage service function of_Retrieve to coordinate retrieval among DataWindows in the linkage chain. You typically call this function from the uppermost DataWindow in the linkage chain; inv_linkage.of_Retrieve cycles through all DataWindows that are linked. Before retrieval can occur, several additional things must be done:

- All detail DataWindows should have retrieval arguments if the PFC uses columns in the master DataWindow as retrieval arguments for the detail DataWindow (linktype of 2).

- The master DataWindow of type u_dw must have code in the pfc_retrieve event to retrieve the master data.

Note: Only the master DataWindow of type u_dw must have code placed in the pfc_retrieve event for retrieving the data. The PFC will build the code and retrieve the detail DataWindows as necessary.

Syntax

dwcontrol.instancename.of_Retrieve ( )

Argument	Description
dwcontrol	Instance name of the u_dw-based DataWindow control.
instancename	Instance name of n_cst_dwsrv_linkage. The u_dw default for this value is inv_linkage.

The return value is an integer. The return is 1 if the function succeeds and -1 if an error occurs.

Example: To retrieve data for dw_master and dw_detail in Fig. 9.10, the following code can be written in the pfc_postopen event of w_mastdetail_sheet, which was inherited from w_sheet, and the pfc_retrieve event of dw_master. A retrieval argument must be added to dw_detail based on the dept_id.
For the pfc_retrieve event of dw_master,

Return this.retrieve( )

For the pfc_postopen event of w_mastdetail_sheet,

```
IF dw_master.inv_linkage.of_Retrieve( ) = -1 THEN
        MessageBox("Error","Retrieve error - master")
        Return -1
ELSE
```

```
            dw_master.SetFocus( )
END IF
```

Invoke other DataWindow functions through the linkage services. Now that we have shown you how to set up a master/detail sheet and retrieve the data, there are additional functions in the linkage service that are useful. Here are just a few of the functions, with some examples of how to use them. You can find more information on the different linkage functions in the *PowerBuilder Online Books* and in the PFC on-line help.

of_FindRoot. Call this function from any DataWindow in the linkage chain to determine the topmost DataWindow.

Syntax

dwcontrol.instancename.of_FindRoot (root)

Argument	*Description*
dwcontrol	Instance name of the u_dw-based DataWindow control.
instancename	Instance name of n_cst_dwsrv_linkage. The u_dw default for this value is inv_linkage.
root	The u_dw-based DataWindow into which the function places a reference to the topmost DataWindow. This argument is passed by reference.

The return value is an integer. The return is 1 if the function succeeds and -1 if an error occurs.

Example

```
u_dw    ldw_root
IF dw_detail.of_FindRoot(ldw_root) <> 1 THEN Return FALSE
```

of_IsRoot. Call this function to determine whether the current DataWindow is the topmost in the linkage chain.

Syntax

dwcontrol.instancename.of_IsRoot ( )

Argument	*Description*
dwcontrol	Instance name of the u_dw-based DataWindow control.
instancename	Instance name of n_cst_dwsrv_linkage. The u_dw default for this value is inv_linkage.

The return value is boolean. The return is TRUE if dwcontrol is at the top of the linkage chain and FALSE if it is not.

Example: In the example from Fig. 9.10, to find if dw_master is the root, the following code could have been called from an event on the window w_masdetail_sheet. The code would return TRUE.

```
IF dw_master.of_IsRoot( ) THEN Return TRUE
```

of_GetDetails.   Call this function from any DataWindow in the linkage chain to access its detail DataWindows.

Syntax

dwcontrol.instancename.of_GetDetails (details[ ])

Argument	Description
dwcontrol	Instance name of the u_dw-based DataWindow control.
instancename	Instance name of n_cst_dwsrv_linkage. The u_dw default for this value is inv_linkage.
details[ ]	The u_dw array into which the function places references to all details of dwcontrol. This argument is passed by reference.

The return value is an integer. The return is the number of elements in the details[ ] array.

Example: In the example from Fig. 9.10, to find the details for dw_master, the following code could have been called from an event on the window w_masdetail_sheet. The code would return one value in ldw_details—dw_detail.

```
Integer  li_details
u_dw             ldw_details[ ]
li_details = &
        dw_master.inv_linkage.of_GetDetails(idw_details)
…
```

of_TriggerEvent.   Call this function to perform application-specific processing through the linkage chain.

Syntax

dwcontrol.instancename.of_TriggerEvent (userevent)

Argument	Description
dwcontrol	Instance name of the u_dw-based DataWindow control.
instancename	Instance name of n_cst_dwsrv_linkage. The u_dw default for this value is inv_linkage.
userevent	String containing the name of a valid user event for the DataWindow control.

The return value is an integer. The return is 1 if the function succeeds, -1 if userevent did not exist (or had no code) in at least one DataWindow, and -2 if an error occurs.

Example: In the example from Fig. 9.10, userevent ue_anyevent was added to dw_master and dw_detail. To trigger this event in both DataWindows, we would write the following code:

```
dw_master.inv_linkage.of_TriggerEvent ("ue_anyevent")
```

of_Update. This function updates the linked DataWindows in the direction specified in the of_SetUpdateBottomUp function. Depending on the arguments specified, this function may call the PowerScript AcceptText function before calling the Update function. You can also specify whether to clear each DataWindow's update flags. In updating data, *inv_linkage.of_Update* cycles through all DataWindows that are linked.

The pfc_update event of w_master already contains this code and is triggered whenever a window of this type is closed.

Syntax

dwcontrol.instancename.of_Update ({ accepttext {, resetflags }})

Argument	*Description*
dwcontrol	Instance name of the u_dw-based DataWindow control.
instancename	Instance name of n_cst_dwsrv_linkage. The u_dw default for this value is inv_linkage.
accepttext	Boolean indicating whether the DataWindow control should automatically perform an AcceptText before performing the update:
	TRUE—perform AcceptText (default).
	FALSE—do not perform AcceptText.
resetflags	Boolean indicating whether dwcontrol should automatically reset the update flags:
	TRUE—reset the flags (default).
	FALSE—do not reset the flags.

The return value is an integer. The return is 1 if the function succeeds and -1 if an error occurs.

Example: The following portion of code is in the pfc_update event of pfc_w_master and is triggered when a window of type w_master is closed.

```
...
// This is a linked PFC DataWindow.
ldw_pfc_dw = ldw_dw
// Update via the linkage service, check rc.
li_rc = ldw_pfc_dw.inv_linkage.of_Update (TRUE, FALSE)
IF li_rc < 0 THEN Return li_rc
...
```

n_cst_dwsrv_multitable (multitable update service)

This is the non-PFC way to update several tables in one DataWindow control or DataStore. It requires you to write code that will do the following:

- Use a Modify statement to change the Update property of columns in each table.
- Preserve the status flags of the rows and columns until all the tables have been updated.

- When all the updates are successfully completed and committed, call ResetUpdate to clear the changed flags in the DataWindow.

In the following non-PFC code example, the DataWindow object joins two tables: department and employee. First the department table is updated, with status flags not reset. Then the employee table is made updatable and is updated. If all updates succeed, the Update command resets the flags and the SQL COMMIT command commits the changes. Note that to make the script repeatable in the user's session, you must add code to make department the updatable table again.

```
integer rc
string err
// The SELECT statement for the DataWindow is:
// SELECT department.dept_id, department.dept_name,
// employee.emp_id, employee.emp_fname,
// employee.emp_lname FROM department, employee
// Update department, as set up in the DW painter
rc = dw_1.Update(TRUE, FALSE)
IF rc = 1 THEN
        //Turn off update for department columns.
        dw_1.Modify("department_dept_name.Update = No")
        dw_1.Modify("department_dept_id.Update = No")
        dw_1.Modify("department_dept_id.Key = No")
        // Make employee table updatable.
        dw_1.Modify("DataWindow.Table.UpdateTable = ~"employee~"")
        //Turn on update for desired employee columns.
        dw_1.Modify("employee_emp_id.Update = Yes")
        dw_1.Modify("employee_emp_fname.Update = Yes")
        dw_1.Modify("employee_emp_lname.Update = Yes")
        dw_1.Modify("employee_emp_id.Key = Yes")
        //Then update the employee table.
        rc = dw_1.Update()
        IF rc = 1 THEN
                COMMIT USING SQLCA;
        ELSE
                ROLLBACK USING SQLCA;
                MessageBox("Status", "Update of employee table failed." &
                +"Rolling back all changes.")
        END IF
ELSE
        ROLLBACK USING SQLCA;
        MessageBox("Status", &
        "Update of department table failed." &
        +"Rolling back changes to department.")
END IF
```

As you can see, updating several tables in one DataWindow is not a trivial task. The code above is not generic, so that similar code must be written over and over when updating DataWindows with multiple tables. The PFC multi-table service solves the complexities of updating a DataWindow that has multiple tables. The PFC multitable service is a collection of functions that facilitate the updating of DataWindows that contain rows from more than one table. By using this service, you will be able to implement the updating of a DataWindow with multiple tables very quickly.

Enabling the service.   To activate the PFC multitable update functionality for the user, the developer needs to first instantiate the service using the *dwcontrol.of_SetMultiTable* function.

Syntax

instancename.of_SetMultiTable (boolean)

Argument	*Description*
instancename	Instance name of u_dw.
boolean	Boolean specifying whether to enable (TRUE) or disable (FALSE) the multitable update service.

The return value is an integer. The return is 1 if the function succeeds and -1 if an error occurs.

Example: To activate the PFC multitable update functionality for the user, the developer needs to first instantiate the service using the *dwcontrol.of_SetMultiTable* function, typically in the constructor event of the DataWindow control:

this.of_SetMultiTable(TRUE)

Register the table and its update characteristics.   In order to update a DataWindow with multiple tables, a modify statement to change the Update property of columns in each table must be written. The PFC multitable service uses a generic modify command that needs the table and its update characteristics. To register this information with the PFC multitable service, call the multitable service *of_AddToUpdate* function once for each table to be updated in a multitable update.

Syntax

dwcontrol.instancename.of_AddToUpdate (table, keycolumns[ ]
{, updateablecols[ ] {, keyinplace, whereoption }})

Argument	*Description*
dwcontrol	Instance name of the u_dw-based DataWindow control.
instancename	Instance name of n_cst_dwsrv_multitable. The u_dw default for this value is inv_multitable.
table	String specifying the table name.
keycolumns[ ]	String array containing the key columns used for update.

updateablecols[ ]	String array optionally containing the list of updatable columns. The default is all columns in the DataWindow.
keyinplace	Boolean optionally indicating whether to update the key in place (TRUE) or to delete and reinsert (FALSE). The default is FALSE. If you specify this argument, you must also specify whereoption.
whereoption	Integer specifying the DataWindow update where option:

0—key columns.

1—key and updatable columns.

2—key and modified columns.

If you specify this argument, you must also specify keyinplace.

The return value is an integer. The return is 1 if the function succeeds and -1 if an error occurs.

Example: To register the table and its update characteristics, call the multi-table update service function *of_AddToUpdate* for each table needed to be updated in the constructor event of the DataWindow control. In the following example, the select statement for the DataWindow is

```
SELECT department.dept_id, department.dept_name,
employee.emp_id, employee.emp_fname,
employee.emp_lname FROM department, employee
```

The code in the constructor event of the DataWindow control is

```
// used for key columns in DataWindows
String ls_depart_keycols[ ] = {"dept_id"}
String ls_empl_keycols[ ] = {"emp_id"}
// used for updatable columns in DataWindows
String   ls_depart_updatecols[ ] = {"dept_id", "dept_name"}
String ls_empl_updatecols[ ] = {"emp_id", "emp_fname", "emp_lname"}

// set table to update first, with all update criteria
this.inv_multitable.of_AddToUpdate ("DEPARTMENT", ls_depart_keycols, &
ls_depart_updatecols, TRUE, 2)
// set table to update second, with all update criteria
this.inv_multitable.of_AddToUpdate ("EMPLOYEE", & ls_empl_keycols, &
  ls_empl_updatecols, TRUE, 2)
```

Issue an update. The table can now be updated by triggering the u_dw pfc_update event. This event will determine if the multitable update service is instantiated and will call the pfc_update event of n_cst_dwsrv_multitable.

Syntax

instancename.Event pfc_update (accepttext, resetflags)

Argument	*Description*
instancename	Instance name of u_dw.

accepttext	Boolean specifying whether the DataWindow control should automatically perform an AcceptText prior to performing the Update (TRUE) or not (FALSE).
resetflags	Boolean specifying whether the DataWindow control should automatically reset the update flags (TRUE) or not (FALSE).

The return value is an integer. The return is 1 if the function succeeds and -1 if an error occurs.

n_cst_dwsrv_printpreview (print preview service)

The PFC DataWindow print preview service provides typical Windows print preview functionality for the user. This extension of the existing DataWindow object functionality supplies both the developer and the user with a straightforward interface to its functions.

This service comes complete with a zoom control with zoom preview. As with many of the DataWindow services, the cost to the developer is but a few lines of code, or *one* line of code when using a menu derived from pfc_m_master (which has menu items to invoke the print preview, set the zoom, and turn on the ruler).

The Zoom dialog box invokable by the user is shown in Fig. 9.11.

Enabling the service. To activate the PFC print preview functionality for the user, the developer instantiates the service using the *of_SetPrintPreview* function. Once the nonvisual object is instantiated, the print preview functions are available to be invoked.

Syntax

dwcontrol.of_SetPrintPreview (boolean)

Argument   Description

dwcontrol   Instance name of the u_dw DataWindow control.

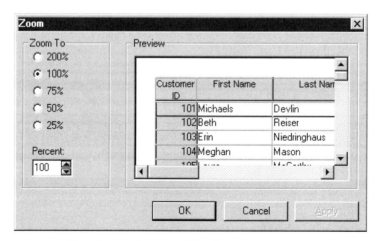

Figure 9.11 The print preview zoom dialog box.

boolean   Boolean specifying whether to enable (TRUE) or disable (FALSE) the print preview service. This service is automatically destroyed upon the destruction of the DataWindow control.

The return value is an integer. The return is 1 if the function succeeds and -1 if an error occurs.

Example: In order to instantiate the service n_cst_dwsrv_printpreview, the following function is called, typically in the constructor event of the DataWindow control:

    this.of_SetPrintPreview(TRUE)

The actual print preview display is typically invoked by the user's selecting File →Print Preview on the menu. This menu item triggers the pfc_printpreview event of the active DataWindow using the message router. The pfc_printpreview event of the DataWindow control then calls the n_cst_dwsrv_printpreview function of_SetEnabled, which actually places the DataWindow object in print preview mode by setting the print.preview attribute of the DataWindow object to TRUE as shown below:

    dwo.object.DataWindow.print.preview = TRUE

Similarly, the zoom and ruler functions are invoked by the menu items View →Zoom and View→Ruler, respectively, which in turn trigger the pfc_zoom and pfc_ruler events of the active DataWindow, which call the of_SetZoom and of_SetRuler functions, which ultimately, as above, set the appropriate DataWindow object attributes.

n_cst_dwsrv_querymode (querymode service)

Like the PFC filter service, the n_cst_dwsrv_querymode service adds some very nice extensions to the already existing DataWindow object querymode functionality. The non-PFC querymode and querysort functionality allows the developer to provide a query by example (QBE) search capability to the user; however, as with the non-PFC filter functionality, there are a number of shortcomings in using the non-PFC querymode that are addressed by using the PFC querymode service.

The PFC querymode service enhances the non-PFC functionality by allowing developers to restrict the columns eligible for querymode by the user (again, similar to the PFC filter service), as well as giving the user the ability to save and restore queries entered in querymode. In many ways, the PFC querymode service can be thought of as a front end to the DataWindow object's querymode functionality.

Note: Querymode *cannot* be invoked on DataWindows that have linkage service relationships enabled. Therefore, to successfully implement querymode on a DataWindow involved in a linkage relationship (e.g., a master/detail), one must first destroy the linkage service, enable querymode on the master DataWindow using the of_SetEnabled(TRUE) function, then, upon disabling querymode using the of_SetEnabled(FALSE) function, reinstantiate the linkage service.

Enabling the service.   To activate the PFC querymode service, the developer needs to instantiate the service by using the *dwcontrol.of_SetQuerymode* function of u_dw.

Syntax

dwcontrol .of_SetQuerymode (boolean)

Argument	*Description*
dwcontrol	Instance name of the u_dw DataWindow control.
boolean	Boolean specifying whether to create (TRUE) or destroy (FALSE) the querymode service. This function call does not place the DataWindow into querymode, it simply instantiates the service. This service is automatically destroyed upon the destruction of the DataWindow control.

The return value is an integer. The return is 1 if the function succeeds and -1 if an error occurs.

Example: In order to instantiate the service n_cst_dwsrv_querymode, the following function is called, typically in the constructor event of the DataWindow control:

this.of_SetQuerymode(TRUE)

The querymode service is not set up to function as autonomously as some of the other services; for example, there are no menu items built into pfc_m_master to invoke querymode. Therefore, a bit more work is required to get this service off the ground.

Performing the query.   The query itself is implemented by first toggling the querymode attribute of the DataWindow object on, allowing the user to enter a QBE, and then finally turning the querymode attribute off, which by default performs a query against the entered QBE parameters.

Querymode is toggled on (as differentiated by instantiating the service) as well as off by calling the of_SetEnabled object function of n_cst_dwrv_querymode.

Syntax

dwcontrol.instancename.of_SetEnabled (boolean)

Argument	*Description*
dwcontrol	Instance name of the u_dw DataWindow control.
instancename	Instance name of the n_cst_dwsrv_querymode object, inv_querymode.
boolean	Boolean specifying whether to turn querymode on (TRUE) or off (FALSE), i.e., setting the DataWindow object attribute *querymode* to *yes* or *no*.

The return value is an integer. The return is 1 if the function succeeds and -1 if an error occurs.

Example: In order to toggle querymode on and off from a command button on the window, the following code is added to the clicked event of that button:

```
IF dw_1.inv_querymode.of_GetEnabled() THEN
  cb_1.text = "Query"
  dw_1.inv_querymode.of_SetEnabled(FALSE)
ELSE
  cb_1.text = "Retrieve"
  dw_1.inv_querymode.of_SetEnabled(TRUE)
END IF
```

The button begins with the text Query on it; upon clicking on it, the DataWindow dw_1 is placed in querymode and the button text is changed to Retrieve. Clicking it once more turns querymode off and restores the button text to Query. The default behavior upon turning querymode off with of_SetEnabled(FALSE) is to perform a retrieve based on the QBE parameters (if any) entered by the user. The default retrieval behavior can be controlled with the of_SetRetrieveOnDisabled object function.

Syntax

dwcontrol.instancename.of_SetRetrieveOnDisabled (boolean)

Argument	Description
dwcontrol	Instance name of the u_dw DataWindow control.
instancename	Instance name of the n_cst_dwsrv_querymode object, inv_query-mode.
boolean	Boolean specifying whether to retrieve (TRUE) or not (FALSE) upon turning querymode off.

The return value is an integer. The return is 1 if the function succeeds and -1 if an error occurs.

Example: To alter the default querymode behavior to not automatically retrieve on disabling querymode, the following function is called, typically after the instantiation of the querymode service in the constructor event of the DataWindow control:

```
this.of_SetQuerymode(TRUE)
this.of_SetRetrieveOnDisabled(FALSE)
```

Controlling the queryable columns. As with the filter service, it is advantageous to control which columns are available to the user for querying. The default upon using the querymode service is to allow all columns to be queryable (that is, any column that is enterable can be used in the query). However, one can populate an array with the columns that one wishes to allow querying on, thereby excluding all other columns, by using the of_SetQueryCols function. This function simply sets the protect attribute on columns that are not in this list.

Syntax

dwcontrol.instancename.of_SetQueryCols (querycols[])

Argument	Description
dwcontrol	Instance name of the u_dw DataWindow control.
instancename	Instance name of the n_cst_dwsrv_querymode object, inv_querymode.
querycols[]	String array specifying the columns to allow querying on.

The return value is an integer. The return is 1 if the function succeeds and −1 if an error occurs.

Example: In order to allow just the employee and department names to be queryable, this function is called after instantiating the querymode service, typically in the constructor event of the DataWindow control:

```
string ls_querycols[]
this.of_SetQuerymode(TRUE)
ls_querycols[1] = "emp_name"
ls_querycols[2] = "dept_name"
this.inv_querymode.of_SetQueryCols(ls_querycols)
```

Saving and restoring queries. Queries performed in querymode can be saved and restored by making calls to the of_Save and of_Load object functions of n_cst_dwsrv_querymode. These functions would typically be invoked from a button or menu item while in querymode. The of_Save object function calls Powerscript file I/O functions to save the QBE parameters to a file, while the of_Load object function utilizes the ImportFile Powerscript function to load the previously saved QBE parameters into the DataWindow.

Syntax

dwcontrol.instancename.of_Save (title, pathname, filename {, extension {, filter } })

Argument	Description
dwcontrol	Instance name of the u_dw DataWindow control,
instancename	Instance name of the n_cst_dwsrv_querymode object, inv_querymode.
title	String specifying the title of the File Save dialog box.
pathname	String specifying the default pathname.
filename	String returned containing the name of the file chosen.
extension	String specifying the default file extension (optional).
filter	String specifying the contents of the listbox in the File Save dialog box.

The return value is an integer. The return is 1 if the function succeeds, 0 if the user has canceled, and −1 if an error occurs.

Example: To save the query parameters from a command button on the window, the following code is added to the clicked event of that button:

```
IF dw_1.inv_querymode.of_GetEnabled() THEN
  dw_1.inv_querymode.of_Save("Query Saver", ls_path, ls_file)
END IF
```

Syntax

dwcontrol.instancename.of_Load (title, pathname, filename, extension, filter)

Argument	Description
dwcontrol	Instance name of the u_dw DataWindow control.
instancename	Instance name of the n_cst_dwsrv_querymode object, inv_querymode.
title	String specifying the title of the File Open dialog box.
pathname	String specifying the default pathname.
filename	String returned containing the name of the file chosen.
extension	String specifying the default file extension (optional).
filter	String specifying the contents of the listbox in the File Open dialog box.

The return value is an integer. The return is 1 if the function succeeds and -1 if an error occurs.

Example: To load previously saved query parameters from a command button on the window, the following code is added to the clicked event of that button:

```
IF dw_1.inv_querymode.of_GetEnabled() THEN
dw_1.inv_querymode.of_Load("Query Loader", ls_path, ls_file)
END IF
```

Tip: To make the querymode service more like the other *set and forget* DataWindow services, one can extend the u_dw object in the PFE layer by adding user events to toggle querymode, save queries, and load queries (see the code in the above examples) and extend the m_master object by adding menu items to invoke those events in the active DataWindow (via the message router).

n_cst_dwsrv_report (report service)

The PFC report service provides an extremely rich set of functions that concentrate on the use of DataWindows for reports, especially with regard to printing and modification of the DataWindow. This service includes a number of functions which provides a development interface for the setting and getting of object attributes (e.g., color, font, etc.), as well as the addition of objects to and their deletion from a DataWindow object (e.g., lines, pictures, text, and computed columns). These functions will rearrange other objects on the DataWindow as necessary, and also adjust the band size as necessary. The report service also provides for the automated creation of a composite DataWindow.

Enabling the service.   To activate the PFC report, the developer needs to instantiate the service using the *dwcontrol.of_SetReport* function.

Syntax

dwcontrol.of_SetReport (boolean)

Argument	Description
dwcontrol	Instance name of u_dw.
boolean	Boolean specifying whether to enable (TRUE) or disable (FALSE) the report service.

The return value is an integer. The return is 1 if the function succeeds and -1 if an error occurs.

Example: In order to instantiate the service n_cst_dwsrv_report, the following function is called, typically in the constructor event of the DataWindow control:

this.of_SetReport(TRUE)

Call report DataWindow service functions, as needed.   Once the service has been instantiated, report DataWindow service functions can be called as needed. Table 9.10 lists and describes the functions available through this service.

You can find more information on the different report service functions in the *PowerBuilder Online Books* and in the PFC on-line help.

n_cst_dwsrv_reqcolumn (required column service)

When a user is performing data entry using a DataWindow, some of the fields on the DataWindow are required. Typically you write code in some validation routine to make sure the required fields are entered before an update is performed. If the user didn't enter all the required fields, an error message is typically displayed. Because this type of edit is performed many times in an application, it makes sense to have a service that provides functionality for determining if the user did not enter a value in a required field on a DataWindow. The PFC required column service provides this functionality.

This service allows you to defer required fields processing until the user completes data entry. It also allows you to specify columns for which PowerBuilder should still perform required fields processing. When enabled, this service writes null values to empty fields with the nilisnull property, suppressing required fields messages.

This service applies only to DataWindow columns that use the nilisnull property. For example, EditMasks don't have this property, so the required column service doesn't apply to edit masks.

Figure 9.12 shows a sample error message that is displayed when this required column service is enabled and the user does not enter a value in a required field.

TABLE 9.10   Report DataWindow Service Functions

Function	Description (from the *PowerBuilder Online Books*)
of_AddCompute	Adds a computed column to the DataWindow object.
of_AddLine	Adds a line object to the DataWindow object.
of_AddPicture	Adds a picture to the DataWindow object.
of_AddText	Adds a text object to the DataWindow object.
of_CreateComposite	Creates a composite DataWindow from an array of DataWindows.
of_GetDefaultBackColor	Gets the default back color.
of_GetDefaultBorder	Gets the default border.
of_GetDefaultCharset	Gets the default character set.
of_GetDefaultColor	Gets the default color.
of_GetDefaultFontFace	Gets the default font face.
of_GetDefaultFontSize	Gets the default font size.
of_GetPictureSize	Gets the size of a picture object.
of_GetTextSizePos	Gets the size and position of a text object.
of_SetBackground	Sets the background.
of_SetBorder	Sets the border.
of_SetColor	Sets the color.
of_SetDefaultBackColor	Sets the default back color.
of_SetDefaultBorder	Sets the default border.
of_SetDefaultChar	Setsets the default character set.
of_SetDefaultColor	Sets the default color.
of_SetDefaultFontFace	Sets the default font face.
of_SetDefaultFontSize	Sets the default font size.
of_SetFont	Sets the font.
of_PrepPrint	Adjusts objects on a DataWindow for optimal printing (e.g., black text on a white background).
of_PrintReport	Calls of_PrepPrint, prints the DataWindow, then undoes the of_PrepPrint function.
of_ResetUndo	Resets the undo stack.
of_Undo	Undoes undo levels.
of_GetUndoLevels	Gets the number of undo levels.
of_SetRelativeZoom	Sets the DataWindow zoom.

Enabling the service.   To activate the PFC required column service for the user, the developer needs to first instantiate the service using the *dwcontrol.of_SetReqColumn* function.

Syntax

instancename.of_SetReqColumn (boolean)

Argument	Description
instancename	Instance name of u_dw.
boolean	Boolean specifying whether to enable (TRUE) or disable (FALSE) the required column service.

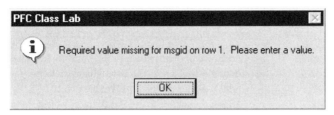

Figure 9.12 Sample error message displayed by the required column service.

The return value is an integer. The return is 1 if the function succeeds and −1 if an error occurs.

Example: In order to instantiate the service n_cst_dwsrv_reqcolumn, the following function is called, typically in the constructor event of the DataWindow control:

```
// set required column validation service
this.of_SetReqColumn(TRUE)
```

To optionally force the standard DataWindow required column processing on specific columns, the function of_RegisterSkipColumn is called.

Syntax

dwcontrol.instancename.of_RegisterSkipColumn (column)

Argument	Description
dwcontrol	Instance name of the u_dw DataWindow control.
instancename	Instance name of the n_cst_dwsrv_reqcolumn object, inv_reqcolumn.
column	String specifying the column that will not be subject to the deferred required column processing.

The return value is an integer. The return is 1 if the function succeeds and −1 if an error occurs.

Example: In order to have deferred required column processing on all columns but emp_id, the following function is called, typically in the constructor event of the DataWindow control after the instantiation of the required column service:

```
this.of_SetReqColumn(TRUE)
this.inv_reqcolumn.of_RegisterSkipColumn("emp_id")
```

Change the DataWindow properties. In order to have the required column service work properly, you must change the properties for each required column in the DataWindow. In the DataWindow painter, you need to bring up edit properties for each required column and make sure the Empty String is NULL prop-

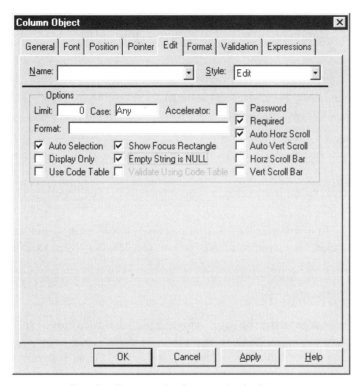

Figure 9.13 Sample edit properties for a required column.

erty is checked and the Required property is checked. Figure 9.13 shows an example of these two properties being set.

n_cst_dwsrv_rowselection (row selection service)

The PFC row selection service allows you to implement different versions of how you can select rows on a DataWindow of type u_dw. The following are the different ways a user can select rows using the row selection service:

- The single-row selection handles row selection when you want to allow one row to be selected at a time.

- The multirow selection handles row selection by allowing you to select multiple rows with single clicks. These rows can be contiguous or noncontiguous. When multirow selection is enabled, users toggle a row's selected state by clicking it. This capability is similar to a listbox's MultiSelect property.

- The extended selection handles row selection by allowing you to select multiple rows with Shift + click, Ctrl + click, and Ctrl + Shift + click. This capability is similar to a listbox's ExtendedSelect property.

Enabling the service.   To activate the PFC row selection service for the user, the developer merely needs to instantiate the service using the *dwcontrol.of_SetRowSelect* function.

Syntax

instancename.of_SetRowSelect (boolean)

Argument	Description
instancename	Instance name of u_dw.
boolean	Boolean specifying whether to enable (TRUE) or disable (FALSE) the row selection service.

The return value is an integer. The return is 1 if the function succeeds and -1 if an error occurs.

Example: In order to instantiate the service n_cst_dwsrv_rowselection, the following function is called, typically in the constructor event of the DataWindow control:

this.of_SetRowSelect(TRUE)

Specify the row selection option.   The simple instantiation of the service using the function of_SetRowSelect provides the default PFC row selection service behavior, however, one can optionally set the style of the row selection. The default behavior of the row selection service is single-row selection.

To set the row selection option, use the of_SetStyle function.

Syntax

dwcontrol.instancename.of_SetStyle (selectoption)

Argument	Description
dwcontrol	Instance name of the u_dw-based DataWindow control.
instancename	Instance name of n_cst_dwsrv_rowselection. The u_dw default for this value is inv_rowselect.
selectoption	Integer specifying the row selection option:
	0—single-row selection.
	1—multirow selection.
	2—extended row selection.

The return value is an integer. The return is 1 if the function succeeds and -1 if an error occurs.

Example: To set the row selection option, the function of_SetStyle is called, typically in the constructor event of the DataWindow control:

this.inv_rowselect.of_SetStyle(2)

n_cst_dwsrv_rowmanager (row manager service)

The PFC row manager service is used to handle modifications to a DataWindow. You can insert rows, delete rows, and undelete rows. If you use this service's functions to delete one or more rows, you must still code an Update function to apply the changes to the database. Be careful about allowing deletes when the linkage service is instantiated. Because the master DataWindow might contain data that is a foreign key to data on a detail DataWindow, updates to deletes with foreign keys must occur from the bottom up. When data is inserted or updated, the update must occur from the top down.

The service provides functions to do the following:

- Add an empty row to the end of the DataWindow.

- Insert an empty row between two existing rows.

- Delete one or more rows.

- Reverse the last delete from the DataWindow.

These services are provided in two ways: through functionality available from the right menu button (RMB) pop-up menu, and through sheet menu items (via the message router).

Instantiate row manager service. To activate the PFC row manager service for the user, the developer merely needs to instantiate the service using the *dwcontrol.of_SetRowManager* function.

Syntax

instancename.of_SetRowManager (boolean)

Argument	Description
instancename	Instance name of u_dw.
boolean	Boolean specifying whether to enable (TRUE) or disable (FALSE) the row management service.

The return value is an integer. The return is 1 if the function succeeds and -1 if an error occurs.

Example: In order to instantiate the service n_cst_dwsrv_rowmanager, the following function is called, typically in the constructor event of the DataWindow control:

this.of_SetRowManager(TRUE)

To prevent the RMB pop-up menu. When a user clicks the right mouse button when the focus is on a DataWindow control of type u_dw in an application, the DataWindow pop-up menu of type m_dw appears. This menu was described in earlier sections of this book. This menu can be disabled so that it won't appear by placing the following code in the constructor event for any DataWindow control of type u_dw in your application:

```
ib_rmbmenu = FALSE
```

To enable/disable specific menu items in the RMB pop-up menu.   The DataWindow pop-up menu described above has many menu items on it. For example, there is a menu item for inserting, deleting, and adding rows. Sometimes you may not want the user to have access to some of these menu items. You have access to these menu items by means of the DataWindow object u_dw event called pfc_prermbmenu. This event is triggered in the PFC every time the right mouse button is clicked. When the PFC triggers this event, it passes a reference, am_dw, to the pop-up menu of type m_dw that is created. You can now enable, disable, or hide any menu items of the DataWindow popup menu.

Example: To disable the Delete menu item on the DataWindow pop-up menu, place the following code in the pfc_prermbmenu event of any DataWindow control of type u_dw:

```
// disable the menu item
am_dw.m_table.m_delete.enabled = FALSE
```

n_cst_dwsrv_sort (sorting services)

The PFC sort service provides DataWindow sort functionality to an application. The service can be used by several display options:

You can choose among four styles of Sort dialog boxes.

You can allow the user to sort by clicking on column headings.

Enabling sorting services.   To activate the PFC sort service, the developer needs to invoke the *of_SetSort* function for each DataWindow control.

Syntax

```
instancename.of_SetSort ( boolean )
```

Argument	Description
instancename	Instance name of u_dw.
boolean	Boolean specifying whether to enable (TRUE) or disable (FALSE) the sort service.

The return value is an integer. The return is 1 if the function succeeds and -1 if an error occurs.

Specify whether the PFC sorts on display values or data values.   The developer can specify whether to use display values instead of data values by calling the of_SetUseDisplay function.

Syntax

dwcontrol.instancename.of_SetUseDisplay (boolean)

Argument	Description
dwcontrol	Instance name of the u_dw-based DataWindow control.
instancename	Instance name of n_cst_dwsrv_sort. The u_dw default for this value is inv_sort.
boolean	Boolean specifying whether to use display values (TRUE) or data values (FALSE) for sorting.

The return value is an integer. The return is 1 if the function succeeds and -1 if an error occurs.

Specify how the sort dialog boxes will display DataWindow column names.   The developer can specify whether Sort dialog boxes should display database column names, DataWindow column names, or column header names by calling the n_cst_dwsrv of_SetColumnNameSource function.

Syntax

dwcontrol.instancename.of_SetColumnNameSource (source)

Argument	Description
dwcontrol	Instance name of the u_dw-based DataWindow control.
instancename	Instance name of n_cst_dwsrv. The u_dw default for this is inv_base.
source	Integer specifying the column name source: 0—DataWindow column names (default). 1—database column names. 2—DataWindow column header names.

The return value is an integer. The return is 1 if the function succeeds and −1 if an error occurs.

Specify the sort style.   The sort style determines the dialog box that displays when the of_SetSort function is called.

Syntax

dwcontrol.instancename.of_SetStyle (sortstyle)

Argument	Description
dwcontrol	Instance name of the u_dw-based DataWindow control.
instancename	Instance name of n_cst_dwsrv_sort. The u_dw default for this value is inv_sort.
sortstyle	Integer specifying the sort style: 0—PowerBuilder Sort dialog box (default). 1—w_sortdragdrop dialog box. 2—w_sortsingle dialog box. 3—w_sortmulti dialog box.

The return value is an integer. The return is 1 if the function succeeds and -1 if an error occurs.

Example: Place the following code in the constructor event for the u_dw (after sorting is set):

    inv_sort.of_SetStyle(1)

Figure 9.14 shows what the Sort dialog box looks like when the sort style is 1.

Enable column header sorting

Syntax

    dwcontrol.instancename.of_SetColumnHeader (boolean)

Argument	Description
dwcontrol	Instance name of the u_dw-based DataWindow control.
instancename	Instance name of n_cst_dwsrv_sort. The u_dw default for this value is inv_sort.
boolean	Boolean specifying whether the service implements column header sorting (TRUE) or not (FALSE).

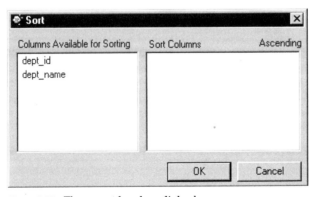

Figure 9.14 The w_sortdragdrop dialog box.

The return value is an integer. The return is 1 if the function succeeds and -1 if an error occurs.

Invoke the service. Call the of_SetSort function or the pfc_sortdlg event, as appropriate.

Syntax

dwcontrol.instancename.of_SetSort (sort)

Argument	Description
dwcontrol	Instance name of the u_dw-based DataWindow control.
instancename	Instance name of n_cst_dwsrv_sort. The u_dw default for this value is inv_sort.
sort	String containing a valid DataWindow sort expression. Column names must be preceded by a pound sign (#). If this argument is NULL, the function displays a Sort dialog box.

The return value is an integer. The return is 1 if the function succeeds, 0 if the user cancelled out of the Sort dialog box, and -1 if an error occurs

DataWindow debugger

There are many times when it would be nice to be able to display different properties of the DataWindow you are currently looking at. When a developer is debugging code, it is sometimes necessary to know the row status, column status, and values of the different DataWindow buffers. The PFC DataWindow debugger window provides all this information and more. Figure 9.15 shows what this window looks like when it is instantiated.

Enable the dataWindow debugger menu item. In order to use the DataWindow debugger, menu item m_debug on the DataWindow menu m_dw must be enabled and made visible. This can be done by adding the following code to the pfc_prermbmenu event of any DataWindow control of type u_dw:

```
am_dw.m_table.m_debug.enabled = TRUE
am_dw.m_table.m_debug.visible = TRUE
```

Instantiate the DataWindow debugger window. When the DataWindow RMB menu is visible and the DataWindow Properties menu item is clicked, the pfc_debug event is triggered for the DataWindow control. Code must be added here to instantiate the DataWindow debugger window. The following code can be added to the pfc_debug event of any DataWindow control of type u_dw to instantiate the window:

```
s_dwdebugger    lstr_parm
lstr_parm.DW_obj = this
```

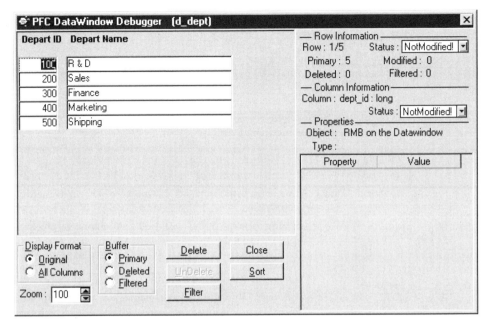

Figure 9.15 PFC DataWindow debugger window.

```
lstr_parm.tr_obj = SQLCA
OpenWithParm(pfc_w_dwdebugger, lstr_parm)
```

GSI TimeMaster Example

Included on the CD that comes with this book is the GSI TimeMaster application. The application gives many examples of ways in which many of the DataWindow services can be implemented. Take notice of how the linkage services have been implemented for the sheet by placing the code in the sheet's open event. This is to make sure that all DataWindow controls have been instantiated. Also notice that many of the other services have been implemented in the constructor event of the DataWindow control on the sheet to ensure encapsulation. Documentation on the GSI TimeMaster application will go into further details of the types of DataWindow services used in the application.

Summary

As you can see, the PFC has included many services for the DataWindow user object u_dw. This will allow you to offer your users many more features in the applications you write without having to do much coding. This chapter has tried to give you an overall understanding of the different services available to the DataWindow user object u_dw. This chapter has also pointed out some of the most important services and how to implement those services. There is no way we can go into detail on every function and event in all the services provided for the DataWindow user object u_dw. You can find more information on the different PFC services provided to the DataWindow user object u_dw in the *PowerBuilder Online Books* and in the PFC on-line help.

10

Other PFC Services

Introduction

Among the services provided by the PFC are a handful of utility services. These are the most loosely coupled of the PFC services, and typically can be instantiated at different scoping levels according to their use within the application. In this chapter, we will show you how to use the utility and associative services that are provided with the PFC.

Chapter Objectives

This chapter will teach the reader to understand and use the utility and associative services of the PFC. These services will be examined in detail:

- Menu message router
- SQL Spy
- DataWindow Debugger
- PFC security
- Conversion
- Date/datetime
- File handling
- INI file processing
- Cross platform
- Selection

- SQL parsing
- String handling
- Numerical

Menu Message Router

Message router

We discussed the message router in detail in Chap. 5. We bring it up again here to point out that this is a general-purpose message delivery service that you can use from within any window that has an attached menu. For instance, in an MDI application, you can address the menu's of_SendMessage function like this:

```
// In this example, the frame window is called w_frame
w_frame.menuid.FUNCTION DYNAMIC of_SendMessage("gsi_event")
```

The effect of this is the same as if the of_SendMessage function were called from within one of the menu item's clicked events. Notice the use of the DYNAMIC keyword. You need to specify DYNAMIC because the w_frame.menuid instance variable is of type *menu* and has no function of_SendMessage(). You could avoid this by assigning menuid to a local variable of type m_master, like this:

```
// Use local variable to establish addressability to of_SendMessage()
m_master m_temp
m_temp = w_frame.menuid
m_temp.of_SendMessage("gsi_event")
```

Either of these approaches gives you access to the general-purpose message routing capability provided by the PFC's of_SendMessage() function. Just to refresh your memory, the sequence the message router follows is:

- If the application is not MDI, call the pfc_messagerouter event on the menu's parent window.
- If the application is MDI, call the active sheet's pfc_messagerouter event first.
- If the passed event does not exist on the active sheet, call the frame's pfc_messagerouter event.
- The pfc_messagerouter event then attempts to trigger the event on the window, followed by the current control, and finally on the last active DataWindow.

Using the of_SendMessage function in this way will allow you to use the PFC's message-routing capability from anywhere within your application, taking full advantage of its generic architecture.

PFC Utilities

The PFC includes a substantial number of utility services that are specifically window or DataWindow services. These utilities can be instantiated at any scope within your application—global, instance, or local. Most of these services are defined with the *Autoinstantiate* option. That is, you only need to declare a variable of the appropriate type, without coding any explicit CREATE or DESTROY statements. This makes them even easier to use, and more attractive to the developer.

DataWindow debugger

The DataWindow debugger provides a simple interface that allows you to view and directly modify the properties of a DataWindow while the program is running. The steps that you take to use the DataWindow debugger are:

- Populate a structure with a pointer to the DataWindow and a transaction object.
- Open the w_dwdebugger window, passing the structure as a parameter.

Figure 10.1 shows the DataWindow debugger in action over the GSI TimeMaster sample application. To make the DataWindow debugger easier to use, we simply added the code that starts the w_dwdebugger window to the u_dw object:

Step 1: Add a user event, gsi_dwdebug, to u_dw.

Step 2: Add code to populate the debugger structure and open w_dwdebugger. In the user object painter, add the following code to the gsi_dwdebug event:

```
// Declare structure for DataWindow debugger information

s_dwdebugger lstr_parm

// Populate the structure with a DataWindow pointer and a transaction object

lstr_parm.dw_obj = This
lstr_parm.tr_obj = SQLCA

OpenWithParm(w_dwdebugger, lstr_parm)
```

You will find that this script won't compile when you first enter it. That is because the w_dwdebugger extension-layer object was omitted from the PFE libraries. Powersoft did this quite deliberately, feeling that it was unlikely that anyone would change the window, and that it would be used only by developers. You can use the pfc_w_dwdebugger window instead, or create your own extension window. If you choose to do the latter, you'll need to comment out the line that opens w_dwdebugger, close the user object painter and save your work up to this

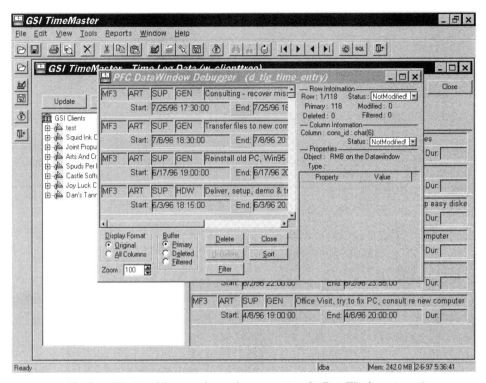

Figure 10.1 The DataWindow debugger shows the properties of a DataWindow at runtime.

point, and create the w_dwdebugger window. You will find the pfc_w_dwdebugger ancestor window in PFCDWSRV.PBL. To create the window:

- Open the Window painter.
- Choose Inherit.
- Select PFCDWSRV.PBL.
- Select pfc_w_dwdebugger and press OK.
- Close the Window painter, saving the window as w_dwdebugger in the PFEDWSRV.PBL. (The sample application's PBLs are prefixed with ATG instead of PFE, so our w_dwdebugger is found in ATGDWSRV.PBL.)

Once you have created the DataWindow debugger window, you can open u_dw in the user object painter and uncomment the line that opens w_dwdebugger.

Since the DataWindow debugger code is in the u_dw object, the service is available at any time. We need to add code to the right mouse button menu to invoke the debugger event. Follow these steps to add a menu item for the DataWindow debugger:

- Add code to the u_dw pfc_debug event to open the debug window:

```
IF CON.IB_DEVELOPMENT THEN
       s_dwdebugger lstr_parm

       lstr_parm.dw_obj = this
       lstr_parm.tr_obj = this.itr_object
       OpenWithParm(w_dwdebugger, lstr_parm)
END IF
```

- Add code to the u_dw pfc_prermb event to enable the "Datawindow Properties..." pop-up menu:

```
IF CON.IB_DEVELOPMENT THEN
       boolean lb_debug
       lb_debug = IsValid(gnv_app.inv_debug)
       am_dw.m_table.m_debug.visible = lb_debug
       am_dw.m_table.m_debug.enabled = lb_debug
       am_dw.m_table.m_dash13.visible = lb_debug
END IF
```

With these few simple changes, you will have added DataWindow debugging capabilities to every u_dw-based DataWindow in your application.

Tip: The capabilities of the DataWindow debugger should not be available to the end user. Before you deploy or ship your application, you need to hide or remove the menu item that gives access to the DataWindow debugger. If you want to keep the debugger capabilities available after deployment, consider using a nonintuitive keystroke sequence to invoke the service. The *PowerBuilder Online Books* show a technique that uses a combination of the right mouse button and a Ctrl + Shift + D keystroke to activate the datawindow debugger service. A better way is to have checkboxes on the login window for debug services. If debug services are instantiated, the DataWindow debugger is available. Yet another method of enabling the debug service is to use the windows status bar service to add a bitmap to the status bar. The effect is similar to the Windows 95 tray bar. Clicking on a bitmap would toggle the service and change the bitmap to reflect the current service status. See Chap. 8 for a detailed description of this technique. To remove the access to the debug code from the production version, a boolean constant IB_DEVELOPMENT should be created. This constant should be checked before any call to the debug service. Using a constant causes conditional compile behavior; when the constant is FALSE, the code inside the IF statement is optimized out by the compiler. See Chap. 7 for more detail.

Using the DataWindow debugger

Now that you have installed the DataWindow debugger functionality, let's see it in action. You can open any window with a DataWindow on it (based on u_dw, of course). Then invoke the DataWindow debugger using the Tools | DataWindow

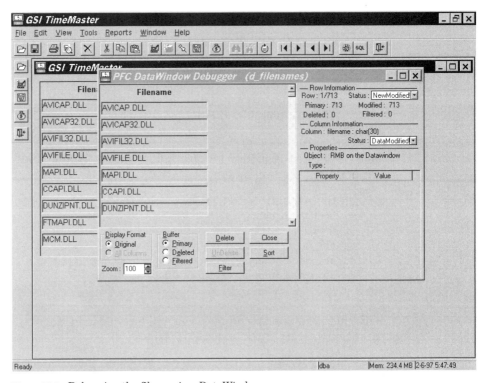

Figure 10.2 Debugging the file services DataWindow.

Debugger menu item. As an example, Fig. 10.2 shows the DataWindow debugger open over the Tools | File Services demonstration window.

As you can see from Fig. 10.2, the DataWindow debugger shows a copy of the DataWindow control. You choose an object on the DataWindow by right-clicking over the DataWindow. You can choose a column, a band, or the DataWindow in this manner. Once you have selected an object, its properties will show in the property list in the lower left of the debugger window. You can change any property by typing a new value into the property list. In this example, we have set the color of the DataWindow background to 995, which produces a particularly bilious red.

You can also use the DataWindow debugger to change the status of a column or a row with the status drop-downs in the upper right.

Tip: If you want to specify a filter for the DataWindow, just press the Filter button. Press it *once,* though. You won't see the Filter dialog box until you move the DataWindow debugger window, which is sitting on top of the Filter dialog box.

Tip: A DataStore version of w_dwdebug could be created by copying the window and changing the type of idw_remote from DataWindow to DataStore. This creates a powerful debugging feature. You can view and manipulate the DataStore data!

SQL Spy

PFC provides a comprehensive SQL Spy utility. You can view and modify SQL for DataWindows and EXECUTE IMMEDIATE embedded SQL statements. This can be very useful if you are not getting the results that you expect from your DataWindows or embedded SQL statements.

Table 10.1 shows the functions defined within the PFC SQL Spy service.

The usual place to enable the SQL Spy utility is from the pfc_open event of the application manager. However, the SQL Spy utility is used in a slightly different way from most PFC services. SQL Spy is implemented as an instance variable on the PFC debug user object. Because of this, you must first enable the debug services:

```
// Enable the debug service (application manager pfc_open event)
this.of_SetDebug(TRUE)
```

Next, enable the SQL Spy utility by calling the debug service's of_SetSQLSpy function:

```
// Enable the SQL Spy service (application manager pfc_open event)
this.inv_debug.of_SetSQLSpy(TRUE)
```

As an option, you can specify a log file for SQL Spy:

TABLE 10.1   The PFC SQL Spy Service Functions

Object name	pfc_n_cst_sqlspy	Object type	Abstract client
Ancestry	nonvisualobject	Extension	n_cst_sqlspy
Description	SQL Spy debugging services user object.		
Usage	Used to view and modify SQL statements.		
Reason for use	This service allows you to view and modify SQL statements before they are sent to the database, or to review a log of SQL statements that have already been executed. It is intended to be used as a debugging aid, and is not for the end user.		
Events	Constructor	Initialization.	
	Destructor	Clean-up	
Functions	of_OpenSQLSpy	Opens the SQL Spy log window.	
	of_SetBatchMode	Controls whether the SQL Spy Inspect dialog box is presented before each update.	
	of_SetLogFile	Sets the name of the log file.	
	of_SQLSyntax	Logs a SQL statement manually.	
Services	N/A		
Layered extensions	Extend by insertion.		

```
// Specify a log file for the SQL Spy service
string ls_filename
ls_filename = "c:\logs\atg_sql.log"
this.inv_debug.inv_SQLSpy.of_SetLogFile(ls_filename)
```

After you have enabled the SQL Spy service, you can display the latest entries to the log by calling the of_OpenSQLSpy function to display the SQL Spy pop-up window:

```
gnv_app.inv_debug.inv_SQLSpy.of_OpenSQLSpy(TRUE)
```

Note: If you are using an ODBC connection, you should set DisableBind to 1 in the Connect string.

Tip: You can leave the SQL Spy window open to view the SQL Syntax as it is sent to the database.

Finally, you can instruct SQL Spy to display each SQL statement and allow modification by calling the of_SetBatchMode() function:

```
// Enable the w_sqlspyinspect dialog box
gnv_app.inv_debug.inv_sqlspy.of_SetBatchMode(FALSE)
```

When you update a DataWindow, the w_sqlspyinspect dialog box will appear. The SQL commands for each row in the DataWindow will be displayed, one by one. You can review each SQL statement and make modifications as needed. There are four command buttons on the SQLSpyInspect window:

- *Step.* Updates the current row and displays information about the next row to be updated.
- *Resume.* Updates the current row and all remaining rows. The SQL Spy inspect capability is disabled.
- *Cancel.* Does not update the current row and displays the next row to be updated.
- *Cancel All.* Does not update all remaining rows.

Security

The PFC provides a security utility that allows you to create a database with user and group access rights for individual on-screen objects. The information kept in the database includes:

- Windows
- DataWindow columns
- Standard visual user objects

- Custom visual user objects and the controls within them
- Menu items

The security system consists of three components:

- *Security administration utility.* Allows you to define users, groups, and access to secured items.
- *Security scanner.* Scans windows to gather information on items that can be secured.
- *Security database.* Contains information on users, groups, items to be secured, and access to those items. Note that if another database is to be used, you must migrate the tables in this database to your own database. It is the pfc.db.

Note: The security scanner must be run as a single executable file. The application modifies its library search path and must not use PBDs.

Using security

The security administration program.   The first step in using the security system is to run the security administration program. The security administration program allows you to create users and groups, associate users with groups, and assign access rights to secured items (windows and controls). Within the security administration program, you will perform the following actions:

- Define users and groups.
- Associate users with groups.
- Run the security scanner.
- Define security for windows and controls.
- Associate users and groups with windows and controls.

The security service grants default rights to items that are not in the security tables. That is, no action is taken to grant or restrict access to items that are not in the database. To reduce the size of the security database and maintain performance, scan only those windows that contain objects you want to restrict.

Tip: The PFC security system ships with a default local SQL Anywhere database. You will need to use a server database for an application that has multiple users.

Scanning applications.   The security scanner program is run from within the security administration program. Select File | Scan Application from the menu bar. You will see a list of the applications defined in your PB.INI file. Choose one of these applications and press the Select button. The Select Windows dialog box will appear. Use Ctrl + click and Shift + click to select the windows that you want to scan. When you have selected the windows, press the Scan button. When scanning is complete, press Exit.

Customize controls.   Now you can customize the controls that you have scanned into the database. The File | Templates menu selection allows you to modify the descriptions of the secured items and delete any items that don't need to be secured. Try to make your descriptions as clear as possible. This will help when you are associating users and groups with each control.

Define security for users and groups.   Select File | Users/Windows from the menu to associate users with windows and controls. When the User/Window Management window displays, select a user or group from the Users drop-down. Double-click on the application that you want to establish security for and select the All radio button. Use the status drop-down listbox associated with each object to specify the security access that the selected user or group will have for that object. The status choices are

- Enabled
- Disabled
- Invisible
- Not set

Enabling security in an application.   Now that you have created the security database, you need to implement security in your application's objects. To enable security in an application, you will need to

- Enable the security service.
- Establish a database connection to the security database.
- Enable the security service on the appropriate windows.

To enable the security service for an application, call the of_SetSecurity function on the application manager:

```
gnv_app.of_SetSecurity(TRUE)
```

To establish a connection to the security database, create a transaction object based on n_tr, populate it, and connect it to the database.

Note: If the security database is on the application's database, you can just pass in the default transaction object on the of_InitSecurity call.

```
// application manager instance variable: n_tr itr_security
gnv_app.itr_security = CREATE n_tr
gnv_app.itr_security.of_Init(gnv_app.of_GetAppINIFile(), "Security")
gnv_app.itr_security.of_Connect()
```

Call the of_InitSecurity function to initialize the security system:

```
Integer li_return
li_return = gnv_app.inv_security.of_InitSecurity &
    (gnv_app.itr_security, "SAMPLE", gnv_app.of_GetUserID(), &
    "Default")
```

Enable security on each applicable window:

```
// window open or pfc_open event
gnv_app.inv_security.of_SetSecurity(This)
```

For more information. This discussion has only skimmed the surface of PFC security. The PFC security system is a large and capable application. To get detailed information on its use, consult the *PowerBuilder Online Books.*

PFC Associated Services

Conversion

The PFC conversion service allows you to convert from one datatype to another. It is especially useful for storing configuration and user preference values in INI files or the registry. You enable the conversion service by declaring a variable of type n_cst_conversion.

Tip: You don't need to CREATE or DESTROY the variable you use for n_cst_conversion. It is defined with the autoinstantiate option. Therefore, all you need to do is declare it. It will be destroyed automatically when it goes out of scope.

Table 10.2 shows the services defined within n_cst_conversion.

The conversion services make it easy to save and recall configuration information to an INI file. This is an example from the GSI TimeMaster sample application. The following code saves the frame's toolbar alignment value to the user INI file:

```
// application manager pfc_close event
n_cst_conversion lnv_conversion
// Save the toolbar alignment value as a string in the INI file
SetProfileString(gnv_app.of_GetUserINIFile(),"Options","Toolbar", &
    lnv_conversion.of_String(gnv_app.of_GetFrame().toolbarAlignment))
```

And this code restores the toolbar alignment when the frame window is opened:

```
// w_timelogframe open event
n_cst_conversion lnv_conversion
```

TABLE 10.2   Functions Defined within PFC n_cst_conversion Service

Object name	pfc_n_cst_conversion	Object type	Abstract client
Ancestry	CommandButton	Extension	n_cst_conversion

Description	Conversion service user object.
Usage	Used to convert from one data type to another.
Reason for use	This service provides a simple, standardized way to convert between data types, and gives you the ability to use a string or integer representation to save and manipulate PowerBuilder enumerated types and booleans.
Events	N/A

Functions		Converts:
	of_Boolean	Integer or string to boolean
	of_Button	String to enumerated button type
	of_Integer	Boolean to integer
	of_Icon	String to enumerated icon type
	of_SQLPreviewType	String to enumerated SQLPreview type
	of_String	Boolean, SQLPreview, toolbar alignment, icon, or button to string
	of_ToolbarAlignment	String to enumerated toolbar alignment type
	of_WindowState	String to enumerated window state type
Services		
Layered extensions	Extend by insertion.	

```
toolbaralignment ltb_align
string ls_tb
// Save the toolbar alignment value
ls_tb = ProfileString(gnv_app.of_GetUserINIFile(), &
    "Options","Toolbar", "Top")
// Convert from the profile string to the enumerated type
lnv_conversion.of_ToolbarAlignment(ls_tb, ltb_align)
// Set the toolbar alignment to the saved value
this.ToolbarAlignment = ltb_align
```

Date/datetime

The PFC date/datetime services allow you to do computations on date and datetime values. Issues such as rollover to the next or previous year are handled automatically. The n_cst_datetime service provides you with a set of utility functions that allow you, among other things, to

- Check for valid dates.

- Get the first or last day of the month.

- Check if a date is a leap year, or if it is a weekday or a weekend day.

- Convert dates between the Gregorian and Julian calendars.

- Compute relative dates.

Table 10.3 shows the functions included in the n_cst_datetime service.

Tip: You don't need to CREATE or DESTROY the variable you use for n_cst_datetime. It is defined with the autoinstantiate option. Therefore, all you need to do is declare it. It will be destroyed automatically when it goes out of scope.

File handling

The PFC file-handling functions provide a common entry point for platform-specific file manipulation functions.

You use the of_SetFileSrv() global function to enable the file-handling services. The function examines your environment and instantiates the appropriate descendant object for your operating platform. The Windows 16-bit and Windows 32-bit (NT or 95) platforms, Apple Macintosh, and UNIX/Solaris are currently supported.

Table 10.4 lists the functions defined on the abstract ancestor, n_cst_filesrv.

The platform-specific functions in pfc_n_cst_filesrvWin16 and pfc_n_cst_filesrvWin32 extend the ancestor functions to perform processing appropriate to the given platform. Table 10.5 lists the Windows 16-bit specific functions. Table 10.6 lists the Windows 32-bit specific functions. Tables 10.7 and 10.8 list the details of the Macintosh and Solaris file service objects.

Figure 10.3 shows a window incorporated in the GSI TimeMaster sample application. This window uses the of_DirList function to populate a DataWindow with a list of the .DLL files in the Windows\System directory. We created a window, w_filesrv_test, to demonstrate the use of the of_DirList function. This is the code from the DirList command button:

```
String ls_currdir
Integer li_cnt, li_entries
String ls_import
n_cst_dirattrib lnv_dirlist[ ]
SetPointer(HourGlass!)
ls_currdir = "c:\Windows\system\*.dll"
li_entries = &
inv_filesrv.of_DirList &
(ls_currdir, 0, lnv_dirlist)
IF li_Entries < 0 THEN
        MessageBox("File Services", &
        "Directory not found")
        Return
ELSEIF li_Entries = 0 THEN
        MessageBox("File Services", "No files found")
```

TABLE 10.3   The PFC Date/DateTime Service Functions

Object name	pfc_n_cst_datetime	Object type	Abstract client
Ancestry	nonvisualobject	Extension	n_cst_datetime

Description	Datetime services user object.
Usage	Used to perform calculations on date and datetime values.
Reason for use	This object provides services that allow you to do computations on date and datetime values. You also get functions to test the validity of dates, check if a date falls within a leap year, and whether it falls on a weekday or weekend, and convert between Julian and Gregorian dates.
Events	

Functions	of_DayOfWeek	Returns the day of the week of the passed date.
	of_Days	Calculates the number of days from seconds.
	of_FirstDayOfMonth	Returns the first day of the month from the passed date.
	of_Gregorian	Converts a Julian date to a Gregorian date.
	of_Hours	Converts seconds to hours.
	of_IsLeapYear	Checks if the passed date occurs in a leap year.
	of_IsValid	Checks if the passed date is a valid date.
	of_IsWeekDay	Checks if the date passed is a weekday.
	of_IsWeekEnd	Checks if the date passed is a weekend day.
	of_Julian	Converts a Gregorian date to a Julian date.
	of_JulianDayNumber	Calculates the day number of the passed date.
	of_LastDayOfMonth	Returns the last day of the month for the passed date.
	of_MilliSecsAfter	Calculates the number of milliseconds between two times.
	of_MonthsAfter	Calculates the number of months between two dates.
	of_RelativeDateTime	Computes a datetime relative to the passed datetime.
	of_RelativeMonth	Calculates a date that is the passed number of months relative to the passed date.
	of_RelativeYear	Calculates a date that is the passed number of years relative to the passed date.
	of_SecondsAfter	Calculates the number of seconds between two datetimes.

TABLE 10.3   The PFC Date/DateTime Service Functions (*Continued*)

of_Wait	Waits a specified number of seconds, or until a specified datetime.	
	of_WeekNumber	Returns the week number of the passed date.
	of_WeeksAfter	Returns the number of weeks between two dates.
	of_YearsAfter	Returns the number of years between two dates.
Services		
Layered extensions	Extend by insertion.	

```
        Return
END IF

for li_cnt = 1 to li_entries
dw_1.ImportString(lnv_dirlist[li_cnt].is_filename)
next
```

As you can see, the operation of the of_DirList function is very simple. You pass it a directory specification, an attribute byte, and a reference to an array of n_cst_dirattrib objects. The of_DirList function populates the array with information for each file matching the passed directory mask and attribute byte. Once the array is returned, we take the filenames out and import them into the DataWindow.

INI file

The PFC INI file service provides the capability to delete INI file entries or sections, or to enumerate the sections within a file or the keys within a section. Table 10.9 shows the functions available in pfc_n_cst_inifile.

Tip: You don't need to CREATE or DESTROY the variable you use for n_cst_inifile. It is defined with the autoinstantiate option. Therefore, all you need to do is declare it. It will be destroyed automatically when it goes out of scope.

Cross platform

The PFC cross-platform functions provide a common entry point for platform-specific operations. You use the of_SetPlatform() global function to enable the cross-platform services. The function examines your environment and instantiates the appropriate descendant object for your operating platform. The Windows 16-bit and Windows 32-bit (NT or 95), Apple Macintosh, and UNIX/Solaris platforms are currently supported.

Table 10.10 lists the functions defined on the abstract ancestor, n_cst_platform.

TABLE 10.4   The PFC File Service Abstract Ancestor

Object name	pfc_n_cst_filesrv	Object type	Abstract client
Ancestry	nonvisualobject	Extension	n_cst_filesrv

Description	File services user object.
Usage	Abstract ancestor object for file services. Used to provide abstract functions for each of the platform-specific functions defined in pfc_n_cst_filesrvwin16 and pfc_n_cst_filesrvwin32.
Reason for use	Used to provide a common entry point for platform-specific file services. The functions on the abstract ancestor are called, and the code in the specific descendant object will be executed.

Protected functions	of_CalculateFileAttributes	Used internally—calculates attribute byte.
	of_IncludeFile	Used internally by of_DirList.
Public functions	of_AssemblePath	Assembles a fully qualified path.
	of_ChangeDirectory	Abstract function only.
	of_CreateDirectory	Abstract function only.
	of_DelTree	Deletes a directory, its files, and its subtrees.
	of_DirectoryExists	Abstract function only.
	of_DirList	Abstract function only.
	of_FileCopy	Copies one file to another.
	of_FileRead	Reads a file into a BLOB or string array.
	of_FileRename	Abstract function only.
	of_FileWrite	Writes a file from a BLOB or string.
	of_GetAltFilename	Abstract function only.
	of_GetCreationDate	Returns the file's creation date.
	of_GetCreationDateTime	Abstract function only.
	of_GetCreationTime	Returns the file's creation time.
	of_GetCurrentDirectory	Abstract function only.
	of_GetDiskSpace	Abstract function only.
	of_GetDriveTypeM	Abstract function only.
	of_GetFileAttributes	Abstract function only.
	of_GetFileSize	Abstract function only.
	of_GetLastAccessDate	Abstract function only.
	of_GetLastWriteDate	Returns the last date on which the file was modified.
	of_GetLastWriteDateTime	Abstract function only.
	of_GetLastWriteTime	Returns the last time at which the file was modified.
	of_GetLongFilename	Abstract function only.
	of_GetSeparator	Returns the directory separator character.
	of_ParsePath	Separates a filename into its parts.

TABLE 10.4   The PFC File Service Abstract Ancestor (*Continued*)

	of_RemoveDirectory	Abstract function only.
	of_SetCreationDateTime	Abstract function only.
	of_SetFileArchive	Sets the file's archive attribute.
	of_SetFileAttributes	Abstract function only.
	of_SetFileHidden	Sets the file's hidden attribute.
	of_SetFileReadonly	Sets the file's read-only attribute.
	of_SetFileSystem	Sets the file's system attribute.
	of_SetLastAccessDate	Abstract function only.
	of_SetLastWriteDateTime	Abstract function only.
	of_SortDirList	Sorts the of_DirList output
Services	N/A	
Layered extensions	Extend by insertion.	

The platform-specific functions in pfc_n_cst_platformWin16 and pfc_n_cst_platformWin32 extend the ancestor functions to perform processing appropriate to the given platform. Table 10.11 lists the Windows 16-bit specific functions. Table 10.12 lists the Windows 32-bit specific functions. The specific functions for Macintosh and Solaris are shown in Tables 10.13 and 10.14.

Selection

The PFC selection service gives you the ability to open a window from which a user can select any number of rows, and which returns the data from the selected rows. The data that the user selects from comes from a DataWindow. The DataWindow can be passed in any of three ways:

1. Retrieved rows
2. Rows passed in as arguments
3. Data stored with the DataWindow object

Tip: You don't need to CREATE or DESTROY the variable you use for n_cst_selection. It is defined with the autoinstantiate option. Therefore, all you need to do is declare it. It will be destroyed automatically when it goes out of scope.

Table 10.15 shows the functions defined in pfc_n_cst_selection. There are three different calling syntaxes for of_Open.

Syntax 1: to display retrieved rows for a DataWindow. This syntax displays the w_selection dialog box, retrieving rows from the database for the specified DataWindow object.

TABLE 10.5   The PFC 16-Bit File Service Functions

Object name	pfc_n_cst_filesrvWin16	Object type	Abstract client
Ancestry	n_cst_filesrv	Extension	n_cst_filesrvWin16
Description	Platform-specific (Windows 16-bit) file services user object.		
Usage	Platform-specific ancestor object for file services. Used to provide 16-bit Windows functionality for each of the platform-specific abstract functions defined in pfc_n_cst_filesrv.		
Reason for use	Allows platform-independent file manipulation through the use of the pfc_n_cst_filesrv ancestor object.		
Events			
Protected Functions	of_ConvertDate	Internal use—converts to PowerBuilder date.	
	of_ConvertTime	Internal use—converts to PowerBuilder time.	
Public Functions	of_ChangeDirectory	Changes the working directory.	
	of_CreateDirectory	Creates a new directory.	
	of_DirectoryExists	Determines if directory exists.	
	of_DirList	Returns an array of files and attributes in the passed directory.	
	of_FileRename	Renames or moves a file or directory.	
	of_GetCurrentDirectory	Returns the current working directory.	
	of_GetDiskSpace	Returns space information for the specified drive.	
	of_GetDriveType	Returns the drive type for the specified drive.	
	of_GetFileAttributes	Gets the attributes for a file.	
	of_GetFileSize	Gets the size of a file.	
	of_GetLastWriteDateTime	Returns the last datetime a file was modified.	
	of_RemoveDirectory	Deletes an empty directory.	
	of_SetFileAttributes	Sets the attributes for the specified file.	
	of_SetLastWriteDateTime	Sets the last date and time the file was modified.	
Services	N/A		
Layered extensions	Extended by insertion.		

Syntax

instancename.of_Open (dataobject, returnval[ ] {, transobj {, columns[ ] {, arguments[20] {, title } } } })

Argument	Description
instancename	Instance name of n_cst_selection.
dataobject	String specifying the DataWindow object that w_selection uses to retrieve and display rows.

TABLE 10.6   The PFC 32-Bit File Service Functions

Object name	pfc_n_cst_filesrvWin32	Object type	Abstract client
Ancestry	n_cst_filesrv	Extension	n_cst_filesrvWin32

Description	Platform-specific (Windows 32-bit) file services user object.
Usage	Platform-specific ancestor object for file services. Used to provide 32-bit Windows functionality for each of the platform-specific abstract functions defined in pfc_n_cst_filesrv.
Reason for use	Allows platform-independent file manipulation through the use of the pfc_n_cst_filesrv ancestor object.

Events	

Protected Functions	of_ConvertFileDateTimeToPB	Internal use—convert file date and time
	of_ConvertPBDateTimeToFile	Internal use—convert date/time to file date and time format

Public Functions	of_ChangeDirectory	Changes the working directory.
	of_CreateDirectory	Creates a new directory.
	of_DirectoryExists	Determines if a directory exists.
	of_DirList	Returns an array of files and attributes in the passed directory.
	of_FileRename	Renames or moves a file or directory.
	of_GetAltFilename	Returns the file short name (8.3).
	of_GetCreationDateTime	Returns the date and time a file was created.
	of_GetCurrentDirectory	Returns the current working directory.
	of_GetDiskSpace	Returns space information for the specified drive.
	of_GetDriveType	Returns the drive type for the specified drive.
	of_GetFileAttributes	Gets the attributes for a file.
	of_GetFileSize	Gets the size of a file.
	of_GetLastAccessDate	Returns the date a file was last accessed.
	of_GetLastWriteDateTime	Returns the last datetime a file was modified.
	of_GetLongFilename	Returns the long filename for a file.
	of_RemoveDirectory	Deletes an empty directory.
	of_SetCreationDateTime	Sets a file's creation date and time.
	of_SetFileAttributes	Sets the attributes for the specified file.
	of_SetLastAccessDate	Sets last date and time the file was accessed.
	of_SetLastWriteDateTime	Sets the last date and time the file was modified.

Services	N/A
Layered extensions	Extend by insertion.

TABLE 10.7   The PFC Macintosh File Service Functions

Object name	pfc_n_cst_filesrvmac	Object type	Abstract client
Ancestry	n_cst_filesrv	Extension	n_cst_filesrvmac

Description	Platform-specific (Apple Macintosh) file services user object.
Usage	Platform-specific ancestor object for file services. Used to provide Apple Macintosh functionality for each of the platform-specific abstract functions defined in pfc_n_cst_filesrv.
Reason for use	Allows platform-independent file manipulation through the use of the pfc_n_cst_filesrv ancestor object.

Events		
Protected functions	of_ConvertDate	Internal use—converts to PowerBuilder date.
	of_ConvertTime	Internal use—converts to PowerBuilder time.
	of_IncludeFile	Internal use—called by the DirList function.
Public functions	of_ChangeDirectory	Changes the working directory.
	of_CreateDirectory	Creates a new directory.
	of_DirectoryExists	Determines if a directory exists.
	of_DirList	Returns an array of files and attributes in the passed directory.
	of_FileRename	Renames or moves a file or directory.
	of_GetCreationDateTime	Gets the date and time the file was created.
	of_GetCurrentDirectory	Returns the current working directory.
	of_GetDiskSpace	Returns space information for the specified drive.
	of_GetDriveType	Returns the drive type for the specified drive.
	of_GetFileAttributes	Gets the attributes for a file.
	of_GetFileSize	Gets the size of a file.
	of_GetLastAccessDate	Returns the last access date for a file.
	of_getVolumes	Lists the volumes attached to a user's workstation.
	of_RemoveDirectory	Deletes an empty directory.
	of_SetCreationDateTime	Sets a file's creation date and time.
	of_SetFileAttributes	Sets the attributes for the specified file.
	of_SetLastAccessDate	Sets the file's last access date.
Services	N/A	
Layered extensions	Extend by insertion.	

TABLE 10.8 The PFC Solaris File Service Functions

Object name	pfc_n_cst_filesrvSol2	Object type	Abstract client
Ancestry	n_cst_filesrv	Extension	n_cst_filesrvSol2

Description	Platform-specific (Solaris) file services user object.
Usage	Platform-specific ancestor object for file services. Used to provide Solaris functionality for each of the platform-specific abstract functions defined in pfc_n_cst_filesrv.
Reason for use	Allows platform-independent file manipulation through the use of the pfc_n_cst_filesrv ancestor object.

Events		
Protected functions	of_ConvertFileDateTimeToPB	Internal use—convert file date and time
	of_ConvertPBDateTimeToFile	Internal use—convert date/time to file date and time format
Public functions	of_ChangeDirectory	Changes the working directory.
	of_CreateDirectory	Creates a new directory.
	of_DirectoryExists	Determines if a directory exists.
	of_DirList	Returns an array of files and attributes in the passed directory.
	of_FileRename	Renames or moves a file or directory.
	of_GetAltFilename	Returns the file short name (8.30).
	of_GetCreationDateTime	Returns the date and time the file was created.
	of_GetCurrentDirectory	Returns the current working directory.
	of_GetDiskSpace	Returns space information for the specified drive.
	of_GetDriveType	Returns the drive type for the specified drive.
	of_GetFileAttributes	Gets the attributes for a file.
	of_GetFileSize	Gets the size of a file.
	of_GetLastAccessDate	Returns the date a file was last accessed.
	of_GetLastWriteDateTime	Returns the last datetime a file was modified.
	of_GetLongFilename	Returns the long filename for a file.
	of_RemoveDirectory	Deletes an empty directory.
	of_SetCreationDateTime	Sets a file's creation date and time.
	of_SetFileAttributes	Sets the attributes for the specified file.
	of_SetLastAccessDate	Sets the date and time a file was last accessed.
	of_SetLastWriteDateTime	Sets the date and time the file was last modified.
Services	N/A
Layered extensions	Extend by insertion.

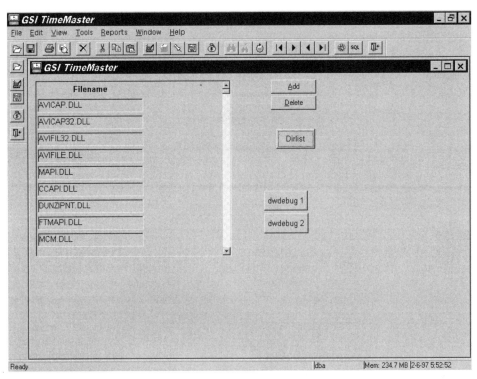

Figure 10.3   The of_DirList returns a list of files matching a specified pattern.

TABLE 10.9   The PFC INI File Service

Object name	pfc_n_cst_inifile	Object type	Abstract client
Ancestry	nonvisualobject	Extension[	n_cst_inifile
Description	INI file services user object.		
Usage	Provides functions to access, delete, and update INI file sections and keys.		
Reason for use	This service allows you to extract the sections and keys present in an INI file and process their values accordingly. You can also delete an entry or an entire section.		
Events			
Functions	of_Delete	Deletes an entry or section in an INI file.	
	of_GetKeys	Returns the keys within a given section.	
	of_GetSections	Returns the sections within an INI file.	
Services	N/A		
Layered extensions	Extend by insertion.		

TABLE 10.10 The PFC Cross-Platform Service Abstract Ancestor

Object name	pfc_n_cst_platform	Object type	Abstract client
Ancestry	nonvisualobject	Extension	n_cst_platform
Description	Cross-platform services user object.		
Usage	Abstract ancestor object for cross-platform services. Used to provide abstract functions for each of the platform-specific functions defined in pfc_n_cst_platformWin16, pfc_n_cst_platformmac, pfc_n_cst_platformSol2, and pfc_n_cst_platformWin32.		
Reason for use	Used to provide a common entry point for platform-specific services. The functions on the abstract ancestor are called, and the code in the specific descendant object will be executed.		
Events			
Functions	of_FindWindow	Abstract function only.	
	of_GetComputerName	Abstract function only.	
	of_GetFreeMemory	Abstract function only.	
	of_GetFreeResources	Abstract function only.	
	of_GetPhysicalMemory	Abstract function only.	
	of_GetSystemDirectory	Abstract function only.	
	of_GetTextSize	Abstract function only.	
	of_GetUserID	Abstract function only.	
	of_GetWindowsDirectory	Abstract function only.	
	of_GetWindowText	Abstract function only.	
	of_IsAppRunning	Abstract function only.	
	of_PageSetupDlg	Displays the w_pagesetup dialog box.	
	of_PlaySound	Abstract function only.	
	of_PrintDlg	Abstract function only.	
Services	N/A		
Layered extensions	Extend by insertion		

returnval[ ]	Array of the Any data type into which the w_selection dialog box places information for the selected columns. This argument is passed by reference.
transobj	n_tr-based transaction object optionally specifying an active connection that the w_selection dialog box uses to retrieve rows.
columns[ ]	String optionally specifying the DataWindow columns that w_selection returns. The default is the first column.
arguments[20]	Twenty-element array of the Any data type optionally specifying retrieval arguments for dataobject.
title	String optionally specifying a title for the w_selection dialog box.

TABLE 10.11   **The PFC 16-Bit Cross-Platform Service Functions**

Object name	pfc_n_cst_platformWin16	Object type	Abstract client
Ancestry	n_cst_platform	Extension	n_cst_platformWin16

Description	Platform-specific (16-bit Windows) services user object.
Usage	Platform-specific services user object. Used to provide 16-bit Windows functionality for each of the platform-specific abstract functions defined in pfc_n_cst_platform.
Reason for use	Allows platform-independent operations through the use of the pfc_n_cst_platform ancestor object.

Events		
Functions	of_FindWindow	Returns a handle for the specified window.
	of_GetFreeMemory	Returns the bytes of available memory.
	of_GetFreeResources	Returns the percentage of free system resources.
	of_GetSystemDirectory	Returns the path of the system directory.
	of_GetTextSize	Returns height and width in PBUs according to passed arguments.
	of_GetUserID	Returns the current network logon name.
	of_GetWindowsDirectory	Returns the Windows directory.
	of_GetWindowText	Returns the text in the window's title bar.
	of_IsAppRunning	Checks if an application is running.
	of_PlaySound	Plays the specified sound file.
	of_PrintDlg	Displays the Print dialog box.
Services	N/A	
Layered extensions	Extend by insertion.	

Syntax 2: to display a passed set of rows. This syntax displays the w_selection dialog box using rows passed in a function argument.

Syntax

instancename.of_Open (dataobject, returnval[ ] {, powerobj[ ] {, columns[ ] {, title } } })

Argument	*Description*
instancename	Instance name of n_cst_selection.
dataobject	String specifying the DataWindow object that w_selection uses to display rows.
returnval[ ]	Array of the Any data type into which the w_selection dialog box places information for the selected columns. This argument is passed by reference.

TABLE 10.12   The PFC 32-Bit Cross-Platform Service Functions

Object name	pfc_n_cst_platformWin32	Object type	Abstract client
Ancestry	n_cst_platform	Extension	n_cst_platformWin32

Description	Platform-specific (32-bit Windows) services user object.
Usage	Platform-specific services user object. Used to provide 32-bit Windows functionality for each of the platform-specific abstract functions defined in pfc_n_cst_platform.
Reason for use	Allows platform-independent operations through the use of the pfc_n_cst_platform ancestor object.

Events		
Functions	of_FindWindow	Returns a handle for the specified window.
	of_GetComputerName	Returns the name of the workstation.
	of_GetFreeMemory	Returns the bytes of available memory.
	of_GetPhysicalMemory	Returns the bytes of physical memory (RAM).
	of_GetSystemDirectory	Returns the path of the system directory.
	of_GetTextSize	Returns height and width in PBUs according to passed arguments.
	of_GetUserID	Returns the current network logon name.
	of_GetWindowsDirectory	Returns the Windows directory.
	of_GetWindowText	Returns the text in the window's title bar.
	of_PlaySound	Plays the specified sound file.
	of_PrintDlg	Displays the Print dialog box.
Services	N/A	
Layered extensions	Extend by insertion.	

powerobj[ ]	PowerObject array containing data that the w_selection dialog box displays in the data object DataWindow.
columns[ ]	String optionally specifying the DataWindow columns that w_selection returns. The default is the first column.
title	String optionally specifying a title for the w_selection dialog box.

Syntax 3: to display data stored with the DataWindow object.   This syntax displays the w_selection dialog box using data stored in the specified DataWindow object.

Syntax

instancename.of_Open (dataobject, returnval[ ] {, columns[ ] {, title } })

TABLE 10.13   The PFC Macintosh Cross-Platform Service Functions

Object name	pfc_n_cst_platformmac	Object type	Abstract client
Ancestry	n_cst_platform	Extension	n_cst_platformmac
Description	Platform-specific (Macintosh) services user object.		
Usage	Platform-specific services user object. Used to provide Macintosh functionality for each of the platform-specific abstract functions defined in pfc_n_cst_platform.		
Reason for use	Allows platform-independent operations through the use of the pfc_n_cst_platform ancestor object.		
Events			
Functions	of_GetComputerName	Returns the name of the workstation.	
	of_GetFreeMemory	Returns the bytes of available memory.	
	of_GetPhysicalMemory	Returns the bytes of physical memory (RAM).	
	of_GetSystemDirectory	Returns the path of the system directory.	
	of_GetUserID	Returns the current network logon name.	
	of_PlaySound	Plays the specified sound file.	
	of_PrintDlg	Displays the Print dialog box.	
Services	N/A		
Layered extensions	Extend by insertion.		

Argument	Description
instancename	Instance name of n_cst_selection.
dataobject	String specifying the DataWindow object that w_selection uses to retrieve and display rows.
returnval[ ]	Array of the Any data type into which the w_selection dialog box places information for the selected columns. This argument is passed by reference.
columns[ ]	String optionally specifying the DataWindow columns that w_selection returns. The default is the first column.
title	String optionally specifying a title for the w_selection dialog box.

SQL parsing

The SQL parsing service allows you to break a SQL statement into its component parts or reassemble a SQL statement from its components.

To enable the SQL parsing service, declare a variable of type n_cst_sql. This variable can be global, instance, or local, depending on the needs of the application.

TABLE 10.14   The PFC Solaris Cross-Platform Service Functions

Object name Ancestry	pfc_n_cst_platformSol2 n_cst_platform	Object type Extension	Abstract client n_cst_platformSol2
Description	Platform-specific (Solaris) services user object.		
Usage	Platform-specific services user object. Used to provide Solaris functionality for each of the platform-specific abstract functions defined in pfc_n_cst_platform.		
Reason for use	Allows platform-independent operations through the use of the pfc_n_cst_platform ancestor object.		
Events			
Functions	of_FindWindow	Returns a handle for the specified window.	
	of_GetComputerName	Returns the name of the workstation.	
	of_GetFreeMemory	Returns the bytes of available memory.	
	of_GetPhysicalMemory	Returns the bytes of physical memory (RAM).	
	of_GetSystemDirectory	Returns the path of the system directory.	
	of_GetTextSize	Returns height and width in PBUs according to passed arguments.	
	of_GetUserID	Returns the current network logon name.	
	of_GetWindowsDirectory	Returns the Windows directory.	
	of_GetWindowText	Returns the text in the window's title bar.	
	of_PlaySound	Plays the specified sound file.	
	of_PrintDlg	Displays the Print dialog box.	
Services	N/A		
Layered extensions	Extend by insertion.		

TABLE 10.15   The PFC Selection Service

Object name Ancestry	pfc_n_cst_selection nonvisualobject	Object type Extension	Abstract client n_cst_selection
Description	Selection service user object.		
Usage	Used to open a selection window.		
Reason for use	This service allows you to display a dialog box based on a DataWindow that allows the user to select one or more rows.		
Events			
Functions	of_open	Opens the w_selection dialog box, allowing the user to select one or more rows for further processing.	
Services	N/A		
Layered extensions	Extend by insertion.		

Tip: You don't need to CREATE or DESTROY the variable you use for n_cst_sql. It is defined with the autoinstantiate option. Therefore, all you need to do is declare it. It will be destroyed automatically when it goes out of scope.

Table 10.16 lists the SQL parsing functions.

The parts of the SQL statements are passed using a SQL attributes object, n_cst_sqlattrib. To assemble a SQL statement from its components, place the component values into the properties of the n_cst_sqlattrib object, then call of_Assemble:

```
// Assumes instance variable: n_cst_sql inv_sql
String ls_sql
n_cst_sqlattrib lnv_sqlattrib[ ]
lnv_sqlattrib[1].s_verb = sle_verb.text
lnv_sqlattrib[1].s_tables = sle_tables.text
lnv_sqlattrib[1].s_columns = sle_columns.text
lnv_sqlattrib[1].s_values = sle_values.text
lnv_sqlattrib[1].s_where = sle_where.text
lnv_sqlattrib[1].s_order = sle_order.text
lnv_sqlattrib[1].s_group = sle_group.text
lnv_sqlattrib[1].s_having = sle_having.text
ls_sql = inv_sql.of_Assemble (lstr_sql)
```

TABLE 10.16 The PFC SQL Parsing Functions

Object name	pfc_n_cst_sql	Object type	Abstract client
Ancestry	nonvisualobject	Extension	n_cst_sql
Description	SQL parser user object.		
Usage	Use to enable parsing of SQL statements.		
Reason for use	This service allows you to break a SQL statement into its component parts. You can manipulate these parts (for example, by adding a more restrictive WHERE clause) and then reassemble the SQL statement.		
Events			
Functions	of_Assemble	Builds a SQL statement from its component parts.	
	of_Parse	Parses a SQL statement into its component parts.	
Services	N/A		
Layered extensions	Extend by insertion.		

To parse a SQL statement into its component parts, call of_Parse, then extract the components from the n_cst_sqlattrib object:

```
String ls_sql
n_cst_sqlattrib lnv_sqlattrib[ ]
Integer li_return
li_return = inv_sql.of_Parse (mle_sql.text, lnv_sqlattrib)
IF li_return > 0 THEN
   sle_verb.text =  lnv_sqlattrib[1].s_verb
   sle_tables.text = lnv_sqlattrib[1].s_tables
   sle_columns.text = lnv_sqlattrib[1].s_columns
   sle_values.text = lnv_sqlattrib[1].s_values
   sle_where.text = lnv_sqlattrib[1].s_where
   sle_order.text = lnv_sqlattrib[1].s_order
   sle_group.text = lnv_sqlattrib[1].s_group
   sle_having.text =  lnv_sqlattrib[1].s_having
END IF
```

String handling

Sooner or later, we all need to process the contents of strings. Perhaps we need to break apart a text file and substitute values for keywords within that file. We might need to extract information from a downloaded file or wire feed. Or we might just want to correct capitalization in a string. PFC provides the string service to allow these and many more operations on strings.

You enable the string service by declaring a variable of type n_cst_string. This variable can be global, instance, or local, depending on your application's needs.

Tip: You don't need to CREATE or DESTROY the variable you use for n_cst_string. It is defined with the autoinstantiate option. Therefore, all you need to do is declare it. It will be destroyed automatically when it goes out of scope.

Table 10.17 lists the string-handling functions available in n_cst_string.

Numerical

The PFC numerical service provides functions to access binary data. This service is useful when dealing with external functions that return bit values, such as the Windows SDK functions.

To enable the numerical service, declare a variable of type n_cst_numerical. This variable can be global, instance, or local, depending on the needs of your application.

TABLE 10.17   The PFC String-Handling Service

Object name	pfc_n_cst_string	Object type	Abstract client
Ancestry	nonvisualobject	Extension	n_cst_string

Description	String services user object.
Usage	Used to provide various string manipulation functions.
Reason for use	This service provides many functions to aid in the processing of string data. It enables you to modify and manipulate strings in many useful ways.

Events		
Functions	of_ArrayToString	Creates a single string from an array.
	of_CountOccurrences	Counts the number of occurrences of one string within another string.
	of_GetKeyValue	Returns the right side of a keyword = value string.
	of_GetToken	Returns the token from a passed string.
	of_GlobalReplace	Replaces all occurrences of one string within another string.
	of_IsAlpha	Checks if a passed string is alphabetic-only.
	of_IsAlphaNum	Checks if a passed string is alpha-numeric-only.
	of_IsArithmeticOperator	Checks if a passed string contains only arithmetic-operator characters. Arithmetic-operator characters are (,), +, -, *, /, and ^.
	of_IsComparisonOperator	Checks if a passed string contains only comparison-operator characters. Comparison-operator characters are <, >, and = .
	of_IsEmpty	Checks if a string is empty or NULL.
	of_IsFormat	Checks whether a passed string contains only format characters. Format characters are all nonalphanumeric printable characters.
	of_IsLower	Checks whether the alphabetic characters in a string are all lowercase.
	of_IsPrintable	Checks whether a passed string contains only printable characters. Printable characters are ASCII 32 through ASCII 126.
	of_IsPunctuation	Checks whether a passed string contains only punctuation characters. Punctuation characters are !, ", ', ., :, ;, ?, and the comma.
	of_IsSpace	Checks if a string contains only spaces.
	of_IsUpper	Checks if the alphabetic characters in a string are all uppercase.

TABLE 10.17   The PFC String-Handling Service (*Continued*)

	of_IsWhiteSpace	Checks if a passed string contains only whitespace characters. Whitespace characters are newline, tab, vertical tab, carriage return, form feed, backspace, and space.
	of_LastPos	Searches backward through a string to find the last occurrence of another string.
	of_LeftTrim	Removes spaces and nonprintable characters from the beginning of a string.
	of_PadLeft	Pads a string with spaces on the left until it is a specified length.
	of_PadRight	Pads a string with spaces on the right until it is a specified length.
	of_Parsetoarray	Parses a string into array elements, based on a delimiter string.
	of_Quote	Encloses a string in double quotes.
	of_RemoveNonPrint	Removes all nonprintable characters from a string.
	of_RemoveWhiteSpace	Removes all whitespace characters from a string.
	of_RightTrim	Removes spaces and nonprintable characters from the end of a string.
	of_SetKeyValue	Sets the value portion of a keyword = value expression.
	of_Trim	Removes spaces and nonprintable characters from both ends of a string.
	of_WordCap	Sets the first letter of each word in a string to uppercase and all remaining letters to lowercase.
Services	N/A	
Layered extensions	Extend by insertion.	

Tip: You don't need to CREATE or DESTROY the variable you use for n_cst_numerical. It is defined with the autoinstantiate option. Therefore, all you need to do is declare it. It will be destroyed automatically when it goes out of scope.

Table 10.18 lists the PFC numerical functions.

Summary

This chapter showed you how to make use of the many utility and associative services provided by the PFC. With these services, you are empowered to manipulate

TABLE 10.18   The PFC Numerical Service Functions

Object name	pfc_n_cst_numerical	Object type	Abstract client
Ancestry	nonvisualobject	Extension	n_cst_numerical
Description	Numerical service user object.		
Usage	Used to access binary values.		
Reason for use	This service gives you the ability to perform operations on binary data, including base conversions and bitwise operations.		
Events			
Functions	of_Binary	Converts base 10 to binary.	
	of_BitwiseAnd	Performs a bitwise AND operation.	
	of_BitwiseNot	Performs a bitwise NOT operation.	
	of_BitwiseOr	Performs a bitwise OR operation.	
	of_BitwiseXor	Performs a bitwise XOR operation.	
	of_Decimal	Converts binary to base 10.	
	of_GetBit	Determines the value of a specified bit in a base 10 number.	
Services	N/A		
Layered extensions	Extend by insertion.		

different data types, perform platform-independent file and operating system functions, parse and assemble SQL, manipulate strings, access binary values, and perform calculations on date and datetime values. You also saw how to make use of the SQL Spy, DataWindow debugger, and security facilities of PFC.

Performance and Tuning

Introduction/Objectives

PowerBuilder 5 allows you to compile your code either to standard p-code or to machine code, depending on the platform you are developing on. Compiling to machine code means that your PowerScript code is translated into C, which is then compiled into a DLL. Is this a performance-booster? For code-intensive operations, most definitely. In fact, a performance boost of up to 50 times can be realized in some cases. Are all operations subject to this performance boost? No! Many operations that we have been doing in PowerBuilder are already calling native C code routines. For example, most DataWindow functions are housed in the PBDWE050.DLL, a C-code library. These are not going to get much faster than they already are unless the base code is modified by Powersoft.

What does all of this mean to us, as average programmers? It means that we are still responsible for ensuring that we develop efficient code and classes to get the most performance out of the tool. Good design and development techniques go a long way to promote performance.

In today's world, however, we find that we are basing our code on a class library written by others. The PFC is a classic example of this. Performance is no longer just in our hands, but also in the hands of the PFC development team. This means our good design and good coding techniques can possibly be offset by a poor technique used in the library. Although Powersoft has some excellent developers working on the PFC, and they use the latest development techniques, they are still human, and the PFC is still in its first public release. This means that there is no doubt room for improvement. New techniques keep coming out, different ways to implement behavior, and improvements in the native code debugger that helps the developer trace through the code to detect problem areas.

Coming down the road is the Profiler, a tool being provided by Powersoft that will be able to trace the code being executed and profile the performance of the code. This, along with the feedback of the thousands of PFC users, will help make a library like the PFC perform better and better over time.

This chapter will dig into some of the myths and realities of performance: Techniques that will help speed up your code; techniques to avoid, as they will slow your code down; the realities of using a class library such as the PFC; size limits that affect performance; and how to measure the performance of your code are all discussed.

Myths and Realities

There are several discussions going on in various groups about the performance of a PowerBuilder application. In some circles, it is said that PowerBuilder is just plain slow. We've had the opportunity to watch PowerBuilder grow over the years, and we'll admit that there are areas of improvement waiting for someone at Powersoft to work on and improve. Overall, however, we'll also admit that performance has improved quite dramatically over the years. One of us still has an old 486/33 machine with 8 Mbytes of RAM sitting in a home office. It's now a child's computer, but there are still a few of our applications on the machine. One of these applications is an application written for PowerBuilder 2. The application was simply ported up through the various versions of PowerBuilder, and the old versions were kept along with their respective deployment kits, just to keep track of what the application does. The application consists of a class library with several levels of inheritance, windows and DataWindows used in different ways, and SQL.

Along with the application is a small and simple application profiler. This application accepts messages from the other application and records start and end times depending on the message type being sent. The overall increase in speed since PowerBuilder 2 is actually quite astonishing. Many areas of the application have improved over 40 times!

We have also taken the opportunity to rearchitect the class library. When PowerBuilder 4 came out, we decided to make the library service-based. With PowerBuilder 5, we added a little loose coupling and brokered request management. The class library, although small, is quite sophisticated, and was the basis for a paper on service-based architecture that was published at the beginning of 1995.* The result of the rearchitecture process was a performance boost in some areas of more than 400 percent!

The point being made here is that new versions of the base product will provide improvements in performance, some of which can be significant. What gives you the most improvement in performance, however, is tight, well-written code. You, the developer, are responsible for much of this.

---

*The latest copy of this white paper is included on the attached CD.

Inheritance

There is and always has been a myth that levels of inheritance have a significant impact on performance. Well, in a way, it's true; 72 levels of inheritance are definitely slower than 3. However, levels of inheritance do not play the most significant part in the performance of your application except under the following conditions:

- You are running in development mode. In development mode, ancestry and the class pool are managed dynamically, and in many cases, an object in a hierarchy will be dynamically regenerated by PowerBuilder if it finds it necessary to do so. This will happen if you make a change to an object that is an ancestor to another object. The descendant object is not regenerated when the ancestor code is saved; rather, when the descendant object attempts to load, it detects that changes have been made to the ancestor, and therefore that the descendant object must be regenerated. This is not necessary when a compiled executable (machine code or p-code) is run, because these resolutions have already been made.

- One or more objects in the hierarchy are greater than 64 kbytes in size. The effect will vary based on the operating system you are running on, and also on the amount of memory available to your PowerBuilder application. There is a boundary above which it simply takes longer to load an object. We have found this limit to be 64 kbytes, and we have seen improvement of 30 percent or more when the object's size is reduced below that boundary.

- You are running your application on a network, and either the source code or the PowerBuilder DLLs reside on the network (or both do). Loading across a network will always be slower than loading on the client machine. For this reason, we heartily recommend spending some time, effort, and possibly money to set up and use an automated distribution mechanism so that your users can load the application and required DLLs locally to ensure best performance. In this case, if objects within a hierarchy reside in different libraries, and each of these libraries must then be accessed across the network, at least your initial loads will be significantly slower than subsequent loads.

A deep hierarchy does not perform like a flat hierarchy or no hierarchy at all. Accessing, loading, and building a six-layer hierarchy is less efficient than loading a single-layer hierarchy. However, this type of discussion about the inheritance tree is not as accurate as one might think. Let's first take a look at how PowerBuilder loads objects.

When an object is first referenced, PowerBuilder loads the object's definition into memory. This is the portion that remains in memory. An instance of the definition is then built based on the definition. If the object is inherited, the ancestor's definition has to be loaded first, then the current object's definition, and then these two combine to build an instance of the object, and so on. The search process for the object's definition can take considerable time if the hierarchy is deep and distributed among various libraries. Table 11.1 compares the

TABLE 11.1   Loading Objects into Memory

Single-layer hierarchy	Multiple-layer hierarchy
Search for object definition	Search for object definition
Load object definition	Discover inheritance criteria
Create instance of object	Search for ancestor definition
	Discover inheritance criteria
	Search for ancestor definition
	Discover inheritance criteria
	Search for ancestor definition
	Load object definition
	Create instance of object

load process of a typical object with a four-layer inheritance tree with that of an object with a single layer.

It becomes immediately obvious that the multiple-layered object will take longer to load. This flat comparison does not do justice to reality, however. Typically, objects are not loaded only once in the life of an application. (If an object is, then you should take steps to make sure that the object *does* have as flat as possible a hierarchy—Frame Windows, for example, fall into this category.)

Case study: Invoice data object and Company data object.   Let's take a little deeper look into what happens in a more typical case of objects that are used several times in an application, and also at the level of functionality that is involved. Take the case of an object that can process Invoice details. A typical hierarchy might look like this:

- Ancestor object
- Business layer
- Application layer

Each of these layers contains functionality. The base-level ancestor performs some initialization and could control some general processing, the business layer might implement some rules about the processing capabilities, and the application layer drives the actual processing for the Company data object. Each layer contains a certain amount of functionality and requires a certain amount of memory. For the purposes of this discussion, we will make the assumptions about size shown in Table 11.2.

If we developed the Company object without a hierarchy, its size probably would *not* be 70 kbytes. After all, the various layers would contain functionality for other object classes as well. It would more likely be about 60 kbytes or less if all of the functionality imbedded in the hierarchy that pertains to Invoice data were to be implemented. This is a key distinction of the two approaches as well. Class hierarchies generally implement higher levels of functionality than nonhierarchical approaches. If we looked at this hierarchy, we would see something like that shown in Fig. 11.1.

**TABLE 11.2   Object Hierarchy
Size—Company Object**

Object layer	Size
Base layer	30 kbytes
Business layer	20 kbytes
Application layer	20 kbytes
Total	70 kbytes

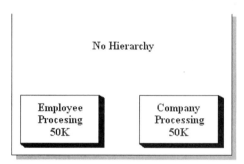

Flat Hierarchy
No Inheritance Used

No Hierarchy

Employee
Procesing
50K

Company
Processing
50K

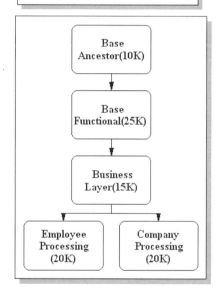

Normal "Treelike"
Hierarchy beginning to
form.

Base
Ancestor(10K)

Base
Functional(25K)

Business
Layer(15K)

Employee
Processing
(20K)

Company
Processing
(20K)

Figure 11.1   Example: flat model vs. traditional inherited model.

Based on our knowledge of how PowerBuilder objects are loaded, we can see that the object load paths follow those described in Fig. 11.2.

The difference begins when the second instance is loaded. Now, with both definitions in memory, the two approaches' load times will be much more comparable. The definitions for both objects are already in memory, so search time is eliminated. Load times are much more comparable. Figure 11.3 demonstrates the load steps.

Now we look at a second object. For example, let's define Invoice as another object class. A similar effect is described in the single vs. layered approach, with one difference: The layered approach inherits from the same tree as the Company object, resulting in the hierarchy shown in Fig. 11.4.

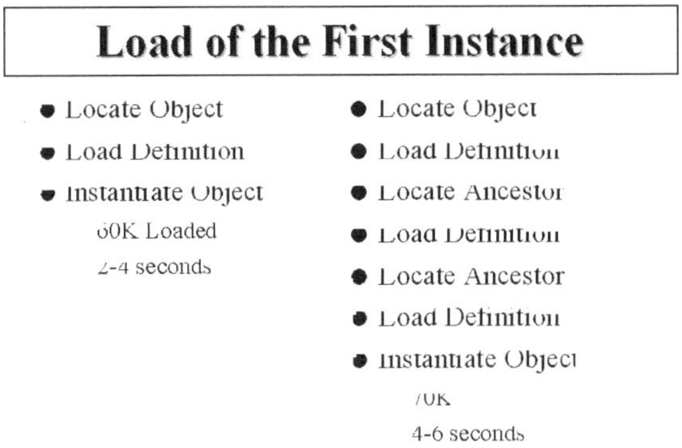

Load of the First Instance

- Locate Object
- Load Definition
- Instantiate Object
  - 60K Loaded
  - 2-4 seconds

- Locate Object
- Load Definition
- Locate Ancestor
- Load Definition
- Locate Ancestor
- Load Definition
- Instantiate Object
  - 70K
  - 4-6 seconds

Figure 11.2 Load of the first instance—the flat model out-performs the inherited model.

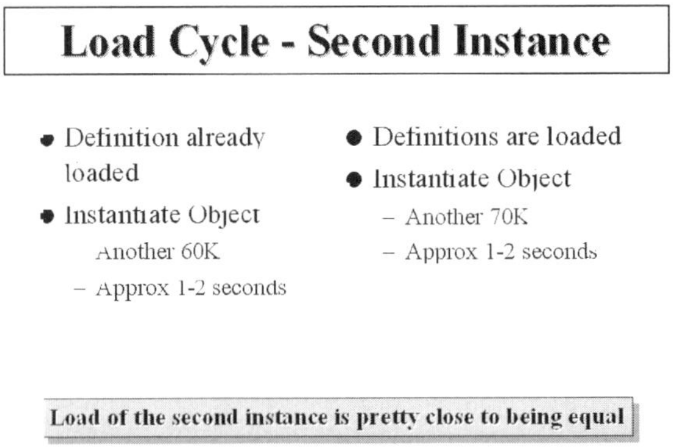

Load Cycle - Second Instance

- Definition already loaded
- Instantiate Object
  - Another 60K
  - – Approx 1-2 seconds

- Definitions are loaded
- Instantiate Object
  - – Another 70K
  - – Approx 1-2 seconds

| Load of the second instance is pretty close to being equal |

Figure 11.3 Loading of the second instance is much more comparable. In some cases, the inherited model may out-perform the flat model.

As you can see, the ancestry for the object uses the same base ancestor and base functional classes. In the flat model, when Invoice information is required, the 60-kbyte Invoice object is searched for and loaded into memory. The search process for the Invoice object in the layered approach is more efficient because the base ancestor and base functional layers are already in memory. The search time is comparable, and in fact you might find that the layered Invoice object loads faster than the flat model. The differences in load times between the first load of an instance and the second are far smaller. The layered approach pays a stiffer penalty once, but then continues to be more and more efficient than the single-layered approach. This can be demonstrated as shown in Fig. 11.5.

As objects continue to be loaded, the total execution time of the flat-model approach would soon exceed the time consumed by the layered approach, and

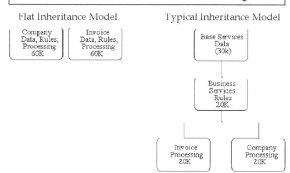

Figure 11.4 Hierarchy extended for Invoice and Company processing.

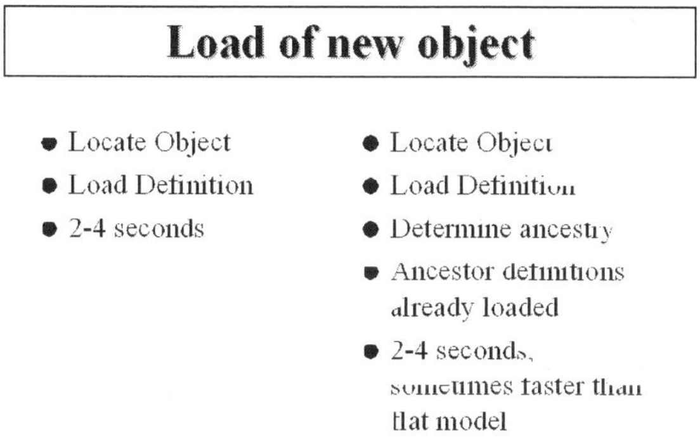

Figure 11.5 Second object load times are reversed in performance. The inherited model will often outperform the flat model.

ultimately you would suffer from performance degradation, even if it is not truly noticeable.

One reason for the myth that the flat model is faster is that the load time with the single-layer approach does not deviate much from object to object, while the layered approach can reduce load times by as much as half, or sometimes more, leading the user to believe that there is a performance problem with the object, at least once. Also, the same object is not always loaded first, so the user sees the Invoice object take a while longer one day, and the Company object run slower the next because of processing flow. Again, this is perception rather than reality and can be avoided by "preloading" specific ancestor objects, either by using them sooner in the application or by physically preloading them. You can preload an object's definition by simply declaring a variable of the object class in an earlier loading object. An example of this is to declare instance variables of the u_dw and w_master windows in the Application Manager. The variables result in class definitions being loaded into memory at application startup time, and you will not see the first window delay that you might have seen before. This avoids the scenario of "The first time is really slow—after that, it's acceptable."

The performance gain with preloading is not a real performance gain. It is a shifting of the load process from a point in the application where it is noticeable to one where it is not as noticeable. The loading has to take place sometime. What preloading does do is make your load times more consistent. Remember, though, that these class definitions remain in memory, so if memory usage is more important to you than performance, you may not want to adopt this approach. I have also found that for large objects (objects which exceed 64 kbytes in size), this approach has a markedly reduced effect.

Runtime environment—development vs. executable, machine code vs. p-code, 32-bit vs. 16-bit

Another myth we need to dispense with is that a library like the PFC becomes much slower when a corporate or enterprise layer is added. What you are seeing is the additional dynamic regeneration of objects required when running from development. Compiled PFC applications with and without the additional layer run virtually equally as fast. It is not a myth that machine-code executables run faster than p-code. What is a myth is the often-spoken-about "50 times faster." In some very specific operations, you will find that machine code runs 50 times faster than p-code. However, the p-code engine developed/enhanced by Watcom is very efficient and very quick. Areas which will typically show this type of performance increase are loop processing cycles, such as For...Next and Do...While...Loop instructions. Straightforward Powerscript execution will also be faster, depending on what the Powerscript is doing.

As for 32-bit vs. 16-bit, 32-bit runs faster on a 32-bit platform, and 16-bit runs faster on a 16-bit platform. Both 16-bit running on a 32-bit platform and 32-bit running on a 16-bit platform are slower than their counterpart executable/operating system match.

Architecture

The architecture you choose to use plays a part in determining the overall impact on performance in your application. We present the following example. We have worked with a major class library at a current client for over three years now, and we have watched the library evolve through the architectural generations described in Chap. 1. The library was codeveloped with a third-party vendor, and we utilized the extension layer and service-based concepts a long time ago. Our library was one of those looked at by Powersoft when deciding on the architecture it would adopt for the PFC. The result is that the PFC and our current library are remarkably close in architectural style. The PFC is obviously more advanced in technique, because its developers were able to begin developing using PowerBuilder 5.0, but many of the same features and

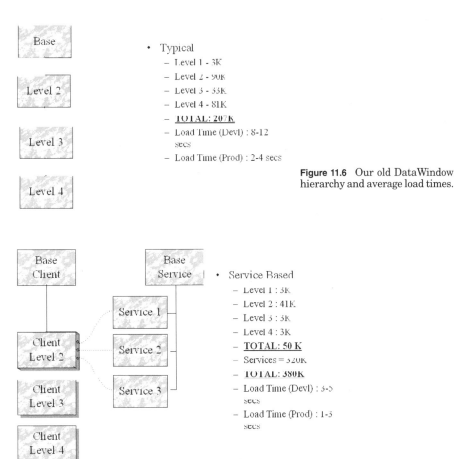

• Typical
  – Level 1 - 3K
  – Level 2 - 90K
  – Level 3 - 33K
  – Level 4 - 81K
  – TOTAL: 207K
  – Load Time (Devl) : 8-12 secs
  – Load Time (Prod) : 2-4 secs

Figure 11.6 Our old DataWindow hierarchy and average load times.

• Service Based
  – Level 1 : 3K
  – Level 2 : 41K
  – Level 3 : 3K
  – Level 4 : 3K
  – TOTAL: 50 K
  – Services = 320K
  – TOTAL: 380K
  – Load Time (Devl) : 3-5 secs
  – Load Time (Prod) : 1-3 secs

Figure 11.7 The new DataWindow class hierarchy and average load times.

techniques are used. As some of the first proponents of service-based architecture, we had the opportunity to investigate the reason for our library's "poor" performance, specifically with regard to our DataWindow hierarchy. What we had was the situation shown in Fig. 11.6.

Quite obviously, one of the major reasons for the slow load time was the fact that two of the objects in the hierarchy exceeded the magical 64-kbyte boundary. We found that when we removed the code from the objects and placed it in service objects loaded on demand, the load times of the objects improved quite dramatically. This led to a rearchitecting of the library, and the results can be seen in Fig. 11.7.

This led us to two conclusions. The first was that objects less than 64 kbytes in size loaded faster, leading us to conclude that a "fat client" was an object that approached or exceeded this limit. The second was that placing code in service objects which were nonvisual resulted in significant improvements in overall performance.

Hardware

One of the biggest performance-enhancers we've seen is bigger and faster hardware. We have witnessed significant performance increases as the development machine grew in size. In moving from a 486/33-MHz machine to a 200-MHz Pentium Pro with 64 Mbytes RAM, object load times obviously improve dramatically. Quite obviously, you can boost the performance of your application by boosting the equipment that the application runs on. Unfortunately, hardware is one of the things we as developers have little or no control over. We write applications for users, so it is the user's machine which will determine the native performance of your application. As an example, the load times shown in Figs. 11.6 and 11.7 were obtained on a 100-MHz Pentium processor with 32 Mbytes RAM. The load times can be halved by running on a 200-MHz Pentium processor with 32 Mbytes RAM or more. If you load the application on a user's machine and that machine is a 486/33 machine with only a nominal amount of memory, your application will run significantly slower.

While the obvious conclusion is that more power means better performance, it is important to realize that good coding techniques and well-written and well-designed applications will perform better than poorly designed or poorly written applications. And design and coding techniques are an element of the overall equation that we do have more control over.

Try to ensure, if it is within your power to do so, that the machine the application will run on is the best equipment your user can provide, and then follow that up by ensuring that you utilize sound design and coding techniques so as to not adversely affect the application's performance.

Perception

When measuring performance, there is one key aspect that is often overlooked, and that is the perception of performance. There will always be an area within a system that we feel can, and should, perform better. What we often overlook is what the user perceives to be lackluster performance. There are some things we can do that will improve the appearance of performance.

Users will recognize performance problems when they are forced to wait for the computer to do something. This often occurs when retrieving data or building large, complex screens. Generally, users want the system to perform at their speed, not the CPU's. Their speed is defined by the function they are attempting to complete and their understanding of how long each process should take. If the process takes 5 seconds to accomplish manually, the computer system should do it in less time, regardless of the level of complexity involved.

This is often difficult to accomplish. A key element in avoiding this is to avoid long blank pauses. When the user stares at an hourglass waiting for something to happen, the entire system will be labeled as slow. When a long process will take place, you need some form of feedback that will keep the user informed and distract him or her for at least a portion of the time.

We recently did a presentation on performance using this technique. The audience members were mostly technical people who were already using

PowerBuilder and knew its strengths and weaknesses. The demonstration involved opening a window and retrieving 120 records from a database. Three scenarios were established.

- *Scenario 1*—The window was opened and data retrieved during the open cycle. The process took about 1.1 seconds on average on a Pentium 90. We opened the window and initiated a retrieve, a normal development style. (We had already loaded the window and DataWindow and retrieved the data once to ensure that all memory-caching would already have taken place.)

- *Scenario 2*—The window was opened and the retrieve posted so that the window opening completed prior to the retrieval taking place. In this case, the average time was around 0.9 second. The difference was not really noticeable to the human eye, but most of the audience agreed that the process seemed faster. The difference was more due to the fact that the window opened and displayed fully before the data came back. The emphasis was that there was some feedback during the processing cycle, resulting in less "dead time."

- *Scenario 3*—The window was opened and the retrieve posted as in scenario 2, but the RetrieveStart event popped up a small dialog window which told the user that a retrieve was about to take place. When the retrieve ended, the pop-up was closed. Based on the processing load, one would assume that this would almost certainly take longer. It did, averaging around 1.4 seconds—significantly longer than the other two methods.

One startling fact emerged: Almost every single person in the room voted scenario 3 as the fastest! When we opened up a small time log embedded within the main window and displayed the average times, there was a buzz in the room. What had happened was that people's perception was altered. Because the pop-up window contained the words "Please Wait" followed by a brief message explaining the cause for the delay, everyone had been distracted for at least half of the processing time. This is time not measured. Therefore the third method appeared to be significantly faster than the other two.

Another presentation using the same example on a slower machine emphasized the result. The third method appears to run significantly faster than the others. The emphasis being made is this: Keep your user informed! If you do so, (1) they know the reason for the delay, (2) they are not staring at a blank screen and hourglass, moving the mouse to watch the mouse trails they have turned on for amusement, and (3) reading the message requires time. This time is not accounted for in measuring the performance of the object in question. The object is perceived to perform better than it actually does.*

To this end, we have established a couple of guidelines to aid in performance perception. These are:

- Slow is slow only if it makes you wait. Only when you wait for a process to do something can it appear to be slow.

---

*The example described is included on the attached CD under ch11.

- Keep your user informed. Even slower processes become more endurable if the reason for the wait is known.

- Use the available tools to provide as much feedback as possible, and use the right tool in the right place. In our example, populating MicroHelp had far less effect. Many people ignored the MicroHelp unless they were looking for something. The pop-up dialog box was much more effective. We also inserted a beep to indicate that the process was done, drawing immediate attention to the fact that it was complete.

- Rule of thumb: Longer than 3 seconds is a long time for a user. Keep updating your feedback (if possible) at least every 3 seconds.

Library search path

An often-discussed topic is the placement of libraries in the search path. The search path determines the sequence in which an object's index entry is placed into the executable. In development mode, it plays a more significant role, because the search for object definitions is much more dynamic. At runtime, there is no real "search time," as only the object table index is scanned, the correct library is identified, along with the object's address, and the object is directly referenced and loaded. Therefore, the search path has a more dramatic effect during development, while its effect on a production application is negligible at best.

Class and instance pools

As discussed earlier, when an object is loaded into memory, PowerBuilder first locates the object, determines its hierarchy, locates any and all ancestor objects, and then loads these definitions into a segment of memory called the *class pool*. The definitions remain in memory. Once all of the object's related ancestors have been loaded, an instance of the complete object is loaded into another segment of memory called the *instance pool*. Further instantiation of the object results in new instances being created in the instance pool. If another object is loaded which shares the class definition of the object that is already loaded, PowerBuilder does not have to load the class definition. It picks up the class definition from the class pool and uses this to create an instance of the new class in the instance pool. When the object is removed from the instance pool, PowerBuilder will determine whether the definition can be removed from the class pool. This can be done by creating a class hierarchy such as that shown in Fig. 11.8.

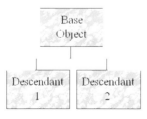

Figure 11.8 Sample object hierarchy to utilize in testing class and instance pool load times.

When object 1 is loaded, the class definition is loaded into the class pool and an instance of the object is loaded into the instance pool. Subsequent creates of the object are achieved in a fraction of the original load time. When an instance of object 2 is created, it too is loaded in a fraction of the original load time. If you remove all of the instances of the class from memory, its definition is also removed from the class pool. Now creation of an instance of object 2 takes as long as the initial load did.

Another thing to remember is that the class pool holds only the functional definition of the class. Variables, both instance and local, are located in the instance pool. Shared and global variables are housed in a private nonremovable segment of memory, accessible to all of the members of the instance pool.

Finally, it is useful to remember that the class pool resides in nondiscardable memory, meaning that it will not be swapped out when memory is needed by another application. The instance pool does not reside there, meaning that it could be swapped out if memory is urgently needed by another application.

Service instantiation in postopen and postcreate events

One of the elements of utilizing a service-based architecture is determining when to load the services the object will use. Obviously, services that are utilized all the time should be loaded as part of the object's constructor event. Most services do not fall into this category, however, and can be loaded after the object has been created in the instance pool. This has the effect of allowing the object to load faster, and shifts the loading of the service classes to a point in time when they are actually being loaded in the background and not affecting the loading of the object. Just as we discussed in the performance perception section, this shifting of the load processing alters the perception of object load times.

One other effect achieved is that of ensuring that instances of objects that might be referenced are loaded into memory. For example, if you place two instances of the u_dw class on a window, you cannot set up the linkage between the two in the constructor event of either object, because you cannot control which object will be loaded into memory first. To avert this problem, we either place the linkage code in the open event of the window the objects are placed upon, or shift the placement of the u_dw setup logic to a post_constructor event which is posted from the constructor, ensuring that object loads are complete before the linkage code that references the other object can run. The window's open event has the same effect, as it will begin executing only after all of the objects housed within the window are loaded.

We prefer the post_constructor approach, as this allows us to utilize dynamic user object creation, something not inherently available in the current version of the PFC.

Preloading objects

There has been some talk about the benefits of preloading certain objects in order to improve performance. Preloading objects is simply another method of shifting the load time of the object from the time when the user is watching to a time when he or she is not, improving the perception of performance. This benefit is limited to the first time the object is loaded into the instance pool, however, so the benefit may not be as large as is first expected. On the downside is the fact that preloading requires that the object definition be loaded into a nondiscardable segment of memory, and that memory is not released until the application ends. This could have a detrimental effect on the application's performance if the number of objects being preloaded grows and the runtime machine is one which is short on physical memory.

Number of PBLs/PBDs and number of objects

When PowerBuilder 2 was launched, some limitations of the product became apparent. One of these was the number of libraries and the number of objects within the libraries. A general guideline given was that a library should hold no more than 50 objects and should be less than 800 kbytes in size. These limitations were removed with the launch of PowerBuilder 3, and should definitely not be a factor when using PowerBuilder 4 or 5. Many applications these days require some sophisticated classes and libraries, resulting in some libraries exceeding the 800-kbyte mark. This has little or no effect on load times of objects.

While these limitations are still recommended today, the reason now is maintenance. It is easier to locate and maintain an object housed in a library with less than 50 other objects. As an experiment, we took our existing class library and copied all of the objects (from 18 PBLs) into a single PBL. Performance was improved when running from development mode, but running an executable showed no difference. The improvement in speed from development mode was far offset by the excessive time it took to load and open the library and then scroll down through the more than 200 objects to find the one you needed to work with.

Compile targets—PBDs, DLLs, EXEs

Where to compile to? This is a question that has been complicated for quite a while, and is now further complicated by the addition of the machine-code DLL target. Obviously, we will always create one EXE for our application. But what should be done with the remainder of our PBLs? Should we create PBDs or DLLs, or should we compile them into the EXE? First, let's look at the last of these. A PowerBuilder EXE is a stub containing the references to the dynamically loadable libraries, be they DLLs or PBDs. This is why the EXE need not be recreated when you recompile a PBD or DLL. When you choose to include a PBL in the EXE, you are in fact simply creating a hidden PBD. The EXE remains a stub, and any libraries included in the EXE are partitioned as if they were a PBD. Objects are still loaded via the same mechanism. The only difference is that if you are running the executable over a network, the initial load time of the application is increased to pull a larger executable file across the network. Once the EXE file is loaded into memory, the objects included as part of the EXE are loaded into swappable memory. This does not mean that any object definitions are loaded, but simply that the location of the object definitions is loaded. This obviously does mean some improvement in the load times of objects housed within the EXE, but this improvement is noticeable only if most of the application is loaded across a network.

Compiling code into machine-code DLLs means that your code is translated into native C code and compiled using a C compiler. Obviously, native C code will run faster than interpreted p-code. On the negative side is the fact that DLLs must be loaded into memory when the application runs. This has a more dramatic impact on memory resources. On the positive side is the fact that if everything is loaded into memory, the access time to the objects is improved, at least for the initial load of the objects.

Choose your compile target with care. Being aware of these facts, and also of your users' runtime environment, may affect your decision.

Performance Enhancement Techniques

Several coding techniques can provide an immediate benefit to your application. Code and design reviews are a vital element in ensuring that good techniques are adhered to, thus ensuring that the code you write is achieving maximum performance. Here are some other techniques to consider.

Building environmental controls

Managing your environment is no easy task. There are so many things that can go wrong, it is almost impossible to allow for all of the conditions you might encounter. One of the most unstable and inconsistent of these is the environment surrounding your application, the windows environment. Every object you develop adds to the burden the windows resources must handle. If you have more than 4 Mbytes of RAM and a permanent swap file, chances are you will not have memory problems before you encounter GDI and USER resource problems. These must be monitored carefully, as they are consumed extremely rapidly. Consider that a program such as Excel can swallow up 20 percent of your GDI resources in a single gulp. If you paint a window with several controls on it, you will consume these valuable and precious resources quickly too.

Try to keep as few individual controls as possible in a single window. This reduces the load on the environment, promotes better graphical performance, and makes maintenance easier. A DataWindow is a great tool for collections of controls. External DataWindows can be built with checkboxes, radio buttons, listboxes, and many other characteristics to simulate a collection of controls. And they use fewer resources. (You also have the flexibility of loading the default attributes of the DataWindow with a single instruction.)

Scripting techniques

There are several techniques that can be utilized to help make your scripts faster and more efficient. The first of these is quite simply to keep each individual function or event as short and to the point as possible. Below are a few other techniques we have picked up.

Array processing.   Have you ever tried to load an array with a list of items? Building a loop to increment the index value and setting each element in the array can be not only time-consuming but painful. Here is a technique to load the entire array with one statement, no indexing required.

```
String MyArrayOfStrings[]
MyArrayOfStrings = {Value1, Value2, Value3, Value4}
```

This loads the values into the first four elements of the array.

Another tip is to try to use fixed-size arrays as much as possible. Fixed-size arrays reserve memory in advance and thus perform much better at load time. Remember to try to free up the array as soon as possible in order to free up the memory it is using. This can be done quickly with a null array of the same type, e.g.,

```
String ArrayOfNulls[]
SetNull(ArrayOfNulls)
MyArrayOfStrings = ArrayOfNulls
```

One final technique is to use the Destroy function on the array if it is an array of structures. For example,

```
s_Structure MyArrayOfStructures[]
...Some processing that loads and uses the array
FOR idx = UpperBound(MyArrayOfStructures) to 1 STEP −1
DESTROY MyArrayOfStructures[idx]
NEXT
```

Avoiding long executing statements.   One of the techniques shown above is a performance no-no—the use of a function to set a boundary in a FOR loop. Used as it is above, it is not as bad as the other way around. For example,

```
FOR idx = 1 to UpperBound(MyArrayOfStructures)
```

Using UpperBound in this type of statement means that the function is executed for each iteration of the loop. Instead, assign UpperBound to a holding variable and use the holding variable to test the range, e.g.,

```
int max
max = UpperBound(MyArrayOfStructures)
for idx = 1 to max
```

Direct DataWindow referencing.   Another area where performance can be improved dramatically using a coding technique is in accessing DataWindows. In PowerBuilder 5, you can access any element of a DataWindow directly, that is, through the use of dot notation. Direct referencing can replace most of the DataWindow functions, such as GetItem, SetItem, and especially Modify and Describe. For example, to get all of the data in a specific row in a DataWindow, we used to rely on a series of GetItem() function calls, being particularly aware of the data types of the columns. Now you can define a structure (or an NVO) which contains elements that mirror the DataWindow columns and obtain all of the data for the row using DataWindowName.Object.Data[row]. Consequently, you can also access all of the rows in the DataWindow by making the receiving structure an array instead and dropping the index reference, i.e., DataWindowName.Object.Data. We highly recommend that you take the extra time and effort to review and study this technique, as it can be beneficial to the performance of your application and, perhaps more importantly, it is absolutely necessary that you understand it when you are developing distributed PowerBuilder applications where data is passed between the application and the application server.

Events to watch out for. Some events do not react kindly to developers and can introduce severe complications if used incorrectly. The list below shows a few of these.

- *retrieverow*—Executes script for each row of data returned. Use this event carefully, if at all, as it will significantly slow your retrieval times.

- *other*—Executed for every message the object is capable of receiving. Do not execute any code which results in the generating of a message.

- *activate/getfocus*—Executed whenever an object receives the focus. Do not execute code which forces the object to lose focus, such as a messagebox.

Use the tools and applications that are already available to you

Using system information. There are different ways to show system resources. Here are a few ideas we have used.

One method is to use a custom status bar that continually updates system resource information and displays this textually in the custom status bar. This is similar to what PowerBuilder shows.

A second method is to have a dialog window that can be opened from the menu that displays resources graphically. A window that does this is included in the example application with PowerBuilder and also with the Application Library in PB3 and PB4. This checks system resources and displays a graph showing the available resources.

If you use Microsoft Office, there is a program that shows detailed system information that you can call from your application. The MSInfo.Exe module can easily be called, and has a display as shown in Fig. 11.9.

About boxes. There are two methods for displaying an about box for your application. The first is obviously to code your own. The second involves a system call to display the standard about box as used by Windows applications. (See the Program Manager about box.) This function is shown in Fig. 11.10.

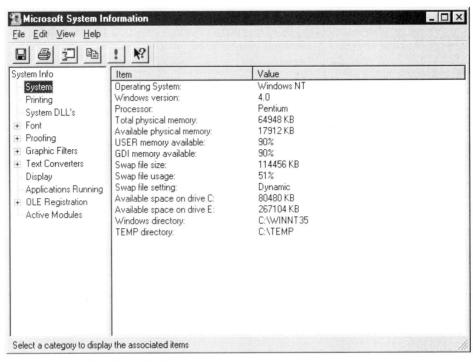

Figure 11.9   MS Office System Info.

```
//** Function Description for ShellAbout
//*****************************************************
// Parameters : hWndParent - can be zero ; The About Box is NON-MODAL if zero
//             lpProgTitle - String with Title
//             lpInfoText - About Two Lines of Text for the About Box
//             hIcon - If Zero or Invalid , Displays Windows Icon
//

/* Local External Declaration

FUNCTION int ShellAbout (int hWndParent, string lpProgTitle, &
string lpInfoText, int hIcon ) &
LIBRARY 'Shell32' ALIAS FOR "ShellAboutA"

*/

ShellAbout(0, "<<Application Name>>",&
+ "An example of using the Shell About program to display" &
+ " an about box for your system", 0)
```

Figure 11.10   Function declaration and call to ShellAbout.

Figure 11.11 Display from ShellAbout.

When this function is called, you will get an about box which looks like the standard Windows about box, as shown in Fig. 11.11.

The point being made is that there are many tools available to us if we take the time to look around. Many of these tools will be on your users' desktops, so you can take advantage of code that has been written and tested many times over (one of the elements that promote performance is the very idea of the product's being used by many users).

Sheet windows

Sheet windows are the mainstay of the MDI application. They contain the processing scripts required by the application. Here are a few tips and techniques regarding sheet windows.

Long-running activate events. Try not to place too much code in the window's activate event. The activate event occurs (1) when you open the sheet and (2) when you switch between sheets. The activate event already has processing overhead built in, as it has to switch your menus from sheet to sheet, a possibly expensive process. Adding to this will visibly slow down the process of switching between windows. A side effect of this is that in debug mode, you cannot step out of the activate event. Why? Because the activate event is the window's getfocus event and is fired whenever the window receives focus. The debugger forces the window to losefocus, and it then gets the focus as soon as the event script is complete, in which case it fires the activate event again. Make sure you put your stops *after* the activate event.

Long-running scripts during the open cycle. Long-running scripts during the open cycle of the window give an artificial appearance of slow load performance. Remember that the building of the objects contained within your window is in process at this time; the objects will already be starting their graphical processes, and your user will potentially see portions of objects drawing and redrawing themselves. You would be much better off *posting* an event to perform processing, so that the window loads quickly and the first step of your processing can display feedback to the user as to what it is doing—for example, retrieving data. (A progress bar or updatable messages prove useful for this.)

Closequery and show. Two other events in the window are often misunderstood: the *closequery* event and the *show* event. The show event is fired *after* the activate and immediately before you see the results on the screen. If you want to affect the appearance of a window, i.e., its position, size, etc., this is the event in which to do so. You will therefore avoid the flickering often seen with applications changing appearance in the open event.

The closequery event fires from the close event automatically, and allows you to control whether or not the window should close. Checking for such things as data that has changed without being saved should be done here. If you wish to prevent the window from closing, return a 1. Windows that must remain open at all times can be controlled here.

Note: Remember that if you use this form of processing to prevent the window from being closed, you need to make sure you provide at least one method whereby it can be closed, or you'll never be able to close your application.

DataWindows

DataWindows are the most often used, and the most powerful, objects in the PowerBuilder repertoire. These objects are used on almost every window in applications to display and manipulate data. These objects are extremely powerful and are well documented. Here are a few techniques we have picked up on that enhance the processing capabilities of DataWindows even more.

Describe, modify, and create. The Describe, Modify, and Create functions are extremely powerful tools that are used to manipulate, create, and describe your DataWindows. The only problem everyone faces is the use of the syntax. Well, there's a simple solution. The dwSyn050.exe program, which is shipped with PowerBuilder Enterprise, allows you to visually select the attributes and various describe and modify syntaxes necessary. This allows you to create the statements you need without the normal fear of syntax overload. Use this program to generate error-free syntax for using these powerful features. Figure 11.12 shows the DW Syntax program in action, displaying the attributes for a modify of the Table.Select clause.

One thing to keep in mind is that for most of the statements you can utilize with Modify and Describe, you can substitute direct attribute referencing. It

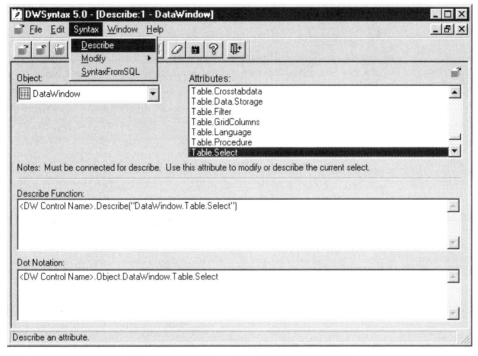

Figure 11.12 DataWindow Describe/Modify syntax—Modify Table.Select.

is still a good idea to build multiple or complex modify and describe statements, execute the group of statements, and parse the results. The cost of parsing the results is offset by the single execution of the describe/modify statement.

ImportString(). How often have you heard this: "SetItem() is too slow"? Well, the truth of the matter is, it *is* too slow. Unfortunately, there are no alternatives for setting individual data elements into a DataWindow, other than keyed data. But when a new row needs to be inserted with default values, remember this function. ImportString() will take a comma- or tab-delimited string of data that matches your columns and insert this data into your DataWindow in one step. Multiple columns of data can be inserted in about the same amount of time as a single SetItem. This capability is also useful wherever you utilize DataWindows to capture manual data, such as an Error dialog window.

Data retained on save DataWindows. DataWindows have another useful capability: to act as a DataStore for static data. Imagine creating the elements of a drop-down DataWindow manually, saving these, and then using the data in a drop-down without accessing your database or using the much slower and more cumbersome SetValue or DropDown Listbox. New data can be added and the data can be filtered, sorted, and manipulated in any fashion, with the final outcome being no change to what you started with.

To use this feature is simple. In any DataWindow, select the Rows and then Data menu items. This will present you with a grid in which data can be entered. Once you enter the data, you can save this data along with your DataWindow; when the DataWindow is loaded, the data is automatically loaded with it. This data can then be sorted, filtered, and otherwise used, giving you data access with a database.

Performance Analysis

Once we have the more easily controlled elements satisfied, you need to analyze the library objects to determine where performance setbacks, if any, occur. The word from Powersoft is that developers are working on an application profiler which will provide the information you need in order to assess your application.* There are, however, means to achieve this today. The first of these, and one that we recommend all applications utilize, is the use of the /pbdebug switch when running the executable. This is part of our standard test suite execution. We run the test suite once with the /pbdebug switch. This provides us with information about the application (and class library) calling sequence, a stack trace, and other information that we find useful. (We also run this with the TRACE keyword set on the database to trace SQL calls.) Going through all of this information is tedious, but necessary to determine where unnecessary code is being executed, or where methods are calling other methods we were not expecting.

Another way to do this is to create your own profiler. To do this, we utilize a small application we created along with very small pieces of code added to various objects. The application is a Remote Log Facility† which traps windows messages targeted for it and registers the time and resources available at that time. Because the application is separate from your application, no additional overhead is added to your application.

What this application needs to be able to do is to trap messages sent to it, determine who the sender was, and keep track of time. This means that your application needs to communicate with a separate application. While a distributed service might seem like a good idea for this, it isn't. In order to have minimal effect on the application, we decided on the sendmessage mechanism. The application sends a message to the operating system and then continues. The profiler, or Remote Log Facility (RLF), picks up the message, does some work to figure out who and what published the message, and logs the results. The first step needed to accomplish this is for both the RLF and the application to register a message class with the operating system that will serve as their dedicated communication link. We do this with an SDK function called RegisterWindowMessage. The function declaration for this, and the other SDK functions we will use, are shown in Fig. 11.13.

*At the time of writing, this was not available to us.
†Both the Remote Log Facility and the PFC InterApp Message Service are included on the CD.

```
FUNCTION unit RegisterWindowMessage(string MsgClassName) LIBRARY
  "User32" ALIAS FOR "RegisterWindowMessageA"
FUNCTION boolean SendMessage(uint Handle, uint msg_no, uint wparam, long
  lparam) LIBRARY "user32" ALIAS FOR "SendMessageA"
FUNCTION boolean PostMessage(uint Handle, uint msg_no, uint wparam, long
  lparam) LIBRARY "user32" ALIAS FOR "PostMessageA"
FUNCTION int GetClassName(uint hWnd, ref string ClassName, int
  StringLength) LIBRARY "user32" ALIAS FOR "GetClassNameA"
FUNCTION int GetWindowText(uint hWnd, ref string wintext, int textlength)
  LIBRARY "user32" ALIAS FOR "GetWindowTextA"
```

Figure 11.13 Function declarations for interapplication messaging.

Tip: Using the alias keyword allows you to continue to use the standard function name for execution, simplifying maintenance of cross-platform code.

In order for the application and the RLF to communicate, we must make a call to this function. This function call is shown in Fig. 11.14.

Now we need to add to the application the capability to send a message to the operating system indicating that this message class should be used. To do this, we created a Profiler service class that we added to the Application Manager's capabilities using the usual extension techniques. Now, wherever we want the profile information captured, we add a call to the SendMessage method such as that shown in Fig. 11.15.

The RLF must be able to capture the message and translate this into something that makes sense. In order to do this, we add code to the main window's Other event. We detect the message class and call the Log method as shown in Fig. 11.16.

The functions executed can then perform whatever processing is required. Your application does not wait for this to happen. It continues processing. When you are done with your testing, you can switch over to the RLF running in the background and look at the results of your testing. We created some output using a DataWindow, and a sample of the results of some application testing is shown in Fig. 11.17.

```
RETURN RegisterWindowMessage(messagetype)
```

Figure 11.14 Registering a message class.

```
IF WindowID = 0 THEN WindowID = 65535
RETURN SendMessage(WindowID, MessageID, wparam, lparam)
```

Figure 11.15 Sending a message to the message class.

```
IF Message.Number = MsgNum THEN

    /* Attempt to interpret message */
    uint wordparm, objecthandle
    long longparm
    int NameLength = 80
    String ObjName, ObjTitle
    wordparm = message.wordparm; objecthandle = wordparm
    longparm = message.longparm

    ObjName = Space(namelength)
    Objname = svc_iApp.ccf_GetClassName(ObjectHandle)

    ObjTitle = Space(namelength)
    svc_iApp.GetWindowText(ObjectHandle, ObjTitle, NameLength)
    IF ObjTitle >" " THEN
    ELSE
        RETURN -1
    END IF

    id = objecthandle
    msg = ObjName+"("+ObjTitle+") Msg( = "+String(longparm)+") -"
    IF dw_Msgs.RowCount() >longparm THEN
        string extmsg
        extmsg = GetItemString(dw_msgs, longparm, "text")
        IF NOT isNull(extmsg) THEN Msg = Msg + extmsg
    END IF

    wf_logclass()
END IF
```

Figure 11.16 Trapping the message and executing code depending on it.

How it works

Basically, both your application and the log facility application register a special windows message class. When one application sends or posts a message to the message queue containing this unique message id, the windows message handler processes the message and notifies the recipient application(s).

Your application is coded to check if the message manager is available before executing the function call, so there is no overhead other than a very fast IsValid() function call if the object is not active. This code looks like this:

IF IsValid(InterAppObject) THEN InterAppObject.SendMessage(hWndRecipient,
   MsgNum, longparm, wordparm)

The hWndRecipient is the handle of the window that is to receive this message, and can be defaulted to hwnd_broadcast (or 65536). The MsgNum is a value returned to you when you register the message with windows, and longparm and wordparm contain the values you can use for processing the mes-

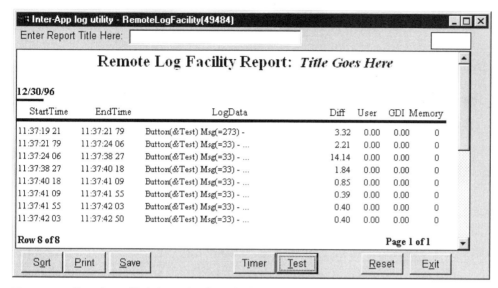

Figure 11.17   Sample profile information from the Remote Log Facility.

sage. (We use longparm to send a identification of the function to the log program, and wordparm can be used to hold other data, such as time, etc.)

This little log facility can then be used to trap the start and end times for any object or script and give you real feedback on performance. The addition of a small profiler service to the PFC can allow you to easily add code to your application to provide you with the information you need.

How to test

This section describes how we are going to test the library to analyze areas of performance that can be improved or require improvement. The tests we plan to run will be run using various machine, network, and environment setups.

Use an automated scripting tool to record and run test.   We use the capabilities of SQA Test Suite to record and run our tests. This will ensure that we apply consistent parameters and criteria for all tests. We run each situation script a total of 20 times and calculate the average time for each test.

Use the Remote Log Facility to record times.   We have developed a module which can record data, including time and resources, which runs remotely from the application. The application communicates with the log facility by means of windows messages, thereby having a minimal effect on the performance of the library.

Use a debug version of the library.   We developed a special edition of the library framework which contains the embedded calls to the Remote Log Facility. As specified, the access to the log functions is simple windows message posts to a special windows message class, reducing the impact on the system.

Analysis.   We recommend that you perform your analysis on various hardware and software configurations. Even if the configuration will not be used in a production environment, it can serve to provide additional information.

Software configurations

PowerBuilder DLLs networked, application EXE/PBDs networked. PowerBuilder DLLs and application EXE/PBDs are all running from the network. This should have the slowest performance of any version of your library.

PowerBuilder DLLs networked, application EXE/PBDs local. PowerBuilder DLLs are running from the network, and application EXE/PBDs are running locally. Performance here should be acceptable.

PowerBuilder DLLs local, application EXE/PBDs networked. PowerBuilder DLLs are running locally, and application EXE/PBDs are running off the network. Again, performance should be acceptable.

PowerBuilder DLLs local, application EXE/PBDs local. PowerBuilder DLLs and application EXE/PBDs are all running locally. This is the highest-performance configuration. However, this is not an optimal condition for running distributed client-server applications, but it will provide feedback on what performance levels *can* be attained.

Development vs. runtime executable. Running the tests with both development and production environments will help us to analyze how much time is being utilized by PowerBuilder itself, as most load time taken by PowerBuilder is eliminated in the development environment.

PowerBuilder DLLs preloaded. Preload the PowerBuilder DLLs using a small "shell" application, (or in fact, the Remote Log Facility, which serves quite nicely as a PowerBuilder DLL loader).

Hardware configurations.   If possible, run the various test scenarios on different client platforms to determine how much of an impact upgrading equipment would have on future use. For example:

- 486/33 with 16 Mbytes RAM
- 486/75 with 16 Mbytes RAM
- Pentium P90 with 16 Mbytes RAM

Analyze for different database accesses.   In order to complete Save Cycle testing, we include tests of using Watcom (ODBC) and Sybase (our choices) in the test cycle. We also try to compare normal DataWindow SQL access with stored procedure access.

What should you test?

Application load time. At application startup, plan to analyze the time it takes to load PowerBuilder and then to load the application.

PowerBuilder load time. PowerBuilder load time is described as the amount of time it takes to load the PowerBuilder runtime DLLs. We are aware of the fact that the PowerBuilder 4.0 loads much more of the runtime environment up front than PowerBuilder 3.0; this is one of the ways in which PowerBuilder is addressing some of the runtime performance issues. Expect the PowerBuilder 5.0 load time to be significantly longer than that for PowerBuilder 3.0 and slightly longer than that for PowerBuilder 4.0. PowerBuilder 5.0 loads faster under Windows NT, but slightly slower under Windows 3.1.

Library or framework load time. Analyze the amount of time it takes to load each element or service of the BCL framework. The results will indicate any areas of suspect performance.

Application initialization. Measure other areas of application initialization, such as splash windows, resource checking, version checking, etc.

Application login. At the login window, we measure the time it takes to connect to various databases and investigate means to improve the connect time required. Various parameter settings will be measured to attempt to determine the optimal settings for each database.

Frame window and menu load. We measure the load time required to load our frame window and frame menu and investigate different techniques now available to improve the performance of the initial frame menu loads.

Often-used dialogs. In this section, we perform analysis of the dialog windows most often utilized in the library and determine how we can improve the performance of any dialog determined to be non-performance-compliant, i.e., performance that does not meet the standards we establish as our goals. For example:

- User preferences
- Window Toolbar dialog
- Help About
- System Info
- Sort/Filter/Find dialogs
- Error dialogs
- User Messagebox dialogs

Other key objects.   Finally, run tests on all of the other objects most often used, such as parent-child (master-detail), data retrieval, etc.

Test results and analysis

In analyzing the results of the tests, we need to make sure we cover the following points:

- Collect all test results for analysis.

- Analyze test results and determine where effort is required for correction, enhancement, no change, etc.

- Create the technical specification for required changes.

- Develop recommendations for developers to improve performance through the use of better techniques.

- Make all required changes to library code *or* make recommendations for change to the vendor for changes which affect the architecture. This effort is very dependent on the results of the analysis, and may be either extended or shortened based on our findings.

Summary/Conclusions

We hope this helps to shed a little light on the differences between what your users might perceive to be performance and what you know is happening in the system. Keep your user in mind when developing. Performance can be affected in more ways than one. Remember that design plays a large part in how you might affect performance, and make use of what's available to you. Finally, we hope we have dispensed with some of the myths surrounding the performance of PowerBuilder and, more importantly, the PFC.

12

Extending the PFC

Introduction/Objectives

The PFC development team had taken on a very challenging task. Their goal was to provide a class library that met the requirements of every developer in a vast Powerbuilder community. Judging by the tremendous response and the fact that you are reading this book, it is clear they have succeeded. They have done so by intentionally omitting any functionality that would force a specific presentation style or would cause the framework to become inflexible. As a result, PFC has a lot of opportunities for extension.

In Chap. 3 the concept of the extension layer was introduced. This chapter will discuss the practical application of the extension layer and other techniques used to customize the PFC library. Although at first it may seem that by providing the extension layer, PFC has dictated the exact method of extension, in reality there is still room for many choices. In fact, there are so many that the topic of extending the PFC remains the source of many debates.

One of the most important decisions on a PFC project involves the selection of the extension method. The choices made regarding the extension techniques are not easily reversed. The extension methods must be selected with care. Unfortunately, the decisions related to extending the PFC architecture must be made on the very first PFC-based project. As is the case with any class library, one of the first questions is: "Where do I place the code?" Finding the right event provides half the answer. You have to determine whether the additional logic belongs in the extension layer. This chapter will provide the answers to these questions and will discuss different alternatives for the object extension. After completion of this chapter, you should have enough knowledge to select the method most appropriate for your specific requirements.

PFC Layer

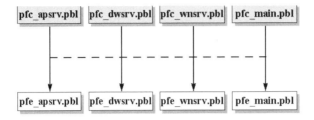

Figure 12.1 Extension layer.

Extension Layer

The Extension Layer

What is it?

PFC is distributed as a set of eight PBLs. All the PFC code is contained in four PBLs; the other four comprise an extension layer (see Fig. 12.1).

The extension layer is intended to allow us to make application-specific changes without affecting the base class objects. Let's examine how the concepts are implemented in PFC. Each object in the PFC layer has a corresponding descendant in PFE. There is no code in the extension-layer objects; they are intended as placeholders for any custom logic. The descendant objects in PFC are inherited from the ones in PFE. The relationship between the objects in the PFC and the extension layers is shown in Fig. 12.2. The circular relationship between the two layers provides the ability to modify any object without placing the code directly in the class library.

In order to come up with an extension-layer mechanism best suited for your needs, you must be aware of the different extension techniques, the different types of logic you are going to add to PFC, and finally the extension requirements specific to your environment.

Extension Techniques

Having the extension layer raises the first question: Should I add the new logic directly to the extension layer, or should I add the logic by inheriting from the extension layer? The answer is both. The difference between the two methods lies in the circular relationship between the PFC and PFE layers. The logic added to the extension layer affects the whole library. The logic added by inheritance will affect only a new descendant object. Let's identify and define the two different techniques.

Definition: **Extension by Insertion**—Extending by adding code directly to the objects in the PFE layer or in any layer between the PFC and PFE layers. These extensions usually are generic in nature.

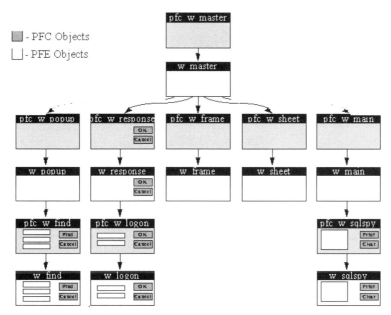

Figure 12.2 Extension-layer object relationship.

Definition: **Extension by Inheritance**—Extending by inheriting an object from the PFE layer and adding code to further specialize the object. This form of extension is usually more specific in nature.

Both of these methods rely on placing the new code within the inheritance structure.

Definition: **Extension by Delegation**—Extending by delegating tasks to new service objects. This form of extension can be generic or specific in nature, but because of the additional complexity, it may be reserved for code intended for reuse.

One point that may be obvious still deserves to be mentioned: Modifying the objects in the PFC layer is not recommended. These objects are subject to change in future releases.

Extension by insertion

Extension by insertion is very powerful. Every PFC object has a corresponding PFE descendant. Every object in the class library can be extended.

For this method to be used, the insertion object must already exist in the class library. Another limitation of this method lies in the fact that any change made by insertion is global for the scope of the PFE layer. Let's take a look at the transaction object n_tr. It contains several precoded and placeholder functions. To make the transaction object functional for Sybase, we need to override of_SetUser and, if autocommit is set to TRUE, of_Begin and of_End as well. This is illustrated in Fig. 12.3.

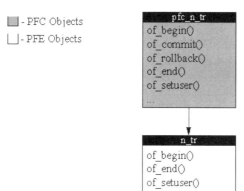

Figure 12.3 Transaction extended by insertion.

This works great for a single-database application, but what happens if you need to connect to different databases? Adding the DBMS-specific functions to n_tr has made every transaction in the application specific to a single DBMS. There are ways around this problem, but as a rule extension by insertion has to be generic enough for the scope of the PFE layer. The extension scope is discussed later in the chapter.

Extension by inheritance

Extension by inheritance can get more specific. Figure 12.4 demonstrates how different windows can be extended by inheritance. In this case, an application

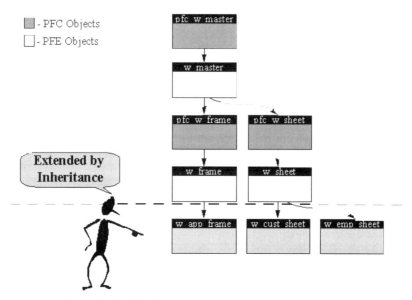

Figure 12.4 Extension by inheritance.

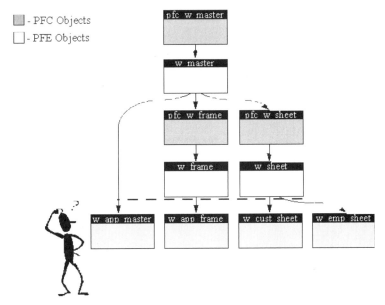

Figure 12.5 Limitations of extension by inheritance.

frame and multiple sheet windows are generated by inheriting from the windows in the PFE layer.

Extension by inheritance works great for the lowest descendant objects. However, there is a problem with using extension by inheritance to add logic to the ancestor object. Because the new object is not a part of the inheritance chain, the functionality added to w_app_master will not make it to w_app_frame. Figure 12.5 shows this limitation.

Extension by inheritance is limited to the lowest-level descendants and concrete classes. It does not work for the abstract classes.

The limitation of extension by inheritance could also be considered an advantage. Extension by inheritance makes it possible to generate very specific objects without affecting the rest of the class library. Let's get back to the transaction example. As you can see from Fig. 12.6, we can generate a DBMS-specific transaction through inheritance.

Note: The transaction object is easily extended by inheritance because it is declared as a global variable. The developer can select a specific transaction. This method may not be appropriate for prereferenced service classes.

Extension by delegation

The two previous methods have added new logic through the use of inheritance. An important alternative that should not be overlooked is extension by delegation or by creating new services. Because the services are associated at runtime, this method opens new opportunities for implementation techniques such

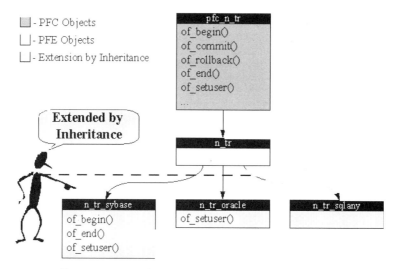

Figure 12.6   Transaction extended by inheritance.

as operational polymorphism, which allows dynamic object association. This method was used to implement the file and platform PFC services. Figure 12.7 demonstrates how the transaction object can be extended using this technique.

The of_Connect function is extended to create the appropriate transaction service.

```
CHOOSE CASE Upper(Left(this.dbms, 3))
      CASE 'SYB', 'SYC'
              this.inv_trsrv = CREATE n_cst_trsrv_sybase
      CASE 'OR7', 'O71', 'O72', 'O73'
              this.inv_trsrv = CREATE n_cst_trsrv_oracle
      CASE ELSE
              // unsupported dbms
              return −1
END CHOOSE
return super::of_Connect()
```

The of_SetUser function is then delegated to the transaction service.

```
IF IsValid(inv_trsrv) THEN
      inv_trsrv.of_SetUser(as_userid, as_password)
END IF
```

Typically, tasks are delegated by client objects to service providers. An application delegates its tasks to the application manager, DataWindow control to DataWindow services, windows to window services, and so on. However, the service delegation is not limited to two levels. The service providers may

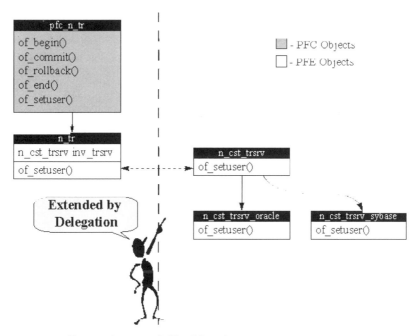

Figure 12.7 Transaction extended by delegation.

assume the role of client objects and transfer some responsibilities to other service objects. Therefore, it is possible to use the extension by delegation technique to extend the PFC's service objects.

Extension Logic

From the examples in previous sections, it has become apparent that not all the logic that needs to be added to PFC is the same. The type of logic that needs to be added will often dictate its placement. This section will discuss the different types of extension logic.

Two important concepts in any object-oriented language are generalization and specialization. In order to achieve a high level of reuse, many requirements have to be combined into a few generic concepts. These concepts can be gradually specialized to meet the more detailed needs of a smaller group. This technique is called *nested generalization* and was described in Chap. 3. Other requirements may be implemented as components of a service-based architecture. Each component may be based on a nested generalization method. PFC has applied a concept of nested generalization and service-based architecture to provide a lot of its functionality. PFC starts with generic concepts of windows, visual and nonvisual controls, applications, and window and DataWindow services. Each of the above is then further specialized.

Definition: **Specialization**—Extracting a more specific concept from an abstract by defining detail behavior.

Definition: **Generalization**—Combining multiple related concepts into a single concept by defining common behavior.

In order to figure out where the specific code should be placed, it is important to determine the purpose of the additional logic. What kind of code is going to be added to PFC? Some of the possible reasons to extend PFC are listed below.

- Adding new functionality to the general classes
- Modifying the behavior of the general classes
- Specializing the existing objects
- Creating new general classes
- Creating new specific classes

All of the above can be categorized into two distinct groups: generalization code and specialization code.

Generalization code

Generalization code includes any modifications to existing general classes or creation of new general classes. The following reasons for extension fall into the category of generalization code:

- Adding new functionality to the general classes
- Modifying the behavior of the general classes
- Creating new general classes

Some examples of the above are adding a new event or function to an existing object, overriding an event or function in an existing object, and creating a new object. The reasons for generalization code are common look and feel, extensions to the existing services, addition of new services, and bug fixes.

Specialization code

The following reasons for extension fall into the category of specialization code:

- Specializing the existing objects
- Creating new specific classes

Examples of new specific classes are application-specific business objects, template window ancestors to generate application-specific presentation, application-specific service extensions, and application-specific services.

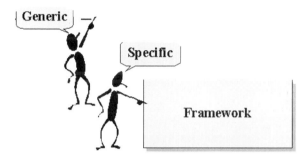

Figure 12.8 Generic-to-specific transition I.

Extension Scope

Where does the generic functionality end and the specific begin? This depends on your point of view. If you are designing a framework on top of PFC, you are specializing the PFC to meet the requirements of a framework. In this case, the PFC contains the generic objects and your framework contains the specific. See Fig. 12.8. Once the framework is completed, you'll specialize it further to generate each application. In this case, the application will contain the specific functionality and anything above will be generic. See Fig. 12.9.

There are numerous reasons to extend PFC. PFC may be customized for a particular industry sector—for example, generating a financial application framework. It may also be further specialized to meet the requirements of a single company. Taking it one step further, a department-level framework may be generated, implementing the business rules specific to the particular department. Finally, at the last level, PFC may be specialized to meet the requirements of a single application. It is important to draw the borders and be aware of different points where the generic code makes the transition to specific. The objects on each side of these borders will have to be insulated from each other.

Extensibility Checklist

Before diving deep into extension-layer implementation, it may be appropriate to determine the extension requirements of your particular project(s).

- Will any part of the application be reused by multiple projects?

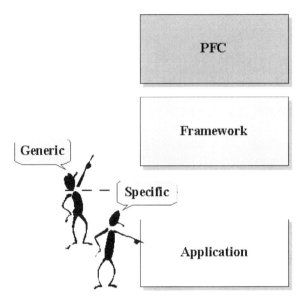

Figure 12.9 Generic-to-specific transition II.

- Will the application be built on top of an in-house framework reused by multiple departments?
- Will the application be based on a third-party framework?
- Will the application or framework be under source control?
- How much additional functionality is planned to be added to the framework on top of PFC?

The answers to these questions will help you select the appropriate extension method.

Extension Methods

Roll up your sleeves; we have reached the point where we are ready to get technical and examine the different extension approaches.

PFE as an application layer

The first extension approach requires the least amount of preparation. This approach is best illustrated by the Quick Start application. In this case, the PFE layer is used for both the generic reusable code and the application-specific logic. Using this approach, a separate PFE layer is maintained for each individual application. The objects in the PFE layer can be directly modified with application-specific code. See Fig. 12.10 for an example.

Class Library

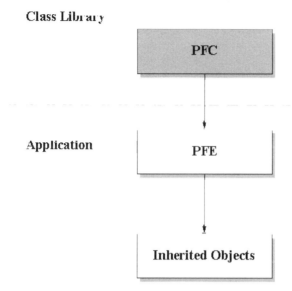

Figure 12.10   PFE as an application layer.

Advantages

- *Does not require any up-front planning.* This is the "out of the box" solution. You can copy the four PFE PBLs into a separate directory and start coding.

Limitations

- *Once the generic framework code is combined with the application-specific, they cannot be easily separated.* This approach is based on an assumption that there is little or no need for reusable code. The extension scope is defined as two components, PFC and application. If you plan to reuse any code or to share it between multiple applications, this approach is not practical.

Note: Do not underestimate the common framework requirement for your application. The reusable framework may be as small as a few PFC bug fixes. Reapplying the same fixes for the next project can be very tedious.

- *A separate copy of PFE and PFC PBLs for each project must be maintained.* The reason for separate PFE PBLs is clear (they are specific to each project), but why PFC? The answer lies in the nature of object relationships between the two layers. The PFC layer contains many objects which are inherited from the objects in the PFE layer; for example, pfc_w_sheet is a descendant of w_master. The same is true for associative and aggregate relationships. The transaction object referenced in PFC objects is n_tr, not pfc_n_tr. In many cases, modifying the PFE objects with the application-specific code makes the PFC objects application-specific as well.

This brings up an important distribution issue: If you create PBDs or DLLs from the PFC PBLs, they may not be compatible between multiple applications!

PFE as a framework layer

Using the second approach, both the framework and application elements are included in the extension scope. The PFE layer is reserved for framework objects only. The application-specific logic is added by inheriting from the PFE layer, as demonstrated in Fig. 12.11.

Advantages

- *PFE and PFC PBLs, PBDs, or DLLs may be reused and /or shared between multiple applications.* The framework and PFC can be treated as a single unit. The application extension is not a part of the extension layer, and therefore it has no effect on the framework and PFC objects. Some companies are distributing the framework using PBDs only. This is the only approach that still allows this type of distribution. Even if the PBLs or PBDs are distributed to different project teams, the framework and the application distribution is simplified.

- *This approach is easier to support.* All the circular references are contained to PFC and PFE. The application-specific code is added below PFE. Once the

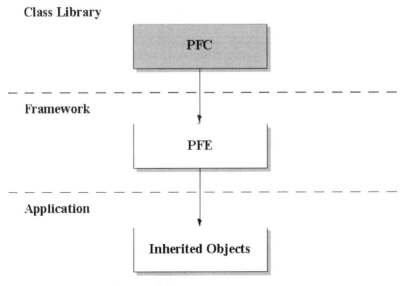

Figure 12.11 PFE as a framework layer.

framework is complete and deployed to different application development groups, there is not much that can be done on the application level to inadvertently change the framework behavior. The framework support is simplified.

- *The approach is lean.* This approach allows separate framework and application components with the minimum number of objects. Other approaches, discussed later, require an additional layer, which increases the number of PBLs and objects.

Limitations

- *The application-specific logic is limited to extension by inheritance and delegation.* Extension by inheritance is limited to the lowest descendant objects. None of the abstract PFC ancestors can be extended with the application-specific logic. For example, application-specific code cannot be placed in w_master; this object is in the PFE layer and is reserved for the framework code.

  There are many objects in PFC that favor extension by insertion. Any PFE object that was referenced from PFC cannot be easily extended by inheritance. Most of the PFC objects cannot be extended by inheritance, but instead may require extension by insertion or delegation. This is because these objects were directly referenced from the _PFC layer. The bulk of these are service objects, but there are some client objects as well.

  This method does allow the generic framework logic to be added by insertion; the PFE layer can be modified directly. The limitation lies only with the application-specific code. Extension by insertion is typically used for the generalization code. Is there a need for generic behavior at the application level? Let's take a look at two examples that do require application-specific logic at the PFE level.

  u_dw is the first example. The events *pfc_prermbmenu, pfc_preprintdlg,* and *pfc_pagesetupdlg* serve as placeholder events that allow customization of the pop-up menu, and the Print and Page Setup dialog boxes. If u_dw is used throughout the application to customize the pop-up menu for the whole application, code must be added to u_dw directly or duplicated for every u_dw placed on the window.

  The second example is the status bar window service. The status bar service allows the addition of standard memory and time objects as well as custom text and bitmaps to the MicroHelp bar. The service allows interaction with the status bar through the use of *pfc_statusbarclicked, pfc_statusbardoubleclicked,* and *pfc_statusbarrbuttonup* events. In this case, application-specific code has to be added directly to *n_cst_winsrv_statusbar* in the PFE layer.

- The workaround for the first case is to create an application-level abstract class u_app_dw inherited from u_dw. Every DataWindow in the application must be of u_app_dw type. It then becomes possible to change the pop-up menu on the applicationwide level by adding code to u_app_dw. The solution for the second case is a little more challenging. The status bar service reference variable is of n_cst_winsrv_statusbar type. See the excerpt from the of_setstatusbar function below:

```
IF ab_switch THEN
        IF IsNull(inv_statusbar) Or not IsValid (inv_statusbar) THEN
                inv_statusbar = create n_cst_winsrv_statusbar
                inv_statusbar.of_SetRequestor (this)
                Return 1
        END IF
ELSE
...
```

Because the inv_statusbar is created as n_cst_winsrv_statusbar, extension by inheritance has no effect. One possible solution for this problem is to use the delegation technique and create another application-specific status bar object, as shown in Fig. 12.12.

A new object, app_n_cst_winsrv_statusbar, is created. All the events are triggered from the corresponding n_cst_winsrv_statusbar status bar object. The new object is instantiated as inv_app_statusbar and serves as a placeholder for application-specific logic.

- *Possible conflict with third-party utilities.* The hard-coded references to the objects in the PFE layer lead to one important benefit: The PFE layer has provided an industry standard. There are a few PFC-related tools available now, with many more on the way. Their contributions range from object modeling to wizard-based template generation. The reason these tools were able to get this far is because they are able to generate code based on the objects in the PFE layer. When objects are extended by inheriting from PFE,

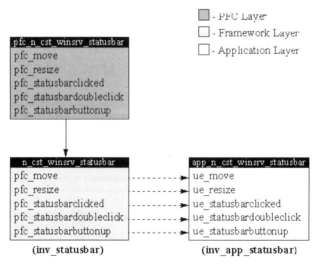

Figure 12.12 Status bar delegation solution.

the new descendant objects fall outside this standard, rendering the tools useless.

- *Cannot be further extended through inheritance.* With some limitations, it is possible to add application-specific code by inheriting from PFE. It is not possible to add another generic framework layer below PFE. As an example, try to inherit from n_cst_dwsrv_sort, add a function called of_MyFunction, and then call of_MyFunction through the existing inv_sort reference variable. The compilation of the code will fail because the inv_sort is declared to be of n_cst_dwsrv_sort type, and of_MyFunction does not exist in n_cst_dwsrv_sort.

  Extension by delegation is still possible. As seen in previous examples, service delegation technique is very powerful and can be used to compensate for inability to extend through inheritance. Nonetheless, loss of the inheritance-based techniques should be carefully evaluated and balanced against the advantages of this approach.

- If you are developing an industry-specific framework or a class library and there may be a requirement to add another generic layer below yours, this method will not work. In other terms, this is a selfish approach. Using the PFE layer for the framework does not leave any room for another generic layer.

Adding an additional Layer

So far, two layers were used the way they were deployed with PFC. The next logical step is to add another layer. This can be accomplished by adding an additional layer between PFC and PFE. The new layer (PFD*) is inserted by changing the inheritance structure of the PFE layer. DataWindow services are utilized as an example to demonstrate this technique. Figure 12.13 shows the DataWindow services relationship in a two-layer approach, before the additional layer is added. The base service object n_cst_dwsrv is inherited from its PFC counterpart, pfc_n_cst_dwsrv.

After an additional layer is inserted between PFC and PFE, the DataWindow service relationship is changed. The new relationship is shown in Fig. 12.14.

A new object, pfd_n_cst_dwsrv, is inherited from pfc_n_cst_dwsrv, and n_cst_dwsrv is changed to inherit from pfd_n_cst_dwsrv. This can be accomplished by saving the old n_cst_dwsrv as pfd_n_cst_dwsrv, then deleting the existing n_cst_dwsrv and creating a new one by inheriting from pfd_n_cst_dwsrv. If the existing n_cst_dwsrv already contains some code, its ancestry can be modified by exporting the object, replacing all the references to its ancestor, and importing it back. The same process is then repeated for every object. The process sounds a lot more intimidating than it actually is. The three-layered extension PBLs enclosed on the companion CD took an hour to generate—a tedious hour, but nonetheless only an hour.

*The naming convention has no significance. The above was chosen in alphabetical order, or it could stand for "Departmental."

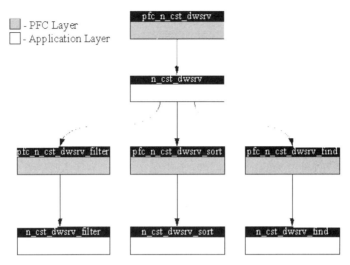

Figure 12.13 Two-layer relationship.

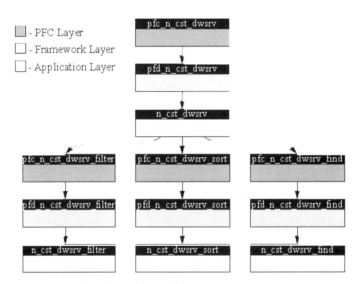

Figure 12.14 Three-layer relationship.

Three-layer approach (PFC, framework, and application layers)

Using a three-layer approach, there is room for a framework in the additional middle layer, leaving PFE to be used for application-specific code. See Fig. 12.15.

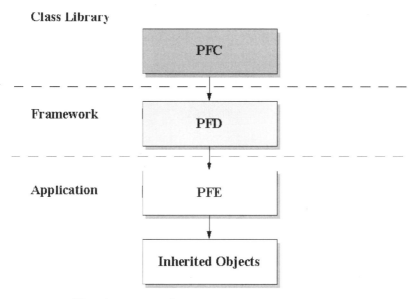

Class Library

PFC

Framework

PFD

Application

PFE

Inherited Objects

Figure 12.15 Three-layer approach.

Advantages

- *Has flexibility.* The PFE layer is available for the application-specific code. The application objects can be extended by insertion, inheritance, or delegation. In the previous example of the u_dw pop-up menu and the status bar service, the application-specific code may be placed directly in the u_dw's pfc_prermbmenu and pfc_statusbarclicked of the n_cst_winsrv_statusbar.

- *Allows further extension by insertion.* In contrast to the last approach, this time the PFE layer is left empty. The users of the framework have the option of adding yet another layer between PFD and PFE. The change of inheritance is easier because PFE is empty. The objects in PFE may be overwritten without the fear of losing any code.

- *Third-party utility is friendly.* When the PFC library is extended by insertion, all the objects in the PFE layer include the new functionality. Any template or code generated by a third-party application will reference the objects in the PFE layer and therefore will automatically include the new functionality.

Limitations

- *Requires maintaining a separate copy of PFE and PFC PBLs for each project.* This is true any time the PFE layer contains application-specific code. Consider the relationship between pfc_u_dw, u_dw, n_tr, and pfc_n_tr. Figure 12.16 demonstrates what happens when two applications share the same

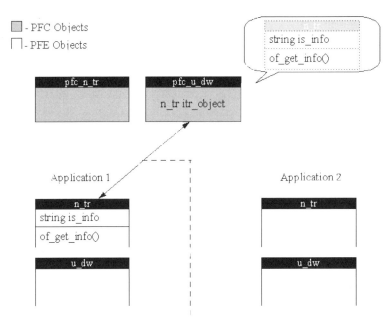

Figure 12.16 Shared library limitation.

PFC PBLs. In the first application, the transaction object was extended. An instance variable and a function were added.

When the first application is regenerated, the definition of n_tr is memorized and the pfc_u_dw object becomes aware of a new instance variable and a function. As shown in Fig. 12.17, when the second application is regenerated, its n_tr definition replaces the first.

If the first application is regenerated, the second will not run successfully because of the n_tr definition mismatch. This may result in a "GPF tug of war"—when the first application is rebuilt, the second breaks, and vice versa.

The same issue applies for the objects related by inheritance. For example, when a function is added to n_cst_dwsrv, in the PFE layer the definition of all descendant DataWindow services will include the new function. As a result, the definitions of both PFC and PFE objects have been indirectly modified.

- *Introduces additional inheritance levels and a larger number of PBLs and objects.* The performance degradation due to the number of inheritance levels in Powerbuilder 5.0 is insignificant. However, the greater number of PBLs and objects may affect the performance in development mode. This is because a lot of optimization performed in the compiled application cannot be done in development mode. See Chap. 11 for a complete discussion of performance issues.

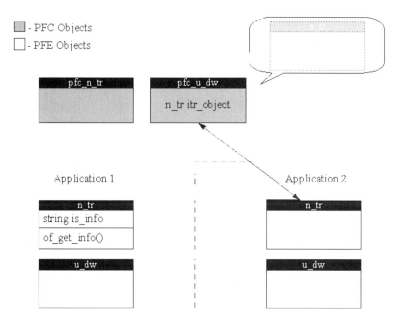

Figure 12.17 Shared library limitation.

Extension effect on framework deployment and maintenance

Whenever a framework is built for use on multiple projects, you must consider the framework deployment and maintenance issues. The framework may be intended for a single project team, a small work group, a department, or a whole company. There are very few issues when the framework is used by a single project team as a reusable object repository. It can be built along with the first project and improved with every future application. Once the framework is used concurrently on two or more projects, possible conflicts between these projects should be resolved before they arise.

- *Framework location.* The most convenient place for the common libraries (PFC and PFD) is on the network. Multiple project teams may modify the application library path to point to the common libraries on the network. Unfortunately, this approach may not be practical. The first issue has to do with the shared library limitation discussed earlier in this chapter. Most of the extension methods do not allow sharing of libraries between projects. The second pitfall lies in the fact that when changes in the common libraries are introduced, they immediately affect each individual application. The project teams are not allowed to examine the changes and resolve any possible integration issues. The conclusion is that a separate copy of all the common libraries should be used by each project team.

■ *Project contentions.* Change is a fact of life. As soon as the framework is deployed, you will receive bug reports and enhancement requests. Typically these will come from a project team early in the development cycle. However, another team may be close to its deployment date. The team members have worked very hard to get to this point and have spent endless days testing every application feature. The mere mention of change is sure to get you off their Christmas list. The only way to allow each team to have control over its own destiny is to implement version control. The changes between versions should be documented, and each team may pick the most appropriate time to migrate to the next version. Support of multiple versions is more complex, so you may want to limit the support to the last two or three versions and make the migration mandatory for all others. The support issues are covered in detail in Chap. 15, but some of the extension method decisions will directly affect the ability to effectively maintain the framework and each application.

When creating a middle layer, there is another issue that should be resolved. There are two possible choices: An interim-layer object may be inserted between every PFC and PFE object or only between the ones that were modified. The latter approach is demonstrated in Fig. 12.18. The framework contains functionality only for the sort and find DataWindow services. Everywhere else the original object relationship was preserved.

When the latter approach is used, the framework objects may be added as required when new functionality is added. This is acceptable for a single-team framework, but it introduces extra maintenance problems for multiple-project environments. When a new object is added to the framework, every application will have to change the inheritance structure to point to the new object instead of to PFC. The complexity is multiplied by the number of applications currently

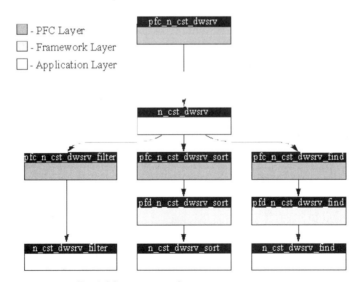

Figure 12.18 Partial-layer approach.

in development or production. An inheritance adjuster utility may simplify this task, but may be still too intrusive to be considered viable. Consider asking every project team to change its application inheritance structure with each framework release. Generating a middle-layer object for every PFC object regardless of changes made will simplify maintenance down the line.

Other extension methods

There are other methods, but they are all either an extension or a mix of the three major ones described in a previous section. Additional layers may be added, bringing the total above three. In the three-layer approach, PFE may be used as a department framework and the layer above reserved for corporate standards. The PFE as a framework layer approach can be made very functional through the use of extension by delegation techniques. All the variations on the theme approaches share the advantages and the shortcomings of the big three.

Extension-Layer Usage

All the extension methods described in this chapter share common implementation techniques. This section will discuss some of these methods.

Extending precoded events

In extending the precoded PFC events, special care must be taken when these events have return codes. Simply placing the additional logic in an extended event will override the ancestor return code. This may cause unpredictable behavior. To illustrate this point let's take a look at pfc_w_master's pfc_postupdate event. This event is triggered automatically by the pfc_save event and is responsible for resetting the update flags upon a successful update. If the update flags were reset successfully, it returns a 1, but if there was an error and the flags were not reset, the event returns −1. A function call is added to perform the required postupdate processing:

```
int li_rc
li_rc = this.of_PostUpdateProcessing()
return li_rc
```

When an event is extended in Powerbuilder. a call to the ancestor event script is added behind the scenes. This can be seen in the exported object code. The lines of code above translate to:

```
event pfc_postupdate;call super::pfc_postupdate;
int li_rc
li_rc = this.of_PostUpdateProcessing()
return li_rc
end event
```

When extending events which return a value, the ancestor return code must be checked by overriding the event and making an explicit call to the ancestor event.

```
int li_rc
li_rc = Super::Event pfc_postupdate()
IF li_rc => 0 THEN
        li_rc = this.of_PostUpdateProcessing()
END IF
return li_rc
```

Although the event is overridden in reality, it is still extended because of the call to the ancestor event on a first line.

Note: The ancestor return value will be available as an event argument in the next major Powerbuilder release.

Extending standard events

For standard Powerbuilder events, the ancestor event return code has to be checked as well. In such a case, there is an additional caveat. Some standard events have default return values. The default value is returned if a return statement is omitted. If the default return code is used in the ancestor event, the call to Super::Event will return a Null and not a default return value. Additional code has to be added to check for this condition. One such case is the updatestart event of u_dw. This event has two possible return values:

0   Continue processing.

1   Do not perform the update.

The example below shows the code necessary to extend the updatestart processing.

```
long ll_rc
ll_rc = Super::Event updatestart()
IF IsNull(ll_rc) THEN ll_rc = 0
//        Extended processing...
return ll_rc
```

Extending placeholder and empty standard events

By definition, placeholder events do not contain any code; therefore, it is possible to extend them without checking the ancestor return code. Unfortunately, there is no guarantee that in the future there is not going to be any code added to these events. To ease code maintenance, these events should be extended the same way as precoded and standard events.

Adding new services

New service objects can be used to add new generic features or to contain application-specific business rules. To create a new service object, follow the steps outlined below:

- Create a nonvisual object with a reference variable to the client object.
- Declare the events needed to communicate with the client object.
- Declare a reference variable to the service on the client object.
- Redirect the client object events to the service provider.
- Create an of_Setxxx function in a client object.
- Call the of_Setxxx(FALSE) function in the client object's destructor event to automatically destroy the service.
- Add the appropriate logic to the service object.

The example below demonstrates the steps required to add a DataWindow surrogate key generation service. This service is used to generate a key when a new row is inserted into a DataWindow. The key is then inserted into a key column. The service can be configured to generate and populate the keys on each insert or prior to update. The required steps and the sample code are listed below.

Create a nonvisual object with a reference variable to the client object.   A nonvisual object, pfd_n_cst_dwsrv_autokey, was inherited from the base DataWindow service, n_cst_dwsrv. The client object reference variable idw_requestor did not have to be declared because it already exists in the base service. The service-specific instance variables were added:

```
Protected:
string is_dw_col_name     // The DataWindow key column name
string is_col_name        // The database key column name
string is_table_name      // The database table name
boolean ib_key_on_update = false
```

Declare the events that are needed to communicate with the client object.   Two events were needed, one to determine when a new row was inserted and the second to signal the beginning of the update. The events were named *pfd_updatestart* and *pfd_insertrow*. The code for both is listed later.

Declare a reference variable to the service on the client object

```
// pfd_u_dw instance variable
n_cst_dwsrv_autokey inv_autokey
```

Redirect the client object events to the service provider.   The pfc_addrow and pfc_insertrow events are redirected to the pfd_insertrow event of the service object. Updatestart is redirected to the pfd_updatestart event.

```
//***********************************************************
// Object: pfd_u_dw
// Method: pfc_addrow
//
```

```
// Arg : none
// Return: long
//
// Desc : Redirect the event to the appropriate services.
//*********************************************************

long ll_row

ll_row = Super::Event pfc_addrow()

IF ll_row > 0 THEN
        IF IsValid(inv_autokey) THEN
                ll_row = inv_autokey.Event pfd_insertrow(ll_row)
        END IF
END IF
return ll_row


//*********************************************************
// Object: pfd_u_dw
// Method: pfc_insertrow
//
// Arg : none
// Return: long
//
// Desc : Redirect the event to the appropriate services.
//*********************************************************

long ll_row
ll_row = Super::Event pfc_insertrow()
IF ll_row > 0 THEN
        IF IsValid(inv_autokey) THEN
                ll_row = inv_autokey.Event pfd_insertrow(ll_row)
        END IF
END IF
return ll_row


//*********************************************************
// Object: pfd_u_dw
// Method: updatestart
//
// Arg : none
// Return: long
//
// Desc : Redirect the event to the appropriate services.
//
//*********************************************************
long ll_rtc

ll_rtc = Super::Event updatestart()
```

```
IF IsNull(ll_rtc) THEN ll_rtc = 0

IF ll_rtc = 0 THEN
        IF IsValid(inv_autokey) THEN
                ll_rtc = inv_autokey.Event pfd_updatestart()
        END IF
END IF

CHOOSE CASE ll_rtc
        CASE 0 // No rows or key service not used. Continue with an update
                return 0
        CASE 1 // Key generated. Continue with an update
                return 0
        CASE −1 // Error. Do not continue with an update
                return 1
END CHOOSE
return 1
```

Create an of_Setxxx function in a client object.   The of_Setxxx function, in this case of_Set_Autokey, is responsible for the service creation and destruction.

Note: The function always refers to the object in the PFE layer— n_cst_dwsrv_autokey.

```
//*************************************************************
// Object: pfd_u_dw
// Method: of_Set_Autokey
//
// Arg(s) : boolean
//                      True - Create the service
//                      False - Destroy the service
// Return :             Integer
//                      1 - Successful operation.
//                      0 - No action taken.
//                      −1 - An error was encountered.
//
// Desc :               Starts or stops the Autokey generation service.
//                      This service generates and inserts a new key value
//                      in the specified column.
//                      Use of_Set_Key_column to specify the above.
//
//*************************************************************

//Check arguments
IF IsNull(ab_switch) THEN
        Return −1
END IF

IF ab_switch THEN
```

```
            IF Not IsValid (inv_autokey) THEN
                    inv_autokey = Create n_cst_dwsrv_autokey
                    inv_autokey.of_SetRequestor ( this )
                    Return 1
            END IF
    ELSE
            IF IsValid (inv_autokey) THEN
                    Destroy inv_autokey
                    Return 1
            END IF
    END IF
    Return 0
```

Call the of_Setxxx(FALSE) function in the client object's destructor event to automatically destroy the service.

```
//*********************************************************
// Object: pfd_u_dw
// Method: destructor
//
// Desc :          Clean up the created services
//
//*********************************************************
of_Set_Autokey(FALSE)
```

Add the appropriate logic to the service object. There are two events and two functions. The events pfd_updatestart and pfd_insertrow contain the code needed to populate the key columns. The function of_Populate_On_Update determines whether the key column is populated on insert or update. The function of_Set_KeyColumn initializes the service by providing the DataWindow and the database column names.

```
//*********************************************************
// Object: pfd_n_cst_dwsrv_autokey
// Method: pfd_updatestart
//
// Arg : none
// Return: long
//
// Desc : Generate the unique key for all the NewModified! rows
//*********************************************************

long ll_new_key, ll_rowcount, ll_idx
int li_rtc
dwitemstatus dwi_rowstatus

// If keys are generated on insert return
IF NOT ib_key_on_update THEN return 1
```

```
// If there are no rows return 0, on error return −1
ll_rowcount = idw_requestor.RowCount()
IF ll_rowcount <1 THEN return ll_rowcount
FOR ll_idx = 1 TO ll_rowcount
        dwi_rowstatus = idw_requestor.GetItemStatus(ll_idx, 0, Primary!)

        IF dwi_rowstatus = NewModified! THEN
                // Get the new key value
                IF IsValid(idw_requestor.itr_object) THEN
                        li_rtc = idw_requestor.itr_object.of_Get_Key (&
                        is_table_name, is_col_name, ll_new_key)
                        IF li_rtc <0 THEN return −1
                ELSE
                        IF IsValid(gnv_app.inv_debug) THEN
                                gnv_app.inv_debug.of_Message("Failed to get the
key for "+is_table_name+" and "+is_col_name)
                        END IF
                        return −1
                END IF

                // Place it in the current row
                li_rtc = idw_requestor.SetItem(ll_idx, is_dw_col_name, ll_new_key)

                IF li_rtc <0 THEN return −1
        END IF
NEXT
return 1

//*************************************************************
// Object: pfd_n_cst_dwsrv_autokey
// Method: pfd_insertrow
//
// Arg : long al_new_row
// Return: long
//
// Desc :
//*************************************************************

long ll_new_key
int li_rtc

// If keys are generated on update return
IF ib_key_on_update THEN return 1

// Get the new key value
IF IsValid(idw_requestor.itr_object) THEN

        IF idw_requestor.itr_object.of_Begin() <> 0 THEN
                idw_requestor.itr_object.of_Populate_Error_Message()
```

```
                              return −1
                END IF

                li_rtc = idw_requestor.itr_object.of_Get_Key ( is_table_name,&
        is_col_name, ll_new_key)

                IF li_rtc <0 THEN
                        idw_requestor.itr_object.of_rollback()
                        return −1
                ELSE
                        idw_requestor.itr_object.of_Commit()
                END IF
        ELSE
                IF IsValid(gnv_app.inv_debug) THEN
                        gnv_app.inv_debug.of_Message("Failed to get the key for "
        +is_table_name+" and "+is_col_name)
                END IF
                return −1
        END IF

        // Place it in the newly inserted row
        li_rtc = idw_requestor.SetItem(al_new_row, is_dw_col_name, ll_new_key)

        IF li_rtc <0 THEN return −1
        return al_new_row

        //************************************************************
        // Object: pfd_n_cst_dwsrv_autokey
        // Method: of_Set_Keycolumn
        //
        // Arg :            string as_dw_col_name
        //                  string as_key_table_name
        //                  string as_key_col_name
        //
        // Return: int
        //                          + 1 success
        //                          <0 failure
        // Desc : Initialize the service.
        //************************************************************

        // Check the arguments
        IF IsNull(as_dw_col_name) THEN return −1
        IF IsNull(as_key_table_name) THEN return −1
        IF IsNull(as_key_col_name) THEN return −1

        IF Trim(as_dw_col_name) = "" THEN return −1
        IF Trim(as_key_table_name) = "" THEN return −1
        IF Trim(as_key_col_name) = "" THEN return −1
```

```
// Save the values in the instance variables
is_dw_col_name = as_dw_col_name
is_col_name = as_key_col_name
is_table_name = as_key_table_name
return 1


//*************************************************************
// Object: pfd_n_cst_dwsrv_autokey
// Method: of_Populate_On_Update
//
// Arg : ab_arg
// Return: none
//
// Desc : Determines when to generate the unique key on update
//                 or on insert.
//*************************************************************
ib_key_on_update = ab_arg
```

Summary/Conclusions

There have been some complaints about how little direction for selecting the appropriate extension method has been provided by Powersoft. After reading this chapter, you may have an idea why. There is no single right answer. Powersoft has delivered a very flexible class library with an extension-layer concept that allows many different choices. Making an educated decision requires a careful examination of your requirements, familiarity with the company's infrastructure, an object-oriented background, and a working knowledge of PFC.

This chapter has outlined the major PFC extension issues and has presented some pros and cons of different extension methods. There is a catch-22: It is difficult to make a decision without knowing the implementation of each object in PFC. However, it is not recommended that you start your first PFC project before selecting the appropriate extension method. This is why in every table in this book describing PFC objects, there is a column specifying the possible extension methods.

Which extension approach is the best? You are going to have to live with the consequences of this decision for the life of the project. Ultimately it is your decision, and at this point you should have enough ammunition to answer the question. Look over the extensibility checklist questions. Research your requirements. Examine the benefits and the shortcomings of each approach. Weigh each benefit and shortcoming against your company's development and deployment procedures.

If you are looking for an extension method to house a custom framework, the first extension method should be quickly eliminated. From its release PFC was marketed as a foundation class library for the development of application frameworks. It has exceeded everyone's expectations and many developers will use PFC alone, but there is definitely room for expansion. PFE as an application-layer method leaves no room for a framework. To rewrite the expansion code for each application is unacceptable.

The two-layer "PFE as a framework layer" approach provides a viable solution. It is especially attractive if you have a need to share PBDs or DLLs between multiple executables, or have a common network location for the framework libraries. It does require that everyone involved be very familiar with service-based architecture techniques. Extension by delegation can be used successfully to resolve many design issues. It can also be overused, resulting in growing complexity, event-timing, and interobject communication issues. Nevertheless, because of its advantages, this method is gaining in popularity.

The three-layer approach is a mainstream solution. It is recommended by Powersoft and is the most flexible of the three methods. It allows extension by insertion, inheritance, or delegation for both application and framework layers. The disadvantage is the development environment performance. This performance speed varies based on the hard disk access speed. It may be more noticeable on a slow network. Testing a simple application such as PEAT or Quick Start with an additional layer should give a good indication of performance. Keep in mind that the performance hit is noticeable only in development mode. The performance degradation in an executable is hardly noticeable.

The three-layer approach is the choice of PFC-based commercial class libraries. They cannot predict their customer base and have to allow further extension by insertion.

If your framework code is based on the insertion techniques, the three-layer method provides the ability to easily move the generic code between the application and framework layers. This may come in useful in "feature procurement" or multiproject conflict resolution. A new framework feature can be added to a single team's application layer. After being proven on one application, the feature can be moved up to the framework layer. Once in a while teams may disagree on what should be added to the common framework. This often comes up when one team is trying to reach a milestone and is not receptive to changes. In this case, a new feature can be temporarily placed on the application level until everyone agrees. These issues can also be resolved with revision control, but it is always helpful to have alternatives.

13

PFC Extensions*

Introduction

The PFC's service-based architecture allows developers to easily extend existing services and build new behavior into the library. In this chapter, we'll discuss some ideas for extensions to the PFC and go through the process of extending some existing services and objects as well as adding completely new services to the extension layer. Chapter 3 introduced you to the extension capabilities of the PFC and Chap. 12 discussed the how-to element of class extension, so that will not be repeated here.

Chapter Objectives

The objectives of this chapter are to discuss the extension of a few PFC classes, either by enhancing an existing class, adding a new service to a client class, and/or creating a new service class so that developers can continue to utilize the benefits of reusable code. From the simplest object to the most complex service, it is important to note that it can be done, it should be done, and you can have fun and be productive while doing it.

Extending an Existing Object

One of the ways to add functionality is to add code to an object. The two objects that you'll most likely make extensions to are w_master and u_dw. These are the core pieces of any PowerBuilder application. There are several scenarios that you'll run into as you make extensions.

---

*Portions of this chapter were contributed by Steve Benfield, Financial Dynamics, Inc.

- If you are merely adding code, then your changes are probably fairly easy; just extend events as needed.

- Sometimes you'll need to extend a function. To extend a function, you'll have to override it and then run the ancestor function by calling super::<function name>. Make sure you capture the return code and act appropriately.

- You may need to extend an event but have code execute *before* the ancestor instead of after it. To achieve this, override the ancestor event, write your code, and then call super::EVENT <eventname>. This is identical to the previous option except for events.

- If you must completely override existing functionality, then make sure you fully document the fact that the event is overridden in the comments for the event.

Make sure that the code you are writing makes no assumptions about which services are currently running. Always check to make sure that any service you are about to call is valid. If it is not, return an error or act accordingly.

Status bar service

One service we really like is the status bar service. Creating custom graphics and text on the status bar is very easy to implement. One example that we've implemented is a debug toggle service. A bitmap is put on the status bar, and when the user double-clicks on the bitmap, the debug service is toggled on or off. Writing code for double-clicking on the status bar is easy; it is already written! If you look at the status bar service (n_cst_winsrv_statusbar), you'll find three events: pfc_statusbarclicked, pfc_statusbardoubleclicked, and pfc_statusbarbuttonup. To write code that responds to the status bar, put code in one of those three events. Simple enough. But wait; where would we put the code? n_cst_winsrv_statusbar—the extension layer. The problem with extension-level changes is that depending on your configuration, the changes could be applicable to multiple applications. Status bar information varies from frame to frame; doesn't it make sense that the code belongs with the MDI frame?

A minor extension that you can add to your PFC implementation is to route the events that normally fire on the status bar service to the MDI frame. To do this, we'll add three events to w_frame: ue_statusbarclicked, ue_statusbardoubleclicked, and pfc_statusbarbuttonup. Then we'll go into n_cst_winsrv_statusbar and code each service event to make the appropriate call to the MDI frame.

As in all windows services, the window that the service is attached to is referenced as iw_requestor. During runtime, iw_requester will point to the MDI frame.

The code in the status bar service is very simple, since it is merely passing control to the MDI frame. Here is the code for the pfc_statusbarclicked event:

```
iw_requestor.EVENT pfc_statusbarclicked( ai_xpos, ai_ypos, as_name )
```

Just add lines like this to the other two events.

Fixing the add and insert row functionality

The PFC is not without bugs or design flaws; no product is. The good thing is that the PFC development team is very open and approachable about the product and has taken action to help fix any errors. One such design flaw is in inserting or adding new rows. The user has two choices when creating a new row: Add or Insert. Add appends the row to the end of the DataWindow, and Insert puts the row at the current row location. Take a look at the code for each of these as shown in Fig. 13.1.

If the row manager is not on, then a row will be inserted using InsertRow. A quick look at the pfc_insertrow and pfc_addrow events of the row manager service show that both call the function inv_rowmanager.of_InsertRow().

The question is: Where do you put common row insert business logic?

The only commonly called function is InsertRow on the DataWindow. So you can add common row insert functionality by overriding the DataWindow's InsertRow() code. The code would look something like the code shown in Fig. 13.2.

If you add this code to each DataWindow that needs insertrow logic, you'll have business logic that is executed regardless of how a row is inserted. However, it really goes against the style of spirit of the PFC. Some programmers don't know that you can override a built-in PowerBuilder function. Moreover, there is a school of thought that says that you should not override built-in functions. So, what we really should do is provide a common placeholder for row initialization logic regardless of how the row is inserted. To do this, we need to

```
//u_dw::pfc_insert
IF IsValid (inv_rowmanager) THEN
   ll_rc = inv_rowmanager.event pfc_insertrow (ll_currow)
ELSE
   ll_rc = this.insertrow (ll_currow)
END IF
//u_dw::pfc_addrow
IF IsValid (inv_rowmanager) THEN
   ll_rc = inv_rowmanager.event pfc_addrow ()
ELSE
   ll_rc = this.insertrow (0)
END IF
```

Figure 13.1   pfc_insert and pfc_addrow extensions.

```
u_dw::insertrow( int newrow )
integer       rc
rc = super::insertrow( newrow )
IF rc >= 0 THEN
   <your insert logic goes here>
END IF
```

Figure 13.2   Insertrow functionality.

extend the DataWindow user object. It makes no sense to make any changes to the row manager, since rows can be added without the service on. To provide our common row initialization functionality, we'll introduce a new event: ue_initializerow. We'll call ue_initializerow from both pfc_addrow and pfc_insertrow after the new row has been created. Our code goes into u_dw in the PFEMAIN extension PBL. The code is shown in Figs. 13.3 and 13.4.

If you look at the code, you'll see that we return the inserted row number if ue_initializerow is successful. If you extend a PFC service by overriding it, you need to make sure that you return the proper value to the calling function. In our case, pfc_addrow and insertrow returned the row number that had just been inserted; therefore, our extension does as well.

```
u_dw::ue_initializerow( long al_newrow )
/*
   Event: ue_initializerow
   Arguments: ai_newrow: New row number that needs initialization
   Returns: integer
     1 if successful
     -1 if error

   Description:
     Used to initialize new rows
     Virtual Event: Developer will enter appropriate code
*/
RETURN 1
```

Figure 13.3   Virtual event for initializerow.

```
u_dw::pfc_addrow()
u_dw::pfc_insertrow()
/*
   Event: pfc_addrow() [or pfc_insertrow()]
   OVERRIDDEN

   Description:
     Adds a call to ue_initializerow after the row is added
*/

integer ll_returncode, ll_insertedrow
ll_insertedrow = SUPER::EVENT pfc_addrow()[or pfc_insertrow()]
IF ll_insertedrow >0 THEN
   ll_returncode = this.EVENT ue_initializerow( ll_insertedrow )
   IF ll_returncode >0 THEN
     ll_returncode = ll_insertedrow
   END IF
END IF
RETURN ll_returncode
```

Figure 13.4   Addrow/insertrow functionality.

Fixing the linkage service

One of the most useful and interesting services is the linkage service. It has a few flaws, however. One of the most major ones involves losing changes when using the retrieval style. When a master row changes while retrieval style is being used, the linkage service does not check to see if any changes have been made in the linkage chain. This means that all changes are immediately lost because no changes are saved to the database.

What we'd like is the ability to have changes saved when the user moved to a different row. The event that fires when the user moves rows is, of course, the rowfocuschanged event of the DataWindow. All we've got to do is put some code in rowfocuschanged to ask the user to save changes if the row is moved. The problem with rowfocuschanged is that it is past tense; once the event is fired, the row has already changed. What we really need is a rowfocuschanging event—but since we don't have one, we'll have to code around it until the time comes.

Before determining how to write this extension to the linkage service behavior, we need to understand what is going on when a row changes. A quick look at pfc_u_dw shows the following code:

```
pfc_u_dw::rowfocuschanged
/* Linkage service */
IF IsValid ( inv_linkage ) THEN
        inv_linkage.Event pfc_rowfocuschanged (currentrow)
END IF
```

This code is simple enough; it merely calls the pfc_rowfocuschanged event of the linkage service. From there, the details are rereterieved. To get our functionality, we'll have to intercept the rowfocuschange and call the linkage only when it is necessary. Also, if the user wants to save the data, we'll have to call pfc_save. These changes will be made to u_dw. The code is shown in Fig. 13.5.

Resize service extension

One of our favorite services is the resize service. Anyone who had to write this type of functionality in the past without library support knows what a pain it can be. The PFC resize service really makes adding resize functionality trivial. However, it requires some annoying maintenance. The resize service normally requires that an of_Register() function call be made for each control on a window; this code is most likely called in the window's pfc_preopen event. Every time a control is added, renamed, or deleted, a line of code calling of_Register must be added, changed, or deleted.

As we began to use the PFC, we realized that this was really a pain and added to the task of maintenance. Why should a window no longer compile just because a command button has been removed?

Instead of writing a line of code for each control, what we need is a way to have the code called for us. To achieve this, we're going to use the tag value of

```
u_dw::pfc_rowfocuschanged
/* OVERRIDDEN */
INTEGER rc, li_numdetails, li_Count
BOOLEAN lb_UpdatesPending = FALSE
BOOLEAN lb_Save, lb_Cancel
u_dw ldw_details[]

IF IsValid( inv_linkage ) THEN
  // If we are moving to the last successful link then do nothing
  IF CurrentRow = il_LastLinkedRow THEN
    RETURN 0
  END IF

  // Check for changes on children
  li_numdetails = inv_linkage.of_GetDetails( ldw_Details )
  FOR li_Count = 1 to li_NumDetails
    IF ldw_Details[li_Count].inv_Linkage.of_GetUpdatesPending() >0 THEN
      lb_UpdatesPending = TRUE
      EXIT
    END IF
  NEXT

  // Updates are pending on at least one child so save
  IF lb_UpdatesPending THEN
    IF inv_linkage.of_GetUpdatesPending() > 0 THEN
      IF ib_AutoSave THEN
        lb_Save = TRUE
      ELSE
        rc = MessageBox( "Updates Pending", &
              "Do you want to save changes?", &
              Question!, YesNoCancel!, 1 )
      CHOOSE CASE rc
        CASE 1 // Save
          lb_Save = TRUE
        CASE 2 // No
        CASE 3 // Cancel
          lb_Cancel = TRUE
      END CHOOSE
    END IF

    IF lb_Save THEN
      ANY      la_ReturnValue
      WINDOW lw
      // Call pfc_save on the parent window
      // if pfc_save not found, call Update on the linkage svc.
      of_GetParentWindow( lw )
      la_ReturnValue = lw.DYNAMIC EVENT pfc_save()
      IF IsNull( la_ReturnValue ) THEN
        rc = inv_linkage.of_Update()
      ELSE
```

Figure 13.5 Rowfocuschanged modified to check dependent children.

```
          rc = integer( la_ReturnValue )
        END IF

        IF rc <0 THEN
          lb_Cancel = TRUE
        END IF
      END IF
      IF lb_Cancel THEN
        this.ScrollToRow( il_LastLinkedRow )
        RETURN 0
      END IF
    END IF
  END IF
END IF

IF super::EVENT rowfocuschanged( currentrow ) > = 0 THEN
  IF IsValid( inv_linkage ) THEN
    il_LastLinkedRow = CurrentRow
  END IF
END IF
```

Figure 13.5 *(Continued)*

the individual controls that need to be resized. Every control on a window (as well as objects on a data object) has a tag attribute. This attribute is not used by any built-in PowerBuilder functionality and is solely for the developer to use as he or she sees fit. You can think of it as a place to code attributes that Powersoft never thought of—such as information for the resize service.

We're going to "tag enable" the resize service of the PFC. To do so, we'll need to write a function that will loop through each control on the window, check the tag value, and call of_Register for each control as needed. All the programmer has to do is enter the phrase resize = <resize behavior> in the tag value and the resize service will pick up that behavior. In fact, if the programmer doesn't put anything in, the resize service will scale any DataWindows and buttons to the right and bottom. You can customize this any way you wish.

Here are the specs for the extension.

The resize service should recognize the following tag values and behavior:

No resize entry	If the control is a DataWindow, tab, or custom visual user object, then scale. Otherwise, FixedToRight&Bottom.
resize = no, resize = none, resize = 0	No resizing
resize = FixedToRight, resize = FR	FixedToRight
resize = FixedToBottom, resize = FB	FixedToBottom
resize = FixedToRight&Bottom, resize = FRB, resize = FBR	FixedToRight&Bottom
resize = Scale, resize = S	Scale

resize = ScaleToBottom, resize = SB	ScaleToBottom
resize = ScaleToRight, resize = SR	ScaleToRight
resize = ScaleToRight&Bottom, resize = SRB, resize = SBR	ScaleToRight&Bottom
resize = FixedToRight&ScaleToBottom, resize = FRSB, resize = SBFR	FixedToRight&ScaleToBottom
resize = FixedToBottom&ScaleToRight, resize = FBSR, resize = SRFB	FixedToBottom&ScaleToRight

Because the current function to register a control is of_Register, we decided to call this function of_Register as well. Through overloading, we'll create a version of of_Register that takes an array of controls (window objects) as an argument. Our new of_Register will be called from a window pfc_preopen event just the way the normal of_Register is in PFC. Here is the code that will be used to register all the controls on a window with the resize service.

```
your_window::pfc_preopen
of_SetResize( TRUE )
inv_resize.of_Register( this )
```

In fact, if you want to have this behavior all the time, you could add the previous code to your w_master extension.

Here is the code for our of_Register function. Notice that calls are made to the PFC string service; the string service has built-in functionality to manipulate "tokenized" strings. The format of the string tokens is "<keyword> = value;". By following this format, multiple attributes can be put into a tag value. For example, you could create tag values such as resize = scale;MicroHelp = Customer Information;.

Note: If you currently use the tag value for MicroHelp, update your MicroHelp code to use the text up to the first semicolon as the MicroHelp. This would allow you to specify tag values such as

Please enter a customer name.;resize = scale

You may also want to enhance your MicroHelp code to look for a tag entry such as MicroHelp = <text>;.

The code sample shown in Fig. 13.6 registers the objects to be resized.

What we've seen so far is extending services in order to either enhance the existing service or correct a set of logic. When you implement corrections to faulty logic, remember that there's a good chance the logic will get fixed in future releases of the PFC, so mark this code carefully so that it can be removed with future releases.

Another way of extending the PFC is by extending the capabilities of client

```
integer of_Register( windowobject agovResizeObject )
/*
  Function: of_Register
  Description: Auto register controls within an object
  Arguments:
    agovResizeObject Object which needs to be auto-registered
  Functionality:
    Scans the controls on a window to determine the resize settings
    for the control. This demonstrates the ability to "tag enable"
    services in the PFC.
*/

n_cst_string     lnv_string
integer          iNumControls, iControlNum, iRegistered
string           sTag, sResizeValue, sError
windowobject     lControlArray[], lCurrentObject
window           lw
tab       lt
userobject       lu

// Check to see if the current control is a DataWindow,
// tab folder, or user object. If it is, then recursively
// call this function for the given control.
CHOOSE CASE agovResizeObject.TypeOf()
  CASE window!
    lw = agovResizeObject
    lControlArray = lw.control
  CASE tab!
    lt = agovResizeObject
    lControlArray = lt.control
  CASE userobject!
    lu = agovResizeObject
    lControlArray = lu.control
  CASE ELSE
    RETURN -1
END CHOOSE

iNumControls = UpperBound( lControlArray )

FOR iControlNum = 1 to iNumControls
  lCurrentObject = lControlArray[ iControlNum ]
  sTag = lCurrentObject.Tag
  sResizeValue = lnv_string.of_GetKeyValue( &
    sTag, "resize", ";" )

  CHOOSE CASE upper(sResizeValue)
    CASE "FR", "FIXEDTORIGHT", "FIXEDRIGHT"
      sResizeValue = "FixedToRight"
    CASE "FB", "FIXEDTOBOTTOM", "FIXEDBOTTOM"
      sResizeValue = "FixedToBottom"
    CASE "FRB", "FBR", "FIXEDTORIGHT&BOTTOM", "FIXEDRIGHT&BOTTOM", &
        "FIXEDTORIGHTANDBOTTOM", "FIXEDRIGHTANDBOTTOM"
      sResizeValue = "FixedToRight&Bottom"
```

Figure 13.6 Register multiple objects for resizing.

```
    CASE "S", "SCALE", "SC"
      sResizeValue = "Scale"
    CASE "SR", "SCALETORIGHT", "SCALERIGHT"
      sResizeValue = "ScaleToRight"
    CASE "SB", "SCALETOBOTTOM", "SCALEBOTTOM"
      sResizeValue = "ScaleToBottom"
    CASE "SRB", "SBR", "SCALETORIGHTANDBOTTOM", "SCALERIGHT&BOTTOM", &
      "SCALETORIGHT&BOTTOM", "SCALERIGHTANDBOTTOM"
      sResizeValue = "ScaleToRight&Bottom"
    CASE "FRSB", "SBFR", "FIXEDTORIGHT&SCALETOBOTTOM", &
      "FIXEDTORIGHTANDSCALETOBOTTOM", "FIXEDRIGHTANDSCALEBOTTOM", &
      "FIXEDRIGHT&SCALEBOTTOM"
      sResizeValue = "FixedToRight&ScaleToBottom"
    CASE "FBSR", "SRFB", "FIXEDTOBOTTOMANDSCALETORIGHT", &
      "FIXEDTOBOTTOMANDSCALETORIGHT", "FIXEDBOTTOMANDSCALERIGHT", &
      "FIXEDBOTTOM&SCALERIGHT"
      sResizeValue = "FixedToBottom&ScaleToRight"
    CASE ""
      // Default value if none given
      CHOOSE CASE lCurrentObject.TypeOf()
        CASE DataWindow!, Tab!, UserObject!
          sResizeValue = "Scale"
        CASE ELSE
          sResizeValue = "FixedToRight&Bottom"
      END CHOOSE
    CASE "NONE", "NO", "0"
      // No resizing wanted
      sResizeValue = ""
    CASE ELSE
      // Error Condition
      // Add to error list and display when finished
      sError = sError+"Invalid Resize Option In: "+&
        lCurrentObject.ClassName()+&
        ", Value = "+sResizeValue+"~r~n"
      sResizeValue = ""
    END CHOOSE
    // Register control with resize service
    IF sResizeValue <> "" THEN
      iRegistered++
      this.of_Register( lCurrentObject, sResizeValue )
    END IF
  NEXT

  // Process error display if debug service is on.
  IF sError <> "" THEN
    IF IsValid( gnv_app.inv_Debug ) THEN
      MessageBox("Resize Service Registration Error", sError )
    END IF
  END IF

  // Return number of columns registered
  RETURN iRegistered
```

Figure 13.6 (*Continued*)

classes. To show an example, we picked the relatively simple command button. Command buttons generally are simple. You drop one on a window (or user object), and then write some code into the command button to execute an event on the parent window. How could this be simplified? How about a button that you drop on a window that will *automatically* figure out what event to fire on the parent window, and fire it—and can even change which event it fires on the fly! Sound like fun? Let's take a closer look.

Enhancing the command button

The goal is self-executing command buttons. The diagram shown in Fig. 13.7 demonstrates the steps we need to follow to accomplish this.

In this sample code, we added the ability for the button to become "aware." The button detects the text property set and triggers a user event on the parent window after adding a user event prefix and removing any special characters. Figure 13.8 shows the variables added.

In Fig. 13.9 we show the code placed into a user function of_EventName() which detects whether the event name is already set and, if not, sets it up.

Figure 13.10 shows that the code is for the button's clicked event. This script

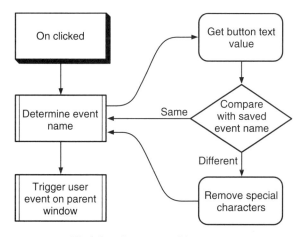

Figure 13.7 Workflow for command button extension.

```
/* Instance variables on the pfd_u_cb object */
Protected:

Boolean        ib_AutoClick = TRUE
String         is_EventPrefix = "UE_"
String         is_EventName
String         is_Text
```

Figure 13.8 Variables set for the auto-click.

```
/*
         of_EventName()
*/
int ilen, idx = 1

/* We are going to use the button's actual text value. If the button text
         is the same as what we already have, then we have the event
         name and do not need to reexecute the code. You could choose
         to use the class name or tag value. The choice is yours.

*/
IF is_text = Trim(this.text) THEN
         RETURN 1
ELSE
         is_text = Trim(this.text)
END IF

ilen = len(is_text)
do
         /* Check if not normal character */
         if (asc(mid(is_text, idx, 1)) <65) &
         OR ((asc(mid(is_text, idx, 1)) >90) &
         AND (asc(mid(is_text, idx, 1)) <97)) &
         OR (asc(mid(is_text, idx, 1)) >122) THEN
                  is_text = Replace(is_text, idx, 1, "")
                  iLen = Len(is_text)
         ELSE
                  idx ++
         END IF

Loop Until idx >iLEN

/* EventPrefix contains the prefix you use, such as "UE_" */
is_EventName = lower(is_EventPrefix + is_text)

RETURN 1
```

Figure 13.9   Sample code to extract event name from button text.

will fire the of_EventName function and then trigger the specified event on the parent window.

Now when the button is placed on a window (or other object), it will automatically trigger an event matching the button text. If the text is changed dynamically, the button will fire a different event. If no event name is found, a default event of ue_buttonclicked will be fired.

Tip: Avoid coding functionality or behavior in a command button after it has been dropped on a window. It is okay to precode a user object version of a command button, as this promotes encapsulation and reuse.

```
/* CLICKED EVENT:

        If AutoClick is active, get the event name and trigger the event; otherwise
        do nothing and execute the user code added later
*/

IF ib_AutoClick THEN
        /* Get the event name to fire */
        of_GetEventName()

        /* Set up a default event if the event name comes back blank */
        IF is_EventName = "" THEN is_EventName = "ue_buttonclicked"

        /* Locate the parent window and fire the event */
        Window Lw_parent
        of_GetParentWindow(lw_parent)
        lw_parent.Event(is_eventname)
END IF
```

Figure 13.10 Trigger the event back on the parent window.

Automatic DDDW caching

Our first PowerBuilder 3.0 application used a new feature called drop-down DataWindows. Life was good. We had an order entry application with roughly 15 drop-downs on it. We had one problem—the order was taking a little too long to come up. After doing all the optimization we could with stored procedures, opening an invisible order window to cache the class, and pushing everything into a postopen event, the order was still taking 4 to 6 s to open. What we found out was that our lovely new drop-down DataWindows were causing 15 SELECT statements to be issued against the database each time an order was opened. Clearly a list of order types or shipping methods doesn't need to be updated on the screen every time it is viewed; clearly something had to be done. Luckily, the news around the user group was that it was possible to share these drop-downs with real DataWindows. The idea of a cache mechanism immediately came into mind. So we created a window that had 15 DataWindows on it and retrieved those DataWindows when the application started. Just to make sure the users didn't mind the wait of retrieving these DataWindows, we put up a pop-up window that said "checking security." There are many tools in the GUI developer's arsenal.

Today, in PowerBuilder 5.0, we don't have to worry about creating hidden windows to simulate a DataWindow cache; we've got DataStores now. In addition, the PFC offers a DataWindow caching service which allows you to cache DataWindows. The caching service is easy enough to use. The code in Fig. 13.11 shows what it takes to cache a drop-down DataWindow.

For each drop-down, the previous steps need to be repeated. It seems logical that we create a function on the drop-down service to take a DataWindow and a column and register it with the service. Figure 13.12 shows the of_AddDDDW

```
DataWindowChild dwc
n_ds           lds
IF IsValid( gnv_app.inv_DWCache ) THEN
  STRING ls_dataobject
  // Get the name of the data object
  ls_dataobject = dw_1.object.state.dddw.name

  IF ls_dataobject <> "" THEN
    IF gnv_app.inv_DWCache.of_IsRegistered( ls_dataobject ) <1 THEN
      // Register the data object using the name of the data object
      gnv_app.inv_DWCache.of_Register( &
        ls_dataobject , ls_dataobject, this.itr_object )
    END IF

  IF this.GetChild("state", dwc ) >0 THEN
    IF gnv_app.inv_DWCache.of_GetRegistered( &
      ls_dataobject, lds ) = 1 THEN
        lds.ShareData( dwc )
      END IF
    END IF
  END IF
END IF
```

Figure 13.11   Drop-down DataWindow caching service.

function to add to the DW cache service.

Now that we've got a function that we can pass a DataWindow and column name to, creating a function that will register all drop-downs based on tag values is now pretty easy. The algorithm is shown below:

```
Loop through the objects on the DataWindow.
  Is the object a column?
    If column then
      Add drop-down to service.
```

The code to loop through the object on the DataWindow is taken from the of_GetObjects code of the base service of the DataWindow. (We could also have called of_GetObjects on the DataWindow by turning on the base service if needed.) We'll just loop through the tag values looking for the keyword "cache." The current function to register a DataWindow is of_Register; we'll follow the PFC convention and overload the function and call ours of_Register as well. This function is shown in Fig. 13.13.

After the DW cache service is modified with the previous two functions, adding drop-down caching to a DataWindow becomes a simple task, as shown below:

```
yourwindow::pfc_postopen()
IF IsValid( gnv_app.inv_DWCache ) THEN
```

```
n_cst_dwcache::integer of_AddDDDW( u_dw adw, string as_column )
DataWindowChild    dwc
n_ds               lds
STRING                 ls_dataobject

IF NOT IsValid( adw ) &
   OR IsNull( adw ) &
   OR IsNull ( as_column ) &
   OR len( as_column ) <1 THEN
      RETURN −1
END IF

ls_dataobject = adw.Describe( as_column+".dddw.name")

IF len( ls_dataobject ) <2 OR IsNull( ls_dataobject ) THEN
   RETURN −1
END IF

IF.of_IsRegistered( ls_dataobject ) <1 THEN
   IF of_Register( &
      ls_dataobject , ls_dataobject, adw.itr_object ) <0 THEN
      RETURN −1
   END IF
END IF

IF adw.GetChild( as_column, dwc ) >0 THEN
   IF of_GetRegistered( ls_dataobject, lds ) = 1 THEN
      lds.ShareData( dwc )
   ELSE
      RETURN −1
   END IF
ELSE
   RETURN −1
END IF

RETURN 0
```

Figure 13.12   Adding a drop-down DataWindow to the caching service.

```
   Gnv_App.inv_DWCache.of_Register( this )
END IF
```

Row manager

The row manager manages row inserts and deletes and, most importantly, row restores! But one feature it doesn't have is autoinsert. This feature would automatically insert a row as the user makes changes to the last row of the DataWindow. The proper event in which to put this might surprise you: It isn't the rowfocuschanged event, it is the itemchanged event. We'd like a new row added if the user has made a change to the last row of the DataWindow. If no

```
n_cst_dwcache::of_Register( u_dw adw )
IF NOT IsValid( adw ) OR IsNull( adw ) THEN
  RETURN −1
END IF

string    ls_ObjString, ls_ObjHolder, ls_Tag
integer   li_ObjCount, li_Start = 1, li_Tab, li_Count = 0

/* Get the object string */
ls_ObjString = adw.Describe("Datawindow.Objects")
/* Get the first tab position. */
li_Tab = Pos(ls_ObjString, "~t", li_Start)
Do While li_Tab >0
  ls_ObjHolder = Mid(ls_ObjString, li_Start, (li_Tab − li_Start))

  // Determine if object is the right type and in the right band
  IF (adw.Describe(ls_ObjHolder+".type")) = "column" THEN
    ls_Tag = Upper( adw.Describe( ls_ObjHolder+".tag" ))
    IF Pos( ls_tag, "CACHE" ) >0 THEN
      of_AddDDDW( adw, ls_ObjHolder )
    END IF
  END IF

  /* Get the next tab position. */
  li_Start = li_Tab + 1
  li_Tab = Pos(ls_ObjString, "~t", li_Start)
Loop
```

Figure 13.13 Register the cache.

change was made, then no new row is added. What we'll need to do is make modifications to u_dw as well as n_cst_dwsrv_rowmanager. The itemchanged event will need to make a call to the row manager service. If autoinsert has been enabled, the row manager will then determine if a new row should be added.

One small hitch in this scheme is the current behavior of the row manager. By default, the PFC scrolls to newly inserted rows, assuming that the user is ready to add data to the row. This behavior just doesn't work when you want to add a row while the user is entering data on the last row. Therefore, we need to make a slight change to the of_InsertRow function of the row manager to have different behavior if autoinsert is being invoked. To accomplish this, we'll overload of_InsertRow and pass an additional boolean to indicate whether the scrolltorow should occur.

Let's take a look at the things we're going to code:

1. Add an instance variable on the row manager to indicate autoinsert mode.

2. Add a Get and Set function for autoinsert on the row manager.

3. Add an event ue_itemchanged on the row manager to call of_InsertRow if autoinsert is needed.

4. Code the itemchanged event of u_dw to call an event on the row manager.

5. Add overloaded of_InsertRow that takes a row number and boolean to just insert a row without scrolling.

Now let's look at the code, as it is seen in Listings 13.1 through 13.5.

LISTING 13.1   Instance Variables

```
n_cst_dwsrv_rowmanager::instance variable
Protected:
Boolean        ib_AutoInsert
```

LISTING 13.2   SetAutoInsert and GetAutoInsert Functions

```
n_cst_dwsrv_rowmanager::integer of_SetAutoInsert( ab_AuoInsert )
ib_AutoInsert = ab_AutoInsert
n_cst_dwsrv_rowmanager::boolean of_GetAutoInsert( )
RETURN ib_AutoInsert
```

LISTING 13.3   ue_itemchanged Event

```
n_cst_dwsrv_rowmanager::
   integer ue_itemchanged( long row, reference dwobject dwo )
IF of_GetAutoInsert() THEN
   IF al_row <= 0 OR IsNull( al_row ) THEN
      RETURN -1
END IF

IF al_row = idw_Requestor.RowCount() THEN
   // insert a new row without scrolling
   of_InsertRow( idw_Requestor.RowCount() + 1, FALSE )
   END IF
END IF

RETURN 0
```

LISTING 13.4   InsertRow Function

```
n_cst_rowmanager::
    long of_InsertRow( long al_beforerow, boolean ab_scrolltorow )
// of_InsertRow( al_beforerow, ab_scrolltorow )
// If ab_scrolltorow is false then don't scroll to the new row
IF ab_scrolltorow THEN
   RETURN of_InsertRow( al_beforerow )
ELSE
   RETURN idw_Requestor.InsertRow( al_BeforeRow )
END IF
```

LISTING 13.5   Itemchanged Event Extension

```
u_dw::ItemChanged
IF IsValid( inv_rowmanager ) THEN
  inv_rowmanager.EVENT ue_itemchanged( row, dwo )
END IF
```

If you run this code, you'll find that when you change the last row of the DataWindow, you'll automatically get a new row added. All the user has to do is change the last row of the DataWindow and just keep tabbing. A new row is added as soon as the change is made. If you do some testing, you'll find that there is a flaw in this technique. If the last column in the DataWindow is the only column updated, a new row will be inserted when the user tabs off, but the DataWindow will lose focus and the next control on the window will get it. What we'd like to have happen if the user changes the last column on the DataWindow is to have a new row inserted.

So how do you trap this situation when the user tabs out of a DataWindow? Are there any events on the DataWindow that could help? Well, there aren't any predefined, but there is one available. The event is pbm_tabout, and it is fired when the user tabs out of the DataWindow. What we're going to do is define a user event and map it to pbm_tabout. Our code will then detect if the user has just had an autoinsert done. If the user has, then we scroll to the last row in the DataWindow and set the focus back on the DataWindow.

Take a look at the code in Listing 13.6.

LISTING 13.6   Tabout Event

```
u_dw::ue_tabout [mapped to pbm_tabout]
long      il_NewRow
IF this.GetRow() = ( this.RowCount() - 1 ) &
  AND ( this.GetItemStatus( this.RowCount(), 0, Primary! ) = New! &
    OR this.GetItemStatus( &
        this.RowCount(), 0, Primary! ) = NotModified! ) THEN
  // Set to default column. Enhancement might be to automatically
  // detect the default column ( one with lowest tabsequence )
  this.SetColumn( 1 )
  this.ScrollToRow( this.RowCount() )
  this.POST SetFocus()
END IF

RETURN 1
```

Let's analyze what this code is doing for us. First, it checks to see if the current row is the next to last one. If we are on the next to last row, we ensure that the status of the last row is New! or NotModified!. If this is the case, it means that the last row is newly inserted and hasn't been touched. Remember, this event fires only when the user tabs out of the DataWindow. When the user tabs out, he or she will be sitting on the last column on the last row. If the user is no longer on the last row when this event fires, it means that a row has been added between the time the user tabbed out and the time this event was fired. If the user changed only the last column/row of the DataWindow, then the item-changed processing would insert a new row.

Notice that we perform a POST SetFocus(). Since the DataWindow is in the process of changing focus because of the tabout, we need focus to return to the DataWindow *after* the current event processing is complete and the focus change has taken place.

Adding a new service

As with the design and development of any other class, it's really useful to have a few guiding principles to keep you on the right track. Design patterns is a hot topic in the OO world that covers exactly this presupposition. What we propose here is not exactly a pattern, but rather a combination of patterns that results in a reusable foundation for building future service classes.

One of the first things you will come up against in the PFC is the need to extend the PFC by adding a new service class. The typical approach is to copy one of the existing PFC service classes, rip its guts out, and then build your service class using the shell. While this practice helps keep your class looking and feeling similar to the existing PFC classes (a good thing), it also locks you into the PFC approach (not such a good thing). This means picking up both the good and the bad features of the PFC architecture. Well, perhaps we can change all that, and we're going to try, using a real-life example to do it.

Another element of service class design is what exactly the service is going to do. Again, the typical approach is to design the service to do what you specify it should do. Sometimes, a little extra thought and effort can raise the value of your service class.

So let's take a look at what it is we want to accomplish, and then we'll figure out how we will get there.

Setting the goal

If you're designing a service class, you should have a goal. When you have a goal, see if that will help others. Remember that a service class is intended to be useful to other classes or applications, so follow the SBA design principles to ensure that you set the goals appropriately.

Our goal for this exercise is relatively simple: We want to detect whether or not our application is already running. It sounds simple enough, so the first thing we do is develop a goal statement.

Goal statement: Develop a service which will detect whether or not the application is already running.

That's simple enough. This is a service that many have asked about since we entered the 32-bit world. Why? In the 16-bit world, we could use the statement

IF Handle(Application) > 0 THEN "application is already running"

This no longer works in the 32-bit world because each application on the 32-bit operating system gets its own address space and is not aware of other applications outside of its memory space. This "protected" operating system made functions such as handle(application) obsolete. So, we figured that the only other constant to applications in both the 16-bit and 32-bit worlds was the windows API.

This is true even under the UNIX version of PowerBuilder, but we are not familiar enough with Macintosh to make the same claim there.

The design. We design the service class showing three important aspects: client class integration, client class interaction, and service class API. The design does not have to be detailed, just informative.

When we do design work, the first thing we do is try to figure out how the whole thing is going to fit together. We use a flowchart to keep this all visual (which is more helpful for us), and in doing so, we often uncover a few aspects that we would not ordinarily cover. We also try to ensure that we show all three service class design requirements, client class integration, client class interaction, and service class API. Figure 13.14 shows what this service class might look like.

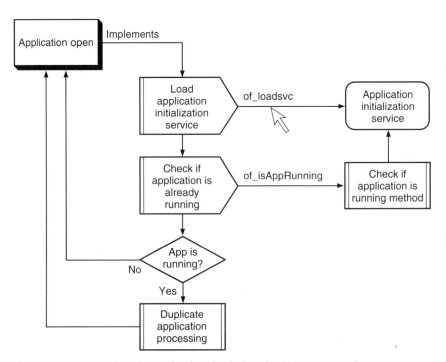

Figure 13.14 Service class design for the "check if application is running" service.

Of course, this is only a skeleton view of the service. We still need to expand the method which will actually look to see if the application is running. The windows API offers a few alternatives for looking at the applications that are running. One of the easiest to use is the FindWindow() function. FindWindow() will allow you to look for an application window by specifying either the window caption (that is, the title that appears in the applications main window title bar and may include the text for a subservient MDI child window) or the class name of the main window, or both. The problem we have with this is that there must be an exact match between the name you supply and the name that appears on the top of the window you are looking for. About 90 percent of the time, that would be enough.

Another method is to execute a DDE call to the application in question. If the call succeeds, the application is there. If not, it is not. Again, this will work about 90 percent of the time.

Our preferred method uses another trio of windows API calls: GetDesktopWindow(), GetWindow(), and GetWindowText(). GetDesktopWindow() accepts no arguments and simply returns that handle to the desktop window, the highest-level window in a Windows, Windows 95, or Windows NT environment. By calling GetWindow() and passing arguments of 'DesktopWindowHandle' and 'Constant gw_child', you will get the handle of a main window for an application. GetWindowText('MainWindowHandle') will get the text from the window title and allow you to use this in determining if this is the window you are looking for. Subsequent calls to GetWindow('MainWindowHandle', 'gw_next') will cycle through the main windows that are served by the desktop window; you can scan this until you find what you are looking for. Figure 13.15 shows the hierarchy of window handles in a typical windows environment and the function you use to interrogate it.

Most of us (including the authors the first time or seven) will stop here, design the service to accommodate this request, implement the service in our favorite framework, and be done with it. This is unfortunate, because it's very easy to extend this service so that it is much more powerful.

Extending the design

When reviewing your design, ask yourself these questions: Is this useful to many applications? What other capabilities would be useful?

When we ask these questions, we find that we can add to our design. When we revisited this design, we found that we could expand it to meet the following needs:

- It would be useful if we could check if applications other than our own were running using this same code.

- It would be useful to know how many other occurrences of an application were running.

- It would really be useful if the service could detect if a specific file were open within an application, for example, an Excel spreadsheet or Word document.

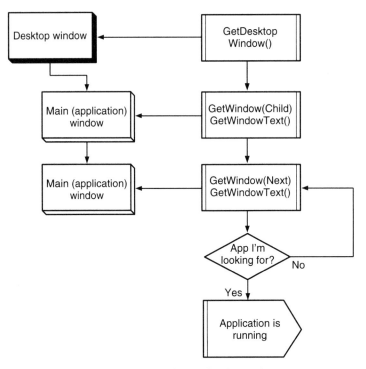

Figure 13.15 API calls to traverse the window hierarchy.

With this in mind, we expanded the design from Fig. 13.14 to look like that shown in Fig. 13.16.

We can do this without any additional API calls, too. Once we detect the application, we accumulate an instance count instead of immediately returning. If a filename is also specified, then we enter an additional seek loop to scan through the window hierarchy of the application to look for the file specified. Figure 13.17 now shows a more complete design.

Now we can see that if a filename is provided—(for example, of_IsAppRunning("Excel", "MySpreadsheet.xls")—then the "check for file" method would be called to interrogate the child windows within the application to see if the file was loaded. This method is described in Fig. 13.18.

Of course, this implies that our entry point will be an overloaded function call. This brings up the point, how exactly should you develop an overloaded function call? We follow a simple set of rules:

Define the main function with the maximum number of arguments. Place all your main code in this function.

Overload the function with other argument combinations, filling in the missing pieces. (This is *not* polymorphism, by the way; it is simply function overloading.)

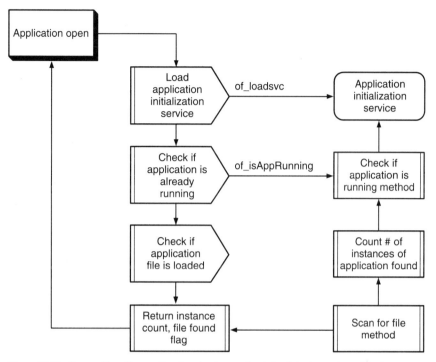

Figure 13.16 Expanding the application instance check to detect number of instances and files within applications.

Our function prototypes would then look like the following:

Long FUNCTION of_IsAppRunning(string AppName, string filename, ref AppInstanceCount)
Long FUNCTION of_IsAppRunning(string AppName, ref AppInstanceCount)
Long FUNCTION of_IsAppRunning(Application AppHandle, ref AppInstanceCount)

This allows us to call the function by passing either the application handle (THIS in the application object), an application name ("My Application"), or an application name and filename ("Excel", "Spreadsheet1.xls"). The second and third functions simply call the first one without a filename; the third also obtains the application name for you.

So, now the design is complete and it is time for us to build this service class.

Building the objects

An architect takes great care in designing something, and the builder should be equally aware of his or her responsibility to the completed product.

Building a service class is a relatively painless process once you have a good design specification. Typically, we would take the design discussed earlier to

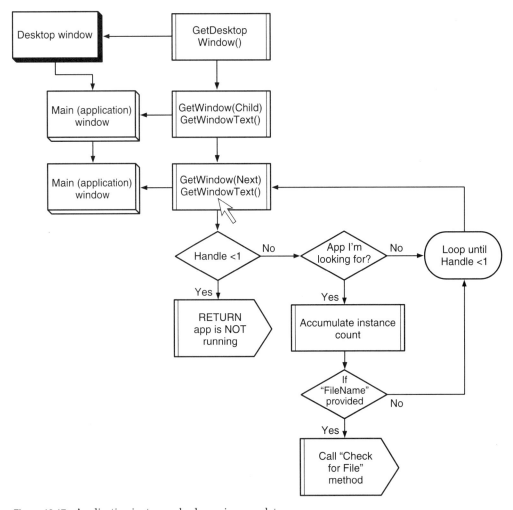

Figure 13.17   Application instance check service complete.

the next level and formally spec out the class, but for the purpose of this article, we'll make the assumption that this has been done,* and move on to building the class.

We like to build classes based upon other proven classes, and this is no exception. We utilize a standard service-class design, which we will detail here briefly.[†]

---

*To see the formal class specification for this class, you can download it from the Web site at http://www.cris.com/~bgcastle.

[†]A detailed discussion of the SBA standards we have developed are available in the latest version of our white paper on service-based architecture available from the above Web site, CompuServe, and various other sites that have chosen to offer the paper.

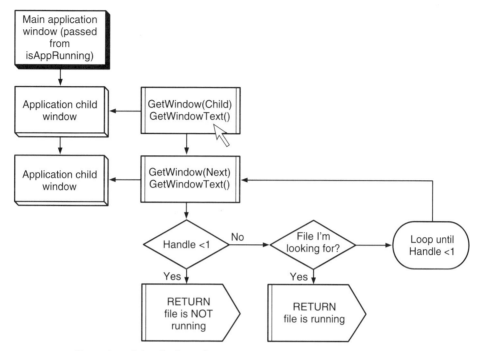

Figure 13.18 Extension of the check application running method—check if file loaded.

We are going to classify this service as a managed service. Let's quickly review the service class hierarchy. We have three levels of service classes, instance or local service class, managed service class, and brokered service class. Figure 13.19 illustrates the SBA standard hierarchy.

Based on the description of these classes, we chose managed service as the implementation choice. Why? We usually try to avoid local services as much as possible, as we prefer to have the services managed for us automatically, and brokered services seem overkill for this implementation. In order to utilize the managed service, we need to implement the SBA service manager. The service manager allows us to utilize service classes in any flavor while ensuring that the service creates and destroys are handled for us. It also allows us to specify the class to use for the service, allowing a much higher degree of extensibility as a result of its loose coupling nature. Figure 13.20 shows how the service manager manages that service for you.

So now, in order to build the service, we will create a new service class inherited from the managed service class, and code the methods that we have designed.* We decided to call the service class "application scanner."

---

*The completed service class, along with service manager, is downloadable from the Web site at http:/www.cris.com/~bgcastle.

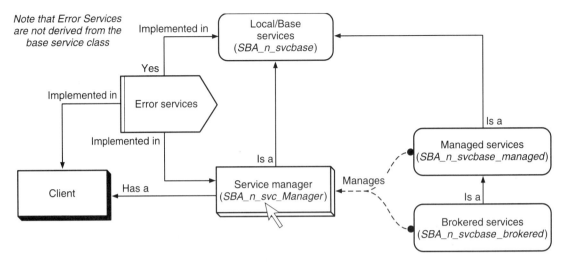

Figure 13.19 SBA service class hierarchy and implementation.

Developing the application scanner class

We've already defined the methods we want on this object, namely an over-loaded of_IsAppRunning() function and an of_IsFileLoaded() function. What we still need to do is to define the external functions that will be used. To do this, we have to extend the existing PFC platform services in order to add the Windows API external functions. Again, whether or not you use a corporate extension layer inserted between PFC and PFE will determine where you place your extended code. We utilize the corporate extension concept and therefore will place the code in the PFD layer. For the sake of discussion here, however, we'll simply put the code in the PFE layer.

n_cst_platformWin16. First we'll add the external function declarations to the platform services. We'll start with the 16-bit version. The external declarations we'll need are

```
FUNCTION uint GetDesktopWindow() LIBRARY "user.exe"
FUNCTION uint GetWindow(uint hwnd, int wflags) LIBRARY "user.exe"
FUNCTION uint GetWindowText(uint hwnd, ref string wintext, int textlength)
  LIBRARY "user.exe"
```

We're done here. We could write a wrapper function to call the external function, which is typical, but not necessary. We choose not to.

n_cst_platformWin32. Now we add the external function declarations for the 32-bit calls. These are:

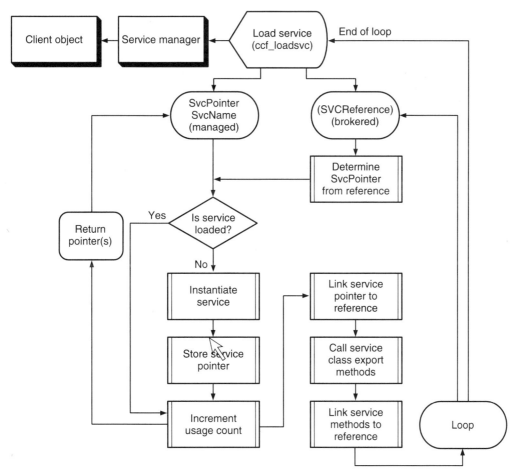

Figure 13.20   Service manager implementation.

FUNCTION uint GetDesktopWindow() LIBRARY "user32"
FUNCTION uint GetWindow(uint hwnd, int wflags) LIBRARY "user32"
FUNCTION int GetWindowText(uint hwnd, ref string wintext, int textlength)
    LIBRARY "user32" Alias for "GetWindowTextA"

Notice that the GetWindowText() function uses an alias. This function is actually already coded in the Win32 platform services as GetWindowTextA(), meaning that you have to write a wrapper so that the wrapper can call the correct function prototype. Using an alias eliminates the need to do this. Regardless of which platform you're running on, you will still call GetWindowText(). The 32-bit function will reroute the function internally to GetWindowTextA() without our interference.

SBA_n_svc_AppScanner. We create our service class by inheriting from SBA_n_svcbase_managed. This ensures that service management features are automatically activated.

Next, we code the main function call, of_IsAppRunning(string AppName, string filename). In this function we place the following code:

```
of_LocateApplication(string a_appname, ref uint h_Application)
of_CountApplicationInstances(string a_appname, ref int a_AppInstanceCount)
of_LocateFileInApplication(string a_appname, string a_filename, ref uint h_filename)
```

The first thing you'll see is that IsAppRunning() is actually a function which makes calls to other functions. IsAppRunning() is provided as an overloaded wrapper function that makes your application developer code simpler and easier to understand. You can call IsAppRunning() and get an answer indicating yes or no (by the returned AppInstanceCount variable), but internally, it works a little differently.

Depending on which overloaded function you call, you might call the internal functions   of_LocateApplication,   of_CountApplicationInstances,   and/or of_LocateFile. of_LocateApplication() performs the first level of our checking. It will do the following steps:

- Obtain the handle to the desktop.

- Obtain the handle to the first child window (child to the desktop).

- Check if this first child is the application window we are looking for. (Remember that the application name may be a portion of the application window name, so the check must be length-specific).

- If not, enter a loop to get the next child window and check its title.

When the loop ends (either handle returned = 0 or we find the application we are looking for), we enter the next phase of the method.

- If the handle = 0, we've discovered that the application is not running and we can simply return an application instance count of zero to the caller.

- If we've found the application, we can enter the function of_CountApplicationInstances, where the loop above is continued, counting each time we find the application.

- If a filename is supplied, the caller is looking for a combination of application and filename. We will call the of_LocateFile() function, where we will do two steps. The first will be to check that the current window we have access to does not contain the filename in its title anywhere. If it does not, we enter a loop, scanning all of the child windows for the particular application, looking for the filename in the title of the child window. If we find it, the file is loaded. If not, the file is not loaded for this particular application and we can continue. This process is repeated for each instance of the application that is found until we can determine whether the application/file-name combination is running or not.

One thing we have not discussed is what to do if the application is found. We've left it up to you to make this decision. When you look at the sample code supplied for this chapter, you'll see how we approached the problem.

Now that the object classes are developed, we're ready to integrate the service into our application.

Integrating the services

Integration of services is like selling real estate. The most important three elements are location, location, location.

Because this is an application service, the choice is quite simple. We implement the service in the application manager. If you've adopted the inserted corporate layer technique, then this new service will be implemented in the corporate layer. If not, you would implement it in whatever you have designated the corporate extension layer to be. In either case, we need to follow a few steps.

- Add an instance variable reference pointer to the application manager for the service manager. (PFC uses classname invo_ServiceName. We recommend that you follow this practice when working with the PFC.) Remember to implement the service manager at the extension level (n_svc_Manager rather than SBA_n_svc_Manager) so that you can extend the service manager for yourself. The service manager is an autoinstantiated service, so create and destroy are handled for you.

- Add an instance variable reference pointer in the application manager for the new service. (We called it SBA_n_svc_AppScanner; therefore we code the instance variable as SBA_n_svc_AppScanner invo_AppScanner). Note that we do *not* declare this service at the extension level. There is no extension level because the service manager allows us to define the class being instantiated at runtime. To extend this service, inherit from it, add your code, and then change the name of the service being loaded to the class you create.

In order to use the service, you must do two things: Load the service, and call the service method. Typically, we add the service load to the application manager constructor event. We need to code the following:

```
invo_SBAMgr.of_LoadSvc(invo_AppScanner, "SBA_n_svc_AppScanner") //Loads the
    application initialization service
```

In future, any new services we add will only need step 2 and the code. The service manager takes care of destroying the service once it is out of scope.

Finally, in the pfc_open event, we will add the code

```
invo_AppScanner(GetApplication().AppName, li_AppCount)
```

With this implementation, we're looking for an instance of our application, so we're using the simple form of looking for the application only. The li_AppCount variable, a local integer, will contain the number of instances of the application that are running, and you can therefore choose what you want to do based on the knowledge you now have.

In other areas within our application, we might want to look for an instance of an Excel spreadsheet. We would simply call that function using the application manager reference pointer as

gnv_App.invo_AppScanner("Excel", "MySpreadsheet.xls", ii_AppInstanceCount)

which would tell us if Excel were running and the file MySpreadsheet.xls were open. Of course, to simply look to see if Excel is running, you would omit the filename argument.

Summary

There are a lot of different ways in which services can be enhanced, replaced, or removed. The examples in this chapter demonstrate various elements of this process. As you can see, there is room for a lot of extension. Does this mean that the PFC is not full-featured? Absolutely not! It shows how easy it is to extend the PFC, customizing it to your environment and allowing you to apply corrective or enhanced code to the objects provided by the PFC development team. It takes a lot to be able to provide this level of flexibility along with ease of use, performance, and a dozen other issues you must be aware of when extending the PFC.

14

Deploying the PFC

Introduction

In this chapter we will discuss the issues involved in deploying applications that use the PFC. We will look at a couple of alternatives and discuss the pros and cons of each. Deployment is perhaps one of the most critical phases of an application's life cycle. This is how we choose to get the application out to the user community, be it a single user, a workgroup, an entire enterprise, or purchasers of an off-the-shelf package.

There are many similarities between the rollout of a class library and the rollout of an application. Both the similarities and the differences are worthy of our attention. In each case, you must deliver a product that satisfies the end user's requirements. Both will require attention to details that are seemingly beyond the scope of the application or library. However, in the case of a library, your attention will most often be directed to issues of access, documentation, and functionality, while an application will focus your attention on ensuring that the target environment is prepared, any information your user might need is accessible, and the necessary files are deployed along with the application executable.

Chapter Objectives

In this chapter you will learn to

- Identify deployment issues and how to solve them.
- Deploy a single executable.
- Deploy using an executable and dynamic libraries.
- Deploying applications using an extended PFC.
- Deploy an extended library based on the PFC libraries.

Deploying PowerBuilder Applications

There are various methods available to the developer to deploy applications. Following is a discussion of these methods and their strengths and weaknesses. When discussing deployment, there are issues within issues. Any of the methods discussed below will work, but which is the best? How do you decide which to use? Should you deploy over a network or locally?

For corporate applications, we prefer to deploy over a network, as this approach makes for easier maintenance when it is time to upgrade the application. However, the performance of the network is a major factor in this strategy. We have seen network deployments that run six to ten times slower than local deployments because of a lack of bandwidth. The approaches to resolve this issue vary from deploying partially on the network and partially to the local drive, to totally deploying locally.

Deploying locally provides for the greatest speed when loading application objects; however, you will face problems in distributing upgrades as the application changes. Fortunately, there are now products available to manage the distribution of upgrades. These applications reside on the network and monitor the software versions on client machines, and will download updated versions when necessary.

Many of these same concerns arise when deploying commercial applications; however, we may be limited in how we choose to deploy by the vendor. These factors should be considered when purchasing software packages.

If the decision is made to deploy locally or if you need to deploy to remote sites, there is the question of how to get the software to the end user. The application may be placed on a network and copied to a local PC. This approach will work well if no files on the existing PC such as odbc.ini or the registry need to be updated. The safest approach is to provide a setup program and installation disks. The disk images may be placed on a network for installation or disks may be distributed to each user. PowerBuilder ships with Install Builder for creating installation disks. There are also several commercially available programs to accomplish this task, such as InstallShield. Figure 14.1 shows the main window of the Install Builder program.

The Install Builder program allows you to define components for your application. These components are made up of files such as help files, the PowerBuilder runtime libraries, and the application files. These files are compressed, and the software will create installation disk images on the system's hard disk. These disk images are then used to create installation diskettes. In addition, the program group for the icons may be defined. Figure 14.2 shows the Install Builder Actions menu and the tasks performed there.

At the time of this writing, it is rumored that Powersoft will starting shipping InstallShield with the next release of PowerBuilder. InstallShield is an integrated software distribution system for Windows 3.1, Win32s, Windows 95, and Windows NT. Some features of InstallShield include:

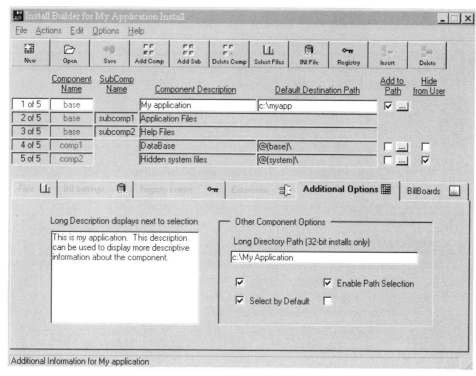

Figure 14.1 PowerBuilder Install Builder program.

Figure 14.2 Install Builder Actions menu.

- InstallShield Wizard EU, a new user interface to guide users through the installation of your application
- Automatic billboard capability
- Transparent bitmaps
- Template scripts—complete ready-to-use installations that you can customize
- Visual debugger
- Component selective installations
- On-line reference

Regardless of the program used to create the installation media, if files or the registry on the end user's machine needs to be updated, this is the best approach you can take to install the software.

The single executable approach

Deploying an application as a single executable is the simplest way to approach application distribution. In this scenario, all libraries and resources are compiled into a single file, which is the only file besides the PowerBuilder runtime libraries that the end user needs to run the application.

This approach will produce a large executable (EXE) file. Contrary to popular belief, if the application is compiled in the interpretive format (p-code), the size is irrelevant. PowerBuilder treats a p-code executable as a PowerBuilder Dynamic Library (PBD). This means that the EXE contains a small bootstrap program that reads the resources from the remainder of the file as they are needed. Only the bootstrap and required resources are loaded into memory. This is true even if some libraries are included in the executable. However, if the application is to be distributed as machine code, the entire EXE must be loaded into memory before it can be run. In this context, the size of the EXE is an important consideration.

The major drawback to this type of deployment is that if you need to make a change to a single object, no matter how trivial the change, the entire application must be recompiled and redistributed.

Figure 14.3 depicts the single EXE deployment.

Deploying with PowerBuilder Dynamic Libraries (PBDs)

While this approach to deploying an application requires the distribution of more files, there are several benefits to be gained. Chief among these are a major reduction in the amount of time it takes to generate an EXE file after the original PBDs are created and, second, the ease of distributing updates to the application.

When applications are deployed in this way, the PBDs for the PFC layer may be shared across all applications. They will need to be rebuilt only when a new version of the PFC layer is needed.

The PFE and application PBLs may also be distributed as PBDs. Figure 14.4 shows this approach.

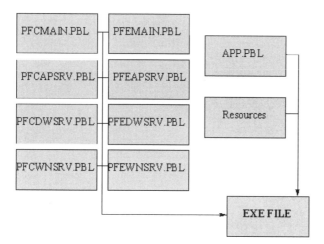

Figure 14.3 Single executable build diagram.

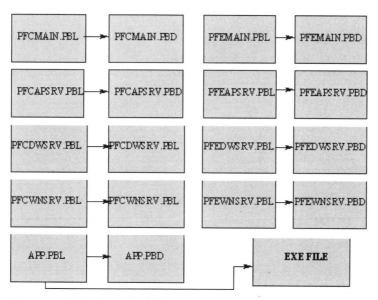

Figure 14.4 Deploying using PBDs.

You can create PBDs in the library painter. Figure 14.5 shows the dialog box for creating PBDs.

When an application using PBDs is rebuilt via the project painter using an incremental rebuild, only items that have changed will be recompiled. Since the PFC layer is seldom modified, the PBDs for it will not be rebuilt unless a full rebuild is requested. This will save considerable time in recompiling the application.

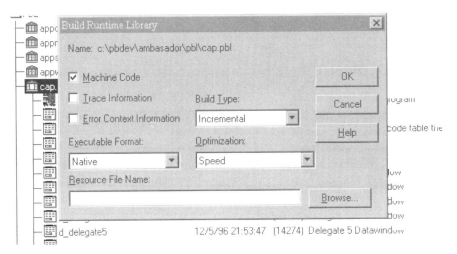

Figure 14.5 Create PBD dialog box.

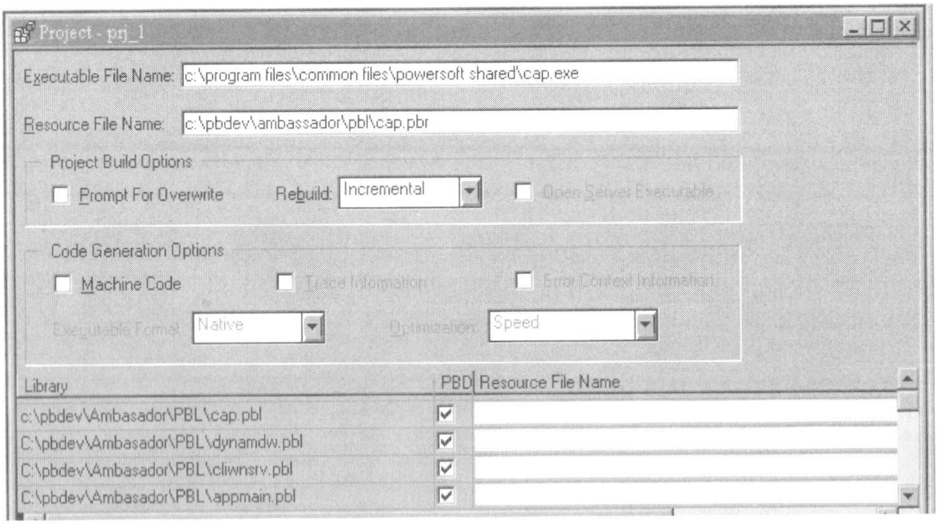

Figure 14.6 PowerBuilder project painter.

Figure 14.6 shows the project painter. This application uses several PBDs.

The application shown in Fig. 14.5 has *all* of its libraries set as PBDs. In this case, a very small EXE will be generated and all the objects that the application uses will be loaded from the PBDs at runtime. This approach also leads to simpler maintenance. In the event that an object changes, only the PBD that it is in needs to be rebuilt and redistributed. The exception to this is when an object is an ancestor to another object, or the change is to a function call. When this occurs, referencing objects must be regenerated. In this case, an incremental rebuild will regenerate all of the libraries involved. The PBDs containing the modified objects and their descendants will need to be redistributed.

If changes are made to ancestor objects that are used across multiple applications, each of the applications that use the object will need to have the appropriate libraries either regenerated or redistributed.

All of the PBDs required for an application must be in the application's working directory or in the application's path.

Deploying PFC Applications

Required files

Some of the PFC services use external DLLs. These must be deployed with your application. The files are platform-specific.

pfccomm.dll	16-bit windows print dialog
pfccom32.dll	32-bit windows print dialog
pfcflsrv.dll	16-bit file service functions
PFCMacFileSrv	Mac file service functions
libkernel32.os	UNIX kernel functions (emulation layer to provide Windows NT system functions to the Unix platform)

Deploying with an extended library

What do we mean by an extended library? There are many ways to extend a class library. First of all, there is adding or enhancing functionality. Second, we may purchase add-on libraries for the PFC. Lastly, we may add additional layers to the PFC.

In some versions of the PFC, developers have added two layers between the PFC and PFE levels. Figure 14.7 shows this structure.

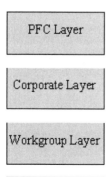

Figure 14.7 PFC with additional layers.

The corporate layer is where all extensions we want at a corporate level are placed. In the workgroup layer, those extensions needed at a department or workgroup level are done. Each department or workgroup would have its own set of these PBLs.

The PFE layer is copied fresh for each new application and is used to house application-specific extensions.

As an example, we might modify the appmanager object at the corporate level to add an instance variable that will be available to all applications within the corporation. In the workgroup layer, we could set that variable to a specific value identifying the department or workgroup.

We have found this structure to be of great value and highly flexible. However, it does complicate the deployment of an application somewhat. Assuming that you will create PBDs out of all PBLs, the directory structure to deploy applications might look like this:

\Application directory	Contains runtime DLLs and PBDs for the PFC and corporate layers.
\Workgroup1	Contains PBDs for the workgroup layer for workgroup 1.
\Apps	Contains application EXEs and remaining PBDs.
\Workgroup2	Contains PBDs for the workgroup layer for workgroup 2.
\Apps	Contains application EXEs and remaining PBDs.

Each individual computer must have the correct path set for this approach to work. This approach also requires a clear definition of the workgroups within your organization. The only problem we have encountered with sharing the PFC libraries in this manner is if the developers are not using the same version of PowerBuilder and someone recompiles a library containing shared ancestors.

Deploying a class library

There are many differences between deploying a class library and deploying an application. The target audience in this case is developers. Developers must be sold on the benefits of the library before they will consent to use it. This means that you must spend considerable effort explaining these benefits. The developers must be convinced of the robustness of the class library, as developers tend to push a library to its limits.

The focus of a class library is on the functionality that it provides, not on workflow. The aim of a class library is to aid the developer to create better, more robust applications faster.

The interface to a class library must remain stable. The underlying structure may change dramatically, but the interface must remain constant. As an example, imagine if the existing interface to the DataWindow control changed with each release of PowerBuilder. New functionality may be added at any time; however, even rare changes to the existing interface that require maintenance to applications will lead to developers choosing not to use a library.

The production environment for a class library consists of

- The PBLs and PBD/DLLs that make up the library
- The directory structure that supports the library
- The network configuration for distributing the library
- The technical support and documentation for the library

All of these must be in place when you introduce the class library to the development team.

When deploying the PFC for use in your organization, you will need to identify the development locations that will need the library. This includes identifying the server(s) on which the library will reside. Create a directory to support the PFC you are using. The one we use looks as follows:

G:\PFC	PFC and corporate-layer PBLs
\doc	Library documentation
\bmp	Bitmaps
\icons	Icons
\workgroups	Fresh workgroup layer to be copied for each workgroup
\workgroup1	Specific workgroup layer
\workgroup2	
\application	Fresh application layer to be copied for each application

Network access rights are controlled so that only our librarian has write access to the PFC and corporate layers. Development teams have read/write access to specific workgroup layers, and read-only access is provided to all on the application layer.

We will add to this structure any other directories that are needed to support any third-party products such as OCXs or additional PBLs. Be sure that you have a clear understanding of the licensing requirements for any add-on software that you choose to use. Development software usually has different licensing requirements for developer copies and runtime copies.

Training is an essential step in the successful deployment of any class library, and this holds true for the PFC. At the time of this writing there are very few courses available, so how do you go about getting training? We did it the only way we could. We played around with the tutorial, then started using the PFC in our applications.

In addition to initial training on the PFC, there needs to be a way to disperse information on upgrades and additions. There are several methods that may be used to accomplish this. They include:

- E-mail
- Ongoing classes
- Bulletin boards
- Memos
- Manual updates

We use a public discussion folder in Microsoft Exchange to discuss proposed changes and keep developers updated on the latest additions to the PFC. We have found that this approach works well for us.

Once the library is in use, some other issues come into play. These include:

- Change requests
- Bug reports
- Change testing

A clearly defined procedure is needed for each of these. These procedures need to be included in your training. Following is a brief discussion of each of these items.

Bug reports.   There should be a clear method for the reporting of bugs. This procedure should include:

- Who to contact and how to contact him or her
- What information to include
- How the report is acknowledged
- How a bug report can be escalated

Having a good bug-reporting and maintenance plan in place will greatly reduce problems associated with using a large class library.

Change requests.   Developers, being who and what they are, will continue to hatch new ideas for additional functionality in their fertile minds. This procedure needs to include a response detailing the expected development time. In many cases, after we have developed some functionality in an application that we believe will be useful across multiple applications, we will send it to our librarian for inclusion into the PFC. This approach does not hinder our development, and it reduces the time required to get the functionality added to the PFC, as the development is already done.

Change testing.   Because a class library spans many applications, testing is of vital importance. Stringent testing methods and procedures need to be developed. Once again, developers will lose confidence in a class library quickly if their applications begin to blow up because of it.

Summary

As can be seen, the more complex the library you use, the more complex the deployment. PBDs provide a good method for the deployment of an application that will ease the maintenance and redistribution of an application. A well-thought-out directory structure and workgroup organization will help to make deployments easier.

Using Powersoft's Install Builder or another program such as InstallShield will make the installation process easier and more secure for the end user.

Our recommendation is to use the PBD approach on a network whenever that is a viable option. This approach will allow for the least amount of maintenance headaches. In PFC applications we always compile all of the PFC libraries into PBDs. We have found this approach to work well in a variety of situations.

Deploying a class library requires addressing several issues that differ from those involved in application deployment. Perhaps the most important of these is the selling of the class library to the development staff.

15

Maintenance and Upgrades

Introduction/Objectives

Remember the days when an upgrade of software meant shutting down the behemoth mainframe for the weekend, and coming back on Monday morning to find the IBM SWAT team swarming around the operations center trying to locate the cause of a problem that occurred during the upgrade? Boy, do those ever seem like the good old days now! It seems that whenever you turn around these days, an upgrade to a critical piece of software is being done. It is amazing that we ever get past the upgrade process!

Take a look at what we go through these days. A typical windows-based client-server environment has, at a minimum, four levels of software going through multiple upgrades every year. We're not talking about major new releases. At least those we can somewhat plan for and allocate time to accomplish. Our environment has the following upgradable components:

- Windows NT
- PowerBuilder
- PFC
- Corporate extension layers
- Applications

This doesn't even consider the database or network software involved, which is usually more removed from the average developer. I once heard a comment which I thought was extremely appropriate: "If the EPA were required to monitor our environment management efforts, they'd shut us down within an hour."

Sadly, this is true. At our current site, a great deal of care is taken to ensure that the rollout of any change is thoroughly tested and the upgrade carefully monitored. This allows us to reduce the impact of the changes we face, but it extends the time between when an upgrade is received and when it arrives on the desktop. Consider this scenario. A maintenance patch arrives for your operating system, let's say NT. This patch must be tested in an isolated environment, so as not to affect the day-to-day work being accomplished. Rollout is typically staggered (because it's difficult to implement on every machine simultaneously), not to mention that you may also have several groups who are using NT 3.51 or Windows 3.1. Next, an upgrade is issued by Powersoft. It's a maintenance release which corrects a bug or two that your developers have been experiencing.

Now you have to test PowerBuilder, not only in an environment that matches your existing environment, but also in the "lab" environment where the latest OS patch is being tested. Of course, your PowerBuilder developers are all using Windows NT and developing 32-bit applications, right? Murphy's law says simply, *not!* So, you have to test both 32-bit and 16-bit fixes, and even though you decide not to include the renegade Windows 95 group, this requires significant resources and effort (an automated regression test suite of a few production applications will go a long way toward accelerating this process).

Now, for those groups who are using the PFC library, you need to ensure that the PFC fixes are tested in your class library environment. More testing, more time, more money. The testing reveals a small inconsistency between the PFC library and your extended corporate-layer objects, which you, as the top developer in the company, quickly correct; then you retest. So far, so good.

Now you need to find the application teams who are developing new applications with the extended PFC class library, as well as those with systems in production. You do *not* want to affect anything that is in production at this point because that would mean retesting each application. Fortunately, you have separate production, test, and development environments. Unfortunately, this means keeping track of all of the above three times over.

Based on this admittedly simplified example, you can see that applying maintenance releases can take a significant amount of time and effort. Powersoft releases a new maintenance release quarterly, so now you're in the position of picking which upgrade you want to implement. This does not take into account upgrades to ODBC and other database drivers, OCX, ActiveX and other componentized controls, browsers, plug-ins, and, last but not least, other commercial applications you use, such as Microsoft Office. Office upgrades affect several DLLs which you may use in your day-to-day work without even realizing it. OLE2.DLL, COMPOBJ.DLL, and COMMDLG.DLL are a few that spring to mind as having caused us a headache or two in the past.

An example of this type of behavior occurred in the installation of a small commercial program. The program utilized a Visual Basic control GRID.VBX, a special type of Visual Basic DLL extension. We received with this program the latest and greatest GRID.VBX, which promptly prevented use of Lotus Notes!

We learned a simple lesson from this: No upgrade should ever be thought of as a single-environment update. Unless you make changes on an nonnetworked PC (and even this environment can be affected), any change made can affect your entire development and user communities and can result in significant losses in revenue.

We learned quickly, although with a great deal of pain, that any change to any DLL can result in chaos and should be handled like nitroglycerin—very carefully.

It becomes easy to see why some companies simply fall way behind in upgrading their software. Staying on the leading edge of the technical world is often a time-consuming (and very costly) process. What can we do about it?

For one, we have to focus on what we, as PowerBuilder developers, can do to ease the pain. The first step, and in our experience the most beneficial, is to establish two things: a set of predefined, tested procedures for applying any upgrade, and a comprehensive automated regression test suite. The first is for sanity. You will be surprised at how much goes on when upgrading. We've seen a few companies that prefer to let the development teams control the upgrades of development software. These companies have several versions of every product installed in places they never even knew they had! Other companies prefer a more disciplined and centralized approach, following very specific steps, and ultimately accomplish the goal. Most of the time they are able to achieve a companywide implementation of maintenance releases before the next one comes out. Anyone who thinks this is easy is in for a surprise.

You may be involved with another form of maintenance if you occupy the position of object administrator with responsibilities including managing your organization's reusable class library (based on the PFC, of course). You have two levels of code you are responsible for: the PFC and your corporate layer (if any). When problems are reported or enhancements requested, you are the person responsible for making the changes, testing the changes, reporting any relevant information back to Powersoft, and then distributing the upgraded software.

This chapter will outline several of the key steps we find necessary in order to ensure that you do the most effective and efficient job in applying upgrades to the PowerBuilder product in general, and to the PFC product in particular. Specifically, we'll focus on

- The "ideal" environment
- Centralized upgrades to the PFC libraries
- Maintaining the PFC layers
- Upgrading your extension layers
- Upgrading your applications
- Testing

The "Ideal" Environment

It's not possible, let alone cost-justifiable, to completely simulate a large corporate environment, so we have to come up with a plan that will help protect our objects from the never-ending stream of upgrades. What has worked for us turns out to be relatively simple, absolutely cost-justifiable, and, most importantly, successful.

We established a "lab" environment which emulates our current production environment. This involves at least one database server and a connected workstation. The server has our database environment resident, and is maintained and updated by our database group, who have a similar lab for testing and maintaining our database environment.

Our workstation is split into two parts, current production and proposed upgrade. The production environment remains protected as if it supported live data and users, and is updated when an upgrade passes all certification tests and is released to our existing production environment. The proposed upgrade area is the area which is of concern to us. We are part of a centralized team that is responsible for managing the centralized code used by the organization. This includes the PFC, our extensions to the PFC, several small applications we have developed using the library, and PowerBuilder. We strongly recommend that a group such as this be established. In our environment, keeping up with the ever-changing code and tools requires a dedicated effort by two individuals.

Ideally, the environment should be set up with three production applications that satisfy the following criteria:

- They utilize different aspects of the development tool and/or the library.
- They utilize your corporate standard database structure.
- They have a formalized regression test plan (preferably automated).

When a maintenance release comes in, it can be applied in this lab environment, under controlled conditions, to see what the effect of the changes will be on existing production applications.

Centralized Upgrades

In the ideal situation, the library components that must be upgraded because of a maintenance release are controlled centrally. If this is not your situation, you face a tough task locating those areas that use the libraries you must upgrade, coordinating the upgrade with that group, and ensuring that the upgrade does not adversely affect their continued use of the library.

As mentioned earlier, you may be responsible for managing the class library within your organization. The importance of centralized upgrading is definitely something not lost on you if you have already attempted this. Consider this scenario. A developer calls you and informs you that a particular function he or she is using is not working as expected. What are the steps you must take to correct the situation? We outlined a series of steps which help us to ensure quick and, more important, accurate response. These are:

- Error analysis
- Library analysis
- Code design
- Code development
- Change management and distribution

When an enhancement is required, the first step is replaced with enhancement analysis, but the remainder of the steps are the same. Let's take a closer look at each step and see what is involved.

Error/enhancement analysis

When an error is reported, the first step is, of course, to determine what the error is. The first step in doing this is to create a repeatable and testable condition within your own environment. If you fail to do this quickly, you must go to the developer who reported the problem, review the steps he or she is following, and see the error condition in action. You then need to detect where the error occurs. Remember that there are as many as four layers of code you are working with: PowerBuilder, the PFC, your corporate layer, and the application code.

Our experience is that it is a good policy to sit with the developer and walk through the code to pinpoint where the code is going wrong, as this indicates that you are willing to work with the developer. Once the point of error is detected, however, your job becomes one of analyzing not only what is being done, but how the function is being used. Incorrect usage should be addressed as a previously undetected potential pitfall that should be documented (and perhaps already has been). Try outlining the correct procedure to the developer, note the error condition and its cause, and schedule an investigation into how this loophole can be addressed via either code or documentation. Reusable code libraries are very sensitive to incorrect usage, and this is a broad-based defect in the reusable world that promotes the need for thorough testing of all conditions.

If the error can be corrected (or bypassed) in the developer's code, your job becomes easier. If not, your next step is to determine exactly where the code needs to be corrected.

Library analysis

As we already know, each layer of code added to a developer's plate means one more layer you have to work through, and understand, before you can take corrective action. If the error condition is in your corporate layer, you can move on to the next step. If the error is in the PFC base code, you need to take other action. You must

- Notify Powersoft of the condition, along with steps to recreate the problem (and also a possible solution if you have one).

- Identify how you can take corrective action immediately, even if short-term, because you may not get the correction back from Powersoft before the next maintenance release.

Some tips to remember when making corrections to the base PFC layer include the following:

- Use a change management product (such as ObjectCycle).

- Make the change to the actual PFC object and test this change. Create a regression test for this case (manual or automated).

- Maintain a separate copy of the changed code only in an archived library (Object Cycle will work for this, too).

- Check the object back into the library and maintain careful and accurate records of changes made.

Why all of this consideration? When a new release of the PFC is distributed, you want to be able to simply overlay your existing PFC libraries with the new ones. Your regression test should test all "error conditions" which you have fixed before; if any are still in the current release, you can reapply those specific changes using the archived text scripts.

If you opt to make the change in an extension layer such as your corporate layer or the PFE layer, remember that future modifications made to the base PFC product can affect your changes, and that your change could affect the PFC code. For example, if you override a PFC event and then write your own replacement code, any future change made to that specific event within the PFC will be ignored. This could mean as little as a bug fix not being applied, or as much as new services being provided that are never usable because you overrode the place where the service is utilized. Be aware of this, and be careful about how you apply the fix, and always keep accurate records of your changes.

Notifying Powersoft is an important step in the cycle. Reusable libraries live and die by their quality, and the only way the PFC will continue to improve is if users report the errors they detect for permanent correction. Remember that the more code Powersoft maintains, the less code you will have to maintain in your corporate layer.

Note: Remember to remove temporary fixes when the correction is applied by Powersoft in a maintenance release. Keep track of applied corrections separately and compare them against the technical bulletin that accompanies every maintenance release.

The other location where an error might exist is in the PowerBuilder code. Here you should follow the defined procedure for reporting product defects within your organization, and then determine where, and if, you can apply a correction or workaround.

Code design

Now that you have a repeatable condition, whether it be an error condition or an enhancement request, record this as a test case in your regression test suite. This has two benefits. First, you will know when your correction/addition works, and second, you will be able to detect if the condition returns. If you are using a tool such as SQA to record the test case, you will be able to alter the expected result prior to making any code changes, so your testing will already fail as an invalid condition and be recorded within SQA as a defect. This will of course cease once the modification has been successfully applied.

It is important that you carefully outline the change you are going to make. If you do this in a visual form such as a flowchart, you will reap the benefit of utilizing an approach we call "visual stimulation." What this does is present your design in a format other than code which triggers a different set of responses within the brain and allows you to visualize the change differently. We have caught several incorrect approaches to a problem-solving effort this way, and we have also found different and better ways to approach a modification. Creating flowcharts that show the flow of code from the PFC through the corporate layer and PFE layers also helps in understanding the impact of changes.

Regardless of which design approach you take, any design is better than no design. Jumping in and coding is the approach many of us have taken because we all know our code is correct first time in, right?

Once you have designed the change and are comfortable with your approach, document it and design the test case you will use to prove the code application. Now you are ready to actually code the correction.

Code development

At this point, we know which objects are affected, and we can make the code change appropriately. Even though we've stated categorically that you should never change the PFC layer, corrections to the base code that are relatively simple can and should be made to the base code library. Keeping in mind that they will be overridden with a new maintenance release, you should export and save any changed scripts in order that they may easily be reapplied. Remember that only a regression test that includes a test case for the condition you are working on will be able to detect if this occurs, highlighting the importance of having a regression test suite.

Most code changes, however, should be applied to your corporate layer, or to the PFE layer if you do not use a corporate layer. The reason is twofold. First, the base code will be overlaid with each maintenance release, and second, the PFC code will be tested by more developers in real-world applications than any corporate layer added. This implies that there is a higher potential for errors to exist in the newer and more focused corporate layers than in the base PFC product.

Change management and distribution

Regardless of whether you are distributing changes made within your organization or you have received a new maintenance release of the base product from Powersoft, the upgrade process should remain the same.

There are typically four components to an upgrade. You update the underlying tool (PowerBuilder), the PFC base libraries, your corporate extension layer (if any), and probably the PFE layer. Let's examine each of these in detail, except for the base PowerBuilder product, which you are all familiar with upgrading already. We follow three steps in rolling out a PFC upgrade.

1. Upgrade the libraries in a remote location (a location separate from your existing production environment).

2. Do a full rebuild using one of your test applications.

3. Upgrade and rebuild the other test applications and run regression tests.

But what if you are a developer on a PFC application without centralized object management? Well, this is, of course, much simpler, because you are not concerned with the effect of change on other projects. Because upgrading the PFC for a single project is a subset of upgrading for multiple projects, if you follow the same approach, you will ensure that you do not miss any possible "gotchas" when upgrading your set of PFC/PFE libraries; therefore, don't think that these steps are outlined for a centralized approach only.

Let's take a closer look at each layer and how it is affected by an upgrade to the product.

The PFC layer.   First, we never modify the PFC layer ourselves, so we have nothing to fear if we replace the existing PFC libraries with the new libraries. While this is true, we still strongly recommend making a backup of your PFC, corporate, and PFE libraries beforehand, then copying all of the libraries to a local workstation away from the normal work environment, and then working in this "work area." There are two reasons for doing this. The first is that you do not want to change working libraries with untested libraries. The second is that working locally allows you to do full rebuilds and/or compiles more quickly than across a network.

Next, you want to go through both your own notes regarding PFC corrections and the release notes that come with the PFC maintenance releases to see which fixes/enhancements the two have in common. Remember to test all of the conditions you have applied fixes for, to determine which conditions have been fixed by the new release and which will have to have fixes reapplied.

The corporate layer.   Of course, this step is necessary only if you have one or more corporate layers with your PFC product. If your upgrade is an internal one, i.e., only your corporate layer has changed and you want to roll this out, follow the same procedures as for the PFC layer, replacing the corporate layer instead with the new corporate layer. If the PFC product is being upgraded, make sure that you create new corporate-layer objects for each *new* PFC object that comes in the PFC libraries (if you opted for the complete layered insertion as described in Chap. 12). The release notes document any new objects that are included. If you maintain the corporate layer, make sure you document any new objects added at the corporate level, as they will have to be added at the PFE level.

If you applied any changes to the PFC via the corporate layer, make sure that these are reviewed carefully to ensure that no change gets overwritten or lost.

The PFE layer.   Surprisingly, this layer causes the most headaches even though you never actually change a single object. You do not replace your existing PFE layer during an upgrade. Instead, you need to read the release notes that come with the release, and determine which objects are *new* to the library. Why? New PFC and/or corporate-layer objects do not have PFE extension objects in the PFE layer. You will need to create these yourself. If you do not have a corporate layer, then simply add any new PFE objects to your PFE libraries. Make a careful note of the objects, because your developers will have to do the same in their copies of the PFE library. If you do have a corporate layer, then you have two steps to follow. First, for each new PFC object, you need to create the corporate-layer object, then reinherit the PFE-layer object from the corporate-layer object. Update the corporate libraries and then add the new objects to the PFE libraries. Again, make a careful note of which objects are added in order to pass these along to your developers. I recommend creating a PFN?????.pbl containing these added objects and using this as a distribution mechanism. The PFN indicates that these are new objects only, to be added to the respective PFE library, and then maintained for historical purposes only. This is a procedure that will be followed by Powersoft as well, where all new objects will be kept in a separate library.

Rebuilding the libraries

Once all of the changes have been successfully applied, you will need to rebuild the entire library. Why? You cannot determine which of the PFC-layer (or corporate-layer) objects that have been modified might adversely affect your existing usage of the object. Using the Full Rebuild option in the library painter is the quickest and safest way to ensure that all objects are rebuilt according to their respective hierarchical dependencies.

Once all the libraries are rebuilt, select each sample, demo, or test application in turn and do a full rebuild of it as well. Although this may seem time-consuming, it is an exercise worth doing. You are going to tell your developers to do the same thing with their applications, so the more applications you can test this out with, the less chance you have of being surprised by a telephone call indicating that their rebuild has failed and now the application needs migration once more (a side effect from a failed full rebuild).

Correct any and all errors (noting informational and obsolete errors as well), and, as when you wash your hair, rinse and repeat until all errors are "cleansed." Now you're ready to do some testing.

Testing

Manual versus automated

If you are in a position where you need to test an application more than once, we strongly recommend an automated testing tool. There are several on the market which perform admirably, notably SQA Test Suite from SQA Inc., QA Partner by Segue Software, and WinRunner by Mecury Interactive. Personally, we prefer SQA Test Suite by SQA. It is relatively simple to install and start using out of the box, although we recommend some training to get a jump start in using some of the more involved features of the tool. (This would apply for the other tools as well.)

Even though it might seem as if an automated testing tool will take up a lot of your time building test cases (which it does; no one will argue about that fact), your returns on this time and effort will be swift and truly satisfying. An indication of this can be demonstrated:

1. Even a small application must be thoroughly tested.

2. If one person spends one week thoroughly testing the application, he or she will have missed testing something.

3. For thorough testing of any kind, you need a complete and detailed test plan or no two test runs will ever be the same.

4. If you spend the time to develop the detailed test plan, you will have accomplished 50 percent of what you need for an automated testing tool, and some tools provide assistance in doing this, so you may spend less time doing it.

5. Once the planning is done, recording test cases is a relatively simple task, although time-consuming. Based on the "small application" referenced here, it should take about a week to do.

6. Even if you spend twice as long building an automated test suite, you will recover this the second time you run the test suite, and you are guaranteed of consistent testing.

7. A new staff member assigned to testing an application does not have to learn every test case (as he or she would if it were done manually), so time can be saved during training.

What to test

There are always a hundred arguments why you should or shouldn't use an automated test suite. Regardless of whether you do or not, you still need to know one major fact: What should you test? This will be answered differently depending on what your job is.

If you are a library administrator responsible for maintaining the central copy of the PFC only, you are in luck! Powersoft has a sophisticated automated regression test suite which is used for testing PFC releases. This means your testing is limited to the effect that new versions of the PFC library have on your organization's applications. While this responsibility is not to be taken lightly, it is eased if you have a few production applications housed in a controlled area where you can perform regression testing. The combined testing of the PFC sample applications, any sample/demo applications you may have developed centrally to demonstrate features or techniques, and the production applications is enough to ensure that the effect of PFC enhancements is endurable in your production and development environments.

If your role includes corporate-layer development/maintenance, your work is a little more complex because you must measure the effect on the corporate-layer extensions as well as everything else.

If you are a PFC developer using the libraries, your role is limited to testing your application with the modified libraries.

Upgrading Applications

As a developer, when a new version of the PFC libraries or your corporate layer is released, you should first ask the question, "Have the libraries been fully tested simulating existing conditions?" If the answer is yes, you can proceed with at least some peace of mind. If the answer is no, your next few days will be, at the very least, interesting.

When you get the new versions of the libraries, take note of any libraries indicating "new objects" that need to be added to your PFE layer. If you have not modified the PFE layer for your application, then adding the new objects holds little danger.

If you have modified the PFE layers, be aware that you may have "created" the very object now being provided to you, and there may be a conflict. We follow a procedure which ensures that our objects maintain sovereign status:

1. Copy the new PFC and corporate layers to a work area we establish on a local workstation.
2. Manually create new PFE libraries in this area.
3. Copy any new objects into the new PFE libraries.
4. Copy existing PFE objects into the PFE libraries (which overlays any like objects).

The reason we can do this is that any PFE-layer object distributed to us is an empty object derived from either the PFC or our corporate layer. If we already have this object, and we have correctly created this object from the PFC or corporate layer, then our object is identical to the newly distributed object plus any changes we have made. Therefore, we are simply readding our changes to the new PFE object.

Now we can rebuild our application (use Full Rebuild), correct any errors (and there really should be none), and we are ready to roll. The next test is to recompile the application (which ensures that it will compile, and gives us something to use for regression testing later). If the application already has a regression test suite, run this and record any differences or defects. Report these immediately and make a decision about whether they are acceptable or not.

Finally, once all is done and we are satisfied, then and only then do we copy the entire set of libraries back into our actual development environment after ensuring that we have a backup of the development environment in its current state. Remember to make sure that all objects being worked on are checked in.

Summary/Conclusions

This chapter has focused on providing solutions to the increasingly difficult task of maintaining our development environments. We've tried to keep it brief and to the point, yet the importance and the degree of difficulty continue to rise. Today's technology is heading off in all directions at once, and it takes significant effort to maintain a level of sanity. Using the techniques described, you will find that at least some of the headaches associated with upgrading a tool such as the PFC are alleviated. Use them to arm yourself with the knowledge necessary to stay afloat. Remember that awareness of situations can offer protection against some of the hazards. And, after all, it's the 1990s. We need protection!

16

Documentation and Help

Introduction/Objectives

Where can I get more information? No matter how much material is covered, this question is sure to come up again and again. This chapter will cover all the currently available PFC documentation, classes, and seminars, as well as the ever-growing list of Internet and other on-line resources.

What Documentation Is Available

Manuals

Two PFC manuals are included in the PowerBuilder documentation:

- *PowerBuilder Foundation Class Library User's Guide*
- *PowerBuilder Foundation Class Library Object Reference*

PowerBuilder Foundation Class Library User's Guide.   The user's guide is broken down into three parts. Part one provides a brief overview of PFC concepts, object-oriented terminology, and PFC components.

The second part contains a tutorial. The tutorial takes you through the basic steps required to create your first "Hello World" PFC application. No prior PFC knowledge is required, all the code is provided. The tutorial does demonstrate some of the fundamental PFC techniques. Your finished application will look like the window shown in Fig. 16.1.

The tutorial lacks a detailed explanation of each topic. However, for a simple application, the tutorial does cover a wide range of concepts. The following topics are covered by the tutorial application:

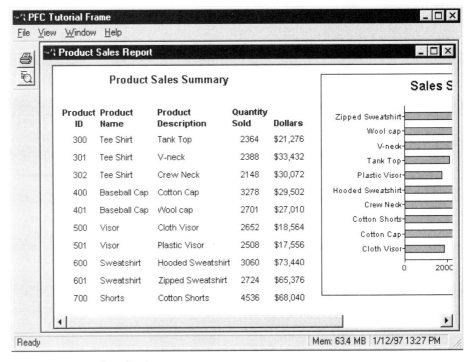

Figure 16.1   Tutorial application.

- Library path
- Application manager
- PFC windows and menus
- Sheet manager service
- Status bar service
- Message router
- DataWindow control
- Row selection DataWindow service
- Row manager DataWindow service
- Sort DataWindow service
- Report DataWindow service
- Print preview DataWindow service

If you have not done so yet, take some time to go through the tutorial. Building a small application will provide instant gratification, build self-confidence, and encourage further exploration of the PFC library.

Part three of the user's guide gets a little more specific. It covers the PFC programming practices, describes the usage of PFC services, outlines the extension strategy, and explains the usage of the PFC utilities. Each object is covered in two steps. An overview section describes the purpose of the object and lists its features. The usage section describes each feature and provides an implementation example.

The *PFC User's Guide* is a very good introduction to PFC. It is not very large, about 200 pages. Subtracting the 80-page tutorial leaves about 120 pages. The *PFC User's Guide* covers many fundamental topics. Reading the *User's Guide* should be considered a prerequisite to your first PFC application.

Note: The information in this book often supersedes the *User's Guide.* Nevertheless, many concepts are easier to comprehend when they are described by different sources.

PowerBuilder Foundation Class Library Object Reference. The *PFC Object Reference* makes up for any lack of detail in the *User's Guide.* It contains a complete description of every PFC object. In contrast to the *User's Guide,* the *PFC Object Reference* is not meant to be read in one session. Just as its name implies, this impressive 800-page manual is intended to be used as a reference. The objects are listed in alphabetical order within the following categories:

- Window objects
- User objects
- Menus
- Global functions
- Global structures and structure objects

Each object is documented using the same outline. The description section defines the object's purpose. The ancestry section provides a bird's-eye view of an object. See Fig. 16.2.

The ancestry diagram illustrates the object's inheritance structure and lists every instance variable, event, and function for each inheritance level. Event, function, and instance variable definitions follow the ancestry section. The syntax, arguments, and return values are described in detail. Usage examples are provided where appropriate.

The thorough coverage, the attention to detail, and the sheer amount of information make the *PFC Reference Guide* an indispensable tool.

On-line reference

The standard package includes the documentation on the *Online Books* CD. PFC documentation can be found in the Advanced Developer Toolkit collection. See Fig. 16.3.

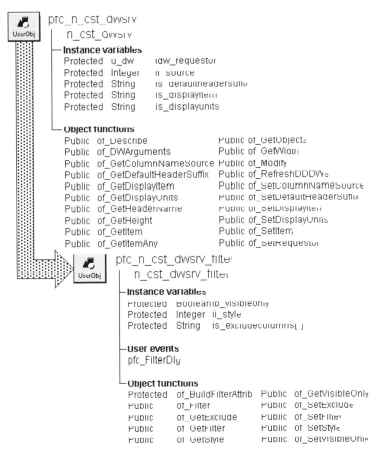

Figure 16.2 Ancestry diagram.

One advantage of the on-line documentation is that the Dynatext engine provides some basic search capabilities. This allows quick access to the topic of interest. See Fig. 16.4.

The on-line reference is better suited for accessing specific information, while the paperback documentation may be easier to read. If you don't have the hardcopy version of the documentation, I recommend generating a printout of the *PFC User's Guide.* You should read the *PFC User's Guide* prior to embracing your first PFC project. The *PFC Object Reference* can be left on CD. The information it contains can be accessed as needed.

Online help

The contents of the on-line help bear a striking resemblance to the *PFC Object Reference.* PowerBuilder inspires reuse even in its documentation. Given the quality and thorough coverage of the Reference Guide, we will be the last to

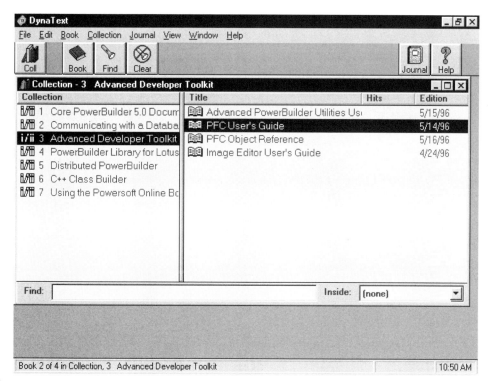

Figure 16.3   On-line PFC documentation.

complain. The on-line help, however, is not an identical twin. The context-sensitive feature allows you to jump directly from the script painter to the topic of interest by highlighting the keyword and pressing Shift + F1. The help file is indexed to provide instant access to related objects.

PFC code

This very valuable resource often gets overlooked. PFC code in itself contains a wealth of information. While researching topics for this book, we asked many experienced PFC developers what was the best way to learn PFC. One answer came up again and again: Read the code!

PFC code contains examples of many interesting techniques. Here are just a few of the things you can learn:

- Use of autoinstantiated user objects to replace structures
- Effective use of recursive events and functions.
- Utilization of any datatype
- New 5.0 language features

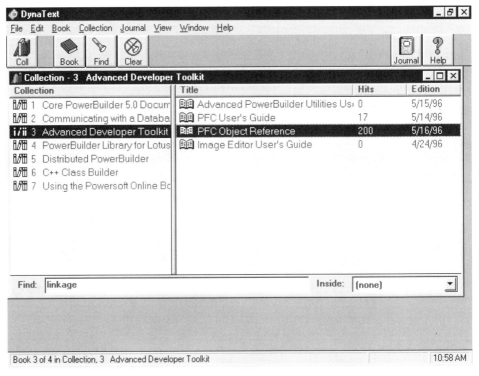

Figure 16.4 Search feature.

- Overloading functions to provide optional arguments
- The use of the standard of_Setxxx() function to instantiate or destroy a service

Reading the PFC code will give you an insight into the programming style. Adopting the PFC programming style and methodology will make your application a natural extension of the PFC. On the other hand, trying to change the default functionality to force a specific behavior may cause unexpected results.

The first PFC users were the PFC developers. PFC uses a lot of its own objects and functions. Many usage examples of the associative services can be found right in the PFC code.

Checking the ancestor script is often just as easy as using the on-line help. This is my preferred method of determining the event/function arguments and return types. While browsing the PFC code, you are sure to come across the comments. The comments offer another documentation source and often contain additional tips.

The Object Browser is another source of up-to-date information on the object functions, events, and properties. While the documentation may fall slightly behind the minor releases, the Object Browser and the source code will always offer the most current information.

Where Can You Find Out More

PFC CBTs

Prior to the release of Powerbuilder 5.0, Powersoft held a series of one-day seminars. In total, five seminars were held, each covering a different feature of 5.0:

- Preparing for distributed computing
- Windows 95–style controls in PowerBuilder 5.0
- Extending PowerBuilder: exploiting OLE and OCX
- Leveraging PowerBuilder 5.0 object-oriented language features
- Accelerating development using PowerBuilder Foundation Classes

After the 5.0 release, each seminar was converted into a CBT course.

Note: Obviously the last title is the one of interest. However, don't bypass the other four titles in this series. Knowledge of all Powerbuilder 5.0 features is crucial to a successful utilization of the PFC library.

Accelerating development using PowerBuilder Foundation Classes CBT course. We have attended the PFC one-day seminar. Although we learned a lot of general PFC concepts, we were slightly disappointed with the amount of in-depth coverage of specific services and examples. We later realized that our expectations were set too high. It is not possible to provide thorough coverage of PFC in a single day.

When we received the CBT course, our expectations were a little lower. This time we were pleasantly surprised. The automated version of the same course seemed to provide more details on each topic. The comparison was not exactly fair, as we had already been exposed to many PFC topics. When we compared the seminar and the CBT course outlines, we discovered that the real difference was in the presentation style. We were able to absorb more information from the computer-based course. This was largely due to the course structure.

Course layout. The PFC CBT course consists of two CDs. Each one is structured as a separate course with its own installation routine. The first CD covers the general topics, and the second goes into more detail. The high-level outline for each CD is listed below:

- Powersoft Foundation Classes I
  Introduction
  PFC overview
  PFC libraries: an example
  Customizing class libraries with extension layers
  The extension layer
  Naming convention

PFC components
What is subclassed
PFC control hierarchy and control features
PFC menu hierarchy
Standard objects
Custom class user object services
PFC architecture
The nonvisual custom class
Noninheritable objects—the application object
Advantages of a service-oriented architecture
Service-aware PFC requesters
DataWindow control ancestor—an example
Encapsulation of functionality
Messaging and polymorphism
Function categories
Customizing PFC services
Conclusion
Summary

- Powersoft Foundation Classes II

Overview
Application services
Creating a new application
DBMS services
Menu services
Window services
DataWindow services
Utility services
Conclusion
Summary

As soon as the course is started, you are given an opportunity to take a pretest. The test consists of ten multiple-choice questions. The same test is presented at the end of the course. This test is intended to give you a sense of accomplishment and provide a way to assess how much you have learned from the course. The posttest will identify those areas that you may need to review.

The next screen displays a course outline. You can start the course from the beginning or jump to a specific topic. The same option is available throughout the course. The main course window, shown in Fig. 16.5, consists of four areas:

- Course title

- Topic text

- Video screen

- Toolbar area

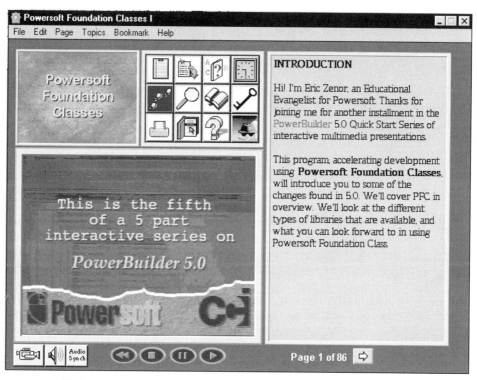

Figure 16.5 CBT main window.

TABLE 16.1   Toolbar Options

Copy	Copy the text window contents.
Notes	Add custom comments for each topic.
Glossary	Present list of terms.
Clock	Display time.
Recent pages	Navigate back to recently covered pages.
Find	Search the entire CD for a specific topic.
Bookmark	Define a bookmark.
Key Points	Display the key points of each topic.
Print	Print the text contents.
Topics List	Jump to a specific topic.
Help	Display the online help.
Posttest	Take the posttest.

Table 16.1 outlines the available toolbar options. These options provide the easy navigation that makes the CBT shine. The course can be taken in comfortable surroundings and, more importantly, at your own pace.

Each topic is presented in three steps. First, the topic is introduced in a short video lecture. The instructors were obviously the best of the crop. Each topic is explained in a clear and precise manner. Next, an example is presented in the video area, or optionally in a full-screen Lotus Screen-cam window. In the last step, you have an opportunity to repeat the example in a "hands-on" lab with the help of the "audio coach." The installation program installs the necessary lab libraries, which are automatically opened by the program. The examples are simple, but the self-paced nature of the course allows you to experiment and extend each exercise as necessary.

What to expect. The structure of Powersoft's computer-based training is very effective. The lecture–example–lab layout reinforces each topic and allows you to retain more information. The flexible navigation allows you to proceed at your own pace and return to any topic. Pre- and posttests enable you to identify areas of weakness that you may need to review.

The single shortcoming of the computer course is that the communication is unidirectional. There is no way to ask questions. Any attempt to do so is typically ignored. There are many other resources, discussed later in this chapter, that offer interactive PFC support.

Powersoft training

Powersoft currently offers a two-day PFC class, "Building Applications Using the PowerBuilder Foundation Class Library." The class is part of a comprehensive suite of educational offerings. The PFC course is part of an advanced "Skill Mastery" series and requires familiarity with object-oriented construction techniques and fluency in the new Powerbuilder 5.0 features.

The course is presented in seven units:

Unit 1, "About Service-Oriented Frameworks"

Unit 2, "Introducing the PowerBuilder Foundation Class Library"

Unit 3, "Using Application Services"

Unit 4, "Using PFC Menus and Windows"

Unit 5, "Using DataWindow Services"

Unit 6, "More DataWindow Services"

Unit 7, "Customizing the PFC"

Appendix A, "Using the Utility Services"

Units 2 through 7 are each followed by several lab sessions. The lab exercises cover the basic steps required to utilize a specific PFC feature.

Table 16.2 lists the topics covered by the PFC class.

What to expect. The course packs a lot of information into two days. The material is covered at a very fast pace. Do not expect an in-depth explanation of every PFC service. The advantage of a class is its interactive environment. The PFC class is a part of an advanced "Skill Mastery" series. In order to teach the advanced class, the instructors have to go through the grueling certification process. As a result, the instructors teaching this course are among the techni-

TABLE 16.2   PFC Class Topics

Framework architectures	Multiple inheritance	Communication with services
Service-oriented basics	Extension layers	Encapsulation
Reference variables	PFC library organization	PFC messaging architecture
Event redirection	PFC components	PFC main services
Nonvisual user object inheritance	Naming conventions	PFC window services
	Hierarchies	PFC DataWindow services
Hierarchy responsibilities	Extending standard class user objects	PFC utility services
Brokers		Migration issues

cally elite and have a lot to offer. To take advantage of their knowledge, you have to go beyond the course curriculum. In order to get the most out of the PFC class, you must come prepared. Some suggestions:

- Read the *User's Guide*.
- Go through the tutorial.
- Build a small application.
- Develop a list of key issues, such as extension strategy.
- Prepare a list of questions.

Other sources

Third-party training.   Since the release of PFC, a few companies have developed PFC seminars and courses. Two that deserve mention are a course offered by BSG Corporation and a seminar from CCS Consulting.

The BSG course is a three-day course segregated into 14 modules and 16 labs. The course follows the outline listed below.

Understanding frameworks

Framework architectures

An overview of the PFC

PFC components

PFC messaging architecture

PFC services—an overview

Application services

    Lab 1: Coding the application objects

    Lab: 2: Application manager

    Lab: 3: Debug services

    Lab: 4: Caching services

Lab: 5: Error services

DBMS services

Menu services

Lab: 6: Menus and messaging

Window services

Lab: 7: Status bar

Lab: 8: Window preference services

Lab: 9: Window resizing services

DataWindow services

Lab: 10: DataWindow linkage services

Lab: 11: DataWindow, rowmanager service, and sorting service

Listview and treeview services

Lab: 12: Listview

Lab: 13: Treeview services

Utility services

Lab: 14: Utility string services

Lab: 15: Utility I/O services

Customizing the PFC

Lab: 16: Customizing the PFC

CCS offers a one- or two-day PFC seminar. The CCS seminar outline is constantly revised. Contact CCS for the current seminar topic and availability.

More information on the courses above is available at each company's Web site.

BSG Corporation   http://www.bsginc.com/

CCS Consulting   http://www.consultccs.com/

What to expect.   The instructors teaching the third-party courses may not be certified by Powersoft. This is not necessarily a disadvantage; these courses are often prepared and taught by working consultants with hands-on PFC project experience. They offer the additional benefit of practical expertise.

Smaller companies can be more flexible with the class curriculum. In contrast to Powersoft's class, the outline of these classes may be constantly revised to incorporate the latest techniques and discoveries.

On the downside, these courses are not as widely available as Powersoft's. They may be offered only in a single area or presented as one-time seminars.

Powersoft guarantees the quality of its courses by controlling the course materials and the instructor certifications. This is not the case with the third-party courses. This does not imply that the third-party educational offerings are inferior, simply that the responsibility for monitoring the quality lies with you.

Internet

Newsgroups. Usenet, an abbreviation of "users' network," is an Internet bulletin board system. It contains thousands of individual newsgroups or forums, each specific to a single topic. The newsgroups can be unmoderated or moderated. Unmoderated newsgroups are uncensored, whereas moderated newsgroups are supervised.

Powersoft maintains a number of moderated support newsgroups at *forums.powersoft.com* newsgroup server. Although it is not currently available, by the time you read this, a PFC newsgroup will have been added. Many PFC-related questions are posted on the unmoderated newsgroup *comp.sys.powerbuilder.* This is the first Powerbuilder Internet newsgroup.

To access a newsgroup, you need a news reader program and access to a NNTP server. A news reader is included with the current version of both Netscape Navigator and Microsoft Internet Explorer. Another program worth mentioning is Forte's Free Agent. It is, as the name suggests, free, and can be downloaded from Forte's Web site, *http://www.forteinc.com.* An NNTP server is typically provided by your ISP or, as is the case with Powersoft's, can be public.

The articles posted on the newsgroup expire. The expiration time depends on the available space and forum traffic. Fortunately, most of the newsgroups are archived. Powersoft plans to distribute all the messages posted on its news server on the Infobase CD. The unmoderated newsgroups are archived by other sources. One such source is Dejanews, *http://www.dejanews.com.*

Mailing lists. Mailing lists provide another way of conducting group discussions on the Internet. A mailing list server forwards any e-mail it receives to every subscriber on the list. To participate in these discussions, all you need is an e-mail address and the e-mail software.

Two current PFC mailing lists are *pfcsig,* maintained by BSG Corporation, and *pfc-users,* by Greenbrier & Russel.

Both mailing lists use the popular mailing list software Majordomo. To join a Majordomo mailing list, you need to send an e-mail to majordomo@<domain.com> with the words "subscribe <list name> <your e-mail address>." For example, to join the BSG list, your e-mail should be addressed to majordomo@rssi.com and the message should contain the phrase "join pfcsig <your e-mail address>." To join the G&R PFC list, send an e-mail to majordomo@gr.com with the following phrase in the message body: "join pfc-users <your e-mail address>."

When you join a mailing list, get ready to get a lot of e-mail. Message traffic on a single list can vary from a few to 100 messages a day. An e-mail software package with an incoming mail filter capability can automatically file all the messages from a specific list in a separate folder. Some mailing lists may offer a digest version, sending one large file of all the messages. Currently a digest option is not available on either pfcsig or pfc-users. The pfcsig list does offer an archive of all the posted messages. The archived pfcsig messages can be found at http://www.reference.com/cgi-bin/pn/listarch?list = pfcsig@rssi.com.

CompuServe.   The CompuServe forum is the oldest of the Powerbuilder automated support forums. For many years it has been a primary source of electronic technical support for PowerBuilder. No one knows who will be left standing after the hurricane Internet blows through. Today the CompuServe forum is still a very valuable source of PFC information.

The forum on CompuServe dedicates a message section to PFC-related questions. The file section contains white papers, code samples, presentations, and demo products.

What to expect.   If we had to pick a single information resource, electronic forums would be it. Newsgroups, forums, and mailing lists are by far the best source of current information. All of the electronic forums are supported by users. If you are facing a problem, chances are that you are following in someone else's footsteps. Joining these forums provides the benefit of sharing the experiences of hundreds of different projects. Electronic support forums offer an opportunity to mature your PFC skills in Internet years.

Summary/Conclusions

As you can see, there is a wealth of PFC information available. The Powersoft documentation provides a good starting point. The *User's Guide* lays the groundwork for fundamental PFC concepts. The *PFC Object Reference* and the on-line help are very valuable lookup resources.

The Powersoft and third-party classes and self-study materials are another source of base PFC concepts. If you do not feel you can take advantage of the interactive class environment, computer-based training may be a better option. CBT may also be used as a preparation for the course. Prior exposure to PFC concepts and terminology will allow you to concentrate on the important issues.

Last but not least, there are electronic forums. This is the only medium that can keep up with the blinding speed of today's technology. This is where you will spend your time long after you master many basic PFC concepts. All of the authors of this book can be found on one or more electronic support forums.

17

Other Inclusions

Introduction

In this chapter we will take a look at what is included with the PFC in addition to its libraries. This includes the tutorial, the PFC QuickStart libraries, and the Project Estimation and Actual Tracking (PEAT) demo application.

Chapter Objectives

In this chapter the reader will become familiar with

- The PFC tutorial
- The PFC QuickStart libraries
- The PEAT demo application

The PFC Tutorial

Using the on-line books

Installation. The PFC tutorial is located on the *PowerBuilder 5.0 Reference* CD-ROM that ships with PowerBuilder. To access it, you will need to install the on-line books. To do this, run the SETUP program in the root directory of the CD-ROM.

Tip: To install any Powersoft product, always run SETUP, not setup32. The SETUP program will determine if you are running under a 32-bit operating system and launch the appropriate program.

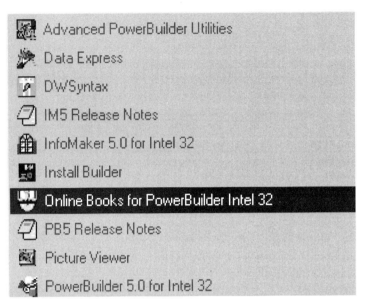

Figure 17.1   On-line books on Start menu.

Answer the queries on the screens and select *PowerBuilder Online Books* as the product to install. This will add the *PowerBuilder Online Books* to the PowerBuilder program group on your computer. Figure 17.1 shows the on-line books in the Windows 95 start menu for the PowerBuilder 5.0 group.

Once the on-line books are installed, they can be accessed by starting them from the start-up menu under Windows 95 or from the PowerBuilder program group in Windows. The CD-ROM will need to be in the drive to access the books. Powersoft uses DynaText to access the on-line books. Figure 17.2 shows the opening screen of the on-line books.

Select collection three, "Advanced Developers Toolkit," and the selection of available volumes on the right side of the screen will change. Figure 17.3 shows the on-line books for the PFC.

Searching for an item.   To search the on-line books for something, enter the word or words you want to search for in the Find box at the bottom of the window. Next, click on the Find button on the toolbar. The number of occurrences found (hits) will be displayed on the right under Hits next to the manual the hits were found in. Figure 17.4 shows 26 hits for the word *tutorial* in the *PFC User's Guide* manual.

Double-clicking on a book's title will open it. Clicking on the + sign to the left of a book part will expand the title to show the chapters within that part. Clicking on the + next to a chapter title will expand it to show the chapter's details. Figure 17.5 shows the *PFC User's Guide* open with the "Tutorial" chap-

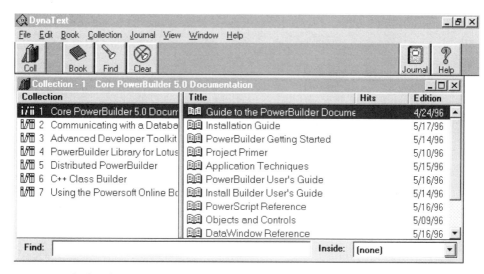

Figure 17.2   On-line books.

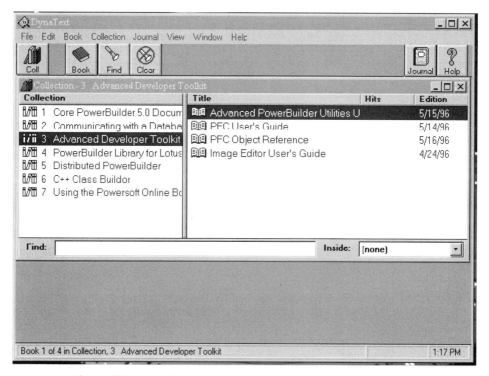

Figure 17.3   Advanced Developer Toolkit on-line books.

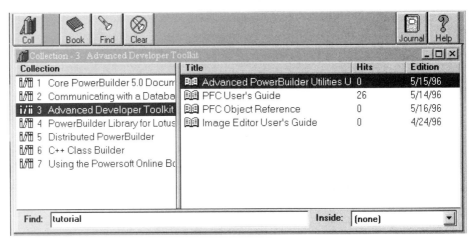

Figure 17.4 Search results.

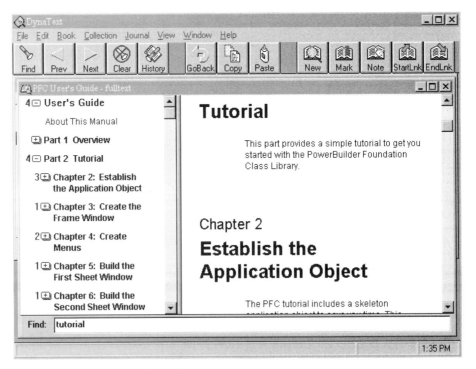

Figure 17.5 Displaying search results.

ter expanded and the first occurrences of the word *tutorial* displayed on the page. Clicking the Next or Prev button on the toolbar will move through the hits.

There are many more capabilities within DynaText, like adding notes and placing bookmarks. Spend some time with the DynaText help files and you should be well pleased with this tool.

The tutorial

The tutorial is designed to provide an overview of some of the PFC's functionality and how to use it. The tutorial consists of a library (pfctutor.pbl) to use with the tutorial. It contains some predefined objects with some precoded events that you will add to during the tutorial.

The tutorial consists of the following five chapters:

1. "Establish the Application Object"
2. "Create the Frame Window"
3. "Create Menus"
4. "Build the First Sheet Window"
5. "Build the Second Sheet Window"

"Establish the Application Object." This chapter will take approximately 20 minutes to complete. In it you will learn how to use the application manager, how to use the PFC's customized transaction object (n_tr), and how to set the library path to use the PFC.

The tutorial provides sample code that you can use in the supplied application. Figure 17.6 shows a sample of this code.

"Create the Frame Window." This exercise will take about 15 minutes. This section of the tutorial will cover the creation of a frame window, how to open a sheet using the PFC message router, how to enable the status bar and sheet management services, and how to connect to the database using the PFC transaction object n_tr.

"Create Menus." This lesson will take about 40 minutes. In it you will learn how to create a descendant of the m_master PFC menu, and how to create frame and sheet menus.

This tutorial uses one approach to supporting menus with the PFC. Others are available, including modifying m_master directly and creating your own menus.

"Build the First Sheet Window." This chapter will take approximately 30 minutes. Here you will learn to create descendants of w_sheet and to use the u_dw user object.

In this lesson, you create a sheet window by inheriting from the w_sheet window. You will define two DataWindow controls on the sheet, use the linkage ser-

5 **Type the following lines.**

```
this.of_SetAppIniFile  &
   ("c:\pathname
\pfc\tutorial\pfctutor.ini")
this.of_SetHelpFile  &
   ("c:\pathname
\pfc\tutorial\pfctutor.hlp")
this.of_SetLogo  &
   ("c:\pathname
\pfc\tutorial\tutsport.bmp")
this.of_SetCopyright("PFC Tutorial
application.")
this.of_SetVersion("PFC 5.0")
iapp_object.DisplayName = "PFC Tutorial"
```

Replace *pathname* with your workstation's path to the pfc directory.

Figure 17.6 Tutorial sample code.

vice to coordinate master/detail processing, and use the row manager to handle inserts and deletes for the detail DataWindow. You also associate the sheet window with the m_products menu.

"Build the Second Sheet Window." This lesson will take about 30 minutes. You will learn how to enable the report service and how to use the retrieve command in the pfc_retrieve event.

In this lesson you create another sheet window. You will define a DataWindow control on the sheet and use the report service to add reporting capabilities.

The remainder of the *PFC User's Guide* manual pertains to using the PFC. Its chapters include "Programming with the PFC," "Using PFC Services," "Extending the PFC," and "PFC Utilities."

It is worth taking the time to work your way through the tutorial to gain an understanding of how the PFC works.

QuickStart

QuickStart consists of five PowerBuilder libraries. Four of these libraries contain objects that are inherited from the PFC layer of the Foundation Class Library. These PBLs are:

Qckapsrv.pbl	Application services
Qckdwsrv.pbl	DataWindow services
Qckmain.pbl	Visual objects
Qckwnsrv.pbl	Window services

The remaining library, Qckstart.pbl, contains an application object along with a couple of other objects to demonstrate how QuickStart works.

These libraries consist of objects that have code added to them to extend the functionality of the base PFC. For example, the following code is contained in the pfc_logon event of the application manager n_cst_appmanager:

```
// Perform logon
sqlca.of_SetUser (as_userid, as_password)
IF sqlca.of_Connect() >= 0 THEN
        return 1
ELSE
        MessageBox (is_title, "Connect failed")
        return -1
END IF
```

Following is the precoded pfc_endtran event from w_master in the Qckmain.pbl file:

```
integer  li_rc

// Commit or rollback based on update
IF ai_update_results = 1 THEN
        li_rc = sqlca.of_Commit()
        IF li_rc >= 0 THEN
                li_rc = 1
        END IF
ELSE
        sqlca.of_Rollback()
        MessageBox (gnv_app.is_title, "Update failed. Changes not saved.")
        li_rc = -1
END IF
return li_rc
```

The above script performs either a commit or a rollback based on the success or failure of an update. Since this code is contained in w_master, it will be available in all windows inherited from Qckmain.pbl.

QuickStart is designed to provide you with a way to utilize the functionality of the PFC in a timely fashion. By changing just a few lines of code and adding some windows of your own, you can have an application up and running in very little time.

Project Estimation and Actual Tracking (PEAT)

The PFC comes with a demo application named PEAT. It was developed using the PFC and is a good starting point to review to see how the PFC may be used. Provided along with the application are analysis and design documents that you should review.

The system is designed to help in the estimation of projects and to track the actual time spent on project tasks. As stated in the analysis document, "An application is needed to track the estimated and actual cost of the development of client/server systems. Each project estimation is made up of two different costs: derived costs and driven costs. Derived costs (i.e., unit testing, project management, etc.) are based on a percentage of the total driven costs. Driven costs are broken down into different categories (i.e. windows, menus, DataWindows, etc.). Each category can have unlimited items. In addition, each item will be assigned a project member role and a complexity."

In the following section, we will take a look at the PEAT application and see how some of the features of the PFC were used.

One of the first steps in developing a PFC application is to create an application and define the library search path to include all of the libraries in the PFC. Figure 17.7 shows the PEAT application's library search path.

The application manager n_cst_peat. Next we need to declare a global variable to use for our application manager. For the PFC to work, this variable must be named gnv_app. Figure 17.8 shows the application manager's global variable declaration.

Next, we need to set the system transaction object SQLCA to use the PFC's transaction object n_tr. Figure 17.9 shows the application's variable types. This object contains functionality for managing database connections.

The open script for the application is as follows:

```
/***
*** Redirect the open message to the application manager
***/
gnv_app = CREATE n_cst_peat
gnv_app.Event Static Trigger pfc_open(CommandParm())
```

This script instantiates the application manager and then triggers the pfc_open event, passing the results of the CommandParm function to it. Any string may be passed to the pfc_open event.

The constructor event of the application manager is used to set application-wide options. Following is the script for this event:

```
// Set the default information needed for this application
iapp_object.DisplayName = "PEAT - Project Estimation and Actuals Tracker"
this.of_SetCopyright("Copyright © 1996 Powersoft Corporation. All Rights Reserved.")
this.of_SetLogo("peat.bmp")
this.of_SetVersion("Version 5.0")
this.of_SetAppINIFile("peat.ini")
```

Here such things as the applications INI file, copyright notice, logo, and version are set. Anywhere in the application that displays these items, these values will be used.

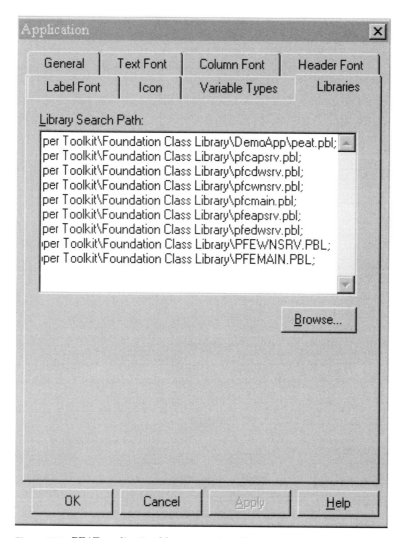

Figure 17.7 PEAT application library search path.

Now the pfc_open event is fired. Following is the script:

```
integer  li_return
string   ls_inifile
// Display the splash window
this.of_Splash(1)
// Initialize the various functionalities of this service
this.of_SetTrRegistration(TRUE)
this.of_SetError(TRUE)
// Connect to database
```

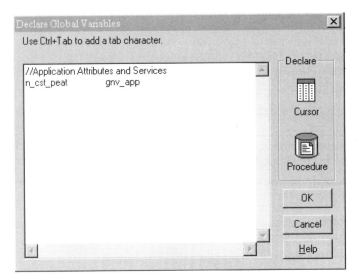

Figure 17.8   Declaring the application manager.

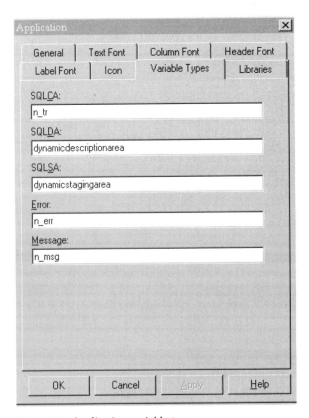

Figure 17.9   Application variable types.

```
ls_inifile = gnv_app.of_GetAppINIFile()
IF SQLCA.of_Init(ls_inifile, "Database") = -1 THEN
        this.inv_error.of_Message(gnv_app.iapp_object.DisplayName, + &
                        "Error initializing connection information, .INI file not
                        found.")
ELSE
        IF SQLCA.of_Connect() = -1 THEN
                this.inv_error.of_Message(gnv_app.iapp_object.DisplayName, + &
                                "Error connecting to Database.", StopSign!, OK!)
        ELSE
                Open(w_f_peat)
        END IF
END IF
```

This script displays the application splash screen for one second, starts the transaction registration and error services, and connects to the database. If the database connection is successful, the window w_f_peat is opened, which in turn opens the w_s_project list window. Figure 17.10 shows the open window.

This window contains a treeview control that shows projects in the treeview and project sections in a listview. Expanding a project in the treeview will display the project sections in the treeview and specific tasks in the listview.

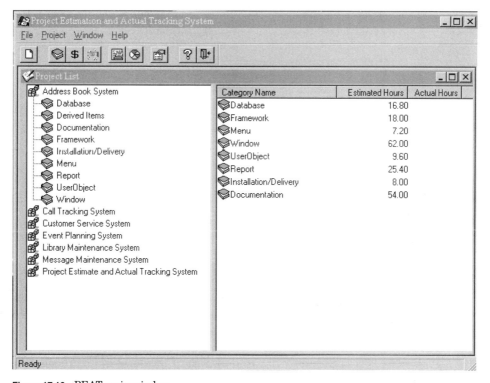

Figure 17.10 PEAT main window.

This window uses a service created for this application. The service, contained in a nonvisual object named n_cst_explorer, provides services to mimic the Windows95 Explorer with a treeview and a listview.

Object name	pfc_n_cst_explorer	Object type	Abstract service
Ancestry	nonvisualobject	Extension	n_cst_explorer
Description	Provides Windows 95 Explorer services.		
Usage	Created as an instance service for a window.		
Reason for use	To mimic Windows 95 Explorer.		
Layered extensions	Extend by inheritance and/or insertion.		
Function (action)	of_Resize		Resizes the listview and treeview controls.
Function (set)	of_SetControls		Associates specific listview and treeview controls to the service.
Function (set)	of_SetDefaultSplitBarPos		Sets the default position for the split bar.
Function (set)	of_SetLeftPane		Sets the object for the left pane of the window.
Function (set)	of_SetRightPane		Sets the object for the right pane of the window.

This is a good example of creating a new service for the PFC. The service is started by issuing a call to the of_SetExplorer function:

```
this.of_SetExplorer(TRUE)
```

The of_Explorer function is contained in the window w_s_projectlist.

```
IF ab_Switch THEN
        IF Not IsValid (inv_explorer) THEN
                inv_explorer = Create n_cst_explorer
                inv_explorer.dynamic of_SetRequestor ( this )
        END IF
ELSE
        IF IsValid (inv_explorer) THEN
                Destroy inv_explorer
        END IF
END IF
RETURN
```

When called with an argument of TRUE, this function checks to see if the service has been created and, if not, creates it. When called with an argument of FALSE, it checks to see if the service was created and, if so, destroys it.

Because this function is contained in the window, the service is usable only from this window or from windows inherited from it. Another approach would be to make this a window service and add the function to w_master, so that it is available to any window that wants to use it.

This also demonstrates another PFC added service, the vertical splitter bar, which automatically manages the size of the "area" of each side.

Summary

The tutorial is a good place to get an introduction to the PFC. It will step you through the process of building an application using the PFC.

The PEAT application will let you see how to use the PFC in much greater depth than the tutorial. It is a well-thought-out application that uses the PFC to good advantage.

18

A Sample Application

Introduction/Objectives

When we started this book, we realized that we should provide a sample application that illustrated the concepts and techniques introduced throughout. The decision concerning which application to use was not easy. Each of us has created a number of applications using the PFC. These applications range in complexity from the very simple to the wide-ranging, complex applications developed for enterprise information systems.

We decided to use an application that was developed for internal use at one of our companies. The application is called GSI TimeMaster, and it is used to collect and report on time and billing information. We chose this application as our sample because it is a real-world example of a need that has been satisfied using the PFC as a basis. The application is also one that most computer practitioners can relate to.

This chapter will introduce you to the sample application, its history, its construction using the PFC, its use, and the various techniques we have illustrated within the application. The sample application is not an exhaustive demonstration of all PFC techniques. That would be artificial, and probably not as helpful. Instead, it is a real application that enjoys current use. The PFC techniques that you will see are there because they satisfy a genuine programming need.

A Sample Application Broken Down—What We Used, When, Why, and How

Background

Gateway Systems, Inc. timekeeping requirements. Gateway Systems, Inc. (GSI), began business in 1984 with several clients and two consultants. We needed a way to keep careful track of the time spent on each activity. We needed to track not only client-billable activities but also such nonbillable activities as marketing, administration, and training, among others. We needed to be able to summarize the time spent on each client for billing purposes, and by each consultant for productivity measurement.

GSI created the first solution using an advanced (for the time) integrated environment, Lotus Symphony.

The Sidekick/Symphony solution. Our first timekeeping application was a spreadsheet-based package. We used a Lotus Symphony spreadsheet to sort, total, and report on the time spent on each activity. The input side of the equation was handled by Borland's Sidekick program. Sidekick was loaded as a terminate-and-stay-resident (TSR) program (it's DOS, remember?) and was available at the touch of a hot key. That way, the consultant could pop up the Sidekick timekeeping notepad at any time, even while running another program. Once the notepad was popped up, the consultant entered a keystroke that produced a timestamp, then typed three three-letter codes, one each for client, project, and task, and then a description of the work performed. This established the start time for the activity. Then Sidekick was popped down again while the activity was performed. At the end of the activity, Sidekick was popped up again and a timestamp was entered on the next line, followed by a percent-billable figure. (In practice, the percent-billable figure turned out to be always either 100 or zero.) This entry established the end time for the activity.

This system worked well. Time entries were easy to make. They were also tied in great detail to the actual time spent on each activity within each project for every client. The immediacy of the pop-up TSR program, plus the simple timestamp and ASCII text interface, made it convenient for the consultant to keep accurate time records.

The spreadsheet was a masterpiece. It included macros to read, parse, sort, and summarize the entries, then produce billing reports. The macros did a lot of text processing and needed a lot of manual intervention. Compared to any manual process, it was a remarkable timesaver. But after we had been using it for some time, it became apparent that the entire process was slow. As the number of time entries increased, the labor and time required to produce the billing reports became prohibitive. A new solution was needed.

The Turbo Pascal solution. In an effort to streamline the process, we created a replacement for the spreadsheet macros using Turbo Pascal. We retained the pop-up notepad method of data collection because it worked and was convenient for the users. But by replacing the slow and labor-intensive macros with a custom-written 3GL program, we were able to target the slowest and most error-prone part of the timekeeping and billing process. The end result required no manual intervention and ran in a fraction of the time needed for the spreadsheet macros. A side benefit that we experienced was improved management reporting.

However, nothing lasts forever. The advent of Windows as a standard operating environment made the TSR Sidekick far less attractive, and in fact almost unworkable, as an entry method. We made some adaptations as time went on, of course. Borland had a follow-on product, Sidekick Plus, that could be loaded in nonresident mode and left running in the Windows background as a DOS task. This let us run it in a window and switch to that window with the Alt + Tab key combination. This worked better, but it was certainly not perfect. Another problem was that the data was not held in a database. The ASCII notepad files produced from Sidekick were the repository for the data. This made any additions or changes to the reports a whole new programming effort.

The PowerBuilder and PFC solution

In 1996 we decided to rewrite the entire system using PowerBuilder 5.0 and the PFC. Starting with one of the example applications, we created an explorer-style interface for the entry of the time records. We designed a very simple database using S-Designor. Then we added enough reporting to be able to summarize activity on a per-client basis for any given period. The result is still quite primitive, but it already has enormous advantages over the old method. As time permits, we continue to make incremental improvements to the program. The application and its accompanying database are part of a larger system that will eventually supporting billing, time-tracking, purchasing, and other activities.

The Design

Requirements

This section details the basic requirements for the application. The primary requirements are already in place, having been defined by the existing system. Additional requirements are based on experience and need.

Input requirements

- *Enter client information.* The system must allow you to establish, change, and delete client records.

- *Enter projects for each client.* The system must provide a way to establish, change, and delete project records for each client.

- *Enter tasks for each project.* The system must provide a way to establish, change, and delete task (or activity) records for each project.

- *Enter consultant information.* The system must provide a way to establish, change, and delete a record for each consultant.

- *Enter time spent on each task.* Time entries consist of client, project, and task identifiers; consultant identifier; description; and start date/time, end date/time, *or* a duration. The following actions must be available for a time entry:

1. *Start.* This will begin a new entry. The current time will be entered for start time as a default. End time will be blank.
2. *Stop.* This will place the current time into the end time of the selected time entry.
3. *Elapsed.* This will allow the entry of an elapsed time for an activity where the exact start and stop times are unknown.
4. *Continue.* This will copy the client/task/project IDs from a selected entry, create a new entry, and default the start time to the current time.
5. *Delete.* This will delete the selected entry (with confirmation).

All input fields for time entries must be user-editable.

Interface requirements

- The application must follow the multiple document interface (MDI) standard.

- The time entry screen must follow a Windows 95 Explorer–like format. The treeview on the left will display the client/project/task hierarchy. The view on the right (*not* a listview) will show the time entries, filtered to the level that is selected. That is, if a client is selected, all time entries for that client will be displayed. If a project is selected, only entries pertaining to that project will be displayed.

- The application must be based on the PFC QuickStart PBLs. This will allow easy startup and integration of PFC features.

- The application must incorporate a Tools menu item for illustrations and tests. This is our one departure from the real-world aspect of the program. The production version of the application does not contain the illustrative menu items.

Output requirements

- *Report on client list.* The application must produce a report detailing the clients that are in the database.

- *Report on client/project/task hierarchy.* The application must produce a report hierarchy of tasks within projects within clients.

- *Reports on activity.* The application must produce reports detailing time entries as follows:
  1. *Weekly for all clients.* This report will show the recorded activity for one or more consultants for all clients for a selected one-week period.
  2. *Weekly for single client.* This report will show the recorded activity for one or more consultants for a single client.
  3. *Monthly for all clients.* This report will show the recorded activity for one or more consultants for all clients for a selected one-month period.
  4. *Billing report for specified time period for single client.* This report will

show the billable activity for a single client, sorted by task within project, for a given time period.

5. *Billing report for specified time period for all clients.* This report will show the billable activity for all clients, sorted by task within project, for a given time period.

Application workflow

We used the cooperative business modeling (CBM) methodology to direct the design of the application. One of the steps in the CBM methodology is the construction of an application workflow diagram. Figure 18.1 shows the application workflow diagram for the GSI TimeMaster application.

Database

Data model.   We used S-Designor to create the data model for the application. Figure 18.2 shows the conceptual data model.

SQL Anywhere.   The Sybase SQL Anywhere product was chosen as the target database environment. This is the database that is shipped with each copy of PowerBuilder 5.0. Listing 18.1 shows the final database schema DDL for SQL Anywhere.

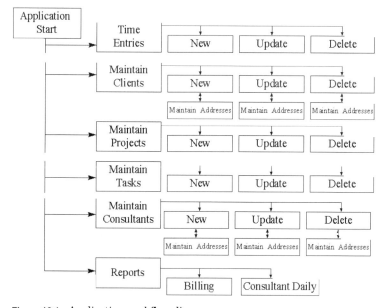

Figure 18.1 Application workflow diagram.

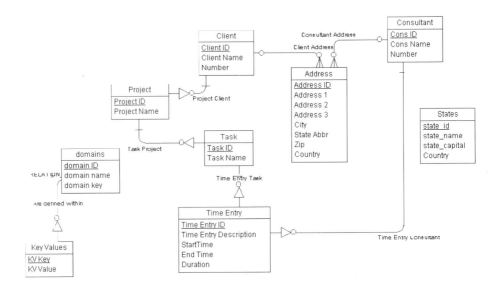

Figure 18.2   Conceptual data model.

Techniques illustrated

Application setup.   The application object (gsi_time) must contain a declaration of the gnv_app global variable. This is the only global variable used in the PFC, and it is a pointer to the application manager object.

```
n_cst_appmanager          gnv_app
```

The application object has six events. Each of these events must be redirected to the application manager service. The QuickStart PBLs contain an application object that already has these events redirected. For each event, it is a simple matter to call the appropriate service on the application manager.

In the application open event, it is necessary to create the application manager object before redirecting the event to the application manager's pfc_open event:

```
gnv_app = create n_cst_appmanager
gnv_app.event pfc_open (commandline)
```

The connectionbegin event is used for Distributed PowerBuilder and also must create the application manager:

LISTING 18.1   Final Database Schema DDL for SQL Anywhere

```
%% ==========================================================
%%     Database name:    TIME_LOG_TABLES
%%     DBMS name:        Sybase SQL Anywhere
%%     Created on:       3/8/97 2:01 AM
%% ==========================================================

if exists(select 1 from sys.sysindex where index_name = 'KEY_VALUES_PK') then
    drop index KEY_VALUES_PK
end if;

if exists(select 1 from sys.sysindex where index_name = 'RELATION_253_FK') then
    drop index RELATION_253_FK
end if;

if exists(select 1 from sys.systable where table_name = 'KEY_VALUES' and table_type = 'BASE') then
    drop table KEY_VALUES
end if;

if exists(select 1 from sys.sysindex where index_name = 'ADDRESS_PK') then
    drop index ADDRESS_PK
end if;

if exists(select 1 from sys.sysindex where index_name = 'CLIENT_ADDRESS_FK') then
    drop index CLIENT_ADDRESS_FK
end if;

if exists(select 1 from sys.sysindex where index_name = 'CONSULTANT_ADDRESS_FK') then
    drop index CONSULTANT_ADDRESS_FK
end if;

if exists(select 1 from sys.systable where table_name = 'ADDRESS' and table_type = 'BASE') then
    drop table ADDRESS
end if;

if exists(select 1 from sys.sysindex where index_name = 'TIME_ENTRY_PK') then
    drop index TIME_ENTRY_PK
end if;

if exists(select 1 from sys.sysindex where index_name = 'TIME_ENTRY_TASK_FK') then
    drop index TIME_ENTRY_TASK_FK
end if;

if exists(select 1 from sys.sysindex where index_name = 'TIME_ENTRY_CONSULTANT_FK') then
    drop index TIME_ENTRY_CONSULTANT_FK
end if;

if exists(select 1 from sys.systable where table_name = 'TIME_ENTRY' and table_type = 'BASE') then
    drop table TIME_ENTRY
end if;
```

LISTING 18.1   Final Database Schema DDL for SQL Anywhere (*Continued*)

```
if exists(select 1 from sys.sysindex where index_name = 'TASK_PK') then
    drop index TASK_PK
end if;

if exists(select 1 from sys.sysindex where index_name = 'TASK_PROJECT_FK') then
    drop index TASK_PROJECT_FK
end if;

if exists(select 1 from sys.systable where table_name = 'TASK' and table_type = 'BASE') then
    drop table TASK
end if;

if exists(select 1 from sys.sysindex where index_name = 'PROJECT_PK') then
    drop index PROJECT_PK
end if;

if exists(select 1 from sys.sysindex where index_name = 'PROJECT_CLIENT_FK') then
    drop index PROJECT_CLIENT_FK
end if;

if exists(select 1 from sys.systable where table_name = 'PROJECT' and table_type = 'BASE') then
    drop table PROJECT
end if;

if exists(select 1 from sys.sysindex where index_name = 'DOMAINS_PK') then
    drop index DOMAINS_PK
end if;

if exists(select 1 from sys.systable where table_name = 'DOMAINS' and table_type = 'BASE') then
    drop table DOMAINS
end if;

if exists(select 1 from sys.sysindex where index_name = 'CONSULTANT_PK') then
    drop index CONSULTANT_PK
end if;

if exists(select 1 from sys.systable where table_name = 'CONSULTANT' and table_type = 'BASE') then
    drop table CONSULTANT
end if;

if exists(select 1 from sys.sysindex where index_name = 'CLIENT_PK') then
    drop index CLIENT_PK
end if;

if exists(select 1 from sys.systable where table_name = 'CLIENT' and table_type = 'BASE') then
    drop table CLIENT
end if;

if exists(select 1 from sys.sysindex where index_name = 'STATES_PK') then
    drop index STATES_PK
end if;
```

LISTING 18.1   Final Database Schema DDL for SQL Anywhere (*Continued*)

```
if exists(select 1 from sys.systable where table_name = 'STATES' and table_type = 'BASE') then
    drop table STATES
end if;

%% ===========================================================
%% Table: STATES
%% ===========================================================

create table STATES
(
    STATE_ID               char(3)                                      not null,
    STATE_NAME             char(24)                                     ,
    STATE_CAPITAL          char(24)                                     ,
    COUNTRY                char(20)                                     ,
    primary key (STATE_ID)
);

%% ===========================================================
%% Table: CLIENT
%% ===========================================================

create table CLIENT
(
    CLIENT_ID              char(6)                                      not null,
    CLIENT_NAME            char(30)                                     ,
    NUMBER                 char(20)                                     ,
    primary key (CLIENT_ID)
);

%% ===========================================================
%% Table: CONSULTANT
%% ===========================================================

create table CONSULTANT
(
    CONS_ID                char(6)                                      not null,
    CONS_NAME              char(30)                                     ,
    NUMBER                 char(20)                                     ,
    primary key (CONS_ID)
);

%% ===========================================================
%% Table: DOMAINS
%% ===========================================================

create table DOMAINS
(
    DOMAIN_ID              integer                                      not null,
    DOMAIN_NAME            char(12)                                     ,
    DOMAIN_KEY             integer                                      ,
    primary key (DOMAIN_ID)
);
```

LISTING 18.1   Final Database Schema DDL for SQL Anywhere (*Continued*)

```
%% ==================================================================
%% Table: PROJECT
%% ==================================================================
create table PROJECT
(
    CLIENT_ID                   char(6)                                 not null,
    PROJECT_ID                  char(5)                                 not null,
    PROJECT_NAME                char(30)                                ,
    primary key (CLIENT_ID, PROJECT_ID)
);

%% ==================================================================
%% Table: TASK
%% ==================================================================

create table TASK
(
    CLIENT_ID                   char(6)                                 not null,
    PROJECT_ID                  char(5)                                 not null,
    TASK_ID                     char(5)                                 not null,
    TASK_NAME                   char(30)                                not null,
    primary key (CLIENT_ID, PROJECT_ID, TASK_ID)
);

%% ==================================================================
%% Table: TIME_ENTRY
%% ==================================================================

create table TIME_ENTRY
(
    CONS_ID                     char(6)                                 not null,
    CLIENT_ID                   char(6)                                 not null,
    PROJECT_ID                  char(5)                                 not null,
    TASK_ID                     char(5)                                 not null,
    TIME_ENTRY_ID               integer                                 not null,
    TIME_ENTRY_DESCRIPTION      char(60)                                ,
    STARTTIME                   timestamp                               ,
    END_TIME                    timestamp                               ,
    DURATION                    numeric(6,2)                            ,
    primary key (CONS_ID, CLIENT_ID, PROJECT_ID, TASK_ID, TIME_ENTRY_ID)
);

%% ==================================================================
%% Table: ADDRESS
%% ==================================================================

create table ADDRESS
(
    ADDRESS_ID                  integer not null
        default autoincrement,
    CONSULT_CLIENT_ID           char(6)                                 ,
    CLIENT_ID                   char(6)
```

LISTING 18.1   Final Database Schema DDL for SQL Anywhere (*Continued*)

```
        default '',
    CONS_ID                    char(6)
        default '',
    ADDRESS_1                  char(30)                                    ,
    ADDRESS_2                  char(30)                                    ,
    ADDRESS_3                  char(30)                                    ,
    CITY                       char(30)                                    ,
    STATE_ABBR                 char(5)                                     ,
    ZIP                        char(15)                                    ,
    COUNTRY                    char(20)                                    ,
    primary key (ADDRESS_ID)
);


%% ============================================================
%% Table: KEY_VALUES
%% ============================================================

create table KEY_VALUES
(
    DOMAIN_ID                  integer                          not null,
    KV_KEY                     integer                          not null,
    KV_VALUE                   char(30)                                   ,
    primary key (DOMAIN_ID, KV_KEY)
);

alter table PROJECT
    add foreign key FK_PROJECT_PROJECT_C_CLIENT (CLIENT_ID)
        references CLIENT (CLIENT_ID) on update restrict on delete restrict;

alter table TASK
    add foreign key FK_TASK_TASK_PROJ_PROJECT (CLIENT_ID, PROJECT_ID)
        references PROJECT (CLIENT_ID, PROJECT_ID) on update restrict on delete restrict;

alter table TIME_ENTRY
    add foreign key FK_TIME_ENT_TIME_ENTR_TASK (CLIENT_ID, PROJECT_ID, TASK_ID)
        references TASK (CLIENT_ID, PROJECT_ID, TASK_ID) on update restrict on delete restrict;

alter table TIME_ENTRY
    add foreign key FK_TIME_ENT_TIME_ENTR_CONSULTA (CONS_ID)
        references CONSULTANT (CONS_ID) on update restrict on delete restrict;

alter table KEY_VALUES
    add foreign key FK_KEY_VALU_RELATION__DOMAINS (DOMAIN_ID)
        references DOMAINS (DOMAIN_ID) on update restrict on delete restrict;
```

```
gnv_app = create n_cst_appmanager
return gnv_app.event pfc_connectionbegin (userid, password, connectstring)
```

The application close event must destroy the application manager as well as redirecting the event:

```
gnv_app.event pfc_close()
destroy gnv_app
```

Likewise, the connectionend event must also destroy the application manager:

```
gnv_app.event pfc_connectionend ()
destroy gnv_app
```

The other events simply invoke the associated event on the application manager. For the idle event:

```
gnv_app.event pfc_idle()
```

For the systemerror event:

```
gnv_app.event pfc_systemerror()
```

You do not need to add any of this code if you are using the QuickStart PBLs. However, if you are using a blank application, you will need to redirect each event as shown.

Application manager setup.   The application manager (n_cst_appmanager) controls the properties and behavior of the application. This is the code from the application manager's constructor event:

```
// Name of the application
iapp_object.DisplayName = "GSI TimeMaster"

// MicroHelp functionality
of_SetMicroHelp (TRUE)

// The filename of the application INI file
of_SetAppINIFile ("app.ini")

// The filename of the user INI file
of_SetUserINIFile ("TimeMst2.ini")

// Application registry key
of_SetAppKey
  ("HKEY_LOCAL_MACHINE\Software\GatewaySystems\TimeMast2")

// User registry key
of_SetUserKey ("HKEY_CURRENT_USER\Software\GatewaySystems\TimeMast2")

// The filename of the application's on-line help file
of_SetHelpFile ("gsi_time.hlp")

// The application version
of_SetVersion ("Version 1.0")
```

```
// The application logo (bitmap filename)
of_SetLogo ("timproc2.bmp")

// Application copyright message
of_SetCopyright ("Copyright © 1997 Gateway Systems, Inc")

// Wrapper property for application display name
is_title = iapp_object.DisplayName
```

As you can see, the constructor event is used to set up variables that control the appearance and behavior of the application. This code is present in the QuickStart application manager, but you need to customize it for each application.

The pfc_open event contains code to initialize SQLCA from the declared initialization file. This event also opens the frame window. This code is standard in the QuickStart application manager. The code that controls the debug flag has been added to customize the open event for this application. We added a function plus two checkboxes on the logon window.

```
n_cst_conversion lnv_conversion
boolean lb_debug, lb_SQLSpy
string ls_DebugString, ls_SQLSpy

// SQLCA can be initialized by platform
// The code is commented, as it is only an example

//IF of_IsRegistryAvailable() THEN
//        sqlca.of_Init (of_GetUserKey()+"\Profile Powersoft Demo DB V5")
//ELSE
        IF sqlca.of_Init (is_userinifile, "Gateway Systems Time Master") = −1 THEN
                MessageBox (is_title, "Initialization failed from file "+is_userinifile)
                halt
        END IF
//END IF

// Get debug flag
ls_debugstring = ProfileString(gnv_app.of_GetUserINIFile(),"Debug","Debug",
  "FALSE")
lb_debug = lnv_conversion.of_Boolean(ls_debugstring)
IF lb_debug THEN
        //Enable debug service
        this.of_SetDebug(TRUE)
        // Get debug flag
        ls_SQLSpy =
          ProfileString(gnv_app.of_GetUserINIFile(),"Debug","SQLSpy", "TRUE")
        lb_SQLSpy = lnv_conversion.of_Boolean(ls_SQLSpy)
        IF lb_SQLSpy THEN
                //Enable SQLSpy Service
                this.inv_debug.of_SetSQLSpy(TRUE)
```

```
                              //Specify a log file
                              this.inv_debug.inv_SQLSpy.of_SetLogFile("c:\logs\sql_spy.log")
               END IF
END IF
Open (w_timelogframe)
```

The pfc_logon event contains code to connect to the database. The connection information was obtained in the initialization step in the pfc_open event.

```
// Perform logon
sqlca.of_SetUser (as_userid, as_password)

IF sqlca.of_Connect() >= 0 THEN
        return 1
ELSE
        MessageBox (is_title, "Connect failed")
        return −1
END IF
```

Finally, the pfc_close event disconnects from the database:

```
// Disconnect from the database
sqlca.of_DisConnect()
```

Treeview object. The main window of GSI TimeMaster uses a PFC treeview control to display the client–project–task hierarchy. The w_clienttree window (in ATGSTART.PBL) contains code in its open event to populate the treeview. Each level of the treeview takes its data from a DataStore. The DataStore for each successively higher level can take retrieval arguments, and the retrieval arguments can be based on the preceding level:

```
Long                                            ll_Root
TreeViewItem        ltvi_Root

this.title = this.title+' ('+this.ClassName()+')'
is_consultant_id = "MF3"

tv_1.AddPicture("custom041!")
tv_1.AddPicture("custom048!")
tv_1.AddPicture("custom067!")
tv_1.AddPicture("custom075!")
tv_1.AddPicture("custom085!")
tv_1.AddPicture("library!")
tv_1.AddPicture("custom076!")
tv_1.AddPicture("custom050!")
// Register the data source for each level of the tree
// Parameters are: level, DataWindow object, transaction object, column to display
as the label,
// the retrieval arguments, and whether the DW object is to be used recursively.
```

```
// Optional parameters are: picture index, selected picture index, state picture
   index, and overlay picture index
tv_1.of_SetDatasource(2, "d_tlg_client", SQLCA, "client_name", "", False, 1, 8)
tv_1.of_SetDatasource(3, "d_tlg_project", SQLCA, "project_name",
   ":parent.1.client_id", False, 2, 2)
tv_1.of_SetDatasource(4, "d_tlg_task", SQLCA, "task_name", ":parent.1.project_id,
   :parent.1.client_id", False, 3, 3)
// Add the root item
ltvi_Root.Label = "GSI Clients"
ltvi_Root.PictureIndex = 6
ltvi_Root.SelectedPictureIndex = 6
ltvi_Root.Children = True
ll_Root = tv_1.InsertItemLast(0, ltvi_Root)
tv_1.Post Function ExpandItem(ll_Root)
dw_1.retrieve()
```

The PFC treeview object relieves us of much of the tedium of populating the PowerBuilder treeview object. By setting up the relationships between the DataStores with the of_SetDatasource function, the tree items are populated as necessary and the flags that show if lower levels exist are automatically maintained.

The of_RefreshItem function refreshes the specified item and the levels above it. The following code is from the window's gsi_refresh event:

Note: Events preceded with the identifier gsi_ were specifically created for the GSI TimeMaster example program.

```
Integer li_rc
long ll_row
datastore lds_datastore

IF ib_Changed THEN
        li_rc = MessageBox("Warning", "You have made changes to the data. " + &
                                "Do you wish to save them before you refresh the
Tree?", Question!, YesNoCancel!, 1)
        Choose Case li_rc
                Case 1
                        cb_update.Trigger Event Clicked()
                Case 3
                        Return
        End Choose
END IF

Integer  li_return
Long     ll_current
TreeViewItem            ltvi_item

ll_current = tv_1.FindItem (CurrentTreeItem!, 0)
li_return = tv_1.GetItem(ll_current, ltvi_item)
```

```
li_return = tv_1.of_GetDataRow(ll_current, lds_datastore, ll_row)
IF li_return = -1 THEN
        MessageBox("TreeView", "Find error looking for row")
ELSE
        li_return = tv_1.of_RefreshItem(ll_current, ll_row)
        IF li_return = -1 THEN
                MessageBox("TreeView", "Refresh failed")
        ELSE
                gnv_app.of_GetFrame().SetMicroHelp &
                ("Refresh succeeded for level " &
                +String(ltvi_item.level))
                tv_1.ExpandItem(ll_current)
                tv_1.SelectItem(ll_current)
                tv_1.SetFocus()
        END IF
END IF
```

Note the of_GetDataRow function in this script. This function returns the DataStore and row associated with the specified treeview item (ll_current). The row number is then passed to the of_RefreshItem function. The row number argument defaults to the current row and so is not needed in this case unless underlying key information has been changed. It is important to know the technique, though.

Finally, the gsi_update event on the window updates the treeview for levels 3 and above:

```
ib_Changed = False
tv_1.of_update(3)
```

Custom right mouse button menu. The GSI TimeMaster application needs a right mouse button menu to implement functionality on the treeview of clients, projects, and tasks. The PFC treeview user object, u_tv, does not support a right mouse button menu. Here are the steps taken to implement a RMB menu on a treeview object.

To add a RMB menu to an object, you will need to

- Create a RMB menu object. The easiest way to accomplish this is to inherit from the pfc_m_ object that best matches your requirements. This also gives you access to the of_SetParent() function on the ancestor.

- Code the script to create, setparent, and invoke the menu in the rbuttonup or rightclicked event in the object.

- Code the script in the RMB menu to call the appropriate event on the parent object.

- Add custom user events and scripts as necessary on the parent object to implement the desired behavior.

Create a RMB menu object. We inherited from m_edit to create the treeview RMB menu. See Chap. 5 for details on the menu.

Create the right mouse button script. Next we created a custom event, gsi_rmb-menu, on the treeview object. Then we added code to the rightclicked event to post the gsi_rmbmenu event:

    this.event Post gsi_rmbmenu()

We copied the code in the gsi_rmbmenu event from the pfc_u_dw user object. We deleted the code specific to DataWindow operations, and added code to enable the treeview menu items and dynamically alter the text of the New menu item:

```
///////////////////////////////////////////////////////////////
//
//        Event: gsi_rmbmenu
//
//        Description: Pop-up menu
//
///////////////////////////////////////////////////////////////
//
//        Revision History
//
//        Version
//        5.0 Initial version
//
///////////////////////////////////////////////////////////////

boolean  lb_frame
m_tvedit              lm_tv
window                        lw_parent
window                        lw frame
Long    ll_current, ll_return, ll_row
n_ds             lds_datastore
string ls_dataobject
string ls_newtext
// Determine if RMB pop-up menu should occur
IF NOT ib_rmbmenu
        return 1
END IF
// Determine parent window for PointerX, PointerY offset
this.of_GetParentWindow (lw_parent)
IF IsValid (lw_parent) THEN
        // Get the MDI frame window if available
        lw_frame = lw_parent
        do while IsValid (lw_frame)
                IF lw_frame.windowtype = mdi! or lw_frame.windowtype = mdi
```

```
                    help! THEN
                            lb_frame = true
                            exit
                    ELSE
                            lw_frame = lw_frame.ParentWindow()
                    END IF
        loop
        IF lb_frame THEN
                    lw_parent = lw_frame
        END IF
ELSE
//        return 1
END IF

// Create pop-up menu
lm_tv = create m_tvedit
lm_tv.of_SetParent (this)
// Set the New item text according to the level selected
ll_current = this.FindItem(CurrentTreeItem!, 0)
ll_return = this.of_GetDataRow(ll_current, &
        lds_datastore, ll_row)
IF ll_return = -1 THEN
        /* New Client */
        ls_newtext = is_newclient
ELSE
        ls_dataobject = lds_datastore.dataobject
        ls_newtext = ""
        choose case ls_dataobject
                CASE "d_tlg_client"
                        /* New Project */
                        ls_newtext = is_newproject
                CASE "d_tlg_project"
                        /* New Task */
                        ls_newtext = is_newtask
                CASE "d_tlg_task"
                        /* New Time Entry */
                        ls_newtext = is_newtimeentry
                CASE ELSE
        END CHOOSE
END IF

is_newtext = ls_newtext
// Allow for any other changes to the pop-up menu before it opens
this.event pfc_prermbmenu (lm_dw)
lm_tv.m_edititem.m_new.enabled = TRUE
lm_tv.m_edititem.m_new.text = is_newtext

// Pop-up menu
lm_tv.m_edititem.PopMenu (lw_parent.PointerX() + 5, lw_parent.PointerY() + 10)
destroy lm_tv
//return 1
```

The strings used for the New menu item text are declared and initialized as instance variables. This centralizes their definition and eases maintenance.

Create RMB menu script to call events on the parent object.   Each new menu item must have code to call the corresponding event on the parent treeview object. This is the script for the clicked event of the Delete menu item:

```
idrg_parent.dynamic event gsi_delete()
```

This code is replicated, except for the name of the event, for the New item.

Create scripts on the parent object to implement the desired behavior.   This is the script for the treeview's gsi_new event:

```
// Execute appropriate event depending on is_newtext

CHOOSE CASE is_newtext
        CASE is_newclient
                w_timelogframe.event gsi_clientmaint()
        CASE is_newproject
                w_timelogframe.event gsi_projectmaint()
        CASE is_newtask
                w_timelogframe.event gsi_taskmaint()
        CASE is_newtimeentry
                /* New Time Entry */
                dw_1.event gsi_start()
END CHOOSE
```

That's all there is to it. The treeview object now has context-aware right mouse button support, courtesy of the PFC.

Conversion service.   The conversion service is used to convert the PowerBuilder enumerated types to their string equivalents. We used the conversion service to retain the toolbar alignment in the application INI file. This code is from the pfc_close event of the frame window (w_timelogframe):

```
n_cst_conversion lnv_conversion

// Save the toolbar alignment value
IF not isnull(lnv_conversion) THEN
        IF IsValid(lnv_conversion) THEN
        SetProfileString(gnv_app.of_GetUserINIFile(),"Options","Toolbar", &
                lnv_conversion.of_String(This.toolbarAlignment))
        ELSE
                MessageBox("Error in Object", "lnv_conversion not valid")
        END IF
ELSE
        MessageBox("Error in Object","lnv_conversion is null")
END IF
```

The n_cst_conversion object is automatically instantiated when it is declared (n_cst_conversion lnv_conversion). When it goes out of scope at the end of the script, it is automatically destroyed.

DataWindow debugger.   The DataWindow debugger provides a simple interface that allows you to view and directly modify the properties of a DataWindow while the program is running. The steps that you take to use the DataWindow debugger are:

- Populate a structure with a pointer to the DataWindow and a transaction object.
- Open the w_dwdebugger window, passing the structure as a parameter.

To make the DataWindow debugger easier to use, we simply added the code that starts the w_dwdebugger window to the u_dw object:

Step 1: Add a user event, gsi_dwdebug, to u_dw.

Step 2: Add code to populate the debugger structure and open w_dwdebugger. In the user object painter, add the following code to the gsi_dwdebug event:

```
// Declare structure for DataWindow debugger information
s_dwdebugger lstr_parm
// Populate the structure with a DataWindow pointer and a transaction object
lstr_parm.dw_obj = This
lstr_parm.tr_obj = SQLCA
OpenWithParm(w_dwdebugger, lstr_parm)
```

This code opens the DataWindow debugger whenever the event is executed.

Debug services.   The debug services are used in the client and consultant maintenance windows to indicate that a menu message did not find a recipient. The following code is from the overridden of_SendMessage function in the m_maint object:

```
// Debug message if message could not be received
IF li_rc = −1 and IsValid (gnv_app.inv_debug) THEN
        MessageBox (gnv_app.inv_debug.ics_pfc, "Message "+as_message+&
                                    " was not received.")
END IF
```

The debug services are instantiated when the dw_debug checkbox on the logon window is activated.

File services.   We created a window, w_filesrv_test, to demonstrate the use of the of_DirList function from the PFC file services. This is the code from the DirList command button:

```
String ls_currdir
Integer li_cnt, li_entries
String ls_import
n_cst_dirattrib lnv_dirlist[ ]
SetPointer(HourGlass!)
ls_currdir = "c:\Windows\system\*.dll"
li_entries = &
  inv_filesrv.of_DirList &
  (ls_currdir, 0, lnv_dirlist)
IF li_Entries <0 THEN
        MessageBox("File Services", &
        "Directory not found")
        Return
ELSE IF li_Entries = 0 THEN
        MessageBox("File Services", "No files found")
        Return
END IF

for li_cnt = 1 to li_entries
  dw_1.ImportString(lnv_dirlist[li_cnt].is_filename)
next
```

As you can see, the operation of the of_DirList function is very simple. You pass it a directory specification, an attribute byte, and a reference to an array of n_cst_dirattrib objects. The of_DirList function populates the array with information for each file matching the passed directory mask and attribute byte. Once the array is returned, we take the filenames out and import them into the DataWindow.

Status bar.   The PFC status bar services are used in the frame window of GSI TimeMaster. The status bar is set up to display the time, free memory, and user id. This code is from the pfc_preopen event of w_frame:

```
// Set status bar
of_SetStatusBar(TRUE)
inv_statusbar.of_Register('userid', 'text', "", 380)
inv_statusbar.of_SetMem(TRUE)
inv_statusbar.of_SetTimer(TRUE)
```

And in the pfc_postopen event of w_frame:

```
// Change the status bar to the userid
inv_statusbar.of_Modify('userid', gnv_app.of_GetUserID() )
```

Master/detail (linkage services).   The client and consultant maintenance windows demonstrate the use of the linkage services. The following is from the w_client_maint open event:

```
dw_master.SetFocus()
//idw_consultant = tab_1.tabpage_consultant.dw_consultant

// Set dw to link to
dw_master.of_SetLinkage(TRUE)
dw_1.of_SetLinkage(TRUE)
//
//// Set dw to link to
dw_1.inv_linkage.of_LinkTo(dw_master)
//
//// Set columns that are linked
dw_1.inv_linkage.of_SetArguments("client_id","consult_client_id")
//// Indicate retrieve option
dw_1.inv_linkage.of_SetUseColLinks(2)
//
dw_master.inv_linkage.of_SetTransObject(SQLCA)
//
// Retrieve data
IF dw_master.inv_linkage.of_Retrieve( ) = −1 THEN
        MessageBox("Error","Retrieve error - master")
ELSE
        dw_master.SetFocus( )
END IF

IF dw_1.rowcount() = 0 THEN
        dw_1.Event pfc_addrow()
END IF
```

This code links the address DataWindow to the client DataWindow. The same code, with the exception that it links by consultant ID instead of client ID, is used in w_cons_maint.

To ensure that a client ID has been entered, the following code is placed in the pfc_validation event of w_client_maint dw_1:

```
LONG L_RETURN
String ls_id

// Call the PFC validation event and preserve the return code
l_return = super::Event pfc_validation()

// IF there was an error in the PFC validation return
IF l_return <0 THEN
        return l_return
END IF

ls_id = dw_master.inv_linkage.of_GetItem(dw_master.getrow(), "client_id")
inv_linkage.of_SetItem(getrow(), "consult_client_id", ls_id)

RETURN 1
```

Drop-down search.   The drop-down search service is demonstrated in the client and consultant maintenance windows. The following code is from the constructor event for dw_1 on w_cons_maint:

```
// Enable drop-down search service
this.of_SetDropDownSearch ( TRUE )
```

The drop-down search service must be notified when editchanged and itemfocuschanged events occur. This code is from the editchanged event for u_dw:

```
// Send event notification to drop-down search service if available
IF IsValid (inv_dropdownsearch) THEN
         inv_dropdownsearch.event pfc_editchanged (row, dwo, data)
END IF
```

And this is from the itemfocuschanged event for u_dw:

```
// Send event notification to drop-down search service if available
IF IsValid (inv_dropdownsearch) THEN
         inv_dropdownsearch.event pfc_itemfocuschanged (row, dwo)
END IF
```

Resize services.   The resize services are used in the basic sheet ancestor, w_timelogsheet. You can see the resize service in action in the file services demonstration window. The open event of w_timelogsheet contains the following code:

```
// Enable the resize service
of_SetResize (TRUE)

// Specify how the window will be resized
inv_resize.of_Register (dw_1, "ScaletoRight&Bottom")
inv_resize.of_Register (cb_1, "FixedtoRight")
inv_resize.of_Register (cb_2, "FixedtoRight")

dw_1.SetFocus()
```

Documentation—the user's guide

This section contains an abbreviated user's guide for the GSI TimeMaster application. The complete user's guide can be found on the accompanying CD.

Installing the application.   The application is provided on the included CD. It is provided in executable form as well as development source code PBLs. However, we do not provide the PFC PBLs. You will need to copy the PFC PBLs from your PowerBuilder 5.0 installation.

To set up the application executable, do the following:

1. Create a directory for the PFC sample application on your hard disk.

2. Copy all files from the directory \PFCSAMP\BIN32 or \PFCSAMP\BIN16 on the CD to the newly created directory. The files include the application .EXE file, the required .PBD files, and the sample database.

3. Create an ODBC data source, "PFC Sample," that points to the PFC_SAMP.DB file in the newly created directory.

4. Create an application shortcut (Windows 32-bit) or program manager icon (Windows 16-bit) for the <app name here> executable file. Use the application directory as the working directory.

To set up the application development environment, do the following:

1. Create a directory for the PFC sample application development on your hard disk.

2. Copy all files from the directory \PFCSAMP\DEV on the CD to the newly created directory. The files include the application .PBL files and resources.

3. Copy the PFC .PBL files and .DLL files from the PowerBuilder PFC directory to the newly created directory. Do not copy the PFE PBL files.

4. From the PowerBuilder Application or Library painter, open the application GSI_TIME in ATG_APP.PBL.

5. Select PROPERTIES for the application and choose the Libraries tab. Add all of the ATG PBLs and PFC PBLs to the library search path.

6. Close and save the application.

7. Rebuild the application before running.

Preparing the database. You need an ODBC data source called PFC Sample. The prepopulated PFC_Samp.db database is provided in this package. You can use this database as your starting point, or you can use the database schema DDL shown in Listing 18.1.

How do I...

Get started? Run the program. The login ID is dba, and the password is sql. Select File | Open | Time Entries. The treeview on the left displays the Client–Project–Task hierarchy. The DataWindow on the right displays the time entries, filtered to whatever level is selected in the treeview.

Add a time entry? Expand the entries in the treeview to the desired client, project, and task. Left-click to select the task. Move the mouse to the time entry DataWindow, press the right mouse button, and choose Start. A new time entry record will be created, with the current time filled in for the start time. Add a description of the work you are doing. Choose File | Save or click the diskette toolbar button to save your changes. When you're done working on the task, right-click on the same time entry and choose Stop. Again the current time will be filled in, this time for the end time. Save again. You can change either of the times to anything you choose. However, be sure to enter a complete datetime.

Maintain consultants? Select File | Open | Consultant Maintenance to open the consultant maintenance window. This is a master-detail window with the consultant information in the top (master) DataWindow and the consultant's address in the bottom (detail) DataWindow. You can edit any field, delete a consultant record, or insert a new consultant record. (Do not change the ID for an existing consultant.) Choose File | Save or click the diskette toolbar button to save your changes. You can edit, delete, or insert an address record for the consultant that is shown in the master DataWindow. Again, choose File | Save or click the diskette toolbar button to save your changes.

Maintain clients? Select File | Open | Client Maintenance. This is a master-detail window with the client information in the top (master) DataWindow and the client's address in the bottom (detail) DataWindow. You can edit any field, delete a client record, or insert a new client record. Choose File | Save or click the diskette toolbar button to save your changes. You can edit, delete, or insert an address record for the client that is shown in the master DataWindow. Again, choose File | Save or click the diskette toolbar button to save your changes.

Do not change the ID of an existing client.

Maintain projects? Select a client in the treeview. Right-click and choose New Project. This will open a project maintenance window that allows insert, update, and deletion of projects. Do not change the ID of an existing project.

Maintain tasks? Select a project in the treeview. Right-click and choose New Task. This will open a Task maintenance window that allows insert, update, and deletion of tasks. Do not change the ID of an existing Task.

Produce a billing report? Select Reports | Billing Report. Choose the desired period. When you choose the period, keep in mind that the start date must be before the end date.

Summary/Conclusions

The GSI TimeMaster application is a real-world example of how to use the PFC to serve your business needs. Many PFC services and techniques are illustrated in the application's objects.

As GSI TimeMaster matures, Gateway Systems will be adding more PFC features to the application and extending its scope. Some of the enhancements we have planned include full implementation of the error services and report services. We encourage you to experiment and add your own features to this application.

19

Distributed PowerBuilder and the PFC

Introduction of the Topic

Distributed PowerBuilder is a new technology that only recently became available to PB developers with the release of PowerBuilder 5. It should be noted that Powersoft's distributed object technology will need to become more advanced to accommodate all the demands of industrial-strength applications. You can expect Powersoft to continue to improve this technology over time so that it will be able to meet the needs of the most demanding of applications. In the meantime, developers should adopt this technology carefully in measured steps to ensure the best results. As with any new technology, many developers will need to see practical applications for the technology before it is commonly adopted. Throughout this chapter you will see some practical uses for the technology as well as some guidelines for implementation.

Distributed objects require the developer to use a more definitive architecture for his or her applications. Developers will be more successful using distributed PowerBuilder when their applications utilize more object-oriented techniques, such as application partitioning and encapsulation. You will need to be comfortable with using user objects to hold significant portions of your application's logic. If you are new to using application-partitioning techniques, you will find your libraries getting filled with more and more user objects and fewer objects such as windows and menus.

The decision to use Distributed PowerBuilder will be made by the software designer. End users are not apt to have any idea of the why or wherefore of its

---

Contributed by Kent Marsh, Millenium Inc.

implementation. The designer should decide to implement Distributed PowerBuilder only when it achieves the technical requirements of an application. Distributed objects provide significant feature capabilities. However, your applications will be more complex and have more system dependencies to coordinate. Keep in mind that each Distributed PowerBuilder application adds additional possible points of failure. Before embarking on the implementation of Distributed PowerBuilder, you should seriously consider the costs and benefits of that decision.

Chapter Objectives

The best way to understand a new technology is to start using it. This chapter will provide you with some introductory information that we hope will encourage you to begin experimenting with Distributed PowerBuilder—that is, if you are not already using it. You should understand the basics of setting up a Distributed PowerBuilder application before beginning any serious application effort. We will discuss some of the architectural design concepts involved.

Unfortunately, the initial PB 5 version of PFC does not provide any significant functionality for distributed computing. What functionality there is will be discussed, as well as ways to extend those classes. You will find some actual coding examples using the PFC with distributed applications. It is expected that future releases of the PFC will provide some functional features that address the needs of DPB (Distributed PowerBuilder).

This chapter will discuss the following:

- What is Distributed PowerBuilder?
- What is in the current version of the PFC that supports DPB?
- How to extend the PFC to support DPB
- An example of using DPB with the PFC
- The future of PFC and DPB

What Is Distributed PowerBuilder?

Fundamentally, Distributed PowerBuilder gives you the ability to have more than one PowerBuilder application working together to run your application. Distributed objects allow separate PowerBuilder applications to communicate over a network connection and share the workload. Distributed applications are totally separate executables that can run locally or anywhere on your network. Distributed objects can communicate through a variety of network protocols. So, exactly where a process resides and with whom it communicates are limited only by your network architecture and your creative genius!

The concept of distributed objects should not be at all new to PowerBuilder developers. In fact, you've been doing distributed processing already! Think about how talking to a client-server database works. Your PowerBuilder appli-

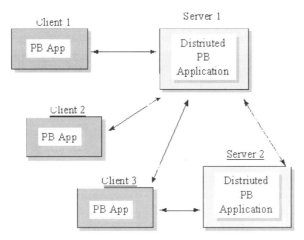

Figure 19.1   A typical distributed application architecture.

cation and the database engine are two separate applications. You communicate
to the database engine, making requests and getting responses, through a standardized API. The database engine could be on any server in your network or
locally on your client machine. Your application acts as a client, and the DBMS
is a server. In the same way, PowerBuilder distributed objects allow you to create additional applications that can act as servers to your client applications!

A common configuration of distributed objects is to have an application on a
centralized server that performs services for a number of client applications
running on various user PCs. A database engine is usually running on a server
and can have numerous PC client applications making calls for its services.
Likewise, using DPB (Distributed PowerBuilder), you can build a PowerBuilder
application to run on a centralized server that is accessed through network protocols by multiple PowerBuilder applications running on client PCs.

A PowerBuilder distributed application is not limited to being either a server or a client. An application can function as both a client and a server! Now,
this opens up some really interesting possibilities. A client application can call
a server application, which in turn calls another server application, and so
forth. You can even have a client call a server, which then makes calls to the
client. This architecture offers a great deal of freedom. Figure 19.1 depicts a
typical distributed application architecture.

Connecting a client application

The steps used by PowerBuilder applications to communicate with one another
is analogous to the way PowerBuilder applications communicate with a remote
database. PowerBuilder applications use the *transaction* object to communicate
with databases. This process of communicating, familiar to any PB developer,
first requires that a valid, instantiated transaction object is used (typically
SQLCA). Then, several transaction object attributes need to be initialized, such

as the DBMS, server ID, user ID, and password. Next you start the communication by issuing the CONNECT command. Additional transaction object attributes provide feedback on the success of messages—for example, SqlErrText, SqlDbCode, SqlCode, and SqlNRows. Distributed PowerBuilder objects communicate with one another in much the same way.

When a client application wants to communicate with a distributed server application, you will need to use a *connect* object. Just as with a transaction object, you first need to properly declare and instantiate a connect object. (References to your connect object must always use a valid object reference variable, so consider the scope of your variable declaration as per its use.) Some of the connect object properties are used to specify how the connection will be established. The properties used will vary depending upon the communication driver used. Finally, use the ConnectToServer() function to establish a connection with a distributed server application.

1. Declare the connect object.

2. Instantiate the connect object.

3. Initialize connection attributes.

4. Connect using the function ConnectToServer().

The code example shown in Fig. 19.2 follows the four steps required for establishing a connection with a distributed PowerBuilder application.

When the client application no longer needs to communicate with the server, you should issue a disconnect command. The disconnect process will free memory space on both the server and the client and allow the server to serve other clients more efficiently. The disconnect process is performed by simply issuing

```
// 1. Declare
long      l_ErrNo
connection i_connect1

// 2. Instantiate
i_connect1 = create connection

// 3. Initialize connection attributes
i_connect1.application = "server_app"
i_connect1.driver      = "WinSock"
i_connect1.location    = "server01"

// 4. Connect
l_ErrNo = i_connect1.ConnectToServer( )
IF l_ErrNo <> 0 THEN
        // Process Error...
    END IF
```

Figure 19.2   Code sample for connecting to a DPB server.

```
i_connect1.DisconnectServer()
DESTROY i_connect1
```

Figure 19.3 DPB application disconnect.

the DisconnectServer() function. As a matter of good housekeeping, you should also destroy the connection object if there is no further use for it.

The disconnection process is shown in the code example in Fig. 19.3.

Starting a server application

A client application cannot communicate with a server application unless the server application is running and listening. How and when you start up a server application will depend upon your production environment and the needs of your application. Typically, a server application that is used by multiple client applications will be managed by some kind of a system administrator or IS operations person. Applications can also be created to automatically start up servers without the need for human intervention. Regardless of your strategy for starting servers, each server application will need to perform the following actions before being able to service clients:

1. Declare

2. Instantiate

3. Initialize transport attributes

4. Listen

In Fig. 19.4, the server application uses the mytransport transport object to begin listening for client connections.

```
// 1. Declare
transport i_transport

// 2. Instantiate
i_transport = create transport

// 3. Initialize transport attributes
i_transport.application = "server_app"
i_transport.driver = "WinSock"

// 4. Listen
i_transport.Listen( )
```

Figure 19.4 The server "listens" for client requests after executing this code.

```
// Stop listening for client connections
i_transport.StopListening()
```

Figure 19.5 Tell the server to stop listening to client requests.

Note: The application name and driver used by the client and the server must match in order for a connection to succeed. Avoid confusion and conflict by assigning each server application a unique name and location combination.

Client applications cannot connect to a server unless it is listening. Once a server application has successfully created a transport object and started listening, then client applications will be able to connect using the same driver as the transport object. A server can instantiate multiple transport objects and thus can listen to multiple protocols simultaneously!

Use the StopListening() function to instruct the server to stop listening for client connections. When the StopListening function is called, no additional client applications will be able to connect. Clients that were connected when the StopListening function was called will no longer be able to communicate to the server. The code in Fig. 19.5 shows a call to the function.

Note: Clients use the *connect* object to communicate to a server. Servers use the *transport* object to listen to clients. A server can connect to itself.

In order for a connection between a client and a server to be successful, you need to have the following conditions set:

Server

1. Server application running

2. Transport object instantiated

3. Application name and driver declared

4. Transport object listening—Listen()

Client

1. Client application running

2. Connect object instantiated

3. A matching server application name and driver declared

4. ConnectToServer() function called

Connectionbegin event

When a client calls the ConnectToServer function, the server application object is notified of the attempt through the *connectionbegin* event. You can use the *connectionbegin* event to control which clients are allowed to connect to a server and to control their access rights. There is also a corresponding call to the application object's connectionend event when a connection ends.

Server applications built using the PFC will use the global variable gnv_app to reference the application object service. By design, all PFC applications must use gnv_app as an application object service. Each of the application object events will trigger a corresponding event in gnv_app. Because connectionbegin and connectionend are both standard application object events, you will find that the gnv_app object also has a corresponding PFC event, *pfc_connectionbegin*.

```
// Event: Connectionbegin
RETURN gnv_app.Event pfc_connectionbegin(userid, password, connectstring)
```

The server can use the event arguments *userid* and *password* to determine the user's access rights. There is also a *connectstring* argument, which is an undefined string for you to use in any way you desire. Powersoft suggests using connectstring as a way to pass application-specific information such as database connection parameters from a client to a server. The event returns the enumerated data type connectprivilege.

If you are a PFC user, you know that you can specify the class declaration used by the global gnv_app as long as it is a descendant of n_cst_appmanager. In the gnv_app event pfc_connectionbegin, use the arguments to determine the access rights of the client that is establishing a connection and return the appropriate connectprivilege.

Whenever a client makes a request to connect to a server application, the server should validate the request. If the client has the proper authority to establish the connection, the server can permit the request and grant the appropriate connection privileges. If the client does not have the proper authority, the server can reject the request.

Use the pfc_connectionbegin event to handle client requests for connections. If the server application uses a specific database connection for each client or uses transaction pooling, you may also want to include the logic to connect to the database in the pfc_connectionbegin event using information stored in the connectstring argument.

Your return code choices for the connectprivilege enumerated data type are:

ConnectPrivilege!

ConnectWithAdminPrivilege!

NoConnectPrivilege

Return NoConnectPrivilege when the user ID and password fail validation. Return ConnectPrivilege if the connection is allowed. Return ConnectWithAdminPrivilege if the connection is allowed and the user ID is found to be an administrator. You may want to validate user IDs against a list of users and administrators in a database. Of course, not all servers need a user ID and password for performing services. The validation used is up to your application needs. But, when using pfc_connectionbegin, you must return some value for the connectprivilege.

An example of the pfc_connectionbegin event in which the userid, password,

```
// Event: pfc_connectionbegin

// Validate User ID
IF userid = "" THEN RETURN NoConnectPrivilege!
IF IsNull(userid) THEN RETURN NoConnectPrivilege!

IF NOT this.uf_IsValidUser(userid, password) THEN
        RETURN NoConnectPrivilege!
END IF

// Connect to DBMS using connectstring values
IF NOT this.uf_ConnectToDBMS(connectstring) THEN
        // Error "Unable to connect to DBMS"
        RETURN NoConnectPrivilege!
END IF

// Check if user is an administrator
IF this.uf_IsAdministrator(userid) THEN
        RETURN ConnectWithAdminPrivilege!
ELSE
        RETURN ConnectPrivilege!
END IF
```

Figure 19.6 Sample code for the connectionbegin event to validate a user.

and connectstring arguments are used to determine the access rights of the client application is shown in Fig. 19.6.

General constraints

When you work with PowerBuilder's distributed objects, you will need to recognize the boundaries within which you frame your application. Powersoft has made a major step forward in this technology, but the company is not all the way there yet in some important aspects. Because of this, some developers have been slow to use PowerBuilder's distributed objects for applications that require industrial-strength objects. We should hasten to mention that Powersoft plans to address these shortcomings in future releases of PowerBuilder. Expect to see some important moves to strengthen distributed objects in release 5.1.

Synchronous processing

One major constraint of PowerBuilder's distributed objects is that they are limited to synchronous processing. This means that when you call a function in a distributed object, the program control in the client is lost to the distributed object until the function call is completed. This is the standard way PowerBuilder executes code in the applications you are used to. When you call a function from a script, the script loses processing control until the function completes and returns.

Synchronous processing is a greater concern in distributed processing because you may be dealing with applications on disparate systems. Say a server application servicing 50 client processes makes a call to one of the clients. If during the time the client has control an interrupt occurs that hangs the process, then the server is no longer available to the 49 other clients! (The word we have received from the developers at Powersoft is that asynchronous processing will be available, perhaps as part of release 5.1.)

Design note: When you build a system, try to construct it so that applications have a minimal amount of exposure to a distributed process which potentially could cause a hang-up. You can accomplish this by emphasizing client calls to a central server and carefully limiting the duration and number of calls by a server to other distributed processes.

Number of concurrent clients

A server application can service any number of client applications. However, each time a client connects to a server, the server application will require some additional memory space specifically for that client. At some point, as more and more clients connect to the server, the server will run out of memory. The current memory allocation scheme works but is somewhat simplistic (not uncommon for a first release). Powersoft will need to improve the memory allocation scheme in order to support larger numbers of clients connecting to a server process. Look for improvements in this area in future releases.

Network protocols

Powersoft's distributed objects can use a number of common network protocols. The protocols available depend upon the platform and the networks available. The list of possible protocols will also vary depending on whether the application operates as a client or a server.

Platform	Driver	Server support	Client support
Windows 3.1	NamedPipes	No	No
	WinSock	No	Yes
	OpenClientServer	No	Yes
Windows NT	NamedPipes	Yes	Yes
	WinSock	Yes	Yes
	OpenClientServer	Yes	Yes
Windows 95	NamedPipes	No	Yes
	WinSock	Yes	Yes
	OpenClientServer	No	Yes

Note: When testing remote objects used by a client application, you can use the special local driver which simulates a networked connection on a single PC. The proxy and user objects must be in the library search path of the client application being tested. During your testing, the PowerBuilder development environment will use the same memory space for both the client application being tested and the "remote" objects being called. Therefore, the names of your remote objects and the names they reference should not conflict with object names used in the client. A server is not really used, so there is no way to "listen" when using the local driver. The server application's other features are best tested using a real connection by real clients.

Limited to PowerBuilder executables

At this point, PowerBuilder distributed objects can communicate only with PowerBuilder executables. At some point you can expect Powersoft to adopt some more open communication protocols, such as CORBA. Then you will be able to have programs written in other languages, such as C, Visual Basic, COBOL, and Java, communicate with your distributed PowerBuilder objects. Until then, your distributed software solution is limited to programs written in PowerBuilder.

What Is in the Current Version of the PFC to Support DPB?

There is very little in the current version of the PFC that supports DPB. Obviously, DPB was not a major concern for the first release of the PFC. Keep in mind that DPB was available only with PB5 and that the developers of the PFC were trying to develop the PFC while PB5 was being developed. It stands to reason that the functionality provided in the PFC was driven in large part by the needs of PB4 applications. The developers of the PFC did a good job of addressing PB4 functional needs with the new features that were available in PB5. The PFC did include some extensive work on some of the new controls available in PB5 (e.g., treeview, listview, and tab). But when you think about it, developers were already making these types of controls and building features for them in PB4. So what the PFC did was incorporate the features developers wanted in PB4 with the new control capabilities of PB5. Distributed PowerBuilder was altogether new, so there wasn't any demand for features addressing its needs.

What is not quite as obvious is that because of the PFC's service-based architecture, many of the PFC services can be used outside of the realm for which they were initially intended. Good examples of this are all of the autoinstantiated utility services, the platform services, and even some of the DataWindow service classes, such as the SQL manager service, which is useful in parsing SQL, something needed on the server application if SQL access is required.

About the only thing in the PFC that directly addresses DPB is the classes based on the connect and transport classes:

```
pfc_n_cn
        n_cn
pfc_n_trp
        n_trp
```

pfc_n_trp

The base class pfc_n_trp is simply a subclass of the system transport class. There are no additional functions, events, or instance variables.

pfc_n_cn

The base class pfc_n_cn is little more than a subclass of the system connect class. There are two additional functions, but no additional events or instance variables. Even the two functions that are included are limited in what they do.

of_Init().   of_Init is an overloaded function with two versions. One version initializes a connection object's properties using values from an INI-file section; the second uses a Registry key. Instead of hard coding the settings used to connect to a remote server application, consider storing the application name, driver, and other connection object properties required for a connection in a more maintainable location.

Note: You may want to further overload the of_Init function with a version that gets connection information from other locations, such as from a database or even another distributed application.

How to Extend the PFC to Support DPB

Whenever you extend existing PFC classes, you first have to make a conscious decision as to whether you are going to alter PFC extension classes directly or create an additional layer below the PFC extension layer. If you are directly altering PFC extension classes, then you will edit n_cn and n_trp. If you make an additional layer below the PFC extension layer, then you will inherit from n_cn and n_trp and edit their descendants. In the example below, we chose to do the latter. By doing this, you can still edit the extension layer and use the example objects.

What's Coming in Future Versions of the PFC?

As of this writing, the PFC development team has not yet determined what enhancements for distributed computing they will include in future versions of the PFC. The following ideas are speculative and are not based on any inside knowledge of what the PFC development team is planning or even hoping to do. We have based these ideas on the current style and directions implied in the current PFC product.

In keeping with the service-based architecture (SBA) style of the PFC, you should expect to see some services for client applications and some services for server applications. The user interface of both client and server applications can benefit from PFC functionality and features. Obviously, client applications are the most likely users of PFC classes, but server applications that have an extensive UI can also benefit from PFC classes.

Currently, the n_cn (connect object class) and n_trp (transport object class) class declarations are hardly anything more than subclasses of the standard system connect and transport classes, respectively. Our expectation is that the PFC will eventually extend the connect and transport objects further to include many more enhancements through additional methods, attributes, and events.

Error handling on a client is often different from error handling on a server. A client application typically will notify the user through a message box when an error occurs. A server application may not want to have a modal dialog box like a MessageBox() tie up the server's processing. Imagine having a multitude of client applications unable to perform because their server application is waiting for some operator to hit the Enter key on a MessageBox window! Or, let's say the front-end application is a Web browser that is accessing remote PowerBuilder user objects. How should error messages be handled in that case? So, the methods used by PFC error messaging may be enhanced so that the context of the user interface will determine how the error message is handled.

PowerBuilder provides a number of monitoring features for distributed processing, but there are no ready-made objects available for applications. I would expect that the PFC would include some windows that would allow users to input information for starting and stopping a server's listening process. We could also see a window for the client side that would allow user input for connections to servers. Monitoring information about client connections and processes will probably be available through a standard PFC window. Another possible window would be a monitor of servers on the network. Each of these windows will probably be packaged in much the same way as DataWindow services, à la SQLspy, find, and sort. The actual window used in your application could be directly from PFC, an extended version, or entirely your own fabrication.

The PFC libraries provide a great deal of functionality that is mainly aimed at the user interface. Remote applications will often need little or no user interface. Also, the PFC library set has a large footprint. It is beneficial to have small, efficient remote applications that load quickly and don't waste resources. So, many developers choose not to use the PFC with remote applications.

Summary and Conclusion

At this time the PFC does not address Distributed PowerBuilder. For future releases of the PFC, there has been talk of releasing some sort of "PFC Lite" for use with distributed applications. Until then, it is up to the application developer to use some of the services provided in the PFC. We feel that there are some excellent services provided in the PFC that can be used with Distributed PB. Take a look at the different nonvisual objects in the PFC, decide which objects are good candidates for Distributed PB, and use them.

20

PFC, DP, and the Internet

Introduction and Objectives

In this chapter, we will address utilizing PowerBuilder and the PFC to push the envelope—to go beyond the boundaries of the typical client-server implementation. After completing this chapter, the reader will be better equipped to further explore the possibilities of deploying applications on the Internet or on intranet platforms. We will attempt to demystify the Internet and give you a brief description of its origins and what the future holds for client-server technologies.

The Internet Unraveled

What is the Internet?

The Internet is, put simply, a network of networks. Stretching around the globe is a vast network connected by extremely high speed lines, which brings together busy metropolitan areas and remote wilderness locations. These wide "data pipes" (called the *backbone*) connect regional networks of Internet service providers, bringing connectivity to a vast number of individual end users and corporate intranets.

MCI recently spent $60 million to upgrade the technology supporting a portion of the Internet backbone, as it estimates a 30 percent increase in Internet traffic each month. If current growth rates continue unabated, there will be 502

This chapter was written by William Rompala, Rompala Consulting, romwil@rompalaconsulting.com, http://www.rompalaconsulting.com.

million people connected to the Internet by January 2000. This represents 8.37 percent of the world's population.

ActivMedia estimated the volume of sales generated by the World Wide Web in 1995 as $436 million. It further estimates that in 1998, that figure will be $46 billion.

This is the future of computing. This is the next stage of client-server processing.

What now supports more than 50,000 networks globally began with one simple network during the Cold War.

In 1962, the Cuban missile crisis brought the reality of a possible nuclear conflict into the living rooms of millions of Americans. The U.S. Department of Defense turned its thoughts to scenarios that would need to be dealt with in the wake of a nuclear holocaust. It was evident that the country's telecommunications systems would be one of the primary targets, in order to try and cripple valuable data communications. Neither typical long-distance telephone services nor the military command network would be expected to survive the first-round nuclear attack if one of the centralized switching systems was destroyed. What was needed was a decentralized computer network that wouldn't have a single "point of failure."

The Department of Defense turned to the RAND Corporation, one of its largest "think tanks," for the answer.

RAND researcher Paul Baran conceived a distributed system that allowed communications to automatically route around problems. In the event of the destruction of major portions of the physical network, its methodology would allow it to continue to operate, for it had no centralized control system—the data would be able to route itself instead of having systems doing the routing.

All of the nodes in this unusual network would have equal status, would be autonomous, and would be capable of receiving, routing, and transmitting information. Under Baran's concept of distributed communications (a.k.a. packet switching), data was broken into packets which had addressing information contained within them, along with the information needed to reassemble the original message. Each packet of information would be able to reach its destination via its own route. These individual entities could take many different paths through the network and might arrive in a different order from the one in which they were sent. Upon receipt of the packets, the client would reassemble the message.

A series of small tests proved Baran's theory. In 1969 the first large-scale implementation of the distributed communication network was brought to life. It consisted of four nodes: University of California at Los Angeles, Stanford Research Institute, University of California at Santa Barbara, and the University of Utah in Salt Lake City. It was around Labor Day in 1969 that the four-node network came alive for the first time:

> A pioneering computer science professor at UCLA and his small group of graduate students hoped to log onto the Stanford computer and try to send it some data.

They were to start by typing "login," and see if the letters appeared on the far-off monitor.

"We set up a telephone connection between us and the guys at SRI...," Kleinrock said in an interview in the *Sacramento Bee*.

"We typed the L and we asked on the phone, 'Do you see the L?'

'Yes, we see the L!' came the response.

"We typed the O, and we asked, 'Do you see the O?'

'Yes, we see the O!'

"Then we typed the G, and the system crashed." (*Knight-Ridder Newspapers*)

This was a landmark moment in the history of the Internet. Rumors that this was the first documented GPF are unfounded, however.

The Advanced Research Projects Agency (ARPA) began sponsorship of the fledgling network, lending the agency's name, thus causing ARPANET to be born. During the 1970s, more and more nodes were added to ARPANET. The net users began to utilize the high-speed network to exchange e-mail and project notes. With a high-speed network available around the clock, geographical and time constraints were no longer barriers to communication. Nothing would now stand in the way of the discussions by the members of the first mailing list: Science Fiction Lovers.

The net continued to grow.

A common protocol needed to be developed if users of dissimilar mainframes, as well as smaller networks, were to be able to communicate with one another. In 1977, the standard that was destined to unite the world was invented: Transmission Control Protocol/Internet Protocol (TCP/IP). This was the network protocol that met the challenges of a packet-based, decentralized network. A packet-switched network sends information across the net in small fragments, called *packets*. If one workstation forwards a file to another workstation, the file is first split into many packets at the sending location and then reassembled at the destination. The TCP/IP protocols define the composition of these packets, including the origin, destination, length, and type of each packet, and how intermediate computers on the network are to act upon the packet upon receipt.

TCP/IP is composed of three layers that work in tandem:

1. *IP.* This layer is responsible for moving packets from node to node. IP forwards each packet based on a 4-byte site address (the IP number, e.g., 204.170.243.139).

2. *TCP.* This layer is responsible for verifying the correct delivery of data from client to server. It is also responsible for detecting errors and triggering retransmission until the data is correctly and completely received.

3. *Sockets.* This is the package of subroutines that allows access to the TCP/IP protocol from applications on most workstations.

Because of TCP/IP, connectivity to and from the ARPANET backbone was now easily available. In 1983, MILNET was created when the military-oriented portion of ARPANET discontinued its relationship with ARPANET. The same year, TCP/IP was made a standard and became used by everyone. It linked all parts of the branching complex networks, which soon came to be called the Internet.

In the early 1990s, the Internet experienced explosive growth. At that time it was estimated that the number of computers connected to the Internet was doubling every year. The main catalyst of this expansion was the creation of the World Wide Web.

The World Wide Web was created at CERN, the European Laboratory for Particle Physics in Geneva, Switzerland. The concept was revolutionary: Information could be collected into units called pages. These pages would be collections of text, graphics, sound, music, etc. The author of a page could also embed links to other pages directly in the body of his or her own page, allowing the reader to select a link from a page to view detail on another. These pages would be transmitted via the hypertext transmission protocol, or HTTP.

Until the World Wide Web, the world of the Internet was inhabited mostly by technically oriented people, as it was necessary to understand the underlying mechanisms in order to utilize it. Now, the information and technology needed to access the Internet and the World Wide Web is available to even the most casual home user. Today you do not even need a computer to access the masses of information available via the Internet. The World Wide Web adds living images and color to the Internet, changing the once text-only interface into an affordable communication tool for the foreseeable future.

The client-server metaphor is used extensively when we examine the Web. The role of thin client is played by the Web browser, while the server could be any of the millions of Web servers.

The Web page

A Web page document is a plain text file that contains the commands that are required to produce the Web page's content in the browser window. These commands, or tags, are collectively called HTML, or hypertext markup language.

In order to understand how HTML works, let us examine the steps that an Internet browser takes to produce a Web page.

1. First the browser requests the document from a Web server via HTTP.

2. The server sends the document to the browser.

3. The browser begins interpreting the document from beginning to end one tag at a time, requesting images, sounds, or additional information as necessary.

Let's examine some HTML.

The line shown in Fig. 20.1 is a complete HTML document on its own. The <HTML> tag denotes the beginning of an HTML command string; the string is turned off by the </HTML> tag. A tag prefixed with the / character is an "off"

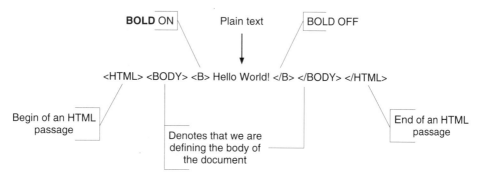

BOLD ON   Plain text   BOLD OFF

<HTML> <BODY> <B> Hello World! </B> </BODY> </HTML>

Begin of an HTML
passage

Denotes that we are
defining the body of
the document

End of an HTML
passage

Figure 20.1   Breakdown of HTML tags.

toggle. We see this again in the <B> </B> pair—these are "bold on" and "bold off" tags.

The output of this HTML page therefore would look much like

Hello World!

Not much on content or style, but good for nostalgia. We could have surrounded our global greeting phrase with <P ALIGN = "CENTER"></P> to have it centered on the screen, and so forth.

Going a step further

We can define data input and output areas that make our HTML truly interactive. This is usually achieved through the <FORM> tag. A form is defined as a collection of data elements with actions assigned to buttons. Let's examine a form (see Fig. 20.2).

This form definition will place an Edit field and a button on the Web browser screen. When this code is interpreted by a browser, the result would look like that shown in Fig. 20.3.

In HTML, a single-line edit is defined using the <input> tag. The properties used in the single-line edit input in Fig. 20.2 are defined within the <input> tag as shown in Table 20.1. The edit field will have the default text of "Joe Shmoe," and the button label will be "Submit Name."

A special case of the <input> tag is the type "submit." When a submit type is defined, it is interpreted as a button that will cause the form's defined action.

```
<FORM METHOD = "GET" ACTION = "/scripts/someprogram.exe">
Enter value: <input name = "customer" value = "Joe Shmoe">
<input type = "submit" value = "Submit Name">
</form>
```

Figure 20.2   Sample HTML code showing the necessary tags for an input field and button.

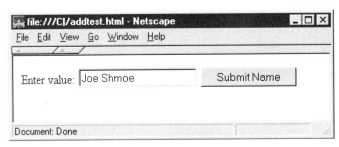

Figure 20.3   Visual depiction of the HTML code.

TABLE 20.1   **Breakdown of Two HTML Keywords**

Property keyword	Meaning
name	The name of the control
value	A default text represented in the control

Upon clicking on the button, the form knows to take the contents of the controls defined in the form (in this case, an edit field named "customer") and pass it as an argument to someprogram.exe in the /scripts directory of the Web server.

Note: We have included a selection of good resources available on the Internet for learning HTML and using CGI on the accompanying CD-ROM in Chap20\HTMLHLP.DOC.

How Does the PFC Fit In?

The PFC does not natively support HTML or Web-based applications, but by extending the PFC and creating your application logic to access business objects, you can both take advantage of the service-based architecture that the PFC offers and utilize the power of distributed objects.

Deployment Issues

Utilizing what we have learned about Distributed PowerBuilder (DPB), we can deploy our objects on a Web server to be accessed by Web browsers. Normally, a distributed PowerBuilder application is deployed as shown in Fig. 20.4.

When we add the Internet element, and deploy on a Web server, we have the situation shown in Fig. 20.5. web.pb acts as the client application, connecting with the DPB application to request information. It then, upon a successful request, sends the information back to the Web browser. When a client requests a PowerBuilder object from the Web server, web.pb steps in and acts as the client for the DPB application.

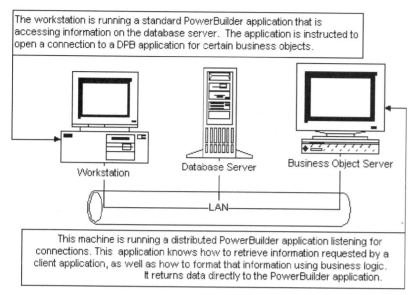

The workstation is running a standard PowerBuilder application that is accessing information on the database server. The application is instructed to open a connection to a DPB application for certain business objects.

Workstation   Database Server   Business Object Server

LAN

This machine is running a distributed PowerBuilder application listening for connections. This application knows how to retrieve information requested by a client application, as well as how to format that information using business logic. It returns data directly to the PowerBuilder application.

Figure 20.4   Typical Distributed PowerBuilder application deployment.

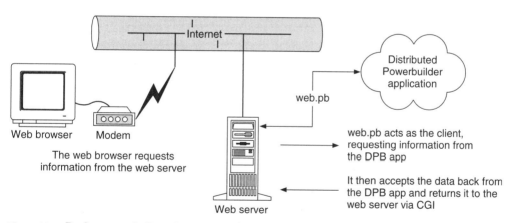

Internet

Distributed Powerbuilder application

web.pb

Web browser   Modem

The web browser requests information from the web server

web.pb acts as the client, requesting information from the DPB app

It then accepts the data back from the DPB app and returns it to the web server via CGI

Web server

Figure 20.5   Deployment of a Distributed PowerBuilder application over the Internet using web.pb.

Obtaining web.pb

Note: web.pb is just one of the components that are included in the Internet Developer's Toolkit, available from Powersoft. This collection of tools is invaluable for the PB developer who wishes to explore deploying on the Internet or an intranet.

At the time of this writing, web.pb is available for downloading at the Powersoft Web site at http://www.powersoft.com/download/index.html#web.pb.

Extensive documentation in the form of Web documents is installed when you install web.pb, including information on how to configure your specific server, how to install your distributed application, and how to call your objects/methods from Web-based forms.

Deploying on the Web: an example

We have seen how to create a distributed PowerBuilder application. To add Web services, we need to create another user object that returns HTML. We will define a series of functions that return HTML strings in this simple introductory example.

The best way to manipulate and retrieve data in this case is through the use of DataStore objects—basically nonvisual DataWindows that you define and create dynamically. First we generate the DataWindow and save it into the PBL library that will be available during runtime. During execution, we create the DataStore object and assign the DataWindow object to the DataStore. The following example illustrates a function on nvo_web_svc that takes a string argument and uses it to retrieve a DataStore. If rows are returned, it returns an HTML string that includes the data.

> **Function 1: of_Get_Address (string a_cons_id) returns string**
> //This function returns the address for a consultant given a consultant id.
> //Return type is an HTML string
>
> string ls_HTML
>
> ds_addresses = create datastore // Create a DataStore object, stored in the
>   // instance var ds_addresses (declared on the uo)
>
> ds_addresses.dataobject = "d_address" // Set the DataWindow object to the
>   // datastore.
>
> ds_addresses.settransobject(sqlca) // Need to set the transaction.
>
> IF ds_addresses.retrieve(a_cons_id) >0 THEN // If rows returned
> ls_HTML = ds_addresses.object.datawindow.data.htmltable //This is a built-in
>   //feature of 5.0 DataWindows
> ELSE   // If no rows returned
> ls_HTML = 'No address found for this consultant ID.'
> END IF
>
> // Let us add a header to make it look good.
> ls_HTML = of_Add_Header(ls_HTML, 'Consultant Address Information')
>
> // Wrap it up by adding the footer information
> ls_HTML = of_Add_Footer(ls_HTML)
>
> DESTROY ds_addresses // Since we created it, we have to get rid of it.

RETURN ls_HTML

Two supporting functions that are called in of_Get_Address are of_Add_Header and of_Add_Footer. This is done to centralize any standard headers and footers for Web pages that you dynamically produce.

Function 2: of_Add_Header(string a_html, string a_information_type) returns string

string
ls_header

```
ls_header = '<HTML>
<HEAD><TITLE>' + a_information_type + '</TITLE></HEAD><BODY><BR><HR>'

return ls_header + a_html
```

By passing a_information_type, the dynamic Web page is given a custom title, such as we see in of_Get_Address—of_Add_Header is passed "Consultant Address Information."

Notice that in of_Get_Address we need to set the DataStore to a transaction object. This could be an instance variable on the user object that is set during the constructor event of the user object, depending on the complexity of the environment.

We can create any number of business objects composed of nonvisual objects and include them in the distributed application deployed on the Web server by simply having the distributed application instantiate them upon opening and including them in the library.

Deploying our application on the Web server

To access the user object that we have installed on our Web server from our HTML form, we can use the following syntax in the definition of our form:

ACTION = "cgipath/Type_of_CGI/Serveralias/Object/Method

where the arguments are as described in Table 20.2.

You would use this action string in the same manner as we examined previously. The results of the form would be passed directly to the method that you specify, and the results of the method will be passed back to the browser.

In order to look up a consultant's address from a Web-based form, the form declaration would be as follows:

```
<FORM METHOD = "GET" ACTION =
"/scripts/PBCGI050.EXE/MYSERVER/nvo_web_svc/of_get_address">
Enter Consultant ID: <input a_cons_id = "a_cons_id" value = "MF3">
```

TABLE 20.2   ACTION Tag Components

Argument	Description
cgipath	Location of the cgi directory (server configuration), usually /scripts or /cgi-bin
Type_Of_CGI	This would be the web.pb program that you installed on the Web server. Standard CGI uses PBCGI050.EXE.
Serveralias	This is specified in the PBWEB.INI file on the Web server.
Object	The name of the object that you created that is contained in the distributed PB application.
Method	The function you wish to execute in the object.

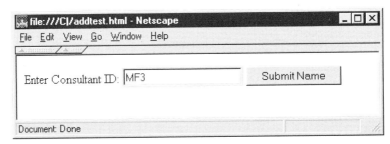

Figure 20.6   Consultant ID entry form.

<input type = "submit" value = "Submit Name"></form>

The resulting form would look like that shown in Fig. 20.6 in Netscape 4.0.

When the form is submitted, the result page is automatically returned to the browser, as web.pb announces the result set automatically. Figure 20.7 depicts the display that would be returned.

A Real-World Example

Now that we have discussed the concepts and the related technologies, let's apply them to a real-world problem, an automatic code update facility.

Imagine an application that was intelligent enough to determine if there was a newer version of itself, dynamic enough to seek out and obtain the new patches, and flexible enough to apply them. This may sound out of reach, but by applying what we have just seen, we can make it happen, and in such a way that *any* application can be easily adapted to behave in the same manner.

First, we will break the requirements into manageable pieces, then discuss the means of achieving them. Remember, we want the solution to this implementation to be flexible enough to enable any PB application to be easily plugged into it. The optimal method: a versioning service.

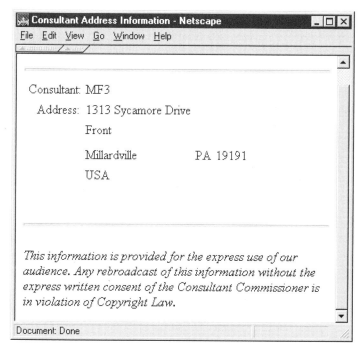

Figure 20.7   Results of the consultant data lookup.

Step 1: Determining current version information. The application would have to know how to determine if there has been a newer released version of itself. This could be achieved by having the versioning service contact a distributed portion on a centralized server to obtain current release information. Figure 20.8 shows what this might look like.

An added bonus would be that the distributed application that connects to the versioning database could also listen for Web-based clients, to connect and request versioning information and return the appropriate HTML.

Step 2: Obtain the latest release. If the results from the "latest version query" tell us that there is a later version of the application, we can request the location, filenames, version number, and so forth from the versioning database in much the same manner. This information will be used to obtain the latest version—via the ftp service, for example. We could launch a "retrieval program" with command-line parameters that would ftp the latest version to our desktop and apply the patch, or simply have the versioning service itself obtain the file via ftp and then shut down and spawn the installation of the new version. This all depends on the complexity and intelligence of the installation programs that apply the updated software.

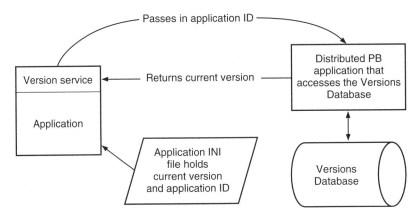

Figure 20.8   Versioning service lookup via the Internet/intranet.

Where Do We Go from Here?

Try it out! Deploy, create, use, learn, design, dream, formulate. The boundaries are only as limiting as you allow them to be. In order to fully explore the possibilities, the following is recommended:

- If you are not currently on-line, get on-line, preferably with a full-fledged SLIP-style account. Most providers offer 24-hour-a-day, 7-day-a-week unlimited access for a flat fee of around $200 a year.

- Make sure you are running PowerBuilder 5.0 so that you can create distributed PB applications.

- For local testing, obtain a Web server package. There are a large number of freeware or shareware servers available on the Internet. We have collected information on a number of them, and this information is included on the attached CD.* Additionally, Sybase SQL Anywhere 5.5 Professional includes a personal Web server.

- Obtain web.pb from www.powersoft.com.

- Start writing Web-based applications.

Powersoft has a Web page that details future features in the PFC available at

http://www.powersoft.com/partners/code/pfc.html

Recently, it was announced there that an HTML service extension for the PFC was "under consideration." We hope to see this feature included in an upcoming release, but until then, we need to write our own extensions.

---

*See Chap20\websrvr.doc.

The Internet Developer's Toolkit

To greatly facilitate the process of developing Internet/intranet applications, Powersoft has released the Internet Developer's Toolkit. The IDT is a collection of utilities that make, 'net development much quicker and easier. It contains a copy of O'Reilly & Associates' WebSite server as well, enabling you to test your deployed objects. A complete installation of web.pb and extensive documentation on configuring and utilizing it are included, making this tool indispensable. A web.pb Wizard writes for you the HTML necessary to access your user objects from your Web page!

The Foreseeable Future

The Web and Internet technologies are the next step in the client-server world. Deploying applications using a multitier architecture is and will be the method of choice in the near future. Taking advantage of the power of distributed logic to allow business objects to be accessed by applications throughout a corporation's intranet will be commonplace soon. The ability to provide true code reusability without needing to recode by connecting new applications directly to existing ones provides shorter development time, a greater standardization of business logic, and lower maintenance costs. Publishing information on the Internet via the Web is quicker and easier when distributed business objects are used. The same distributed objects that are used by internal applications also could listen to CGI calls on the corporate Web site, allowing both internal applications and the Web presence to be concurrently maintained and updated with new business logic with a single code update.

These technologies will be an extremely important part of a PowerBuilder developer's arsenal of skills for the foreseeable future. Creating applications that are more open and object-oriented will be our role in creating stronger and more flexible applications as we proceed into the twenty-first century.

Index

ABOUT THE AUTHORS

HOWARD BLOCK teaches PowerBuilder and leads the PFC Special Interest Group, sanctioned by Powersoft. MILLARD BROWN III, WILLIAM GREEN, BORIS GASIN, and ANDY TAUBER are members of Team Powersoft. Mr. Brown and Mr. Green are coauthors of McGraw-Hill's bestselling *PowerBuilder 5: Object-Oriented Design and Development*.